Winning While Losing

The Alan B. Larkin Series on the American Presidency

UNIVERSITY PRESS OF FLORIDA

Florida A&M University, Tallahassee
Florida Atlantic University, Boca Raton
Florida Gulf Coast University, Ft. Myers
Florida International University, Miami
Florida State University, Tallahassee
New College of Florida, Sarasota
University of Central Florida, Orlando
University of Florida, Gainesville
University of North Florida, Jacksonville
University of South Florida, Tampa
University of West Florida, Pensacola

WINNING
WHILE
LOSING

Civil Rights, the Conservative Movement,
and the Presidency from Nixon to Obama

Edited by Kenneth Osgood and Derrick E. White

University Press of Florida
Gainesville · Tallahassee · Tampa · Boca Raton
Pensacola · Orlando · Miami · Jacksonville · Ft. Myers · Sarasota

This book may be available in an electronic edition.

19 18 17 16 15 14   6 5 4 3 2 1

Library of Congress Cataloging-in-Publication Data
Winning while losing : civil rights, the conservative movement, and the presidency
from Nixon to Obama / edited by Kenneth Osgood and Derrick E. White.
p. cm. — (The Alan B. Larkin series on the American presidency)
Includes bibliographical references.
ISBN 978-0-8130-4908-3 (alk. paper)
1. African Americans—Civil rights. 2. Presidents—United States. 3. Racism—
Political aspects—United States—History—20th century. 4. African Americans—
Social conditions. 5. Conservatism—United States. 6. United States—Race
relations—Political aspects—History—20th century. I. Osgood, Kenneth Alan,
1971– II. White, Derrick E. III. Series: Alan B. Larkin series on the American
presidency.
E185.615.W547 2014
323.1196'073—dc23
2013020091

The University Press of Florida is the scholarly publishing agency for the State
University System of Florida, comprising Florida A&M University, Florida Atlantic
University, Florida Gulf Coast University, Florida International University, Florida
State University, New College of Florida, University of Central Florida, University of
Florida, University of North Florida, University of South Florida, and University of
West Florida.

University Press of Florida
15 Northwest 15th Street
Gainesville, FL 32611-2079
http://www.upf.com

In Memory of Alan B. Larkin (1922–2002)

CONTENTS

PREFACE

This volume explores the paradoxical nature of civil rights politics in the years following the 1960s civil rights movement in the United States. The book originated in the 2009 Alan B. Larkin Symposium on the American Presidency at Florida Atlantic University (FAU), which focused on the impact of the conservative moment on civil rights and the presidency since 1968.

The volume's core theme of progress in the face of defeat, or defeat in the face of progress, was first proposed by Mary Frances Berry, the former chair of the U.S. Commission on Civil Rights. At her keynote address for the symposium, she spoke about how civil rights during the Reagan era followed a pattern of "winning while losing." The other conference participants, who were exploring the civil rights policies of other presidents, agreed that her idea seemed to capture well, if imperfectly and unevenly, the larger trajectory of civil rights in the era that followed the landmark legislative victories of the mid-1960s.

Yet this was an odd moment to be talking about "losing" in the civil rights arena. The planning for the symposium had begun long before Barack Obama emerged as a contender for the Democratic Party's presidential nomination. His victory in the primary and subsequent election to the presidency came as a surprise to the conference participants, who now found themselves discussing the connection between race and the presidency just weeks after the inauguration of the country's first black president. It was a remarkable coincidence. Ultimately, Obama's victory did not affect the historical judgments rendered on the four decades separating his inauguration in 2008 from Martin Luther King's assassination in 1968. The intervening years saw highly visible achievements in the realm of political rights, as Obama himself demonstrated, but persistent setbacks in the quest for full socio-economic equality, as told in the ever grim statistics about black poverty and incarceration. Such a pattern of winning while losing seemed to define the post-1960s era of civil rights politics. This new era was shaped less by liberal activism than by the broader conservative turn in the American electorate, a mood that constrained the ability of civil rights activists to advance their agenda through public policy. If anything, Obama's victory seemed to accentuate the curious paradox of winning while losing in the realm of civil rights.

We are grateful to the Larkin family for the generosity that made the symposium—and this book—possible. Their gift to FAU's History Department has been a gift to history itself and is a fitting tribute to the late Alan Larkin's personal fascination with America's past. We also thank Zella Linn and Patricia Kollander for their efforts to organize and support the symposium, as well as Jane DeHart and Laura Kalman for their helpful suggestions in the planning stages of this work. We also owe an extraordinary debt of gratitude to Meredith Babb of the University Press of Florida and to Helen Laville, Harvard Sitkoff, David J. Garrow, and the other anonymous readers of the manuscript who offered tremendously thoughtful and insightful critiques. Their responses helped us craft a more sophisticated volume that we hope will frame the debate about civil rights politics in the post-1960s era.

A few months following our symposium, we were saddened to learn of the passing of one of our authors and presenters, Ronald Walters. He was a leading scholar and activist on issues related to civil rights and American politics. He also mentored editor Derrick White and contributor Robert Smith—students who were deeply affected by Walters' scholarship and teaching. We mourn his loss as a colleague and as a thoughtful analyst of American politics. Before he died, Walters attended Obama's inauguration in Washington, D.C., and then spoke to our symposium about the meaning of Obama's victory for the future of American politics. His remarks, which were recorded by C-SPAN and can be seen online, were edited by his student and colleague Robert Smith and are included in this volume.

Kenneth Osgood
Colorado School of Mines

Derrick E. White
Florida Atlantic University

INTRODUCTION

THE PARADOX OF SUCCESS

Civil Rights and the Presidency in a New Era

KENNETH OSGOOD AND DERRICK E. WHITE

A year before an assassin's bullet claimed his life in April 1968, Martin Luther King Jr. published his last and most prophetic book: *Where Do We Go from Here: Chaos or Community?* King had just suffered a major defeat in Chicago, where intense northern racism and big-city machine politics thwarted a campaign against housing discrimination. The setback left King wondering about the path forward. Retreating to a small house in Jamaica, with no phone, he put the finishing touches on a manuscript that would receive mixed reviews at the time but would appear ever more prescient with the passage of time. As King wrote, the future of the American civil rights movement looked uncertain indeed. Civil rights activists had just scored their greatest legislative triumphs with the passage of the 1964 Civil Rights Act and the 1965 Voting Rights Act, the culmination of decades of legal and grassroots challenges to the oppressive system of legal segregation in the United States. But the very success of the movement raised a deceptively simple question: What now?

The answer to that question shattered the civil rights consensus. To some—including many white allies of African American civil rights activists—the answer was: Not much. Segregation had ended and it was time to move on. To others, however, it was time for more militant agitation. Years of patient nonviolent protest had yielded too little, too slowly in the areas of economic justice and structural racism. As white liberals abandoned the civil rights movement, black-power activism, urban rebellions, and rioting shattered for good the civil rights coalition King had helped construct over the preceding decade. So when King posited the question "Chaos or Community?," many reviewers at the time perceived the book as an assault on the separatism and militancy of black power.[1] It was, but it also was much more.

King argued that the civil rights movement had moved into a "new phase." The fight for racial equality had just begun. The fracturing of the movement and the long-awaited death of Jim Crow were causes for sober reflection and renewed activism, not complacency. It was past time to address the wide-ranging repercussions of centuries of slavery and segregation. "A society that has done something special against the Negro for hundreds of years must now do something special for him," King wrote. As he well knew, for African Americans the legacy of this discrimination meant inequality at all levels: grinding poverty, substandard education, limited access to jobs, dilapidated housing, a discriminatory criminal justice system, and a disproportionate share of front-line service in the rapidly escalating Vietnam War. King thus argued that the difficult campaign in Selma, Alabama, which had paved the way for the landmark Voting Rights Act, did not mark the end of the civil rights movement but the opening of a new front focused on "the realization of equality." This would be in many ways a more difficult and divisive battle for economic equality, and King now spoke bitterly about the white allies who "had quietly disappeared." He saw a movement betrayed. "The Negroes of America had taken the President, the press and the pulpit at their word when they spoke in broad terms of freedom and justice," King complained, but "the word was broken, and the free-running expectations of the Negro crashed into the stone walls of white resistance."[2]

That resistance came from surprising quarters: not just from traditional opponents of racial equality but also from white liberals who had once joined forces with King to oppose racial injustice. The march on Selma now looked like the apex of black and white unity. A core ideological disagreement divided black activists on the one hand from many former white allies and conservative opponents on the other. "Negroes have proceeded from a premise that equality means what it says," King wrote, "but most whites in America in 1967, including many persons of good will, proceed from a premise that equality is a loose expression for improvement." Behind these differing definitions of equality stood, according to King, a "fantasy of self-deception and comfortable vanity" that relied on the belief that "American society is essentially hospitable to fair play and to steady growth toward a middle-class Utopia embodying racial harmony." For King, the very real persistence of structural racism called for a broad economic program designed to counter the legacy of slavery and segregation. Yet, when faced with the "real costs" of equality—including full employment, the eradication of slums, and truly equal education—many whites rejoined simply: "the Negro has come far enough."[3]

Thus when King asked, "Where do we go from here?" he was asking Americans to consider the deeper, more fundamental challenges that would dominate the political debate over civil rights into the twenty-first century. To ensure civil rights, was it enough merely to guarantee individual freedom by stripping away formal vestiges of discrimination in the law? Or were more extensive actions required to remedy centuries of injustice and create genuine economic and social equality? Such questions highlighted significant differences of political ideology and historical interpretations that separated those who wanted equal opportunity, no more and no less, and those who sought equitable results. For those stressing equal opportunity, the years 1964 and 1965 marked the final resolution to Gunnar Myrdal's "American Dilemma." Their interpretation of the civil rights movement hinged solely on the elimination of legal racial discrimination. With that task now complete, Americans could be satisfied with their color-blind support of opportunity for all. For King and others, however, the elimination of discriminatory laws was but the first phase of a larger movement for civil and human rights. They pointed to centuries of stolen black labor, through slavery and Jim Crow, and saw much more that needed to be done. Addressing the human and economic costs of this legacy was the next and most important phase of the movement.

These issues defined the political divide over civil rights in the years ahead. They also pointed to a new reality of American politics in an increasingly conservative era. In "the Age of Reagan," civil rights leaders could reap meaningful victories in one area, the erosion of legalized discrimination that opened the door to freedom and achievement for individual African Americans, while continuing to lose in the other, the elusive search for economic and social equality that would close the door of opportunity for African Americans as a group.[4] This curious phenomenon of winning while losing took many different shapes in the decades to come, but it nevertheless defined the central paradox of civil rights that came into focus during the last years of King's life. King's attempt to organize the next phase of the movement was cut short by his assassination in April 1968, leaving the civil rights paradox unresolved.[5]

Had King lived to his eightieth birthday on January 15, 2009, he would have seen a world that looked very different—but still uncomfortably familiar. Many euphoric pundits saw that day, on the eve of Barack Obama's historic inauguration, as signifying at long last the fulfillment of King's dream. Yet a few commentators noted that the dream of economic equality, so central to King's activism, remained unfulfilled. The online journalist Sadiq Green was one of the few to dampen the celebrations over Obama's inauguration by noting dourly, "The journey from slavery to Jim Crow to full participation in American society is not yet complete." Too many African Americans, Sadiq Green wrote, "are still trapped by the structural inequalities of American society . . . [and] many appear to be spiraling in the chaos he [King] warned of in his last book." Persistent poverty, unemployment, and a prison system bursting at the seams with incarcerated black men made King's message in *Where Do We Go From Here* "newly resonant," observed *The Nation's* Mark Engler. The message was "especially appropriate right now," added King's former associate Jesse Jackson Sr. after Obama's receipt of the Nobel Peace Prize in December 2009. "Hope is up," Jackson noted ironically, "but unfortunately so is poverty."[6]

Two years later, as President Obama stood beside Jackson and others to dedicate a memorial to King in Washington, Charlene Crowell in the *Philadelphia Tribune* again reminded Americans of King's campaign for economic and social justice and the persistent relevance of *Where Do We Go From Here*. When that book was published in 1967, forty million people lived in poverty, a figure that grew to forty-six million in 2011. "For African Americans one in four people today live in poverty" and unemployment rates are double that of the general population. Add to these facts the "disturbing inequalities, predatory lending with triple-digit interest for payday and car title loans, or dealer-mark-ups on auto financing, and disproportionate foreclosed homes" and it becomes clear that "there is a measurable tax for being Black or Latino in America." Crowell could have mentioned an even more worrying sign. Even as the nation graced King with a handsome memorial on the Washington Mall, fully one half of the country's prison population was black. In light of these worrisome facts, observers could be forgiven for seeing Obama's election not as a dream fulfilled but as a dream deferred.[7]

The sober responses to Obama's historic presidency highlight the ambiguous nature of civil rights progress after the 1960s. In the four decades separating King's assassination and Obama's inauguration, there continued to be notable advances on political civil rights—as Obama himself would symbolize—and in the larger softening of racial prejudice. But there were also meaningful and persistent setbacks on the road to full economic and social equality. To shed light on this phenomenon, this book explores the complex and contested evolution of civil rights priorities by focusing on two overlapping issues: presidential politics and the conservative movement. Bringing together scholars from several different disciplines—history, political science, legal affairs, and sociology—the volume analyzes the impact of conservative trends in American politics on the struggle for racial justice. The authors focus on the civil rights agendas of each administration from Richard Nixon to Barack Obama (with the exceptions of Gerald Ford and George H. W. Bush), analyzing how the broader conservative turn in American life affected their politics and policies. While focusing primarily on the use of executive power, the volume also explores the broader political, legal, and social trends that influenced the national debate on civil rights. The essays collected here are concerned mostly with civil rights for African Americans, although some essays touch on women, Latinos, and others who were affected by, and contributed to, larger conversations about minority rights and equality. While the volume is meant to make a meaningful scholarly contribution to historical understanding of the recent past, the editors also strove to make the volume accessible to a broader audience, including students and the general public, whose popular understanding of these issues is often shaped more by the contemporary political climate than by detailed historical knowledge.

The Conservative Ascendancy

King's death in 1968 happened to coincide with the beginning of a titanic shift in American politics. The progressive movements for social change that had begun with the civil rights movement moved to new terrain—women's liberation, gay rights, and environmentalism—but they also encountered a significant counterforce: a burgeoning conservative movement that, by the 1980s, would decisively shift American politics to the Right. This was the era of the "conservative ascendancy," as the political historian Donald Critchlow so aptly dubbed it.[8] It was an era in which presidential politics on civil rights would be both circumscribed and defined by a powerful grassroots conservative movement and by the increasingly conservative mood of the electorate writ large. This right turn bolstered political leaders who wanted to define civil rights narrowly as merely encompassing political rights and equality of opportunity, while constraining those who wanted to broaden the meaning of equality to accord with King's more comprehensive vision of economic and social justice.[9]

Although movements for reform would continue into the 1970s, the 1968 election was a harbinger of the new conservative era.[10] That election saw three major candidates: Lyndon Johnson's vice president, Hubert Humphrey, who ran on the Democratic ticket, Dwight Eisenhower's vice president, Richard Nixon, who ran on the Republican ticket, and the segregationist governor of Alabama, George Wallace, who ran as an independent. Although Nixon secured the presidency by receiving less than 1 percent more popular votes than Humphrey did, his "law and order" platform won him electoral votes from thirty-two states. Tellingly, Wallace, who ran a virulently racist campaign, garnered nearly 14 percent of the vote and carried five southern states—a remarkable feat considering that no subsequent third-party candidate has won an entire state's electoral votes. Together, the two conservative candidates, Wallace and Nixon, secured nearly 57 percent of the popular vote and carried thirty-seven states. This was a sign of things to come. Beginning in 1968, Republicans would capture seven of the next ten presidential elections.

The entire political landscape had changed. Southern discontent over liberal activism on civil rights meant that the South, which had been a stronghold of the Democratic Party since the Civil War, defected to the Republicans. A new coalition took shape. The Republican Party displaced the New Deal Coalition that dominated American politics from the 1930s through the 1960s. For the next forty years, conservatives held the upper hand in Washington. With a vibrant intellectual base and committed grassroots organizations, the conservative ideology of the Republican Party emerged as the dominant force in the closing decades of the twentieth century—so much so that even Democratic politicians like Jimmy Carter and Bill Clinton were forced to adopt center-right positions on many key issues, especially on social welfare, racial integration, affirmative action, and poverty.[11]

Epitomized by Ronald Reagan's transformative presidency in the 1980s, the conservative ascendancy was fueled partly by a desire to roll back government activism in civil rights.[12] As Thomas B. and Mary D. Edsall argued in their landmark study *Chain Reaction*, race and taxation issues were central components of the Republican Party's successful bid to create a new electoral majority in the 1980s.[13] Resentment over civil rights remedies like affirmative action, school busing, and welfare helped fuel the conservative movement. Many Americans came to believe that the government was trampling on individual rights in the name of rectifying past wrongs. Accordingly, the New Right coalition sought to limit the impact of civil rights initiatives, especially affirmative action, by championing an idea of individual rights to supplant that of "group rights" for minorities.

This volume, then, engages not just debates about civil rights and the presidency but also conversations about the larger meaning of the conservative movement, which shaped much of the political agenda of post-1960s America. It addresses a fast-growing body of work on the conservative movement, much of it focused on grassroots activism and the intellectual foundations of modern conservatism.[14] In exploring the roots of the conservative revival, some authors stress the importance of social and cultural issues, like abortion and the Equal Rights Amendment, while others emphasize national security concerns and conservative opposition to détente in the Cold War.[15] A common thread in the scholarship points to the importance of race and civil rights in forming the modern conservative coalition, which was based in no small part on Republican control over the South and the rural heartland.[16] Constituents from these regions had once been at odds, but they now became linked by concerns about racial status. As Mary Frances Berry points out, the new conservative coalition appealed to both "southern whites' concerns for their region's racial status quo" and "northern whites' fear for their economic status and their all-white neighborhoods and schools."[17]

Nevertheless, scholars debate just how significant a role race played in the conservative revival. Because retrenchment on civil rights was a crucial issue to the new southern base of the Republican Party, and because politicians like Richard Nixon deliberately courted southern resentment in their electoral strategizing, some scholars explain the American Right turn by emphasizing the white backlash against civil rights policies as well as the "southern strategy" employed by conservative politicians to win Dixie's disaffected whites. Scholars such as Dan T. Carter and Kevin Kruse, for example, document the impact of backlash politics on the South as the new base for the Republican Party.[18] James T. Paterson's authoritative history of the period similarly points to Richard Nixon's "genteel" catering to the growing backlash as key to his campaign for the presidency, concluding: "Backlash was indeed the dominant force in the exciting campaign and the election of 1968."[19] Other scholars, however, have raised questions about the significance of the backlash phenomenon and the extent to which race or racism was instrumental in the rise of the Right. Matthew D. Lassiter, for example, argues that instead of a southern strategy that relied on explicit racial hostility to fuel the white backlash, white suburbanites employed a color-blind "suburban strategy." In exploring the rise of the Right in the suburbs and the sunbelt, Lassiter documents a grassroots politics that "charted a middle course between the open racism of the extreme right and the egalitarian agenda of the civil rights movement, based in an ethos of color-blind individualism."[20] Consequently, by the mid-1970s politicians of both parties supported versions of the color-blind suburban strategy, as in their opposition to the busing of children to achieve school integration. Whether motivated by backlash appeals, implicit racism, or color-blind individualism, the paradigm for civil rights gradually evolved away from King's broad-ranging definition of equality of economic and social justice to a more restrictive notion of civil rights that reinforced the status quo by avoiding any analysis of structural racism, the lasting legacy of segregation and white supremacy. The result was a conservative turn in attitudes toward civil rights that allowed for what some scholars call "racism without racists."[21] Policies that were framed as color-blind in principle were anything but color-blind in impact.

The Presidency and Civil Rights after the 1960s

Over the course of the closing decades of the twentieth century, the debate about civil rights gradually but fundamentally changed. The political battles revolved less around whether or not to have civil rights protections enshrined in the law and more around how far those protections should go. This volume suggests that the executive branch played a critical but evolving and inconsistent role in these debates. It explores the ways in which conservative attempts to contain or roll back civil rights measures succeeded in some areas but failed in others, while also detailing the mixed achievements of black activists and their liberal supporters. The core political and legal rights won in the 1960s were sharply contested in the ensuing decades, yet they also managed to remain mostly intact—a modest but important victory for civil rights advocates. At the same time, however, the economic policies promoted by Republicans and Democrats alike failed to address racial disparities in wealth and opportunity that were legacies of past discrimination. Progress was stymied by an illusion of victory. Not only did the end of formal segregation and legalized disfranchisement fail to produce full economic and social equality, but the perception of political equality that those developments engendered may also have impeded progress toward economic equality by suggesting to some that civil rights had been achieved. This was precisely the paradox of success that King confronted so forcefully in his last book.

While this overarching argument is not new in itself, the volume does complicate our understanding of recent civil rights politics by detailing how various presidential administrations confronted civil rights in the post-1960s era as well as how the conservative movement affected those policies. It also suggests new ways of thinking about post-1968 political history, particularly about issues pertaining to the presidency, civil rights, and conservatism. The essays in this volume examine these issues from differing perspectives, with judgments that are sometimes contradictory but mostly complementary. Five key themes permeate the essays.

First, the authors explore the ways in which racial and civil rights issues fused with political ideologies in the post-1960s era. Conservatives played a key role in redefining the ideological context in which civil rights policies were debated and formulated, but it was not a linear or monolithic process. The 1970s were a period of political learning for both Republicans and Democrats as they sought to adjust to a landscape transformed by the passage of civil rights legislation. Over time, and especially during the Reagan Revolution of the 1980s, conservatives influenced the public debate through a multifaceted approach that involved the redefinition and restriction of civil rights policies and programs. The conservative movement's strength stemmed from its ability to rearticulate opposition to government efforts to promote racial equality in ways that were not explicitly racist and had broad appeal to Americans across the political spectrum. They redefined the meaning of civil rights to the narrowest possible framework of individual rights, leaving broader notions expressed by King to rest meekly on the margins of public debate. The core rhetoric of conservatives—stressing "states' rights" and "law and order," while opposing "big government" and "government intrusion in our private lives"—comprised key themes of an emotional political language that served to restrict government involvement in promoting racial equality while at the same time masking the racialized implications of many conservative objectives.[22] As the explicit racism of segregationists like Wallace became discreditable, a new political language coalesced around retrenchment on civil rights that was subsumed by a broader assault on government itself.[23] Opposition to big government and regulation grew symbiotically with opposition to government activism to promote racial equality. These were not identical processes, but neither again were they separate. Each was pivotal to the rise of the other.

Yet, as a second theme, the essays also complicate the simple picture of a "liberal" or "conservative" approach to civil rights at the level of partisan politicking. There was more fluidity across party lines and political ideology than conventional wisdom suggests. Both ideology and policy evolved over time. The essays in these pages do not tell a simple story of Democratic support for civil rights and Republican opposition to it, nor merely of liberal defeat and conservative success. The story is messier and less partisan, with ebbs and flows, battles won and lost. There was considerable inconsistency. Even conservative presidents, as John Skrentny suggests, pursued liberal "zigs" and conservative "zags" in their approach to civil rights. To be sure, the years of Ronald Reagan's presidency marked a low point for civil rights reform, as his administration had a dramatic and long-lasting impact on the restriction of the civil rights agenda. (The administration's impact was so significant that three essays address different facets of the issue.) Yet this volume also reveals, for example, that Republican presidents Richard Nixon and George W. Bush may have had a more significant, if not also flawed, impact on racial equality than Democratic president Bill Clinton, despite reputations to the contrary. Similar surprises emerge in the legislative arena. Liberal Democrats like Senator Joe Biden—later to become vice president to the first black president—were at the forefront of efforts to combat the use of busing to desegregate schools, pushing back hard against Jimmy Carter on the issue. Conversely, moderate Republicans like Senator Bob

Dole joined forces with Democrats to oppose Ronald Reagan's efforts to weaken civil rights enforcement and emasculate the U.S. Commission on Civil Rights. There may have been a conservative-liberal divide on civil rights, but it did not always break down neatly along party lines.

This seeming contradiction—that the conservative movement restricted civil rights in key ways while some conservatives expanded or defended them in others—is addressed by the volume's third theme: often, but not always, political pragmatism did more to influence civil rights policies than political ideology. Although personal conviction had some impact on how individual presidents approached such issues as affirmative action, welfare reform, school integration, and judicial action on civil rights, electoral maneuvering and the broader political context had a greater impact on presidential decision making. Admittedly, presidents were affected and constrained by the larger conservative ideological currents in the body politic. Yet, for both Democrats and Republicans, official ideologies mattered less than rudimentary political calculations—a factor that mitigated against both conservative retrenchment on and liberal expansion of the civil rights agenda. Partly as a result, civil rights attitudes and policies changed incrementally rather than dramatically. If there was a trend of "winning while losing" on civil rights policies, then it applied in differing ways to liberals and conservatives alike.

This points to a fourth theme of the volume, which emerges implicitly rather than explicitly in several of the essays: the remarkable extent to which the presidential impact on civil rights took place below the proverbial radar screen. In the aftermath of the landmark legislation of the mid-1960s, complex issues of enforcement, interpretation, and implementation of civil rights laws would comprise the key terrain on which civil rights battles were fought. The presidency could exert great influence here without necessarily attracting great attention. Although some issues like affirmative action and school desegregation through busing aroused considerable controversy and played out visibly in mainstream political debates, oftentimes presidential administrations exerted the greatest impact on civil rights policies through actions executed in the shadows. Conservatives found, in the Reagan period especially, that frontal assaults on civil rights could provoke formidable resistance. But opponents of civil rights reform could still restrict and reconstruct the civil rights environment through complex administrative mechanisms, judicial rule-making and appointments, and the rhetorical redefinition of civil rights policies as "reverse discrimination" or "government intrusion" on individual freedom. Such measures effectively stymied the further expansion of the civil rights agenda without at the same time provoking a mainstream national debate about their racialized impact. Likewise, hot-button issues such as taxation, welfare, and health care were often discussed and pursued with little meaningful consideration of their effect on civil rights and racial equality. Race and the legacy of discrimination were often marginalized in the public debate. As a consequence, civil rights advocates and their liberal supporters were often unable to get meaningful traction.

The fifth theme of the volume is one foreshadowed by King's last book: the persistent tension between two differing definitions of civil rights—economic equality versus political rights. These were the issues around which many of the policy debates revolved. Success in the move toward legal and political rights created an illusion of broader equality that counterintuitively undermined the movement for economic and social equality. As King foresaw, winning in one area, political rights, in fact and paradoxically made it harder to advance in the other area, economic rights.

Civil Rights in a New Era

As the civil rights movement fractured in the last years of King's life, many Americans grappled with the question King asked in his last book: Where do we go from here? When Richard Nixon triumphed in the 1968 election, he faced the difficult task of defining the political meaning of civil rights in a new era, one transformed by the end of legalized segregation and black disenfranchisement. In this new era, would the presidency become a focal point for continuing civil rights reforms or for retrenchment? For Nixon's political advisors the answer was both.

In the first chapter, the sociologist John Skrentny reveals that Nixon based his approach to civil rights, as he did for so many of his policies, on cold political calculations. His presidency marked a period of ideological transformation as both liberals and conservatives sought to stake out new positions in a country transformed by civil rights reforms. Nixon's first term, Skrentny writes, "was a period of tremendous policy development, but it was also a period where conservatives and liberals were negotiating the role and meaning of ideology in a new and important policy area." The meaning of civil rights was in flux. In sharp contrast to Ronald Reagan, who would draw from personal convictions to redefine the conservative approach to civil rights, Nixon personally and politically lacked an ideological stance. His pragmatism produced both surprises and contradictions. Nixon, who transparently pursued a "southern strategy" through carefully calibrated appeals to white southern resentment over desegregation, also endorsed affirmative action and federal support to develop economic self-sufficiency among minority communities. He left unadulterated the civil rights reforms enacted by his liberal predecessor while appealing rhetorically to white resentment over those same reforms. Moreover, it was the Republican Richard Nixon who crafted several of the key civil rights policies—such as using the IRS to go after discriminatory private schools—that would, with great irony, later mobilize conservative attacks on the Democratic Party and Jimmy Carter.

Political opportunism dictated Nixon's approach. While conceding the African American vote to the Democrats, Nixon maneuvered his civil rights policies to attract greater numbers of women and Latinos to the Republican fold. Thus, for example, Nixon adopted a sluggish and half-hearted support for affirmative action for blacks while vigorously promoting—"with little restraint"—affirmative action for Latinos as part of a concerted effort to woo them to the Republican Party. Similarly, the Nixon administration directed federal funds for minority business development to Latino business owners as part of an overarching effort to construct a new conservative coalition. In the case of women, Nixon had no specific plan. He struggled to find a conservative stance on women's rights, but—in striking contrast to his approach to African Americans and Latinos—was unable to formulate a coherent political strategy. Gradually, political realities helped produce a new conservative approach to civil rights as "the Nixon administration and future Republicans learned what conservatives should say and believe about civil rights in America." By the end of Nixon's second term, conservatives had realized that opposition to policies that sent categorical benefits to minorities would constitute the new orthodoxy on civil rights.

The uncertain and experimental aspects of civil rights policy continued during the Carter administration. The president from Plains, Georgia, recognized both individual and institutional forms of racism but pursued an inconsistent and at times contradictory approach to civil rights in response to an evolving political climate. During his presidency, conservative opposition to such civil rights remedies as affirmative action, tax penalties for discriminatory private schools, and busing came into sharp relief. Such measures were swept up in a larger anti-regulatory tide in American politics. Conservatives successfully framed busing and affirmative action as un-American and discriminatory, as well as standing for big government and red tape. In this context, just as Nixon had struggled to discern the Republican civil rights orthodoxy, so too did Carter cast about for the new Democratic framework on civil rights. The historian Joseph Crespino and his co-author Asher Smith reveal that Carter's administration—like Nixon's before—struggled to stake out a middle course on civil rights. Carter found it difficult to navigate between his minority constituents and liberal supporters of civil rights on the one hand and a growing section of the electorate that was increasingly alarmed by policies like affirmative action and busing on the other.

Carter's approach was contradictory as a result. As a candidate, he opposed busing to desegregate schools. Yet, as president, he took a fairly strong position in support of it. His efforts were stymied by a coalition of Republicans and Democrats that passed legislation undermining the administration's ability to use busing to enforce desegregation. On affirmative action, Carter walked a fine line. He spoke out in favor of affirmative action in principle, but rejected quotas by universities as argued in the *Bakke* case. Conversely, he later strongly supported private business use of minority set asides, as challenged in the *Weber* case. Conservatives viewed affirmative action in both cases as reverse discrimination, and Carter's muddling support for the principle of affirmative action but vehement rejection of racial quotas ceded ideological ground to conservatives. His tepid approach reflected the changing mood of the white electorate as well as a larger anti-regulatory ethos in the body politic. As the authors note, "programs denounced as racial quotas became important props for conservative critics in their larger attack on what they considered to be big government run amok." In this context, Carter and many other Democrats adopted conservative language about government that militated against an expansive civil rights agenda. Carter offered no compelling counter-narrative, thus setting the stage for Reagan and other conservatives to wrest control of the terms of the civil rights debate.

And seize control they did. By the end of the 1970s, a highly polarized environment on civil rights had taken shape. Ronald Reagan both capitalized on this environment and contributed to it. He constructed his New Right coalition in no small measure by appealing to white resentment on matters of race and civil rights. The era's sharpest and most consequential political battles on civil rights played out under his watch as president. Although Reagan experienced some defeats and had mixed success in these fights, his administration exerted a fundamental and long-lasting impact on both the legal and political frameworks in which subsequent civil rights debates would be contested, especially on matters of economic justice.

In the legislative arena, as the historian and former chairperson of the United States Civil Rights Commission Mary Frances Berry reveals, the Reagan administration came out swinging. It waged one battle after another to turn back the clock on civil rights. The Reagan White House attempted to dilute the Voting Rights Act, to defeat fair housing legislation, to provide tax exemptions and federal funds to schools and colleges that still practiced discrimination, and to appoint the controversial judge Robert Bork—who had a worrisome record on civil rights—to the Supreme Court. Remarkably, Reagan failed in each of these areas. He was stymied by the Leadership Conference on Civil Rights (LCCR), a coalition of over 180 national organizations representing various minority groups, and by legislators on both sides of the aisle. These setbacks in the legislative arena caused Reagan to change strategy. He took aim at the Civil Rights Commission. He sought to transform the commission from a government watchdog into the administration's "lap dog" by replacing liberal members (including Berry herself) with conservatives. Reagan's attempts to snooker the commission were partially successful, but a coalition of Democrats and moderate Republicans ultimately protected the commission from becoming thoroughly politicized.

Reagan then shifted his attention to the federal courts. He appointed an astounding number of conservative judges to the bench, making more judicial appointments than any other president to date. Half of the judiciary was composed of Reagan appointees by the time he left office. Although Reagan named 376 judges to the federal courts, only six new appointees were African American. Chosen primarily for their fidelity to conservative principles and for their youth, Reagan's judicial appointees exerted a tremendous impact on the legal environment for civil rights that persists to this day. As time passed, the Supreme Court and lower courts announced narrow interpretations of civil rights laws that fundamentally restructured the legal landscape. Much of this was due to the Reagan appointees. For this reason, Berry argues that Reagan's defeats in the legislative battles to overturn civil rights policy were overshadowed by his successful bid to move the judicial system and public opinion against the civil rights policies of the 1960s.

The legal impact of Reagan's maneuvering was revolutionary. Whereas the courts had championed civil rights through much of the twentieth century, Reagan successfully shifted the courts from being the most important governmental advocate for racial equality to being the opposite: a force for rolling back civil rights legislation. This impact is further explored by the legal scholar and political scientist Richard Pacelle Jr. He argues that the administration applied three overarching strategies for using the courts to turn back the clock on civil rights: first, the replacement of federal judges with those who supported retrenchment on civil rights; second, the redefinition of rights and responsibilities to facilitate the rewriting of legal precedent; and third, the reconstruction of government mechanisms that deal with civil rights policies. This three-pronged plan was anything but conservative, Pacelle notes, since it aspired to use the courts and the bureaucracy to pursue social change.

Of special consequence was the politicization of the Justice Department. Part of Reagan's reconstruction strategy involved remaking the Office of the Solicitor General (OSG), a powerful and important arm of the Justice Department that determines which cases will be argued before the Supreme Court and serves as the government's advocate in the court cases. Since Harry Truman's day, both Republican and Democratic presidents had used the OSG to extend the frontiers of civil rights. But Reagan moved in the opposite direction. He stacked the OSG with conservative political appointees who led the effort to compel the courts to alter civil rights precedents. Similarly, Reagan appointees micromanaged attorneys and officials in the Civil Rights Division and the Equal Employment Opportunity Commission in an attempt to weaken enforcement of civil rights laws. The administration's attempts to create a conservative Department of Justice resulted in a reconstructed Office of the Solicitor General with the new politically appointed position of Principal Deputy, who micromanaged the attorneys and sought to move the OSG to the right. Ironically, as a result of all of these efforts, the agencies that had been charged with defending and advancing civil rights became "agents of retrenchment."

Reagan's most significant impact was negative, argues the political scientist Robert Smith in an essay that looks at both the Reagan and Clinton eras. Reagan was a "reconstructive president" not for what he accomplished, Smith argues, but for what he prevented. He brought an end to New Deal liberalism, thus closing off opportunities for liberal, activist government. Reagan's ideological influence, as well as his economic and legal policies, placed constraints on his successors. So too did the larger conservative turn in the electorate. Indeed, by the time Bill Clinton won the 1992 presidential election, the Republican Party had controlled the White House for twenty of the previous twenty-four years. In order to wrest control from the Republicans, Clinton usurped conservative language on civil rights. Although Clinton possessed a deep personal commitment to racial equality, this conviction was not matched by initiatives that could address ingrained inequalities. Clinton became a "preemptive president" because of his ability to co-opt or manipulate conservative policies and ideas and make them a part of a reformulated Democratic Party. Clinton's waffling on affirmative action and welfare reform stemmed from his attempts to co-opt aspects of the conservative approach to civil rights while maintaining the African American base of the Democratic Party. Smith concludes, "Bill Clinton was a highly successful preemptive president" because the president hijacked conservative policy on civil rights and welfare reform while managing to preserve high levels of African American support.

Smith also contextualizes the larger cultural and intellectual divide that separated conservatives and liberals on civil rights. He reveals that the rise of the neoconservatives, which would be so pivotal in making the presidency of Clinton's successor, George W. Bush, was rooted in domestic, rather than foreign, policy. Neoconservative intellectuals were mobilized by their opposition to the liberal activism of the 1960s and 1970s. By the time of Reagan's election, they had reframed the debate on race and civil rights. They argued that the responsibility for dealing with racialized poverty belonged not to the government or to the country as a whole but to the black community itself. African American leaders and their liberal allies disagreed, blaming economic forces and structural racism for the disproportionate representation of blacks on welfare rolls. Neoconservatives, by contrast, argued that the problem was cultural: it stemmed from the laziness, sexual promiscuity, and lack of responsibility in African American communities, especially among men. Attacks on affirmative action and welfare were staples of neoconservative arguments. Ronald Reagan promulgated the neoconservative view throughout his presidency, aggravating racial stereotypes by branding welfare recipients as lazy welfare queens. Despite his personal disagreement with such views, Clinton adopted much of this rhetoric as both a candidate and a president. Pledging to end welfare "as we know it," Clinton pursued a calculated strategy to win working-class whites that paralleled Reagan's approach. His welfare-reform legislation—by requiring recipients to work, but without providing guaranteed employment—reflected the neoconservative argument that it was laziness and dependency, not lack of opportunity, that kept blacks on welfare. Whereas Clinton argued that welfare reform was a means of "reviving liberalism," Senator Daniel Patrick Moynihan rejoined that Clinton's welfare reform constituted "the most regressive event in social policy of the twentieth century." However one assesses Clinton's record, it is hard to dispute Smith's argument that on matters of civil rights Clinton was walking in the shadows of Ronald Reagan.

Clinton's presidency ended with one of the closest elections in American history, a heated contest that exposed the continuing challenges posed by race and racism at the turn of the twenty-first century. In the disputed election of 2000, Clinton's vice president, Al Gore, ran against Texas Governor George W. Bush. Although Gore won the popular vote, the electoral-college tally was so close that the fate of the presidency hung on the state of Florida and its twenty-five electoral votes. The final result was close enough to trigger a recount under Florida state law. While the ensuing media frenzy focused on the hanging chads and butterfly ballots that made the recount so controversial, a largely overlooked but more insidious pattern of minority-voter disenfranchisement may have had a decisive impact on the election. At predominantly minority precincts throughout the state, voters were kept from casting their ballots through complex administrative rules, faulty voting machines, police intimidation, and other tactics. Although a relatively small number of voters were disenfranchised in this way, the political scientist Charles Zelden suggests that voter disenfranchisement could have determined the outcome of the 2000 election, which was eventually decided, with the help of the U.S. Supreme Court, in favor of George W. Bush.

Zelden's analysis serves as a reminder that to understand the relationship between civil rights and the presidency, we need to look not just at presidential decision-making but also at the process through which Americans select their presidents. Comparing the evidence of vote-denial in the 2000 election with patterns of disenfranchisement from earlier and subsequent elections, Zelden reveals the myriad ways in which institutional forms of race-based disenfranchisement have been entrenched in the nation's electoral system. Since the Voting Rights Act of 1965, the disenfranchisement of minority voters has often been implemented through technically race-neutral legal provisions and administrative procedures, but the net effect has been an observable and significant pattern of vote denial and voter intimidation. A racialized pattern of disenfranchisement emanated from numerous sources: faulty voting equipment in heavily minority districts, disputed voter purges, voter intimidation, and other suspicious activities. These highly suspect occurrences stemmed from a much longer legacy of voter disenfranchisement that has consistently benefited opponents of civil rights. Zelden's analysis challenges contemporary assertions that aggressive civil rights enforcement is no longer needed because of the decline of overt racism.

The presidency of George W. Bush reflected the tendency of conservatives to acknowledge individual forms of racism while downplaying the impact of systemic or structural impediments to equality. Yet, as the historian Steven F. Lawson reveals, Bush's legacy on civil rights defies easy categorization. Like others before him, Bush staked out a position between extremes. He departed both from civil rights purists on the Left and from hard-line conservatives on the Right. Having lost the popular vote and won the presidency by the narrowest of margins, Bush never wrote off minority voters. He actively courted Latinos and African Americans through his efforts to combat the AIDS epidemic in Africa, promote minority business enterprises and home ownership, support the extension of the Voting Rights Act, and appoint minorities to high-level government positions. Bush prided himself on the knowledge that his father, as a congressman, had voted for the Civil Rights Act of 1968. Eschewing racism in his private life, Bush viewed the diversity of his cabinet as the ultimate symbol of his own progressivism on matters of race. His closest advisors included Colin Powell as secretary of state, Condoleezza Rice as national security advisor, and Alberto Gonzales as White House counsel and later U.S. attorney general. In Bush's mind, he was no racist, and he took great offense at suggestions to the contrary.

Before the terrorist attacks of 2001 turned Bush's attention to foreign policy, his top priority was educational reform. Keenly aware of the vast achievement gap between black and white schoolchildren, Bush presented his No Child Left Behind legislation as a civil rights act. Educational reform also served a political purpose. It allowed the president to appeal to both white and minority voters without injecting divisive racial issues into the conversation. Bush hoped to steer the public debate away from affirmative action and its controversial racial preferences and toward quality schooling, an idea that played to conservative principles of individual achievement and self-advancement. Nevertheless, the No Child Left Behind Act was not universally supported among conservatives, many of whom were suspicious about federal intervention in education, especially in the South. In part for this reason, Lawson argues, "Bush deserves greater recognition than he has received for departing from the strictures of conservative ideology to reform education in a manner not witnessed since the 1960s. In so doing he enlarged the scope of the traditional civil rights agenda to include reading and math literacy."

Such measures suggest to Lawson that Bush cannot simply be dismissed as hostile to the interests of African Americans and other minorities, nor can his mantra of "compassionate conservatism" be discarded as mere sloganeering. Yet, although Bush parted ways with hard-liners in his party by endorsing a strong federal role for educational reform, he sided with fellow conservatives in his opposition to affirmative action. He also surpassed Ronald Reagan in his politicization of the Justice Department and diluting of civil rights enforcement. Ignoring systemic forms of discrimination that limited opportunities for nonwhite Americans, Bush pursued regressive economic policies that dramatically widened the gap between rich and poor. African American poverty increased perceptibly during his presidency.

For these and other reasons, Bush failed to win support from the civil rights community. In fact, he fared worse than other Republican presidents despite his initiatives to win African American votes. In part this was because many African Americans felt stung by the 2000 election. They felt Bush had won the presidency illegitimately at the expense of disenfranchised black voters. More fundamentally, many African Americans perceived that Bush's brand of conservatism left unresolved and even worsened conditions in their communities. Whereas Bush believed that self-help and hard work could uplift poverty-stricken individuals, the civil rights community countered that remedying conditions of deep racial and economic equality required government involvement on a scale that conservatives like Bush deplored. In the end, Bush's legacy was defined by the government's inept response to Hurricane Katrina. In its destruction of New Orleans, the storm unmasked the tragic consequences of black poverty and the long-avoided ramifications of structural racism. Many blacks remained in the city as the storm approached because they were poor and lacked the means to evacuate. "The hurricane dramatically revealed that the country may have conquered legal inequality," Lawson observes, "but the debilitating effects of race and racial discrimination had pulled a disproportionate share of blacks into poverty and left them less able to flee the storm's wrath." To Bush's critics, Katrina exposed the weakness of the conservative hostility to government as well as the persistent reality of racial inequality in America.

It was with some irony, then, that even as the nation grappled with the consequences of the storm, conservatives used the election of the nation's first black president to argue that racism was over and that special efforts on behalf of African Americans were no longer needed. As the political scientists Ronald W. Walters and Robert C. Smith note, conservatives used Obama's success "as an argument to scale back the enforcement of civil rights." In an essay that explores the meaning and significance of Obama's election in 2008 for the cause of civil rights, the authors suggest that the challenge facing Obama was to advance a broad meaning of civil rights that included political freedom, social and economic equality, and human rights. Such a task was made harder by arguments suggesting that the election of a black president meant that racial equality had been achieved. Moreover, Walters and Smith wonder if the fear of being accused of racial favoritism would limit Obama in addressing the structural issues black communities face. They conclude, "the final contradiction at the heart of the Obama presidency is that if he does little to address both citizenship and human rights dimensions of the civil rights agenda, his election will be a loss" for civil rights in the United States. As a symbol of how far the country has come on the road to racial equality, Obama may paradoxically impede further advancements by suggesting, to some, that the battle has already been won.

Indeed, Obama shows signs of having been constrained by the most consequential impact of the conservative turn in American politics: a broad intellectual current that holds out "free market" and individualistic solutions to socioeconomic problems and rejects more radical solutions. Americans may have become more egalitarian, and more accepting of racial diversity, but they have also become less attentive to the persistent reality of inequality and less receptive to governmental efforts to address that inequality. The broad rejection of government interventionism on social issues has had the effect of constraining the civil rights agenda since the 1970s. In the years following the civil rights movement, government policies to promote equality were increasingly viewed as suspect and as trampling on individual liberty and free markets. This trend was not merely American, nor confined to conservatives, nor restricted to merely civil rights issues; it reflected a global trend away from government activism and toward laissez-faire approaches to social problems, as Tim Borstelmann so aptly suggests in the conclusion to this volume.[24] The United States was not alone in its turn away from government interventionism and in its faith in individualism, factors that may have impeded the goals of civil rights activists but that had diffuse and remarkable impacts worldwide. The global turn toward both egalitarianism and individualism had paradoxical implications for people of color in the United States. On the one hand, the new spirit of egalitarianism opened new doors and discredited open discrimination and racism. But, on the other, the unfettered individualism closed off opportunities for government intervention to advance racial equality.

King himself saw such a paradoxical march to progress at work when he penned his last book. "Ever since the birth of our nation," he wrote:

> white America has had a schizophrenic personality on the question of race. She has been torn between selves—a self in which she proudly professed the great principles of democracy and a self in which she sadly practiced the antithesis of democracy. This tragic duality has produced a strange indecisiveness and ambivalence toward the Negro, causing America to take a step backward simultaneously with every step forward on the question of racial justice, to be at once attracted to the Negro and repelled by him, to love and to hate him. There has never been a solid, unified and determined thrust to make justice a reality for Afro-Americans.[25]

The great civil rights leader, who at last stands memorialized on the national mall in Washington, D.C., anticipated that the paradox of winning while losing on civil rights would continue long after his death.

Notes

1. See for example: Eugene Patterson, "Dr. King Warns Against the Riots," *Atlanta Constitution*, June 27, 1967; Clarence Seidenspinner, "Man's Struggle for Freedom," *Chicago Tribune*, June 25, 1967; "Not Accepting White Help Black Power Weakness," *Atlanta Inquirer*, June 24, 1967; "Negroes Suffer From Riots, King Writes in New Book," *The Oregonian*, June 25, 1967; "King's Book Refutes Black Power," *Los Angeles Sentinel*, June 22, 1967; Paul Hathaway, "An Analysis of Black Power," *Washington Star*, June 26, 1967.

2. Martin Luther King Jr., *Where Do We Go From Here: Chaos or Community?* (Boston: Beacon Press, 1967, 2010), 94, 4.

3. King, *Where Do We Go From Here*, 4–12. See also Thomas F. Jackson, *From Civil Rights to Human Rights: Martin Luther King, Jr., and the Struggle for Economic Justice* (Philadelphia: University of Pennsylvania Press, 2007); Harvard Sitkoff, *King: Pilgrimage To The Mountaintop* (New York: Hill & Wang, 2008).

4. Sean Wilentz, *The Age of Reagan, 1974–2008* (New York: Harper Perennial, 2009).

5. King's death left civil rights organizations and politicians the space to redefine civil rights in differing ways. See for example, Peniel E. Joseph, *Waiting 'Til the Midnight Hour: A Narrative History of Black Power in America* (New York: Henry Holt, 2007); Derrick E. White, *The Challenge of Blackness: The Institute of the Black World and Political Activism in the 1970s* (Gainesville: University Press of Florida, 2011).

6. Sadiq Green, "Op-Ed: Completing MLK's Dream," *Digital Journal*, January 19, 2009, http://www.digitaljournal.com/article/265489; Mark Engler, "Dr. Martin Luther King's Economics: Through Jobs, Freedom," February 1, 2010, *The Nation*, http://www.thenation.com/article/dr-martin-luther-kings-economics-through-jobs-freedom; Jesse Jackson Sr., "Where Do We Go From Here? An Active and Vocal Movement," undated [December 2009], http://www.blackpressusa.com/op-ed/speaker.asp?NewsID=20540. See also, Sean Thomas-Breitfeld, "What's Left Out of Black History Month Celebrations," *The Nation*, February 6, 2012, http://www.thenation.com/article/166085/whats-left-out-black-history-month-celebrations.

7. Charlene Crowell, "Where Do We Go From Here?" *Philadelphia Tribune*, October 25, 2011, http://www.phillytrib.com/commentaryarticles/item/1205-'where-do-we-go-from-here?.'html. See also, Thomas J. Sugrue, *Not Even Past: Barack Obama and the Burden of Race* (Princeton: Princeton University Press, 2011).

8. Donald T. Critchlow, *The Conservative Ascendancy: How the GOP Right Made Political History* (Cambridge, Mass.: Harvard University Press, 2007).

9. Michael Schaller, *Right Turn: American Life in the Reagan-Bush Era, 1980–1992* (New York: Oxford University Press, 2007), 16–22.

10. Much of the historical literature on the 1970s stresses the gradual movement of American politics to the political right. See Bruce J. Shulman and Julian E. Zelizer, eds., *Rightward Bound: Making America Conservative in the 1970s* (Cambridge, Mass.: Harvard University Press, 2008); Dan T. Carter, *The Politics of Rage: George Wallace, the Origins of the New Conservatism,* 2nd ed. (Baton Rouge: Louisiana State University Press, 1995, 2000); Dominic Sandbrook, *Mad as Hell: The Crisis of the 1970s and the*

Rise of the Populist Right (New York: Anchor Books, 2012); and Thomas Borstelmann, *The 1970s: A New Global History from Civil Rights to Economic Inequality* (Princeton: Princeton University Press, 2011).

11. Gareth Davies, *From Opportunity to Entitlement: The Transformation and Decline of Great Society Liberalism* (Lawrence: University of Kansas Press, 1996).

12. For a succinct overview, see Schaller, *Right Turn*, 16–22.

13. Thomas Byrne Edsall and Mary D. Edsall, *Chain Reaction: The Impact of Race, Rights, and Taxes on American Politics* (New York: W.W. Norton & Co, 1992). See also, Kim Phillips-Fein, *Invisible Hands: The Businessmen's Crusade Against the New Deal* (New York: W.W. Norton, 2010).

14. Key overviews of the conservative revival include Laura Kalman, *Right Star Rising: A New Politics, 1974–1980* (New York: W.W. Norton, 2010); Thomas Frank, *What's the Matter with Kansas? How Conservatives Won the Heart of America* (New York: Holt, 2005); Shulman and Zelizer, eds., *Rightward Bound*; Wilentz, *The Age of Reagan*; Schaller, *Right Turn*; Davies, *From Opportunity to Entitlement*; Critchlow, *The Conservative Ascendancy*. On the intellectual origins of the conservative movement, see especially James A. Smith, *The Idea Brokers: Think Tanks and the New Policy Elites* (New York: Free Press, 1991); David Ricci, *The Transformation of American Politics: The New Washington and the Rise of Think Tanks* (New Haven: Yale University Press, 1993); Gary Dorrien, *The Neoconservative Mind: Politics, Culture, and the War of Ideology* (Philadelphia: Temple University Press, 1993); and John B. Judis, *William F. Buckley, Jr.: Patron Saint of the Conservatives* (New York: Simon and Shuster, 2001). On grassroots conservatism among young people see John A. Andrew III, *The Other Side of the Sixties: Young Americans for Freedom and the Rise of Conservative Politics* (New Brunswick: Rutgers University Press, 1997).

15. Works stressing the foreign-policy origins of the conservative ascendancy include James Mann, *Rise of the Vulcans: The History of Bush's War Cabinet* (New York: Viking, 2004); Jacob Heilbrunn, *They Knew They Were Right: The Rise of the Neocons* (New York: Doubleday, 2009); and Adam Clymer, *Drawing the Line at the Big Ditch: The Panama Canal Treaties and the Rise of the Right* (Lawrence: University Press of Kansas, 2008). In looking at the mobilization of grassroots conservatism, Donald T. Critchlow and Lisa McGirr stress both Cold War anticommunism and social issues. See Critchlow, *Phyllis Schlafly and Grassroots Conservatism: A Woman's Crusade* (Princeton: Princeton University Press, 2007); and McGirr, *Suburban Warriors: The Origins of the New American Right* (Princeton: Princeton University Press, 2002).

16. Detailed treatment of the role of race and civil rights in the conservative revival can be found especially in works exploring the political history of the South. See Dan T. Carter, *The Politics of Rage*; Carter, *From George Wallace to Newt Gingrich: Race and the Conservative Counterrevolution* (Baton Rouge: LSU Press, 1996); Edsall and Edsall, *Chain Reaction*; Kevin Kruse, *White Flight: Atlanta and the Making of Modern Conservatism* (Princeton: Princeton University Press, 2005); Joseph Crespino, *In Search of Another Country: Mississippi and the Conservative Counterrevolution* (Princeton: Princeton University Press, 2007); Matthew D. Lassiter, *The Silent Majority: Suburban Politics in the Sunbelt South* (Princeton: Princeton University Press, 2007); Byron E. Shafer and

Richard Johnston, *The End of Southern Exceptionalism: Class, Race, and Partisan Change in the Postwar South* (Cambridge, Mass.: Harvard University Press, 2006); Glenn Feldman, ed., *Painting Dixie Red: When, Where, Why, and How the South Became Republican* (Gainesville: University Press of Florida, 2011). Although much of the literature focuses on the South, racial politics elsewhere in the country are explored in Thomas J. Sugrue, *Sweet Land of Liberty: The Forgotten Struggle for Civil Rights in the North* (New York: Random House, 2009), and Robert O. Self, *American Babylon: Race and the Struggle for Postwar Oakland* (Princeton: Princeton University Press, 2003).

17. See the essay by Berry in this volume.

18. Carter, *From George Wallace to Newt Gingrich*; Carter, *Politics of Rage*; and Kruse, *White Flight*. See also Edsall and Edsall, *Chain Reaction*; Sandbrook, *Mad as Hell*.

19. James T. Patterson, *Grand Expectations: The United States, 1945–1974* (New York: Oxford University Press, 1996), 637–77, 701–2, 707–8.

20. Lassiter, *The Silent Majority*, 4–5. See also Kevin M. Kruse and Thomas J. Sugrue, eds., *The New Suburban History*, (Chicago: University of Chicago Press, 2006).

21. Eduardo Bonilla-Silva, *Racism Without Racists: Colorblind Racism and Racial Inequality in Contemporary America*, 3rd ed. (Lanham, Md.: Rowman & Littlefield, 2010). See also Tim Wise, *Colorblind: The Rise of Post-Racial Politics and the Retreat from Racial Equity* (San Francisco: City Lights, 2010); Stephen Steinberg, *Turning Back: The Retreat from Racial Justice in American Thought and Policy* (Boston: Beacon, 1995); Harvard Sitkoff, *The Struggle for Black Equality* (New York: Hill and Wang, 1981, 2008), 210–36; and Sitkoff, *Toward Freedom Land: The Long Struggle For Racial Equality In America* (Lexington: University Press of Kentucky, 2010).

22. Glenn Feldman, "Epilogue: Ugly Roots; Race, Emotion, and the Rise of the Modern Republican Party in Alabama and the South," in *Before Brown: Civil Rights and White Backlash in the Modern South*, ed. Feldman (Tuscaloosa: University of Alabama Press, 2004), 268–309; Glenn Feldman, "Introduction: Has the South Become Republican?" in *Painting Dixie Red*, ed. Feldman, 1–18; Michael Omi and Howard Winant, *Racial Formation in the United States: From the 1960s to the 1990s*, 2nd ed. (New York: Routledge, 1986, 1994); Derrick E. White, "'Blacks Who Had Not Themselves Personally Suffered Illegal Discrimination': The Symbolic Incorporation of the Black Middle Class," in *Race and the Foundations of Knowledge*, ed. Joseph Young and Jana Evans Braziel (Urbana: University of Illinois Press, 2006); Lassiter, *The Silent Majority*.

23. J.G.A. Pocock, *Politics, Language, and Time: Essays on Political Thought and History* (Chicago: University of Chicago Press, 1989), 3–41.

24. See also Borstelmann's excellent analysis of global political trends in *The 1970s*.

25. King, *Where Do We Go From Here?*, 72.

1

ZIGS AND ZAGS

Richard Nixon and the New Politics of Race

JOHN D. SKRENTNY

In the fall of 1970, Richard Nixon's top domestic policy advisor, John Ehrlichman, found himself frozen out of the Oval Office. Nixon accepted no appointments and offered no responses to his memoranda. After ten days of silence, the president finally gave an indication of the nature of the problem: insufficient conservatism in key areas of domestic policy. Nixon gave to Ehrlichman a newspaper column by Kevin Phillips arguing that Nixon had veered too far to the Left on crucial aspects of the "social issue," or what we now might call the "culture wars."[1] Specifically, Phillips argued that Nixon's support for affirmative action, integration of the suburbs, and welfare and his Presidential Commission on Campus Unrest had revealed excessive liberalism that alienated working-class whites—whites who were needed for an election victory in 1972. Nixon told his domestic policy chief that Phillips offered "a correct view"—and Ehrlichman should "take action to correct this."

Ehrlichman was able to return to Nixon's good graces only by penning a long memo that offered an ideological rationale for these seemingly wayward policy moves. He argued that a totally conservative line on the social issue was misguided and that a "centerist strategy" was best. But since "very few initiatives will be truly in the center," Nixon had to find balance by mixing in with his "conservative zags" some good liberal "zigs." In the matter of race issues, Ehrlichman argued that Nixon's affirmative action, targeted at labor unions, was a good wedge issue to divide blacks and labor unions, two key constituents of the Democratic Party. But he also admitted that suburban integration had to be stopped.

The memo worked. Nixon invited his adviser in for a ninety-minute meeting, and the ten-day freeze was never mentioned again. The larger message from the domestic-policy advisor freeze-out, however, remained: partisan politics after the civil rights movement were a minefield. What was conservative and what was liberal regarding civil rights (that is, regulatory efforts to prevent discrimination and promote equality) were unknown. And as unclear as were the politics of black civil rights, the politics of women's rights and rights for the emerging minority group of Latinos were even less clear.

Enter into this context of political ambiguity the enigmatic Richard M. Nixon. Scholars have tried to understand this complex man for decades.[2] On civil rights in particular, Nixon confounded his supporters and his critics.[3] Nixon's civil rights record before his presidency was one of moderation. Notably, he headed Eisenhower's President's Committee on Government Contracts, which made some progress on equal employment opportunities in employment among government contractors. He was also a longtime supporter of the Equal Rights Amendment, which would have ended discrimination on the basis of sex.[4] But his positions were neither firm nor elaborate. They offer little guidance for his positions during his presidency.

Understanding Nixon's civil rights politics requires understanding the context of his policymaking. Nixon was the first president to enter the completely remade civil rights landscape. Lyndon Johnson has presided over the passage of the historic Civil Rights Act of 1964, remaking racial patterns in education, employment, and public accommodations. Legal scholars have noted the revolutionary impact of this act. William Eskridge calls it a "super-statute,"[5] and Bruce Ackerman describes it as a "landmark statute" that affects interpretation of the constitution itself.[6] But there were other important civil rights initiatives as well in the 1960s. There was the Voting Rights Act of 1965 (ending decades of disenfranchisement) and the less effective but nevertheless pioneering Civil Rights Act of 1968 (ending segregation in housing), and Johnson also issued in 1965 the Executive Order 11246, requiring government contractors to cease discrimination on the basis of race, religion, and national origin as well as to take some undefined affirmative action to ensure nondiscrimination.

Even by 1969, it was still not clear how these policies would affect American politics. The meanings of Left and Right were muddled during the passage of these acts in Congress, as they passed with bipartisan support. Making overtly racist statements in public was, of course, no longer legitimate in American politics. Liberal Democrats, it appeared, would support the new policies and would lend support for what became great expansions of the reach of the American regulatory state. Conservative Republicans needed to offer an alternative. What would be the new conservative position on civil rights? The battle over the *existence* of the policies was over—what (or where) would be the new fault line in American civil rights politics?

The ambiguity of the times can be understood on an even broader basis than the civil rights issue. Every president enters into office in a particular climate that affects what that president can or cannot do. The political scientist Stephen Skowronek has argued that presidential politics are largely shaped by the political context in which the president is elected. How resilient is the prevailing political opposition? How close was the election? These factors as well can help us understand presidential action.[7]

Nixon's first term coincided with a fascinating time in American politics. Except for the eight-year reign of moderate Dwight D. Eisenhower, liberal Democrats had governed America for thirty-six years. But the Vietnam War, the counterculture, and urban unrest by African Americans had led to the "unraveling of America," as the historian Allen Matusow put it—or at least to the unraveling of liberalism.[8] Yet liberals in Washington were still assertive and convinced of their moral superiority and entitlement to rule. Nixon was also challenged by social conservative, third-party candidate George Wallace and moderate liberal Democrat Hubert Humphrey in the 1968 election. Nixon won the popular vote by a hair—43.4 percent of the vote compared to Humphrey's 42.7 percent, with Wallace capturing a respectable 13.5 percent.[9] Though the election was close, it also showed that 56.9 percent of voters picked a conservative candidate.

Overall, liberalism seemed to be on the retreat, if not the defensive. But liberalism still seemed strong on civil rights. Whereas in 1964 there were many national leaders who opposed federal civil rights regulations—including Republican presidential candidate Barry Goldwater— in 1968, federal regulations guaranteeing nondiscrimination on the bases of race, national origin, and religion were the new starting point to the discussion. There was still a lot to debate, of course. But that debate was about how far civil rights regulations should go, not whether or not to have them. Because the endpoints of civil rights were entirely unknown, both liberals and conservatives were unsure of what the appropriate policies should be—and how hard to push.

What we see in the Nixon years, then, is a process of learning. As is clear in the episode with Ehrlichman regarding the huge impact of reading one newspaper column by a young Kevin Philips, Nixon was unsure of what to do in this dynamic but confusing political context and was very open to persuasion. He looked for clues from the voters. And these clues and his concern to uncover them varied by the issue and over time. What we see in Nixon's first term—the term where he made policy that set up his landslide 1972 victory and he operated without the distraction of Watergate—is movement in his civil rights policy as he learned of the political impacts of different policy preferences. And where he did not find clues or signals, his policy could vary a lot—from a misguided certainty to a confusion that led to a kind of paralysis.

Nixon's civil rights politics, and the negotiation of the meaning of civil rights conservatism as well as electoral imperatives, changed over time and even more strikingly varied with the group in question. Three cases show a different set of dynamics regarding conservative ideology, electoral strategy, and the cultural meanings of different groups.[10] First, adhering to conservative principles, Nixon tried to establish a new boundary for civil rights for African Americans but was selective about where he was going to push or accept the boundary. Here, Nixon's concern was more with white voters and their potential for backlash than with the African American electorate. Second, Nixon pursued civil rights for Latinos with little restraint. In this case, his administration showed little concern for ideology or the concerns of non-Latino whites and instead innovated energetically in order to win votes from the Latino population. It is difficult to discern Nixon's sense of limits to civil rights policies for Latinos, and policy moved in a more liberal direction. Finally, the case of women's rights reveals an administration without a plan—unclear of the electoral prospects or ideological constraints, but apparently sensing that women, though similar to ethnic and racial minorities, were also somehow different. Nixon struggled to find a conservative stance on women's rights.

Taken together, these cases reveal a "winning while losing" pattern to Nixon's civil rights policies. In some respects, Nixon looked like an enemy of civil rights. He adopted a political strategy that aimed to woo white southerners by slowing down desegregation and employing polarizing rhetoric. During his presidency, momentum for civil rights reforms, especially for African Americans, eased perceptibly. Yet, in other respects, Nixon's policies resulted in an expansion of civil rights. This was particularly true for Latinos, whom Nixon was seeking to lure into the Republican fold. Although Nixon would sometimes mouth conservative rhetoric that implied a limited role for the government in advancing civil rights, his administration's policies, as Ehrlichman suggested, included both liberal "zigs" and conservative "zags."

The cases also show that the great ideological divide between liberals and conservatives on civil rights that characterizes today's politics simply did not exist during Nixon's years in office—or to be more precise, during his first term. Instead, the new political landscape created by civil rights statutes, as well as Nixon's close election, contributed to a piecemeal, learning approach to civil rights politics. It was not until Nixon and later Republicans began to strongly pursue white, working-class voters that the conservative positions on civil rights that we know today—opposition to affirmative action, especially for blacks but also for Latinos, and opposition to bilingual education and multiculturalism in the schools—developed and became staples of campaign speeches. Women's civil rights remained confusing for conservatives, but Nixon's period of confusion settled into quiet acceptance of civil rights laws that aided economic opportunities but resisted those that challenged traditional gender roles.

Civil rights during the Nixon years are significant for several reasons. It was a period of tremendous policy development, but it was also a period where conservatives and liberals were negotiating the role and meaning of ideology in a new and important policy area. In the end, conservatives would end up mostly in support of what they had previously opposed—nondiscrimination rights for minorities. They would also police the new boundaries of the new conservative orthodoxy: opposition to quotas, multiculturalism, and race-conscious (or more generally, "difference-conscious") justice.

Black Civil Rights: Between Ideology and Opportunism

Richard Nixon, as his biographers are fond of noting, was a moderate on civil rights for most of his career.[11] His presidency, however, presented unique circumstances. His approach to black civil rights was both conservative and liberal—though with a conservative or partisan twist. This story of Nixon and black voters has now become well known, and so only a few points need to be made here.

Most famous was Nixon's so-called southern strategy. This referred to his administration's resistance to the advancement of civil rights, especially where that resistance might benefit southern racial conservatives. Not surprisingly, Nixon never embraced this term, and nor did he or his advisors promote the idea that the president was slowing down civil rights to appeal to southerners. But that is exactly what he appeared to do.

This was most apparent on busing.[12] The Nixon administration came to office when courts were deciding what school desegregation really meant. These unelected officials were at the vanguard of black civil rights in schooling and the progressive interpretation of Title VI of the Civil Rights Act of 1964. Its impact on schools far exceeded that of the Supreme Court's 1954 decision, *Brown v. Board of Education*.[13] It declared that no programs or institutions receiving federal funds could discriminate on the basis of race, national origin, or religion. By the late 1960s, courts were moving toward an interpretation of civil rights where desegregation meant measurable, statistical integration. This sometimes required busing school children across town, and it produced a storm of controversy. Nixon campaigned on the issue. During the 1968 primaries, he told southern delegates for the Republican National Convention, "I think that busing the child . . . into a strange community—I think you destroy that child. The purpose of a school is to educate."[14]

Nixon maintained this position in office. He did not stop the march of progress in school desegregation, but he delayed it to signal to southern white voters that he understood their concerns. Attorney General John Mitchell and Department of Health, Education, and Welfare (HEW) Secretary Robert Finch shocked civil rights liberals when they declared that the Nixon administration would avoid terminating federal education aid funds for still-segregated schools. Instead, they would concentrate on voluntary compliance; the threat of a lawsuit would be held in reserve.

They canceled a previous target date of the 1969–70 school year for desegregation. In fact, there would be no target date at all.

The statement outraged civil rights advocates both inside and outside the government. Sixty-five of the one hundred lawyers in the Justice Department's Civil Rights Division signed a petition declaring that Nixon's new approach was "inconsistent with clearly defined legal mandates" and showed "a disposition on the part of responsible officials of the federal government to subordinate clearly defined legal requirements to non-legal considerations."[15]

Outside the government, the reaction from the Left was equally strong and perhaps more colorful. Roy Wilkins, the moderate liberal head of the National Association for the Advancement of Colored People (NAACP), greeted Nixon's announcement with graphic disdain: "It's almost enough to make you vomit." Wilkins believed that Nixon was actually breaking the law, noting that his approach "is not a matter of too little too late; rather, this is nothing at all."[16] Civil rights advocates began to prepare a lawsuit against the government for failing to enforce the Civil Rights Act. In October 1970, the civil rights activist Joseph Rauh and the NAACP Legal Defense Fund—with the help of unhappy HEW officials—did file a lawsuit against HEW for failing to enforce Title VI.[17]

In other areas, though, Nixon positioned himself at the vanguard of black civil rights—though, as we will see, not consistently. Most prominent here and the focus of much attention from scholars is Nixon's role in the birth of affirmative action in employment. The conservative position now is to oppose racial preferences and quotas. But it was not always thus.

Nixon made his case for supporting black civil rights especially with his support for Labor Department regulations implementing Lyndon Johnson's Executive Order 11246. That order, building on and refining and strengthening similar orders issued by Roosevelt, Truman, Eisenhower, and Kennedy, required that contractors doing business with the federal government could not discriminate on the basis of race, national origin, or religion. Both Kenney and Johnson had included in their executive orders a passage saying that contractors had to also take some undefined affirmative action to ensure nondiscrimination. What this meant remained undefined for years.

However, under Johnson the Labor Department's Office of Federal Contract Compliance (OFCC) began to experiment with different regulations implementing the order in the field of construction. Of course, construction was a massive part of federal procurement and an area with considerable interest from civil rights leaders.[18] This was because these jobs were very visible, often located in poor black neighborhoods, and almost completely dominated by white union members.

The OFCC had developed a series of implementing regulations that sought to force the construction unions to open up to African Americans. Tried over a few years and in a series of cities, including St. Louis, the San Francisco-Oakland area, Cleveland, and finally Philadelphia, these regulations developed pragmatically in a way that eventually settled on a reasonably effective regulatory strategy. By the 1968 Philadelphia edition, the regulations required contractors to commit to making good faith efforts to hire a certain percentage range of minorities ("goals") and to do so by a specified time (the "timetables" requirement). All of this happened during the Johnson administration, but the explicit race-consciousness of what was called the Philadelphia Plan ran into some legal trouble, and the plan was put on the shelf.

It remained shelved until the Nixon administration came into office in search of some pro–civil rights initiative to balance the retrograde politics of the southern strategy. In 1969, Nixon dusted it off, made some minor changes, and pushed it hard when southerners in Congress tried to kill it. The Philadelphia Plan appealed to Nixon for many reasons, including most intriguingly the conundrum it created for Democrats. It targeted the overwhelmingly white unions, who voted mostly for Democrats and whose leadership strongly supported Democrats, and tried to benefit African Americans, who also voted overwhelmingly for Democrats. It forced Democrats to pick one constituency over the other. And in picking African Americans and affirmative action, Democrats added to the alienation of working-class whites that several other initiatives of the Johnson era had already exacerbated.[19]

After getting the race-conscious "goals and timetables" regulations of the Philadelphia Plan established, in 1970, the OFCC, with its Order No. 4, expanded them to apply to all contractors with contracts of at least $50,000. It was a tremendous expansion of civil rights regulatory reach. Was there any role for ideology in this policy initiative?

Nixon's support for affirmative action in employment did, in some ways, fit with conservative ideology. He sometimes discussed it as an example of self-help and pointed out that it was about getting people to work rather than relying on government for a handout—as, presumably, the Democrats preferred. Yet in other ways the policy of affirmative action in employment was a significant violation of conservative principles. Much more so than simple nondiscrimination, the affirmative-action regulations limited liberty. The policy told business owners how they should hire and, when enforced strongly, who they should hire. But this was all before the current conservative orthodoxy on color-blind civil rights regulations.

Latinos: The Unfettered Search for a New Majority

Unlike Nixon's policies regarding African Americans, which were shaped significantly if not consistently by the racial conservatism that came to be a GOP staple, the administration's policy regarding Latinos ran free and easily, shaped more by the limits of the administration's imagination and budget than by anything else. Conservative notions of a limited government, at least in its legal reach, were nowhere to be found. This can be seen most clearly in two different policy initiatives that put the government squarely on the side of diversity and minority rights in ways that conservatives later detested.

The first was affirmative action. Bureaucrats at the OFCC included Latinos (along with Asian Americans and American Indians) in the original Philadelphia Plan employment affirmative-action regulations without fanfare. The same occurred at the Equal Employment Opportunity Commission, which used the same groups in its 1965 decision to have all employers with at least 100 employees report to the commission on the racial makeup of their workforces. None of this occurred with input from the White House of Johnson or Nixon.

But Nixon championed another type of affirmative action in addition to the employment variety. In his campaign, he had talked loosely of the importance of developing black capitalism, or a black entrepreneurial class. In April 1968, he gave the idea a conservative cast, suggesting it did not really involve the federal government at all: "What we need is imaginative enlistment of private funds, private energies, and private talents, in order to develop the opportunities that lie untapped in our own underdeveloped urban heartland . . . It costs little or no government money to set in motion many of the programs that would in fact do the most, in a practical sense, to start building a firm structure of [black] economic opportunity."[20] The idea was not original, and it had gained attention during the long, hot summers of the previous few years. Blacks, the reasoning went, would not burn down their neighborhoods if blacks actually owned the businesses there, which was rarely the case.

Nixon's idea for black capitalism became an executive order in March 1969 to create the Office for Minority Business Enterprise (OMBE). Officially, it was not supposed to do much: its main task was to coordinate federal procurement with minority contractors. It would soon do more than coordinate, however, and it would also become a program to aid the effort to win Latino votes.

By the fall of 1969, Nixon believed that Mexican Americans should be a key target of his team's political efforts. After meeting with Nixon, Chief of Staff H.R. "Bob" Haldeman told political aide (and architect of the southern strategy) Harry Dent that Nixon believed that the Republican National Committee was "not putting nearly enough emphasis on the *key* ethnic groups—Italians, Poles and Mexicans." Efforts with these groups, he argued, could "be really politically productive."[21]

In the next few years, the Nixon administration increasingly began to seek Latino votes. Other key Republicans urged the Latino strategy. For example, domestic policy advisor John Ehrlichman told Nixon in April 1970 that a meeting with Latino appointees was a good idea because it would "demonstrate Presidential concern for the interests of the Spanish-speaking minorities" and show "presidential awareness that Negroes are not the only minority in the country."[22]

In that year, the Nixon White House also decided that Latinos should be given their own program to develop Latino capitalists. The administration created a new, scaled-down OMBE specifically for Latinos. Strangely, the name of the new program, the National Economic Development Association (NEDA), did not reveal its intended beneficiary. The Small Business Administration started it off with a $600,000 grant before OMBE took over. From 1970 to 1972, NEDA oversaw 821 assistance packages amounting to $43.5 million to grow or expand Latino-owned businesses.[23]

In the area of affirmative action, Nixon did not do anything that he was not already doing for blacks. The difference was that in the case of Latinos, he was more proud of it. The strategy was to cede the black vote to the Democrats and to try to make headway with Latinos. When a reporter asked Nixon in 1971 about the perception among blacks that

Nixon opposed civil rights, Nixon switched the topic to Latinos. He said he was happy to meet with African American leaders "and with representatives of other parts of our society, because we have got to move forward not only with black Americans; we have very significant problems . . . in the Mexican American community."[24]

In May 1971, a strategy memo laid out the case for pursuing the Latino vote. That argument and strategy was totally unburdened by ideology. The bottom line: "There are some twelve million Spanish surnamed [sic] Americans" whose demands "are now accelerating" and "most of this population is strategically located in politically doubtful states." The thesis was simple: "If we get or can get momentum going with these people, they will be very loyal and at present they feel neglected." The way to prevent Latinos from feeling neglected was to take everything the administration was doing for blacks and to expand it or modify it to include Latinos because "one of the battle cries of the Spanish Speaking [sic] community is that they want the same type of opportunities as Negroes, and do not want 'to play second fiddle to any minority.'" Therefore, "any action toward Black Demands [sic] should be taken with subsequent Spanish Speaking [sic] requirements in mind, and with awareness that the Spanish Speaking [sic] will ask for parity in treatment. Perhaps package proposals should be considered."[25]

A few months later, Secretary of Commerce Maurice Stans began to push an expansion of the OMBE program to include more efforts for Latinos. In an "EYES ONLY" memo for Ehrlichman, Stans made the case with census data showing the number of Blacks (22.6 million), Spanish-Americans (9.2 million), and Indian and other (2.9 million; presumably including Asian Americans), as well as with data on the number of minority-owned businesses in the United States. These numbers were part of the political case for expansion of the program. The value of the numbers was augmented by geography. Latinos were concentrated in places rich in electoral-college votes (New York, Texas, California) and so more programmatic efforts toward Latinos "could have real political value." For Stans, the minority capitalism program was of great political value, and the number one benefit was that there was "distinct vote-getting potential among the Spanish-Americans in an expanded program."[26]

Stans wanted a commitment of at least $100 million to OMBE, considerably higher than the $60 million of its current budget. George Shultz of the Office of Management and Budget explained to Nixon, with the help of others in the administration, the pros and cons of increasing the budget. Shultz believed the program had a great potential for waste. Both he and Ehrlichman counseled holding the budget at $60 million. Attorney General John Mitchell, who was to soon resign from his post and direct the Committee to Re-Elect the President, counseled moving up to the $100 million. Although Shultz was suspicious of the program (for reasons related either to good accounting or ideology), he included for Nixon a document describing the "distinct vote-getting potential among Spanish-Americans in an expanded minority business enterprise program" for California, Texas, Florida, Arizona, New Mexico, Chicago, and New York. He added, "the Spanish-speaking population responds well to the economic development programs" and that "past experience indicates that a strong new thrust to the Minority Business Enterprise Program will go along [sic] way to further enhance the favorable impression of you and the Administration in the Spanish-American Community [sic]." Nixon's view, scribbled on the memo itself, was that efforts for the Latinos should be strengthened (though he ordered, "Keep the black about where it is").[27]

In a message to Congress about the program, Nixon bragged about increases between 1969 and 1971 in grants and loans to minorities (from $200 million to $566 million) and a growth in purchases from minority companies from $13 million to $142 million. He described the race-targeted program as self-help: "The best way to fight poverty and to break the vicious cycle of dependence and despair which afflicts too many Americans is by fostering conditions which encourage those who have been so afflicted to play a more self-reliant and independent economic role."[28]

If there was anyone in the Nixon administration who was unfettered by conservative ideology, and particularly on the subject of adding Latino votes, it was Charles Colson, Nixon's designated coalition-builder. In late 1971, Colson put together strategy plans for Ehrlichman, explaining, "we could see some significant movement in the voting preferences of Spanish-surnamed Americans next year" and "there is much in the way of fertile ground to be plowed hard." Were there limits on what they should try? Apparently not: "I think we should do everything possible to encourage it." Colson suggested various new policies. One was to develop a computerized network for NEDA and OMBE in order to find Latino contractors and subcontractors.[29]

Apparently following up on Colson's December 1971 initiative, in January 1972, Ehrlichman's aide Ken Cole sent a series of urgent memos through the White House, explaining, "The President has a strong interest in program development of assistance to Spanish-Speaking [sic] Americans" and adding, "We would like to get things out and rolling in a very short time." Ideas related to the minority capitalism program included stationing a Small Business Administration (SBA) development officer in Latino areas and "establish[ing] a computerized Spanish-Speaking minority enterprise capabilities directory to assist both government and private enterprise in finding Spanish-Speaking contractors and Sub-contractors [sic]."[30]

If Nixon's approach to minority capitalism affirmative action for Latinos revealed little influence from conservative ideology in the 1969–71 period, things would change in 1972. Lack of ideological constraint turned into a lack of ethical constraint. The congressional Watergate committee came to be interested in the use of minority capitalism for political purposes. Some of the most surprising lapses in ethics, the committee discovered, related to use of the program as a way to win Latino support.

Perhaps surprisingly, it was a high-ranking Asian American staffer, William H. Marumoto, who was deeply involved with the controversial actions. Less surprising was that Marumoto worked on Latino issues under Colson. Marumoto convened a meeting each week with a group of Latino aides, including his assistant, Antonio Rodriguez, White House aide Carlos Conde, Henry Ramirez, head of the cabinet's Committee on Opportunities for the Spanish Speaking, and Alex Armendariz, director of the Committee to Re-Elect the President (CREEP). Their task was to dream up new ways to add Latinos to the Nixon coalition. What they ended up doing, however, was using OMBE and NEDA to reward Latino friends and punish enemies.[31]

Marumoto was to participate in a strategy called Capitalizing on the Incumbency, which involved using the executive branch's powers of grant-making and hiring to secure (in Marumoto's case) support from Latinos.[32] Fred Malek, a Haldeman aide and deputy director of CREEP, told Marumoto and Armendariz on the Latino side, as well as two counterparts who worked on black issues, "Each of you has expressed concern to me recently about the use of OMBE grants. This, obviously, represents an excellent opportunity to make a contribution and gain headway in the

Black and Spanish-Speaking areas. I have discussed this situation with [domestic policy aide] Ken Cole, and we are in agreement on the importance of the program to our efforts."[33]

Throughout 1972, Marumoto then spent money in ways to make more likely a victory for Nixon. For example, his 1972 "Weekly Activity Report(s) for Spanish Speaking [sic]" described such activities as having an administrator on March 24 "set aside $300,000 for one of *our* Spanish speaking [sic] contractors" (emphasis added). On April 7, he was "reviewing with [Nixon staff members] John Evans, Bob Brown and Wally Henley proposals and grants at OMBE to make sure the right people [were] being considered and receiving grants from OMBE." On May 19, Marumoto logged, "Rodriguez is assisting Ultrasystems, Inc., of Long Beach, California with a $200,000 grant from OMBE. This organization strongly supports the administration."[34]

The Nixon administration also used a congressionally created parallel minority capitalism program, the SBA 8(a) program, in an unprincipled, unethical, and political way. According to Benjamin Fernandez, a Nixon fundraiser who targeted Latinos, the 8(a) program was part of a "major effort on the part of the administration to award contracts to Spanish-speaking businessmen."[35] Here again there was a political rewarding and punishing logic. Marumoto arranged to have an outspoken Democratic firm told that it no longer needed the 8(a) government preferences. And in another example of the politics-over-ideology nature of the process of this type of affirmative action, and especially for Latinos, there was a meeting of various Nixon officials in March 1972 that planned "ways of improving coordination and more effective means of getting political impact in the grant-making process. Discussion pointed out the tremendous need for a centralized computer facility for all Departments and Agencies whereby one could obtain data regarding grants to any congressional district and/or organization."[36]

The other major Nixon initiative for Latinos focused on bilingual education and a civil right to foreign language accommodation in the schools. Congress passed the Bilingual Education Act in 1968, but both the Johnson administration and Congress itself neglected it. It did not do much—its purpose was to authorize federal funds for teaching children with "limited English proficiency" (LEP). Its significance was more for the previously radical idea of federal tax dollars being used to support foreign language teaching to native speakers. Conservatives came to despise this program. But not during the Nixon administration—there, especially the first term, they saw political benefits and no ideological reason to hold back.

Nixon officials then used an obscure symbolic body, the Cabinet Committee on Opportunities for Spanish-Speaking People (CCOSS), to promote the image of his administration as interested in bilingual education and respect for language difference. In October 1971, Nixon's political aides dreamed up a meeting of CCOSS to take place in Texas. The goal was simple: "To help our candidates with the Mexican American vote and the Spanish-speaking vote." They discerned no downside to any of these activities, even though they were to take place in a southern state not known for racial liberalism. They chose Texas because "it could be done in conjunction with a brand new pilot program of bilingual education taking place at an elementary school in Dallas." Ehrlichman's domestic policy assistant Ken Cole spoke for a group of several aides who supported the initiative (Martin Castillo, former chairman of the Inter-Agency Committee on Mexican American Affairs, John Ehrlichman and Leonard Garment, top domestic policy advisors, and Jeb Magruder, public relations expert) when he advocated arranging the meeting to get "maximum mileage" for "our candidates who need help with the Mexican American vote and the Spanish-speaking vote."[37]

Nixon's coalition-builder Charles Colson also developed a strategy for winning Latino support that included promoting bilingual education. Along with an affirmative action plan for public housing to ensure that more Latinos took advantage of that program, and more efforts to develop a Latino capitalist class, in 1971 Colson was giving great support to bilingual education. Although "budget priorities" limited new funding, this would not preclude an unfunded mandate. Colson suggested, "we could require that bilingual education programs be components of any educational institution receiving funds with more than a 10 percent Spanish-speaking service population."[38] In fact, as will be described below, developments away from the White House, and not driven by electoral politics, were already moving the administration to precisely this policy.

Nixon administration support for the bilingual education concept remained high, but support for the Bilingual Education Act weakened. This decline was related to cost and not to the propriety of ethnic targeting or government-supported difference. On January 10, 1972, Cole had aides examine the feasibility of extending bilingual education. Cole expressed no ideological resistance to having the federal government pay to educate children in languages other than English. His concerns were limited to "the budget question involving bi-lingual education [sic]."[39] For the 1973 budget, the Nixon administration proposed $41 million for bilingual education despite a report that, according to the Office of Management and Budget (OMB), "there are serious questions about the effectiveness of this program." For the Nixon team, whether the program actually worked was not a concern. One aide's memo argued, "As far as appearance is concerned, a 17% increase in the program is not that bad," while another scribbled on the memo, "How can we maximize credit w/ the Spanish speaking?"[40]

How widespread in the administration was support for bilingual education? In April 1972, the administration planned further occasions to demonstrate Nixon's support for bilingualism in preparation for the election. A group of seven top policy and public-relations aides, including Colson and speechwriter Bill Safire, urged a half-hour event with Latino leaders and celebrities, including Fernando Lamas and Ricardo Montalban, "to show the President's interest in bilingual education." They all took for granted the Latino community's support and bilingual education's merits. Only press secretary Ron Ziegler opposed it, calling the event "much too obvious."[41] Nevertheless, promotion of bilingual education became a favorite strategy for appealing to Latinos in the 1972 election.[42]

There was another move toward language rights that would later be an affront to conservative ideology. The Nixon administration promoted an interpretation of Title VI of the Civil Rights Act of 1964, promulgated in a May 25, 1970, memo and later affirmed by the Supreme Court, that saw language accommodation in the schools as a civil right. This was less of an affront to conservative notions of national identity than was the Bilingual Education Act. However, *how* LEP students should be accommodated remained undefined, and bilingual education was certainly a dominant and likely approach. Moreover, it was a massive affront to conservative notions of limited federal government, local control of schools, and the undesirability of unfunded federal regulatory mandates.

The "May 25 Memorandum," as it came to be called, bubbled up from the Office for Civil Rights (OCR) bureaucracy. Ideology may have mattered in this setting, far away from the White House, as two of the primary architects were liberal Leon Panetta and Martin Gerry, a Republican civil rights activist. What is significant about these developments, however, is that they trickled up *to* the White House and became part of more nonideological strategies to pursue Latino voters.

Written by Gerry and signed by OCR director J. Stanley Pottinger, the memo declared that OCR reports found "a number of common practices which have the effect of denying equality of educational opportunity to Spanish-surnamed pupils" and were therefore in violation of Title VI. It announced four different responsibilities for local school districts with at least 5 percent "national origin-minority group" students. The memo spelled out four different areas of compliance with Title VI of the Civil Rights Act of 1964 relating to language. The key requirement was that, henceforth, covered school districts must take "affirmative steps to rectify the language deficiency" in order to allow "effective participation" in district educational programs for students who could not speak or understand English.[43]

Although the OCR administrators appeared most concerned with the civil rights issues of Latinos, as well as with pre-empting any criticism they might receive for acting too slowly, they had the support from Nixon's appointee at the top. HEW Secretary Robert Finch showed the political orientation of other Nixonian officials when he later recalled, "I wanted to make it clear that the course I was following at HEW was not motivated entirely by concern for good works or support for social programs." Instead, his focus was "the cutting issues that were affecting the Republican party." Latino votes were a part of these "cutting issues": "I thought it was very important, for instance, that Republicans gain a foothold in the Chicano community."[44]

Finch's successor at HEW, Elliot Richardson, a veteran of the Eisenhower administration, appeared to be a believer in language and cultural rights for Latinos. In a letter to Senator Walter Mondale, chair of the Senate's Subcommittee on Education, Richardson described the recommendations of an Office of Education advisory committee on Latino education that described the psychological injury faced by culturally different children and argued that:

> the most important needs of the national origin minority group
> child are: 1) the need for ethnic or cultural diversity in the educational environment, 2) the need for total institutional reposturing

in order to incorporate, affirmatively recognize, and value the cultural environment of ethnic minority children so that the development of positive self-concept can be accelerated, 3) the need for language programs that introduce and develop English language skills without demeaning or otherwise deprecating the language of a child's home environment and without presenting English as a more valued language.[45]

What was perhaps most surprising about the right to language accommodation, however, was the Nixon administration's pursuit of court enforcement. The Justice Department, for example, pursued a case in Texas where it argued for a local school district to remake itself in line with bilingual and bicultural principles.[46] Better known is the Nixon administration's position in the *Lau v. Nichols* Supreme Court case, where the high court deferred to OCR and supported the interpretation of Title VI that it required language accommodation in the schools. In that case, the staunch conservative judge Robert Bork, then Nixon's solicitor general, was the lead author of a brief (along with former OCR director Stanley Pottinger, who had then transferred to the Justice Department) that strongly advocated an unfunded federal mandate for a right to language accommodation.

The case involved the city of San Francisco and its failure to provide language accommodation to Asian American students. Bork argued for both a statutory and a constitutional right to language accommodation. Bork argued that San Francisco needed to implement HEW's (technically, OCR's) May 25 memorandum order that national origin nondiscrimination required some kind of program to ensure equal opportunity. He pointed out that the Supreme Court had previously given great weight to HEW guidelines in black school-desegregation cases. Bork and the Justice Department maintained that the Fourteenth Amendment and the Civil Rights Act "impose upon the school authorities in such circumstances an obligation to provide some special instruction to national origin-minority students" that would "allow them meaningfully to participate in the educational program which is readily accessible to their English-speaking classmates."

Bork's argument emphasized the inadequacy of equal treatment. He argued that a school district that provides the same facilities and curriculum for all students—when it was clear that some students would not benefit—

used a "narrow and mechanical view of equal educational opportunities" that could not "be reconciled with this Court's holding" in a series of black school-desegregation cases.[47] In cases of limited English proficiency, the failure to provide special instruction led to a "denial of access to the dominant culture."

Stopping short of arguing for bilingual education, Bork instead simply adopted the May 25 memorandum's "effect standard" of discrimination: "The impact of that practice [of teaching in English] is upon a distinct segment of a national origin-minority group, whose members are affected on account of a national origin characteristic." Equating race and national-origin discrimination (and ignoring the fact that there are no languages associated with "races"), the brief argued, in the end, that "simple justice requires that public funds, to which all taxpayers of all races contribute, not be spent in any fashion which encourages, entrenches, subsidizes, or results in racial discrimination."[48]

Considered together, Nixon's policies toward Latinos make a powerful argument for the irrelevance of ideology in these years. The inside story of the minority capitalism affirmative action is completely devoid of any voices saying it violated principles of conservative ideology. The same was true of bilingual education and language rights.

Women's Rights: Delay Tactics and Confusion

For many Americans, women's rights, or women's liberation, as it was called, are strongly associated with the 1960s and 1970s. In a striking contrast to the case of Latino rights, ideology played a significant role in the development of women's rights. That role was mainly to supply brakes on the development of policy. However, in the case of women's rights, the ideology has less to do with the role of government and more to do with notions of what women's role should be or what women wanted.

The key point for understanding Nixon's approach to women's rights is that he had no idea how to approach women's rights. There was little sense of a clear ideological position and even less sense of the likely electoral gain from supporting women's rights. More than anything, there was confusion and delaying tactics.

Nixon's attitude toward women could change rapidly. For example, he saw that appointments of women to key posts in his administration could have political benefits. He placed Rita Hauser as the U.S. representative to the United Nations Human Rights Commission. Hauser knew that her appointment had political benefits—but she was not sure that Nixon did. In February 1969, she reported to Nixon that her appointment "generated publicity in the press and the media." She sought strategically to use this opportunity, she said, to "promote the image of your Administration in the field of human rights" and offered "to fill in any appearance in the human rights area that you may not be able to accept and for which you think I am suited." Nixon approved, which he demonstrated by underlining passages in her note, and then gave it to his chief of staff H. R. "Bob" Haldeman with instructions to "use her as extensively as possible—always non partisan [sic]. Particularly on T.V."[49]

Twenty-four hours later, on February 6, Nixon saw women as a humorous sidelight to the real politics of the day and one woman in particular as the butt of a good-natured joke. Vera Glaser, a Washington journalist, asked Nixon during a press conference if he would neglect women when making appointments to his administration. She was concerned, noting that only three of the administration's first 200 top-level appointments were women. Nixon responded with a question of his own that treated Glaser like she was a child: "Would you be interested in coming to the government?"[50]

Nixon also dithered on the question of whether or not to meet with four Republican congresswomen on the matter of women's rights. Florence Dwyer (R-NJ) wished to meet with the president but was politely brushed off. She was later joined by Margaret Heckler (R-MA), Catherine May (R-WA), and Charlotte Reid (R-IL) in a letter to Nixon asking for a meeting "for the purpose of discussing a number of matters of direct and immediate concern to women generally." Sensing the president's lack of interest or knowledge on the matter, they explained, "We can provide you with information and ideas which should be of value in dealing with these problems."[51] They were brushed off again, forcing a more confrontational approach that Nixon finally responded to.

A memo by Nixon's liberal advisor, Daniel Patrick Moynihan, led to more analysis but revealed more of the administration's confusion and Nixon's lack of leadership on the issue. A few months after the confrontation with the Republican women from Congress, on August 20, 1969, Moynihan predicted, "female equality will be a major cultural/political force of the 1970s." After going through the causes and effects of the new movement, Moynihan argued that Nixon should "take advantage of this" through appointments "but perhaps especially in . . . pronouncements": "This is a subject ripe for creative political leadership and initiative."[52]

Moynihan's memo led to analysis and a set of recommendations from members of Nixon's domestic policy team. Political advisor and speechwriter Jim Keogh said, "I do thoroughly agree with the conclusion and recommendation that the President take every opportunity in word and deed to champion female equality." Peter Flanigan, another political aide who had dealt with Dwyer and company, wrote facetiously, "As a member of the staff who has borne the brunt of women's attack, I am well aware of the increasing use of violence." He added that he was trying to find women for appointments and secure "major news coverage of such appointments." Bryce Harlow said, "Politically, it's gold," but cautioned, "we don't appear to have such a program, nor is one suggested here." In his summary for Nixon, chief domestic policy advisor John Ehrlichman said, "politically this is a golden opportunity and . . . we should, whenever possible, champion female equality."[53]

However, rather than launch into a set of policies that promised political payoff, as they did with Latinos, the Nixon administration instead formed a task force to study the issues involved with women's rights. This was the weakest of the set of recommendations Dwyer had urged. Nixon officially announced the new body on October 1, 1969, calling it the President's Task Force on Women's Rights and Responsibilities. Several months later, when the group submitted its report to the president, a Nixon advisor told Virginia Allan, the group's chair, that the report was being "filed."[54]

Nixon's confusion could also be seen on the signature women's rights issue of the time: the Equal Rights Amendment (ERA). Nixon had supported the ERA throughout his political career, but as with black civil rights he re-evaluated his position once in office. Now, with real political consequences to his decision, the issue became complex and the pros and cons, the conservative and the liberal positions, unclear. Ehrlichman put together an elaborate decision memo that broke down the ERA issue and Nixon's own personal history on it. He also brought together a wide range of administration officials who mostly—though not unanimously—supported the ERA. Due to Nixon's past support in 1960 and 1968, Ehrlichman himself leaned toward Nixon endorsing the amendment. Vice President Spiro Agnew also had publicly supported the ERA.

Labor Secretary George Shultz also supported it, and Jacqueline Gutwillig, chair of the Citizen's Advisory Council on the Status of Women, had testified to a Senate committee in support. Domestic policy aide Leonard Garment was in support though not with great enthusiasm. Assistant attorney general (and future chief justice of the Supreme Court) William Rehnquist was the lone voice against the ERA among administration officials. According to Rehnquist, the amendment would lead to "the sharp reduction in importance of the family unit, with the eventual elimination of that unit by no means improbable."[55] In the end, Nixon supported the ERA, but did nothing to secure its passage.[56]

Because of this indecision and lack of clear policy vision, policy on affirmative action for women was one of foot-dragging and delays. The key fact here is that whereas affirmative action for racial minorities moved quickly, policy development for women took considerably longer. The Philadelphia Plan, which targeted blacks, Latinos, Asian Americans, and American Indians, got its start in June 1969. After it survived a legal battle in December, the OFCC expanded it from construction to include all contractors in Order No. 4 in February 1970. But it did not include women, even though the authorizing executive order had since the Johnson administration amended the executive order to include sex discrimination. The OFCC did not include women in its affirmative-action regulations until August 31, 1971—and then only after more than a year of fierce lobbying by both Democratic and Republican women in Congress and demonstrations and lawsuits by the National Organization for Women and its spin-off, the Women's Equity Action League.

Why the delay? From the perspective of presidential politics, we can say that Nixon offered no leadership on the issue. The archives do not reveal any discussions of the issue by Nixon himself. But that in itself says something, and this fact fits with the discussions above: Nixon did not know what to do. It was simply unclear to Nixon, or to his trusted appointee, Secretary of Labor George Shultz, what to do. Whereas they never once questioned whether Latinos should be expected to pursue jobs in ways that were basically the same as whites and blacks, Shultz's letter to a congressional subcommittee investigating discrimination (Shultz was apparently too busy to show up and an aide read his letter) expressed much hand-wringing about whether or not in the workplace women were different from men. He stated that Order No. 4's affirmative-action procedures for racial minorities did not apply to women because "many women do not seek employment. Practically all adult males do."[57] This sense that women were different led to the delays and the resistance to women's pressure.

The contrast of the politics of women's rights with the politics of black rights and Latino rights is instructive. Because Nixon perceived women differently than he perceived blacks and Latinos, the political logic for dealing with this group was different. Conservatism did not offer clear guidance on women's politics, particularly in the areas of their economic advancement. Oddly, Nixon did not explore public opinion on the issue in any systematic way. Instead, unlike the situation with Latino rights, which were clear and apparently costless, he remained hesitant and indecisive.

Conclusion

The political context can help us understand Nixon's most innovative civil rights policies. First, they developed only a few years after the passage of the key statutes. In this environment, it is quite understandable that the new boundaries of Left and Right were unknown. Second, his policies developed in the context of an election win with a razor-thin margin of victory.

Was Nixon creating a new conservative position on civil rights? A key tenet of conservatism is the belief in limited government, but in Nixon's policy this belief sometimes mattered in civil rights politics and sometimes it did not. In the case of the desegregation of black schools, Nixon voiced conservative principles when seeking to slow down the process and oppose busing. In the case of Latinos, however, it is difficult to find any concern at all with the role of government in improving opportunities for Latinos. There was some concern with cost and the budget for helping Latino capitalists, but there was no expression of whether or not unfunded federal mandates were the correct policy move. Ideology simply did not seem to matter here, and it is not surprising that conservative Republicans would turn away from Nixon's approach, at least until the presidency of George W. Bush. In the case of women's rights, despite significant pressure from women in Congress and from women's activists, the Nixon administration expressed what was at best caution but what could probably be more accurately described as confusion. Some aides saw political gain with women in expansive women's rights, but unlike in the case of Latinos, the Nixon team delayed and continually wondered what woman really wanted. Even on the ERA, which Nixon had long supported, there was confusion and almost embarrassed support.

In developing his civil rights policies, Nixon responded to how he perceived the group in question and how he anticipated the desires of his electoral coalition. Since he pursued southern white voters, their racial conservatism, which was strongly anti–black civil rights, shaped policy. When Nixon pursued Latino voters, he saw no impacts to his white voter coalition because Latino issues were less important to them. And when Nixon wondered about women's rights, he simply was unsure how the conservatism of his coalition viewed the issues.

A more focused assessment of the views of his coalition led to an increasing civil rights conservatism in Nixon's second term. By 1970, Nixon was increasingly equating his "silent majority" of mostly white voters with the white working class.[58] In doing so, Nixon learned of the preferences of these voters—and clear conservative stances on the new civil rights issues emerged. To be sure, issues regarding women's rights remained murky: while the white working class tended to value traditional women's roles, the reality was that many working-class women worked, and policies that aided their economic well-being were beneficial to them. For this reason, it became a conservative position to oppose elements of civil rights laws that challenged traditional gender roles. Conservatives would point to the threat of the most feared effects of the ERA, such as that it would force women into the military, or point to the feared effects of a law signed by Nixon, Title IX of the Education Amendments of 1972, barring sex discrimination by programs or institutions receiving federal funds. This law had the potential to end the fraternity and sorority system at colleges and universities.

On issues involving race and culture, the new conservative position became clear: opposition to policies that sent categorical benefits to blacks and Latinos. Working-class whites remained economically insecure and resented government programs and regulations for racial minorities that excluded whites. Moreover, the language rights that Nixon enthusiastically sought to give to Latinos offended white working-class conceptions of national identity—as well as devalued the assimilation that was forced upon many of them with ancestry from Southern and Eastern Europe. Even Robert Bork, who as solicitor general fought for a *constitutional* right to foreign language accommodation in the schools, came by the 1990s to criticize the bilingual education and language rights that he had helped bring about.[59]

By 1972, then, Nixon was no longer promoting his Philadelphia Plan to help blacks and instead was complaining about racial quotas. While he never took a strong stand against bilingual education, the position opposing bilingual education and multiculturalism had come to define conservative approaches to Latino politics by the mid-1970s. He remained quiet about affirmative action for women, seeking neither to strengthen nor weaken the policy.

Perhaps the best interpretation of the historical record of the Nixon administration's conservatism on civil rights, therefore, shows that Nixon's positions varied according to the issue at hand and that he sought to follow (what he regarded as) the public's view of the issues. Nixon's own conservatism may have mattered less than the conservatism of the sections of the electorate that he sought to appeal to. In exploring and pushing a wide range of civil rights policies, the Nixon administration and future Republicans learned what conservatives should say and believe about civil rights in America. Those conservative positions created in the early 1970s continue to define the Republican Party today. As in Nixon's time, however, they remain subject to change.

Notes

1. Phillips was inspired by a book that gained wide attention in 1970—Richard Scammon and Ben Wattenberg's *The Real Majority: An Extraordinary Examination of the American Electorate* (New York: Coward-McCann, 1970).

2. Some notable attempts include Stephen Ambrose, *Nixon: The Triumph of a Politician, 1962–1972* (New York: Simon and Schuster, 1989); Joan Hoff, *Nixon Reconsidered* (New York: Basic Books, 1994); Dean J. Kotlowski, *Nixon's Civil Rights: Politics, Principle, and Policy* (Cambridge, Mass.: Harvard University Press, 2002); Herbert S. Parmet, *Richard Nixon and His America* (Boston: Little, Brown, 1990); and Garry Wills, *Nixon Agonistes: The Crisis of the Self-Made Man* (Boston: Houghton-Mifflin 1970).

3. The best account of Nixon's civil rights politics remains Hugh Davis Graham, *The Civil Rights Era: Origins and Development of National Policy, 1960–1972* (New York: Oxford University Press, 1990).

4. John D. Skrentny, *The Minority Rights Revolution* (Cambridge, Mass.: Harvard University Press, 2002); Graham, *Civil Rights Era.*

5. William N. Eskridge, *Dynamic Statutory Interpretation* (Cambridge, Mass.: Harvard University Press, 1994).

6. Bruce Ackerman, "The Living Constitution," *Harvard Law Review* 120 (2007): 1738–1812.

7. Stephen Skowronek, *The Politics Presidents Make* (Cambridge, Mass.: Harvard University Press, 1993).

8. Allen J. Matusow, *The Unraveling of America: A History of Liberalism in the 1960s* (New York: Harper and Row, 1984).

9. http://www.presidency.ucsb.edu/showelection.php?year=1968, accessed December 16, 2008.

10. These cases are drawn from John David Skrentny, *The Ironies of Affirmative Action: Politics, Culture, and Justice in America* (Chicago: University of Chicago Press, 1996) and Skrentny, *Minority Rights Revolution*. Also see Graham, *Civil Rights Era*.

11. Joan Hoff, *Nixon Reconsidered* (New York: Basic Books, 1994).

12. Graham, *Civil Rights Era*.

13. Gerald Rosenberg, *The Hollow Hope* (Chicago: University of Chicago Press, 1993).

14. Stephen E. Ambrose, *Nixon: The Triumph of a Politician, 1962–1972* (New York: Simon and Schuster, 1989), 169–70.

15. Stephen C. Halpern, *On the Limits of the Law: The Ironic Legacy of Title VI of the 1964 Civil Rights Act* (Baltimore: Johns Hopkins University Press, 1995), 89.

16. John David Skrentny, *The Ironies of Affirmative Action*, 190.

17. Halpern, *Limits of the Law*, 95.

18. Thomas J. Sugrue, *Sweet Land of Liberty* (New York: Random House, 2008).

19. The story of the Philadelphia Plan can be found in Graham, *Civil Rights Era*; Skrentny, *Ironies of Affirmative Action*; and Terry Anderson, *The Pursuit of Fairness: A History of Affirmative Action* (New York: Oxford University Press, 2004).

20. Maurice H. Stans, "Nixon's Economic Policy Toward Minorities," in *Richard M. Nixon: Politician, President, Administrator*, ed. Leon Friedman and William F. Levantrosser (New York: Greenwood Press, 1991), 239–46, 239–40.

21. Memo from H. R. Haldeman to Mr. Dent, October 31, 1969, paraphrasing Nixon, in *Civil Rights during the Nixon Administration, 1969–1973*, ed. Hugh Davis Graham (Bethesda, Md.: University Publications of America, 1989), Part I, Reel 2, frame 129.

22. Memo from John Ehrlichman to the President, April 20, 1970, folder: CCOSS File, White House Central Files, Staff Member and Office Files, Robert H. Finch, box 15, Nixon Presidential Materials Project, National Archives, College Park, Md.

23. Memo for David Parker from Carlos d. Conde via Herb Klein, April 18, 1972; Memo for Herb Klein from David Parker, April 11, 1972; and Schedule Proposal from Herbert G. Klein via Dwight L. Chapin, March 9, 1972, in Graham, *Civil Rights during Nixon*, Part I, Reel 4, frames 86, 88, 91, 92.

24. "The President's News Conference of May 1, 1971," in *Public Papers of the Presidents of the United States: Richard M. Nixon, 1971* (Washington, D.C.: Government Printing Office, 1972), 613.

25. Memo for Clark MacGregor from William Timmons, May 12, 1971, and attached memo for Clark MacGregor and George Shultz from George Grassmuck, May 10, 1971, in Graham, *Civil Rights during Nixon*, Part I, Reel 3, frame 871–73.

26. Memorandum for John D. Ehrlichman from Maurice H. Stans, September

17, 1971, in Joan Hoff-Wilson, ed., *Papers of the Nixon White House* (Bethesda, Md.: University Publications of America, 1989), Part 6a, Fiche 173, frames 46–51.

27. Memo for the President from George Shultz, September 17, 1971, with handwritten comments by Nixon, in Hoff-Wilson, *Papers of the Nixon White House*, Part 6a, Fiche 173, frames 32–38.

28. "Special Message to the Congress Urging Expansion of the Minority Business Enterprise Program, October 13, 1971," Public Papers of the Presidents of the United States: Richard M. Nixon, 1971 (Washington, D.C.: Government Printing Office, 1972), 1041–46.

29. Other suggested policies included HUD programs and public housing, which Colson said were not reaching Latinos in adequate percentages; he suggested a kind of affirmative action, or "an administrative goal of the number of housing units that can be reasonably provided to Spanish-speaking families under federal programs and that a time-frame be set up to fulfill that goal." Colson also pushed bilingual education, as discussed in chapter 7. Memo for John Ehrlichman from Charles W. Colson, December 20, 1971, in Graham, *Civil Rights during Nixon*, Part I, Reel 3, frames 899–900.

30. See the three memos for Ed Morgan from Ken Cole, January 10, 1972, on education, housing, and economic development, in Graham, *Civil Rights during Nixon*, Part I, Reel 3, frames 896–98.

31. Hearings before the Select Committee on Presidential Campaign Activities, U.S. Senate, 93rd Congress, First session, Watergate and related activities, Phase III: Campaign Financing, Book 13, Washington, D.C., November 1973, 52 Hearings, Watergate and related activities, 74–5277.

32. Hearings, Watergate and related activities, 5279. An original memo describing this strategy is reproduced on 5532.

33. Memo for Bob Brown, Bill Marumoto, Paul Jones, and Alex Armendariz from Fred Malek, March 3, 1972, in Hearings, Watergate and related activities, 5542.

34. All contained in the Weekly Activity Report of the Spanish Speaking (for Chuck Colson and Fred Malek from Bill Marumoto) on the cited dates, in Hearings, Watergate and related activities, 5549, 5557, 5581, 5576.

35. Hearings, Watergate, and related activities, 5365.

36. Memo for Chuck Colson from Bill Marumoto, March 17, 1972, in Hearings, Watergate and related activities, p. 5543. This meeting involved officials from the Office of Economic Opportunity, formerly the cornerstone of Johnson's War on Poverty.

37. Memo for Richard Nixon from Hugh Sloan via Dwight Chapin, October 21, 1971, in Folder: EX FG 145 Cabinet Committee on Opportunities for Spanish Speaking People 1/71-[12/31/72], Box 1, EX FG 145 InterAgency Committee on Mexican-American Affairs as of 12/30/69 through EX FG 145/A [1973–74], Nixon Presidential Materials Project, NA.

38. Memo from Charles W. Colson to John Ehrlichman, December 20, 1971, in Graham, *Civil Rights during Nixon*, Part I, Reel 3, frames 899–900.

39. See Memo for Ed Morgan from Ken Cole, January 10, 1972; Memo for Ed Morgan from Ken Cole, January 10, 1972; Memo for Peter Flanigan from Ken Cole, January 10, 1972, in Graham, *Civil Rights during Nixon*, Part I, Reel 3, frames 896–98.

40. Memo for Ken Cole via Edward L. Morgan from James B. Clawson, January 28, 1972, in Graham, *Civil Rights during Nixon*, Part I, Reel 3, frames 887–88.

41. See Memo for David Parker from Ron Ziegler, April 18, 1972; Memo for David Parker from Dick Moore, April 14, 1972; Memo for Dick Moore, Bill Safire, and Ron Ziegler from David Parker, April 13, 1972; Schedule Proposal from Herbert Klein via Dwight Chapin, April 11, 1972, in Graham, *Civil Rights during Nixon*, Part I, Reel 4, frames 93, 96–98.

42. See, for example, Letter from Alex Armendariz to Frederick Malek, May 31, 1972, Folder: Ethnics [1 of 3], Box 62, White House Special Files, Staff Member and Office Files, Charles W. Colson Papers, Nixon Presidential Materials Project, NA; undated campaign document, "Spanish-Speaking," in Graham, *Civil Rights during Nixon*, Part I, Reel 4, frames 332–36.

43. Memo for School Districts with More Than Five Percent National Origin-Minority Group Children from J. Stanley Pottinger, May 25, 1970, in Graham, *Civil Rights during Nixon*, Reel 3, frame 889. For a discussion, see Iris C. Rotberg, "Some Legal and Research Considerations in Establishing Federal Policy in Bilingual Education," in *Harvard Educational Review* 52 (1982): 149–68.

44. Quoted in A. James Reichley, *Conservatives in an Age of Change: The Nixon and Ford Administrations* (Washington, D.C.: Brookings Institution, 1981), 180.

45. James V. Gambone, "Bilingual Bicultural Educational Civil Rights: The May 25th Memorandum and Oppressive School Practices" (PhD dissertation, University of New Mexico, 1973), 23. Gambone, a doctoral student at the University of New Mexico, took part in the San Diego meeting.

46. United States v. State of Texas, 342 F. Supp. 24 (1971).

47. These included *Brown*, Sweatt v. Painter 339 U.S. 629 and McLaurin v. Oklahoma State Regents 339 U.S. 637.

48. Bork's brief is reproduced in Hearings before the General Subcommittee on Education of the Committee on Education and Labor, House, 93rd Cong., second session, on H.R. 1085, H.R. 2490, and H.R. 1146 bills to amend Title VII of the ESEA, 1974, pp. 10–19. Bork is listed as lead author, followed by Pottinger.

49. Memo from Rita E. Hauser to The President, February 5, 1969, and handwritten note from the President to H (Haldeman), n.d., in Joan Hoff-Wilson, ed., *Papers of the Nixon White House* (Bethesda, Md.: University Publications of America, 1989), Part 6, Fiche 6a-7-44.

50. Graham, *Civil Rights Era*, 397.

51. Letter from Florence P. Dwyer, Catherine May, Charlotte T. Reid, and Margaret M. Heckler to Mr. President, June 9, 1969, in folder: HU 2–5 women beginning 12/31/69, White House Subject Files, Box 21, Nixon Presidential Materials Project, NA.

52. Memo from Daniel Patrick Moynihan for The President, August 20, 1969, in Graham, *Civil Rights during Nixon*, Part I, Reel 23, frames 78–82.

53. Memo from John Ehrlichman for The President, September 29, 1969, and attached Memos for the Staff Secretary from Jim Keogh, August 26, 1969, Peter M. Flanigan, August 25, 1969, Bryce Harlow, September 20, 1969, and Memo from Daniel

Patrick Moynihan for The President, August 20, 1969, in Graham, *Civil Rights during Nixon*, Part I, Reel 23, frames 73–82.

54. Graham, *Civil Rights Era*, 406.

55. Memo from Leonard Garment to John Ehrlichman, May 25, 1970, and Memo from John Ehrlichman for The President, n.d., in Graham, *Civil Rights during Nixon*, Part I, Reel 23, frames 139–74. Ehrlichman's memo also showed that all presidents since Eisenhower had supported the amendment, and Nixon's 1968 opponents, Hubert Humphrey and George Wallace, joined Nixon in supporting it in the 1968 election.

56. Hoff, *Nixon Reconsidered*, 104.

57. Hearings, *Discrimination Against Women*, U.S. House of Representatives, second session, Special Subcommittee on Education of the Committee on Education and Labor, on Section 805 of H.R. 16098, June 17, 19, 26, 29, 30, July 1, 31, 1970, 694–95.

58. Jefferson Cowie, "Nixon's Class Struggle: Romancing the New Right Worker, 1969–1973," *Labor History* 43 (3): 257–83; Skrentny, *Ironies of Affirmative Action*, chapter 7.

59. Robert H. Bork, *Slouching Toward Gomorrah: Modern Liberalism and American Decline* (New York: ReganBooks, 1996).

2

AFRICAN AMERICAN CIVIL RIGHTS AND CONSERVATIVE MOBILIZATION IN THE JIMMY CARTER YEARS

JOSEPH CRESPINO AND ASHER SMITH

In the late 1970s it was an article of faith among conservative Republicans that liberal bureaucrats in Jimmy Carter's administration were enforcing racial quotas. One of the most controversial issues among conservative Christians was an Internal Revenue Service (IRS) policy that denied federal tax exemptions to racially discriminatory private schools. Critics argued that small, independent religious schools were forced to submit to quotas or else face legal harassment from the federal government.

The issue galvanized Protestants and was a critical issue in bringing these voters into the Republican fold. Two of the most influential New Right leaders, Paul Weyrich and the direct-mail guru Richard Viguerie, cited the IRS controversy as critical to conservative mobilization in the 1970s.[1] At the 1980 Republican National Convention, one of the planks in the GOP platform pledged to halt the "unconstitutional regulatory vendetta launched by Mr. Carter's IRS Commissioner against independent schools."[2] In the first year of Ronald Reagan's presidency, conservative Justice Department officials convinced the administration to revoke the IRS policy, which they believed had begun under Carter. In January 1982, the Reagan administration announced that it was dispensing with the policy and ordered that the tax-exempt status be restored to institutions that had been denied it under the old policy, among them

Bob Jones University in Greenville, South Carolina, which maintained a policy against interracial dating.[3]

The problem was that the conservative activists and officials had gotten their history wrong. The policy had begun not under Jimmy Carter but under Richard Nixon in 1970, one of the most contentious years of southern school desegregation. What looked to conservatives like federal harassment of innocent Christian schools appeared to many other Americans like an appropriate and necessary effort by the federal government to enforce school desegregation in the most reactionary parts of the South. Editorial pages across the country charged Reagan with supporting what the *New York Times* dubbed "Tax Exempt Hate." An embarrassed Reagan administration quickly reversed itself, denying any racial motivation and explaining its decision on legal grounds.[4]

The controversy over the IRS policy toward racially discriminatory private schools is a good example of the complex intersection of civil rights, presidential politics, and conservative political mobilization in the years following the landmark civil rights legislation. In the 1940s and 1950s, civil rights battles had taken place primarily in the courts. In the 1960s, the fight moved to Congress, where legislators passed historic legislation that corrected nearly a century's worth of abject discrimination. Those laws created executive branch agencies that moved civil rights battles into presidential politics in novel ways in the 1970s. Congress tasked presidential administrations with enforcing complex civil rights laws that affected vast areas of public life. It was through bureaucratic processes that abstract ideas about racial equality were actually worked out. This was rarely a simple or easy process, yet these efforts significantly advanced the goals of fairness and equality in American life.

During Carter's presidency, these were often small-bore gains achieved through executive branch powers. The administration struggled to remedy past discrimination in a way that appealed to a broad swath of voters or Congress, many of whom like the church-school supporters fell under the sway of a burgeoning reaction against various forms of government regulation. As the Carter administration struggled to make tangible the civil rights movement's demands for greater equality, conservatives criticized the government for going beyond the color-blind proscription of civil rights legislation. Programs denounced as racial quotas became important props for conservative critics in their larger attack on what they considered to be big government run amok.

Jimmy Carter won the Democratic presidential nomination in 1976 as a moderate candidate who would move his party to the political center after its disastrous defeat in 1972. As governor of Georgia he had established a reputation as one of the top New South leaders. Upon winning the governorship in 1971, Carter made an extraordinary announcement that signaled a dramatic break with the state's segregationist past. "I say to you quite frankly that the time for racial discrimination is over," he pledged in front of former Governor Lester Maddox and fellow Georgians. "No poor, rural, weak or black person should ever have to bear the additional burden of being deprived of the opportunity of an education, a job or simple justice." The speech won him national attention and a place on the cover of *Time* magazine.[5]

As president he attempted to stake out middle-ground positions on contentious civil rights issues, such as the policy of busing children to different schools in order to break down patterns of segregation. The administration tried to balance the demands for continued desegregation with conservatives' growing demands to get government out of the private lives of families. It attempted to reach a similar balance in its approach to a high-profile Supreme Court case involving affirmative action in higher education, *Regents of the University of California v. Bakke*. In these and other instances, the middle ground on civil rights became increasingly hard to find. In addition, an emerging antiregulatory ethos, nurtured by a new generation of conservative politicians, helped shift the tone on civil rights issues. In an era of widespread economic stagnation, business groups portrayed federal programs that monitored employment and hiring as one more roll of red tape that the government used to stifle entrepreneurialism and economic development.

Conservative opposition to federal programs made for a diverse and powerful conservative force that coalesced around their opposition to the federal civil rights regulation. Grassroots religious groups like the ones agitated over the IRS policy toward Christian schools worked in parallel with powerful business organizations opposed to the reinvigorated efforts of the Equal Employment Opportunity Commission. An energized conservative punditry united them in an antigovernment chorus.

In many respects, President Carter's successes in preserving affirmative action, streamlining the civil rights regulatory regime, and appointing a historic number of minorities to courts and federal jobs were easy to miss. Aside from the larger political forces at work, regular communications failures between the executive branch and Congress, liberal activists, and the public obscured Carter's progress in these areas. Neither did the administration adequately publicize their achievements. While the White House pursued the middle ground, a galvanized New Right attacked the administration's civil rights efforts. Carter withstood these assaults, yet he and his advisors failed to defend the principles behind civil rights programs as vigorously as they might have. In some cases, the Carter administration found itself co-opting the language of civil rights opponents, a tactic, as noted by old Democratic allies, that harmed the administration with a core constituency. In the process, the infrastructure of the minority rights revolution became an easier mark for its critics.

Public School Desegregation

In the late 1960s, the practice of busing school children to desegregate public schools emerged as one of the country's most controversial domestic issues. Opposition to busing began in southern districts where courts had ordered an immediate end to de jure segregation. By the early and mid-1970s, however, courts had begun to order busing as remedies for de facto segregation—patterns of racial isolation resulting from ostensibly nongovernmental factors such as population density or housing patterns—in districts outside of the South. By the mid-1970s, antibusing protests had become common throughout the country. Among the most notable were those that took place in Boston in 1974, where attacks on blacks by working-class whites created indelible images of the tensions surrounding the issue.[6]

On the campaign trail in 1976, Jimmy Carter had emphasized his moderate position on school busing. He regularly cited his support for the "Atlanta Plan," which had substituted court-imposed busing for a desegregation plan determined by the local community that utilized only voluntary busing.[7] Yet Carter also criticized primary foes who he perceived to be exploiting white opposition to busing for political gain. "If I have to win by appealing to a basically negative, emotional issue which has connotations of racism," he said at an Orlando press conference before the Florida primary, "I don't intend to do it, myself."[8] Opposing busing while also objecting to attempts to exploit the issue politically was the subtle kind of positioning that helped Carter win the Florida primary, besting both Washington senator Henry "Scoop" Jackson and the other southern candidate, Alabama governor George Wallace. After his triumph in November, Carter entered the White House with a clean slate on the issue, unattached to any specific stance.

Carter drew fire from liberals early on with his appointment of Griffin Bell as attorney general. Bell had opposed busing as a Fifth Circuit judge, and the NAACP and the Congressional Black Caucus objected to the nomination of a candidate whose résumé included a stint as chief of staff to segregationist Georgia Governor Ernest Vandiver.[9] As attorney general, however, Bell took immediate action to desegregate schools, and he was unafraid to use busing as a remedy. Long-standing evidence of constitutional violations led to the federal government cutting off funds to Kansas City schools.[10] Though support for busing was not automatic—the Justice Department, for example, opposed an Indianapolis busing plan after determining that suburban schools there were not racially discriminatory—Bell tended to give the benefit of the doubt to allegations of illegal segregation.[11] One week before announcing its position in the Indianapolis case, the Carter administration endorsed a proposed busing plan between the city and suburbs of Wilmington, Delaware.[12] The Justice Department's role in a busing case out of Dayton, Ohio, drew explicit praise from civil rights groups. Nathaniel Jones, counsel for the NAACP, called the amicus brief submitted by the Justice Department a "refreshing document."[13] Attorney General Bell submitted "honest briefs," Jones said, "not the hypocrisy of the Nixon and Ford administrations."[14]

Over the course of Carter's presidency, however, busing opponents in Congress succeeded in limiting the kinds of remedies that the executive branch could pursue in fighting school segregation. The so-called "Byrd Amendment," named for Democratic West Virginia Senator Robert Byrd, was an obstacle for Carter's Department of Health, Education, and Welfare (HEW). First added to the Labor-HEW Appropriations Act in 1976, before Carter entered office, the amendment stipulated that HEW funds could not be used to transport students to any school beyond the one nearest to their home in order to comply with the 1964 Civil Rights Act.[15] Proponents of the Byrd Amendment expected it to ban non-court-ordered busing.

Despite the clear intentions of Byrd Amendment supporters, Carter administration officials found ways to continue to use busing as a desegregation remedy. As Assistant Attorney General for Civil Rights Drew Days III explained in conclusions prepared for the attorney general and distributed to HEW officials, the amendment's transportation limitation was vague. The Ford administration had interpreted the measure literally, yet Carter officials took advantage of the fact that the legislation neglected to specify whether HEW could use other means to achieve integration. In June 1977, the administration announced the new policy requiring school districts to merge their classes, a strategy referred to as grade restructuring, or pairing and clustering that altered the definition of the school "nearest the student's home."[16] In cases in which restructuring methods were inadequate, Justice recommended that HEW refer the matter to the Justice Department so that they could pursue a court order to remedy the discrimination.[17]

Such methods infuriated the Byrd Amendment's backers. The intent of the amendment was obvious, they argued, even if the tactics embraced by the Justice Department were never expressly forbidden. Furthermore, they argued that the Justice Department's request to have HEW refer to it the cases likely to require busing violated the amendment's injunction against "indirect" uses of HEW resources. Almost immediately, Congressional busing opponents took up legislation designed to more firmly restrict HEW's authority.[18]

Senator Joseph Biden of Delaware was among those particularly alarmed by the Carter administration's actions. Public backlash against busing created many strange bedfellows, and Biden was one of several liberal politicians surprised to suddenly find common ground with staunch antibusing conservatives such as North Carolina's Jesse Helms. During the Ford administration, Biden had urged the then–attorney general Edward Levi to use Wilmington as a test case to attempt to limit the scope of busing orders.[19] Although he resisted recommendations from Senators James Eastland and Herman Talmadge that he go home and "demagogue the shit out of the issue," the Carter administration's vocal support for busing between predominantly black Wilmington schools and the surrounding suburbs stoked local anger.[20] Biden encountered epithets and threats at public meetings, as well as organized opposition and pressure from citizens' groups. The outspoken leader of one such group, the Positive Action Committee, threatened to challenge Biden for his Senate seat in 1978.[21]

Biden and the rest of Delaware's Congressional delegation—senior Republican Senator William Roth and Republican Representative Thomas Evans—requested a meeting with President Carter in June 1977.[22] Carter conceded both that Congress had the right to dictate the actions of federal agencies and that, regardless of the president's own personal opinion on the policy, the Byrd Amendment had to be considered a "proper approach." Without explicitly endorsing his Justice Department's narrow interpretation of Congressional policy, Carter expressed his faith in Griffin Bell's judgment on the issue, citing Bell's work overseeing Mississippi schools as a federal judge. Biden would have to wait for Bell's assessment, Carter said, before he could offer an opinion on the antibusing legislation currently being prepared by the Delaware delegation.[23]

The subsequent Biden-Roth bill, which Drew Days described as a classic example of "legislative overkill," drastically curtailed the authority of federal courts to order widespread busing.[24] The most important section of the bill was a requirement that judges tailor their court orders to remedy only the adverse effects of existing segregation. If enacted, this would have limited the desegregation remedies that the government could pursue. Carter opposed the bill, agreeing with the Justice Department that attempts to "impose additional ambiguously phrased restrictions on the federal courts is likely to lead to more confusion and uncertainty in the school desegregation process." The Senate eventually tabled the bill.[25]

Another Biden initiative proved more effective. He and Missouri Senator Thomas Eagleton—another liberal Democrat under pressure from antibusing forces—introduced a revised version of the Byrd Amendment.[26] It included language closing the loopholes that the Carter administration had found to get around the original Byrd Amendment, expressly forbidding "any combination of grade restructuring, pairing or clustering."[27] Motions to delete this language failed, and Carter officials grudgingly accepted the new restrictions. In a signing statement appended to the 1977 Labor-HEW Appropriations Act, Carter bemoaned the additional complications added "to an already complex area of law" and the potential for "additional expense and delay in resolving issues important to parents, students, and school administrators."[28] HEW's only recourse now to desegregate public schools was to refer cases to an overloaded Justice Department and leave matters up to the attorney general.[29]

Later administration filings—including the government's first combined school-housing case against the city of Yonkers, New York—continued to break important new ground, but the potential for further action was severely limited.[30] The Carter administration began on the offensive, utilizing the full arsenal of federal policies in support of school desegregation. It showed little hesitancy in imposing solutions that had become politically fraught, particularly busing. Yet Congress continued the process, begun earlier in the decade, of denying funds for unpopular remedies. Although administration officials initially found technical methods for continuing the fight against discrimination in public schools, Congress soon got wise. Implementation of the Biden-Eagleton Amendment left federal agencies largely stymied, while the remaining years of the administration would pass with Carter failing to craft an argument in favor of busing that would sway the voting public.

Bakke

A month after Carter's inauguration, the Supreme Court agreed to hear the case of Allan Bakke, a white man who sued the University of California after he was denied admission to the medical school at the Davis campus. Bakke objected to the school's special admissions program that reserved sixteen slots for minority candidates. He claimed that the program violated the equal protection clause of the Fourteenth Amendment as well as Title VI of the 1964 Civil Rights Act.

The *Bakke* case presented a number of problems for Carter. During the previous year's campaign, he had been explicit in his rejection of racial quotas, a position strongly held by many whites and Jewish groups. Yet Carter had also enjoyed substantial African American support, and black politicians and civil rights advocates lobbied the administration to take a strong stand in the case. Eleanor Holmes Norton, chair of the Equal Employment Opportunity Commission, warned that "a decision not to file will carry its own strong implications to the Court and will be totally misread by the minority community, which attaches unusually strong importance to the *Bakke* case."[31] Also, the case had implications for an estimated 110 federal affirmative-action plans that provided minority access to federal jobs, including with the military.[32]

Despite disagreement inside the administration, it quickly became clear that the government would favor the University of California's admissions program. The question was how to do so without condoning quotas. Carter's election rhetoric established the narrow guidelines under which they worked: support for affirmative action for disadvantaged applicants (not just ethnic minorities) and disdain for "rigid, inflexible racial quotas."[33] The tension was in how to achieve progress without a clear mechanism or guideline for judging that progress. Two aides in the Justice Department—Solicitor General Wade McCree and Drew Days, both African American—were given the difficult task of drafting a brief that met these requirements.[34]

In early September 1977 McCree delivered an advanced draft to Attorney General Griffin Bell, who proceeded to make what he later called his "greatest mistake with regard to the power centers at the White House." Bell presented the brief to Carter, summarizing it as a stance "for affirmative action but [opposing] rigid quotas to carry out affirmative action programs, a position that meant Bakke would have to be admitted to the medical school."[35] Carter passed the copy to White House Counsel Bob Lipshutz, kicking off administration-wide circulation of the brief.[36]

Every advisor, it seemed, had a different opinion, leading to a cacophony of criticism. HEW Secretary Joseph Califano Jr. took particular issue with the brief's advocacy for application of a standard of strict scrutiny, viewing it as tantamount to declaring all race-sensitive admissions programs "presumptively unconstitutional." This position, Califano argued, would invite legal challenges to both voluntary and statutory affirmative-action programs.[37] It was at odds, he told the president, with Carter's own recently stated civil rights positions.[38] Aides worried that the sympathy shown to Bakke in the brief was a political disaster.[39] "Regardless of what the brief in fact says," warned Eleanor Holmes Norton, "it is the entry of the government on the side of a challenger to affirmative action programs that will have the impact."[40]

Domestic policy chief Stuart Eizenstat and Lipshutz both found the brief "insensitive" and "even offensive."[41] The draft spent sixteen pages elucidating the government's opposition to quotas in the firmest possible language. It even speculated that some of the minorities admitted to the medical school had been unqualified and questioned why Asian Americans were included in the program. Eizenstat circled these troubling sections of the draft, writing the word "No" repeatedly in the margins.[42]

The internal squabble went public after a copy of the draft brief was leaked to the *New York Times*. Veteran Supreme Court reporter Anthony Lewis tore the draft apart, calling the brief's middle way between quotas and affirmative action "an illusion—a dangerous one."[43] The Congressional Black Caucus quickly set up meetings with administration officials.[44] Black congressmen reached out individually to the attorney general and the president, taking the administration to task for what they viewed as a retreat on human rights policies. In response, Carter ordered Eizenstat and Lipshutz to "jump into" the drafting process.[45]

The Justice Department was slow to cooperate with the policy advisors. Attorney General Bell felt that this was another instance of White House policy advisors interfering in a legal matter, grousing in his memoir: "If the [White House] staff had its way, no doubt every major issue that naturally fell to the Justice Department would be considered policy rather than a legal matter."[46] While leaked copies of the first draft were still making news, Justice distributed a revised brief with a new introductory section focusing on evidentiary challenges and a few other changes. Still lacking, though, was an unambiguous defense of affirmative-action programs.[47]

Deficient as these first briefs may have been as political statements, they were in line with Carter's preferences. The President did not want to have the case remanded, and his repeated opposition to quotas mirrored the Justice Department's arguments. It took frank words from Chief of Staff Hamilton Jordan to get Carter to step back: "As non-lawyers, I don't think you or I really understand the implications of [filing a brief] nor the options available to you. A lot of well-intentioned people here and at the Justice Department assume you and I know a hell of a lot more about this than we do."[48] Above all, Jordan argued, the president must keep the brief's audience in mind: "Neither you nor I have been able to understand the legalism in this case—how can we expect illiterate and disadvantaged people to understand when they are told by their leaders and the media that, 'Carter has ruled against the blacks and Hispanics of the country.'" Bell may take comfort in the fact that the brief was written by two African American staffers, but rest assured, Jordan wrote, "it . . . will only tend to discredit Days and McCree in their own community."[49]

On September 10 Eizenstat informed Bell that the president still preferred that Justice find a way to indirectly have Bakke admitted, though this was "only a secondary interest." Revisions continued, and McCree and Days distributed a third and significantly shorter draft that satisfied almost all internal concerns. Eizenstat and Lipshutz now worried that the administration did not go far enough in opposing quotas.[50] This criticism was not incorporated, and the brief filed with the court on September 19 only referenced the issue in passing. Aside from its statement of support for affirmative-action programs, it passed on many of the other legal issues. After requesting reversal of the California Supreme Court on the constitutionality of the University of California, Davis's program, the brief argued for the decision admitting Bakke to be vacated and the case remanded.[51]

It is difficult to evaluate to what extent the government's amicus brief boosted the administration's civil rights bona fides. Parren Mitchell termed the eventual filing "consonant with what we sought in our pleadings with the Justice Department." Civil rights movement veteran Joseph Rauh said of the brief: "We can live with it."[52] Referencing the leaked first draft, New York Times staff writer David Rosenbaum captured the uneasiness of many liberals by pointing out that all evidence indicated that the argument in the leaked first draft was a more accurate representation of the administration's position.[53]

The eventual decision in Bakke—a highly fractured opinion, with Justice Lewis Powell providing the deciding votes by reversing in part and affirming in part—was close to Carter's long-stated positions. Efforts to assist minority applicants were constitutional, strict quotas were not. The University of California, Davis, program was deemed an illegal quota, and the court ordered that Bakke be admitted.[54] Polls suggested that much of the black community viewed the result in Bakke as a defeat for minority rights.[55] The Carter administration, however, took the opposite stance, applauding the decision and emphasizing that federal affirmative-action programs were unaffected. Attorney General Bell said that the administration was "pleased that the court took the same position on affirmative action programs as we took in our amicus brief."[56] The

White House and the Supreme Court may have come down on the same side, but for many Americans the legacy of *Bakke* was a greater sense of confusion and controversy over the future of affirmative action.

Weber and the Opposition to the EEOC

Affirmative action involved access to not only higher education but also federal contracts and jobs. In May 1977 Congress overwhelmingly passed legislation that provided for minority contract set-asides, an affirmative -action program that the Carter administration backed enthusiastically.[57]

Other affirmative-action programs in employment attracted much more critical attention. A lawsuit filed by Brian Weber, a white, male lab analyst at the Kaiser Aluminum plant in Gramercy, Louisiana, attracted less attention than Allan Bakke's case, yet the facts were similar and the implications just as dire for the future of affirmative-action policy. In his own notes, Jimmy Carter wrote that Weber's case was "probably more important" than *Bakke*.[58] At stake were thousands of voluntary programs initiated by private industries as proactive steps to address previous discrimination.

It was just such a program at Kaiser Aluminum to which Brian Weber objected. Kaiser had previously hired skilled craftsmen from outside the company, but in 1974 it instituted a training program for its unskilled production workers, black and white, that would allow it to promote workers from the inside. Blacks had long been excluded from the skilled trades in Louisiana, and their representation among craftsmen at Kaiser was pitifully low. Black employees held only 1.83 percent of the high-paying skilled positions—5 black craftsmen to 268 white craftsmen—despite the fact that blacks made up 46 percent of the local population and 39 percent of the plant's employees. The company decided to take preventative action in order to avoid a potential lawsuit. Working with the plant's union, the United Steelworkers of America, Kaiser agreed to a training program that would admit workers according to seniority with the stipulation that until black representation in the craft positions came closer to that in the general population, 50 percent of the trainee positions would be reserved for black workers. Weber sued the company and the union on the grounds that the program violated the proscription in Title VII of the 1964 Civil Rights Act that made it illegal "to discriminate . . . because of . . . race."[59]

Weber's suit threatened to upend new procedures set up under the Carter administration's Equal Employment Opportunity Commission (EEOC). Carter had reinvigorated the agency, consolidating within it many of the responsibilities that had been handled by competing organizations spread out across the federal government. It was part of a broad reorganization of civil rights enforcement that fit with Carter's priority on modern, efficient governance. He appointed as the head of the revived EEOC Eleanor Holmes Norton, a Yale-trained lawyer with roots in the civil rights movement, who pledged to cut down on the backlog of thousands of cases that had made the agency the poster child of bureaucratic inefficiency. Holmes emphasized class-action lawsuits against major employers. Under her leadership, the EEOC issued new guidelines that curtailed the use of employee tests and protected employers who set up affirmative-action programs from the kind of reverse-discrimination lawsuits like the one filed by Weber.[60]

The president understood the importance of *Weber* as a test case for the legality of voluntary remedies to discrimination. Many private firms were awaiting judgment in the case before moving ahead with their own voluntary programs. Because the government had intervened in a lower court, the United States was a party in the case. The question was not whether to file an amicus brief, as in *Bakke*, but what the government's argument should be. Officials in the administration were confident in the case that had already been made on appeal. Officials anticipated the criticism about the Kaiser program being a quota. Support for Kaiser would surely create "resentment in conservative circles and among blue collar workers toward 'the government,' if not toward you," a presidential advisor wrote.[61]

Carter officials took comfort, however, in the administration's consistent support for voluntary affirmative action as expressed in *Bakke*. The United Steelworkers' position in the case promised to blunt some of the blue-collar reaction. Kaiser had developed the program only after the government had pressured them into doing so, and the program created opportunities that had not previously existed for either white or black workers. Most of all, administration officials argued, to oppose the Kaiser plan would "chill" the affirmative-action efforts of other companies and unions. "Many private firms may be awaiting this judgment before going forward with their own plans," one memo to the president noted.[62] With little of the infighting that marked the administration's earlier *Bakke* deliberations, both Justice and the domestic policy staff urged vigorous action. On January 30, 1979, the administration filed a brief before the Supreme Court defending voluntary compliance with civil rights laws.

In the end, the court ruled against Weber, determining that Title VII's ban on discrimination did not condemn all "private, voluntary, race-conscious affirmative action plans."[63] In his majority opinion, Justice William Brennan pointed to the legislative history of the 1964 Civil Rights Act and emphasized that the program was a voluntary one adopted by private parties, one that was in clear accord with the "spirit" of the law. It would be "ironic," Brennan wrote, "if a law triggered by a nation's concern over centuries of racial injustice and intended to improve the lot of those who had 'been excluded from the American dream for so long' . . . constituted the first legislative prohibition of all voluntary, private race-conscious efforts to abolish traditional patterns of racial segregation and hierarchy."[64]

The conservative authors Terry Eastland and William J. Bennett criticized Brennan's decision for ignoring "the plain language of the sections of the law in question." They applauded Justice William Rehnquist's dissenting opinion that also used the legislative history and quoted from numerous legislators about how the bill would not permit the use of quota systems based on race. The authors lamented that in *Weber* "the Court approved, for the first time ever, preferential classifications on the basis of race in the absence of any proven constitutional or statutory violations. And the Court did so brazenly, failing to mention the genuine harm done Brian Weber."[65]

Bakke and Weber's charges dovetailed with a broader antiregulatory ethos that predominated in the late 1970s. President Carter himself took the lead in this area by deregulating the airline, banking, communications, railroad, and trucking industries.[66] Yet, his administration received little credit for such actions. More commonly, business interests criticized the administration for failing to counter the "regulatory tide" that first began to wash over Washington in the early 1970s. "The federal bureaucracy" was "unrelenting in its search for transgressions in the private sector," the *Wall Street Journal* editorialized in 1978.[67] In the *Journal's* view, a decade of government interference into the affairs of business began in 1971 with wage and price controls and continued with environmental protection, the Consumer Product Safety Commission, and energy regulation. Added to it by 1978 was the newly empowered EEOC. One attorney quipped that the energy regulations alone amounted to a "public service employment program for lawyers."[68] Carter could have pointed out that it was the very government inefficiency about which the *Journal* complained that led him to restructure the EEOC and deregulate various sectors of the economy. Yet Carter failed to get credit for the efforts that his administration had made.

IRS Controversy

Charges of reverse discrimination like those leveled by white men such as Allan Bakke and Brian Weber were difficult enough for civil rights activists and the Carter administration to deflect. In the late 1970s, however, a controversy developed over the tax status of private religious schools that threatened to turn the debate over quotas into a fundamental question of religious freedom.

In 1978 civil rights groups presented the Internal Revenue Service with evidence that racially discriminatory private schools were operating under tax-exempt status. This violated a procedure established by Richard Nixon's IRS in 1970 to deny tax exemptions to private schools that could be shown to be racially discriminatory. At the time, small private schools were springing up across the Deep South, in some cases literally overnight, as federal court decisions finally forced some of the most recalcitrant southern districts to desegregate public schools. After vigorous internal debate between moderate and conservative advisors, President Nixon sided with the moderates and issued an order denying tax exemptions for new white-flight schools. The order was phrased in such a way, however, that conservative southern Republicans, many of whom were key financial supporters of these new schools, spied a way in which they could comply with the order and maintain tax-exempt status without significantly altering the racial exclusivity of their schools.[69]

Civil rights groups were suspicious of such subterfuge, and they tracked the issue closely. In 1976, civil rights activists in Mississippi reopened a case that had originally prompted the 1970 order by the Nixon administration. The plaintiffs claimed that the IRS was not doing enough to identify and deny exemptions to discriminatory private schools. After a 1978 report by the U.S. Commission on Civil Rights provided firm evidence for the claim, the Carter administration IRS commissioner,

Jerome Kurtz, took action. In August 1978, the service issued new guidelines that outlined the measures required for schools to prove that they did not discriminate. It was the numerical formula outlined in the guidelines that touched off the firestorm of criticism from conservative groups and became the basis for the Republicans' charge in the 1980 platform of a "regulatory vendetta" against independent schools launched by the Carter administration.[70]

Under the new IRS guidelines, a private school would have its tax status reviewed if it was created or expanded around the time of public school desegregation and had an "insignificant" number of minority students.[71] The IRS defined insignificant minority enrollment as less than 20 percent of the percentage of the minority school age population in the community served by the school. Church-school defenders fastened on the formula as a racial quota, and the reaction bordered on the apoplectic. Over 120,000 letters flooded the IRS in protest of the new guidelines. One official characterized the response as "more than we've ever received on any other proposal." Some 400,000 more protest letters were sent to members of Congress.[72]

The tumult over the new procedures led the IRS to hold four days of hearings in Washington where church-school supporters from across the country turned out. These activists made a number of arguments against the new guidelines, but the charge that weighed heaviest was that unelected tax officials had created a racial quota for Christian schools, an accusation that IRS officials were quick to reject. The numerical formula was not a quota, the IRS pointed out, but merely a measure for determining which schools would receive closer scrutiny. IRS Commissioner Jerome Kurtz described it as a "safe harbor," a standard that schools could meet to ensure they would not be under review.[73]

This explanation did little to soften the objections of conservative Christians, particularly after the service announced revisions to the original 1978 revenue procedure that allowed exemptions for Jewish day schools, as well as schools for Muslims and the Amish. The revisions also included a provision for "a particular school which is part of a system of commonly supervised schools," language that was intended to exempt Catholic schools. The IRS was trying to be as specific as it could in targeting private schools started to avoid public school desegregation. It did not want to lump in schools that had a history of religious instruction that predated public school desegregation. Yet the changes only further enflamed resentment among conservative Protestants, who felt that the federal government had now intentionally singled out independently run Christian schools. Many church-school supporters interpreted their current struggle in light of a historic pattern of state opposition to religious freedoms, one that was enshrined in the First Amendment. Arno Q. Weniger Jr., for example, the executive vice president of the American Association of Christian Schools, invoked the memory of his Baptist forefathers in Virginia, who had "languished in jail until the establishment of that first amendment."[74]

The church-school lobby was an important subset of what commentators were increasingly referring to as the religious Right. Over the previous decade, conservative Christians had built new private schools at the rate of two per day. By the mid-1980s, Christian academies were educating more than a million children. Church-school supporters founded two important lobbying groups in the 1970s, the American Association of Christians Schools in 1972 and the Association of Christian Schools International, which originated in 1978 directly out of the fight over IRS policies.[75]

The IRS controversy marked a key moment in the formation of modern evangelical politics. Bob Billings, a church-school organizer and former president of Hyles-Anderson College, a private Bible college in Indiana, joined with Paul Weyrich, the conservative activist, to found the National Christian Action Coalition, the chief goal of which was to defeat the IRS efforts to withdraw tax exemptions for racially imbalanced private schools.[76] Republican leaders eagerly joined in the cause. In 1979, Republicans in the House and the Senate proposed amendments to a Treasury Department, Postal Service appropriations bill that blocked the IRS from enforcing its regulations against discriminatory private schools. In the House, Representative Robert Dornan of California and Representative John Ashbrook of Ohio proposed three different amendments that would block the IRS from using funds to enforce its regulations. The Ashbrook Amendment was the only one to survive the House-Senate conference, but it was all that was needed. Ashbrook placed a similar measure in the fiscal 1981 Treasury appropriations.[77] In the Senate, leadership came from Jesse Helms. In the 1960s, Helms' television editorials on WRAL-Raleigh denouncing liberal meddling were rebroadcast as radio editorials on more than 100 mostly southern radio stations; they also commonly ended up as reprints in segregationist publications.

Helms proposed legislation that went even further than the Dornan and Ashbrook Amendments in stopping the IRS from enforcing its 1978 guidelines.[78]

The private-school fight also figured prominently in presidential politics. Several months before conservatives were able to insert into the 1980 GOP platform the language about President Carter's "regulatory vendetta" against independent schools, Ronald Reagan gave a speech before a cheering crowd of over 6,000 students and faculty at Bob Jones University, a fundamentalist Christian school still involved in a suit against the IRS after having its tax exemptions revoked because of a policy banning interracial dating. Referring to Bob Jones as "a great institution," Reagan called for a "spiritual revival" and denounced the 1978 IRS guidelines as an example of government bureaucrats establishing "racial quotas." For Reagan, this was just Jim Crow segregation operating in reverse. "You do not alter the evil character of racial quotas simply by changing the color of the beneficiary," he told the crowd. He received three standing ovations and was interrupted by applause some fourteen times. A reporter traveling with the president called the appearance "one of the warmest receptions of [Reagan's] . . . campaign."[79] Bob Billings, one of the leaders in the church-school lobby, stepped down from his new position as executive director of the Moral Majority to serve as religious advisor to Ronald Reagan's 1980 presidential campaign. Billings stayed on as a special assistant for nonpublic schools in Reagan's Department of Education.[80]

Presidential Appointments and Legacies

Even as civil rights regulations sparked widespread opposition, the Carter administration made notable advances in minority appointments to federal positions. Prominent African American administration appointees included Andrew Young and Donald McHenry as ambassadors to the United Nations; Patricia Harris as Secretary of Housing and Urban Development (HUD) and later as Joseph Califano's successor at Health, Education, and Welfare; Clifford Alexander as Secretary of the Army; Wade McCree as solicitor general for the Civil Rights Division; Drew Days III as assistant attorney general for the Civil Rights Division; and John Reinhardt as head of the U.S. Information Agency. Passage of the Omnibus Judgeship Act of 1978—and with it the creation of 152 new federal judgeships—provided further opportunity for minority advancement. After a great deal of senatorial lobbying and White House coordination with the American Bar Association to modify their screening procedures in order to accommodate more minority and female appointments,[81] the 258 judges appointed by Carter during his administration included fourteen Hispanics, twenty-nine women, and twenty-eight African Americans.[82]

This record was not unassailable. Parren Mitchell, writing shortly after the administration's one-year anniversary on behalf of the Congressional Black Caucus, reminded the president of unfulfilled promises made during a post-election meeting with black leaders in Plains, Georgia. Although satisfied with the volume of black appointees to senior-level posts—and Carter's avoidance of tokenism—Mitchell was disappointed at the lack of black voices among the top advisors in direct day-to-day contact with the president. The Congressional Black Caucus had made recommendations for such an appointee following the inauguration. Members were dismayed by what they perceived as a lack of action on this front.[83]

Over the course of Carter's presidency, however, black appointees in positions of actual responsibility became a point of pride for the administration. At HUD, over one-third of senior level positions were occupied by African Americans. Bragging that no previous administration—or executive agency within the Carter White House—could match their record, a HUD staffer pointed out in an internal memo: "[African American] officials have a combined responsibility for over $27 billion in Departmental resources and they have over 1,800 positions under their supervision. . . . When Secretary Harris arrived at HUD, there were no Black Regional Administrators; we now have two."[84] Administration interest in these appointees did not cease after they were placed in office. In February 1978, the domestic policy staff arranged a special meeting for all 81 top-level African American White House appointees to review the administration's agenda. Approximately 60 attended and sat in on presentations from National Security Advisor Zbigniew Brzenzinski, Stuart Eizenstat, Office of Management and Budget Director James McIntyre, and Walter Mondale.[85]

The purpose of the meeting, as articulated by Presidential Assistant Bunny Mitchell, was both informational and publicity-minded. Mitchell explained to Eizenstat in a memo that "this meeting is designed to give appointees a comprehensive overview of the administration's goals and priorities for the year so that they will be able to better articulate, and support our initiatives over the coming months."[86] The administration was aggravated that Carter did not get more credit for these appointments. Even black publications and radio stations on the White House's mailing list, complained the White House Press Office, were uninformed concerning all the high-ranking black officials within the administration.[87]

During the latter years of his presidency, Carter's administration endeavored to explicitly inform the public and the press of their appointment record. Press releases touting appointments—including many of the judges appointed following the 1978 Judgeship Act—often carried less-than-subtle headlines: "Carter to Nominate Black as Fifth Circuit Judge" (regarding Joseph Hatchett, the first African American to serve on the Fifth Circuit, which covered portions of the Deep South) and "Carter Names Black to ICC" and "Carter Picks Two Blacks for District Judgeships" (regarding the nominations of future Congressman Alcee Hastings and NAACP General Counsel Nathaniel Jones) were but three examples.[88] The administration disseminated regular "Fact Sheets" touting Carter's appointment record.[89] Others touted military appointments—twelve of the twenty-two African American generals in the U.S. Army were appointed by Carter and Clifford Alexander—and provided regular updates on the promotion of new minority White House staffers.[90]

During the 1980 reelection campaign, it was often these appointments that allies chose to remember. Acknowledging that there was much to regret about the events and policies of the past four years (including the Supreme Court's equivocating *Bakke* decision), Rev. Jesse Jackson eventually focused on minority appointments—along with contract set-asides for minority-owned businesses—as the chief reason to endorse Carter in 1980.[91] Although political jobs hardly seemed enough to African American congressmen dismayed by Carter's moderate economic policies, the post-1978 judicial nominations were almost unanimously acknowledged as a breakthrough. "It is doubtful," proclaimed Missouri Representative Bill Clay in a February 1980 floor speech otherwise excoriating Carter's civil rights record, "if any other President would have made such significant appointments."[92]

These appointments were not without political risk. Although open opposition to minority candidates on the basis of race was mostly out of fashion, multiple entries in Carter's *White House Diary* mention strong Senate opposition to these nominees, particularly the women.[93] Carter's loss at the polls in November 1980—despite 90 percent support among African American voters, who tallied a turnout rate of 60 percent, well above the national average of 54.2 percent—was understood by disappointed observers within the Congressional Black Caucus as the end of new black appointments to the federal bench.[94]

Other developments in the weeks following the 1980 election only deepened fears about the fate of civil rights under Republican leadership. The Reagan campaign commissioned a transition team report on the EEOC to be prepared by Jay Parker, a longtime black conservative and head of the Lincoln Institute for Research and Education. Parker's report reflected the attitudes of critics in the business community who saw the EEOC as an "imperial bureaucracy" that imposed excessive requirements on companies through court actions and sweeping guidelines. Reagan's advisers wanted to drain much of the activism from the EEOC. In their view, the agency had "created a new racism in America" by emphasizing "affirmative-action quotas."[95]

Conservative Republicans also took action in the area of busing. Busing opponents in Congress pointed to the election results as a referendum on a range of social policies and decided to take action even before Reagan's inauguration early the next year. As before, Jesse Helms took the lead against the enforcement infrastructure of the civil rights movement. He introduced an amendment that would have largely finished the job started by Senators Biden and Eagleton earlier in the decade by disallowing the Justice Department to bring any sort of judicial action directly or indirectly resulting in busing.[96] Had the amendment become law, the lone remaining remedy allowed to the federal government for fighting school segregation would have been dealt a near-fatal blow.

There were some within the administration who thought it wisest to accept the antibusing measure. White House Counsel Lloyd Cutler offered the hangman's logic that antibusing legislation proposed by the incoming Congress was bound to be even more regressive.[97]

Others in the administration—among them Walter Mondale, Stuart Eizenstat, Presidential Assistant Anne Wexler, and the Justice Department—urged Carter to veto the bill. The civil rights community would rather fight the battle again in January, they argued, than accept defeat during the last days of the Carter presidency.[98] "There is simply no reason," domestic policy staffers argued, "why this President, with his firmly demonstrated commitment to civil rights, should in his last days in office accede to such objectionable legislation." A veto, they added, would carry great symbolic value, "demonstrating that [Carter] and the Democratic Party do not interpret the recent election results as an excuse to turn their backs on long-standing commitments."[99]

Carter did veto the bill, yet even in his veto message Carter remained true to the middle-of-the-road policy preferences.[100] "I have often stated my belief that busing should only be used as a last resort in school desegregation cases," Carter acknowledged. He framed the issue as a congressional invasion of a president's prerogative to carry out the law.[101]

Civil rights advocates may have won this final battle of the Carter administration, but like other such skirmishes to come during the Reagan era it was fought on the other side's playing field and using their language. During the campaign, Ronald Reagan successfully channeled voters' distaste with civil rights policies. He framed his opposition to busing and to a whole range of civil rights regulations as the defense of individuals against an invasive federal government. "Every American who loves freedom," Reagan proclaimed, "should be equally concerned about the encroachment of government forces into our family lives."[102]

Carter offered no winning counternarrative. In part, this was because by 1980 the policy aims of the civil rights movement had advanced from the achievement of core constitutional and democratic principles to more technical, arcane issues of implementation. The fact that many civil rights advocates who could have contributed to the advancement of such a narrative interpreted Carter's conservative economic rhetoric, so focused on budget cuts and decentralization, as ignoring the welfare of African Americans did not help. The injuries incurred by the Carter administration while fighting for civil rights, both self-inflicted and otherwise, would fester throughout the coming decades. Real progress was made during these years in expanding economic opportunity, advancing minorities in government, and making existing government infrastructure more responsive to civil rights concerns, but it was progress obscured by other setbacks.

Notes

1. Joseph Crespino, "Civil Rights and the Religious Right," in *Rightward Bound: Making America Conservative in the 1970s*, ed. Bruce J. Schulman and Julian E. Zelizer (Cambridge, Mass.: Harvard University Press, 2008), 91.

2. John T. Woolley and Gerhard Peters, *The American Presidency Project* [online]. Santa Barbara, Calif.: http://www.presidency.ucsb.edu/ws/?pid=25844.

3. Stuart Taylor, "U.S. Drops Rule On Tax Penalty For Racial Bias," *New York Times*, January 9, 1982.

4. Howell Raines, "President Shifts View On Tax Rule in Race Bias Cases," *New York Times*, January 13, 1982.

5. "The Nation: A New Day A'Coming in the South," *Time*, May 31, 1971.

6. Louis P. Masur, *The Soiling of Old Glory: The Story of a Photograph That Shocked America* (New York: Bloomsbury Press, 2008).

7. Memo to Stuart Eizenstat from Kurt Schmoke, February 18, 1977. Domestic Policy Staff: Abramowitz, Box 3, Busing, Presidential Papers of Jimmy Carter, Atlanta, Ga. (hereinafter cited as PPJC).

8. Jules Witcover, *Marathon: The Pursuit of the Presidency, 1972–1976* (New York: Viking Press, 1977), 257.

9. "The Transition: Surprises and Sparks on the Hill," *Time*, January 24, 1977.

10. Bernard Grofman, *Legacies of the 1964 Civil Rights Act*, (Charlottesville: University of Virginia Press, 2000), 114.

11. Josh Goshko, "Administration Opposed Busing Plan," *Washington Post,* March 23, 1977. Domestic Policy Staff: Gutierrez, Box 15, Desegregation—Busing, PPJC.

12. Josh Goshko, "Administration Opposed Busing Plan," *Washington Post,* March 23, 1977. Domestic Policy Staff: Gutierrez, Box 15, Desegregation—Busing, PPJC.

13. Jack Germond and Jules Witcover, "Germond & Witcover: A Brief On Busing Signed By Griffin Bell," *Washington Star*, May 2, 1977. Domestic Policy Staff: Gutierrez, Box 15, Desegregation—Busing, PPJC.

14. Peter Khiss, "Bell Praised by N.A.A.C.P. Chiefs For Action in 3 Integration Cases," *New York Times*, May 18, 1977.

15. Memo for Stuart Eizenstat from Kurt Schmoke, June 14, 1977. Domestic Policy Staff: Abramowitz, Box 3, Busing, PPJC.

16. Memo for Stuart Eizenstat from Kurt Schmoke, June 14, 1977. Domestic Policy Staff: Abramowitz, Box 3, Busing, PPJC; memo for Joseph Califano from Griffin Bell, May 25, 1977. Counsel's Office: McKenna, Box 120, Byrd Amendment, 5/77–2/78, PPJC.

17. Memo for Doug Huron from John Harmon, June 7, 1977. Counsel's Office: McKenna, Box 120, Byrd Amendment, 5/77–2/78, PPJC.

18. Memo for Joseph Califano from Griffin Bell, May 25, 1977. Counsel's Office: McKenna, Box 120, Byrd Amendment, 5/77–2/78, PPJC.

19. Lesley Oelsner, "Levi May Contest Delaware Busing; Considers Intervention In Wilmington Case to Get Court Clarification," *New York Times*, May 26, 1976.

20. Joe Biden, *Promises To Keep* (New York: Random House, 2007), 127.

21. Jules Witcover, *Joe Biden* (New York: William Morrow, 2010), 140.

22. Memo for Stuart Eizenstat from Kurt Schmoke, June 14, 1977. Domestic Policy Staff: Abramowitz, Box 3, Busing, PPJC.

23. Ibid.

24. Memo for Stuart Eizenstat from Kurt Schmoke, June 15, 1977. Domestic Policy Staff: Abramowitz, Box 3, Busing, PPJC.

25. Memo for the President from Stuart Eizenstat, returned to Eizenstat, July 20, 1977. Counsel's Office: McKenna, Box 120, Busing, 6–7/77, PPJC.

26. Gary Orfield, "Research, Politics and the Antibusing Debate," *Law and Contemporary Problems* 42, no. 4 (Fall 1978): 170.

27. Memo for Ray Calamaro from John Harmon, June 28, 1977. Counsel's Office: McKenna, Box 120, Busing, 6–7/77, PPJC.

28. "Labor-HEW Continuing Appropriations Bill Statement on Signing H.J. Res. 662 Into Law," December 9, 1977. The American Presidency Project: http://www.presidency.ucsb.edu/ws/index.php?pid=7000#axzz1GsSAm4iE.

29. Memo for Margaret McKenna from John Harmon, July 15, 1977. Counsel's Office: McKenna, Box 120, Busing, 6–7/77, PPJC.

30. Grofman, *Legacies of the 1964 Civil Rights Act*, 115.

31. Memo to Wade McCree from Eleanor Holmes Norton, August 5, 1977. Counsel's Office: McKenna, Box 120, Bakke v. University of California Board of Regents 7–8/77, PPJC.

32. Memorandum for the Heads of Executive Departments and Agencies, July 20, 1978. Counsel's Office: McKenna, Box 120, Bakke v. University of California Board of Regents 7/78, PPJC.

33. Notes by Margaret McKenna, April 1977. Counsel's Office: McKenna, Box 120, Bakke v. University of California Board of Regents 4–6/77, PPJC.

34. Griffin Bell and Ronald Ostrow, *Taking Care of the Law* (Macon, Ga.: Mercer University Press, 1986), 29.

35. Bell and Ostrow, *Taking Care of the Law*, 30.

36. Ibid.

37. Memo to Griffin Bell, Wade McCree from Joseph Califano, September 7, 1977. Counsel's Office: McKenna, Box 120, Bakke v. University of California Board of Regents, 9/1–8/77, PPJC.

38. Memo to the President from Joseph Califano, September 9, 1977. Domestic Policy Staff: Eizenstat, Box 149, Bakke 2/77–9/77, PPJC.

39. Memo to Bob Lipshutz and Stuart Eizenstat from Doug Huron, September 2, 1977. Counsel's Office: McKenna, Box 120, Bakke v. University of California Board of Regents, 9/1–8/77, PPJC.

40. Memo to the President from Eleanor Holmes Norton, September 9, 1977. Counsel's Office: McKenna, Box 120, Bakke v. University of California Board of Regents, 9/9/77, PPJC.

41. Memo to the President from Bob Lipshutz and Stuart Eizenstat, September 6, 1977. Counsel's Office: McKenna, Box 120, Bakke v. University of California Board of Regents, 9/1–8/77, PPJC.

42. First draft of the United States' amicus brief in Bakke v. University of Califor-

nia Board of Regents, Stuart Eizenstat's copy. Domestic Policy Staff: Eizenstat, Box 149, Bakke 10/77–11/77, PPJC.

43. Anthony Lewis, "The Bakke Brief," *New York Times*, September 8, 1977.

44. Letter to Stuart Eizenstat from the Congressional Black Caucus, September 10, 1977. Chief of Staff: Jordan, Box 33, Bakke Case, 9/77, PPJC.

45. Memo to the President from Bob Lipshutz and Stuart Eizenstat, September 6, 1977. Counsel's Office: McKenna, Box 120, Bakke v. University of California Board of Regents, 9/1–8/77, PPJC.

46. Bell and Ostrow, *Taking Care of the Law*, 30.

47. Memo to the President and Vice President from Bob Lipshutz and Stuart Eizenstat, September 10, 1977. Counsel's Office: McKenna, Box 120, Bakke v. University of California Board of Regents, 9/10–30/77, PPJC.

48. Memo to the President from Hamilton Jordan. Chief of Staff: Jordan, Box 33, Bakke Case, 9/77, PPJC.

49. Ibid.

50. Memo for the President and Vice President from Bob Lipshutz and Stuart Eizenstat, September 16, 1977. Counsel's Office: McKenna, Box 120, Bakke v. University of California Board of Regents, 9/10–30/77, PPJC.

51. Brief for the United States as amicus curiae, filed September 19, 1977. Regents of the University of California v. Bakke, 483 U.S. 265, 1978.

52. Robert Reinhold, "U.S. Backs Minority Admissions But Avoids Issue of Racial Quotas," *New York Times*, September 20, 1977, A1 and A34.

53. David Rosenbaum, "U.S. Role in Bakke Case: Hard Questions Deferred," *New York Times*, September 20, 1977.

54. Regents of the University of California v. Bakke, 438 U.S. 265 (1978).

55. Cardell Jacobson, "The Bakke Decision: White Reactions to the U.S. Supreme Court's Test of Affirmative Action Programs," *The Journal of Conflict Resolution* 27, no. 4 (December 1983): 691.

56. Press briefing by Attorney General Griffin Bell, Office of the White House Press Secretary, June 18, 1978. Counsel's Office: McKenna, Box 120, Bakke v. University of California Board of Regents, 6/28–30/78, PPJC.

57. Hugh Davis Graham, "Civil Rights Policy in the Carter Presidency," in *The Carter Presidency: Policy Choices in the Post New Deal Era*, ed. Gary Fink and Hugh Davis Graham (Lawrence: University Press of Kansas, 2001), 206–10.

58. Nancy MacLean, *Freedom Is Not Enough: The Opening of the American Workplace* (Cambridge, Mass.: Harvard University Press, 2008), 251.

59. MacLean, *Freedom Is Not Enough*, 250.

60. Graham, "Civil Rights Policy in the Carter Presidency," 204–6; "EEOC Adopts Final Guidelines Covering Hiring," *Wall Street Journal*, December 12, 1978.

61. "Memo for the President, From the Vice President; Hamilton Jordan; Bob Lipshutz; Stuart Eizenstat. Re: Weber," January 13, 1979. United Steelworkers of America v. Weber, 1/78–7/79, Box 145, Margaret McKenna Papers, PPJC.

62. Ibid.

63. MacLean, *Freedom Is Not Enough*, 252.

64. United Steelworkers of America, AFL-CIO-CLC v. Weber et al., 443 U.S. 193 (1979).

65. Terry Eastland and William J. Bennett, *Counting By Race: Equality from the Founding Fathers to Bakke and Weber* (New York: Basic Books, 1979), 204, 209–10.

66. William Leuchtenberg, "Jimmy Carter and the Post–New Deal Presidency," in *The Carter Presidency*, ed. Fink and Graham, 14–15.

67. "The Unrelenting Army," *Wall Street Journal*, January 6, 1978.

68. "The Big Winners," *Wall Street Journal*, January 13, 1978.

69. Joseph Crespino, *In Search of Another Country: Mississippi and the Conservative Counter-Revolution* (Princeton: Princeton University Press, 2009), 227–33.

70. Crespino, *In Search of Another Country*, 253.

71. Internal Revenue Service, news release, August 21, 1978, reprinted in Congress, House, *Tax-Exempt Status of Private Schools*, 20–37, quotation on 32.

72. Peter Skerry, "Christian Schools Versus the I.R.S.," *Public Interest* 61 (Fall 1980): 19.

73. United States Senate, Hearing Before the Subcommittee on Taxation and Debt Management Generally of the Committee on Finance, 96th Cong., 1st sess., *Tax-Exempt Status of Private Schools* (Washington, D.C.: U.S. Government Printing Office, 1979), 44.

74. Ibid., 119.

75. Patrick Allitt, *Religion in America Since 1945: A History* (New York: Columbia University Press, 2005), 186.

76. For a transcript of the IRS hearings, see Claussen and Claussen, eds., *The Voice of Christian and Jewish Dissenters in America*; Robert C. Liebman and Robert Wuthnow, *The New Christian Right: Mobilization and Legitimation* (New York: Adline Publishing, 1983), 60.

77. *1979 Congressional Quarterly Almanac, 96th Congress, 1st Session*, vol. 35 (Washington, D.C.: Congressional Quarterly Inc), 199–202; *1982 Congressional Quarterly Almanac, 97th Congress, 2nd Session*, vol. 38, (Washington, D.C.: Congressional Quarterly Inc), 397.

78. For examples of Helms' contributions to the *Citizen*, see "Northern Racial Violence Exposes Basic Hypocrisy of 'Liberal Views,'" *Citizen*, November 1964, 21–23; "Whatever Became of the 'Checks and Balances,'" *Citizen*, May 1965, 2, 22; "LBJ: Architect of Anarchy?" *Citizen*, September 1965, 20–21; "Guidelines Author On the Griddle," *Citizen*, December 1966, 8–9.

79. Reagan quoted in David Whitman, "Ronald Reagan and Tax Exemptions For Racist Schools," case no. 609.0, Case Studies in Public Policy and Management, John F. Kennedy School of Government, Harvard University, 25; Robert Lindsey, "Reagan to Debate His B.O.P. Rivals in South Carolina," *New York Times*, January 31, 1980.

80. Robert Liebman and Robert Wuthnow, *The New Christian Right*, 60–61.

81. Jimmy Carter, *White House Diary* (New York, N.Y.: Farrar, Straus and Giroux, 2010), 261.

82. Graham, "Civil Rights Policy in the Carter Presidency," 218.

83. Letter to the President from Parren Mitchell, February 2, 1978. Staff Offices: Martha (Bunny) Mitchell, Box 15, Mitchell, Congressman Parren 2/78–9/78, PPJC.

84. Memo from Randolph to Louis Martin, February 13, 1979. Staff Offices: Louis Martin, Box 6, Black Appointees in Government [1], PPJC.

85. Memo for the President from Bunny Mitchell, February 8, 1978. Staff Offices: Martha (Bunny) Mitchell, Box 15, Carter Administration Black Appointees Meeting 2/8/78, PPJC.

86. Memo for Stuart Eizenstat from Bunny Mitchell, February 8, 1978. Staff Offices: Martha (Bunny) Mitchell, Box 15, Carter Administration Black Appointees Meeting 2/8/78, PPJC.

87. Letter from Marc Henderson, November 2, 1978. Staff Offices: Louis Martin, Box 6, Black Appointees in Government [1], PPJC.

88. Press Releases from the Office of Media Liaison, May 18 and May 22, 1979. Staff Offices: Louis Martin, Box 6, Black Appointees in Government [1], PPJC.

89. Fact Sheet 104: Carter Breaks All Records in Appointment of Blacks to the Federal Judiciary and to Regulatory Boards and Commissions, June 1, 1979. Staff Offices: Louis Martin, Box 6, Black Appointees in Government [1], PPJC.

90. Fact Sheet 105: United States Army to Get First Black Female General, June 1, 1979. Staff Offices: Louis Martin, Box 6, Black Appointees in Government [1], PPJC.

91. An Analysis of our 1980 Political Options and My Endorsement, by the Reverend Jesse L. Jackson. Staff Offices: Louis Martin, Box 6, Black Relations [2], PPJC.

92. *Congressional Record*, Proceedings and Debates of the 96th Congress, second session, vol. 126, no. 21, February 12, 1980. Staff Offices: Louis Martin, Box 6, Black Relations [1], PPJC.

93. Jimmy Carter, *White House Diary*, 276–77, 296, 352.

94. "Our New Men," *Ebony*, January 1980.

95. Joan S. Lublin, "Reagan's Advisers Accuse the EEOC of 'Racism,' Suggest Big Cutback," *Wall Street Journal*, January 30, 1981.

96. Memo for Lloyd Cutler and Joseph Onek from Zoe Baird, November 19, 1980. Counsel's Office: Cutler, Box 54, Anti-Busing, 11–12/80, PPJC.

97. Memo for Stuart Eizenstat from Frank White, November 14, 1980. Domestic Policy Staff: White, Box 1, Anti-Busing Amendment, PPJC.

98. Ibid.

99. Memo for Stuart Eizenstat from Frank White, November 17, 1980. Domestic Policy Staff: White, Box 1, Anti-Busing Amendment, PPJC.

100. Letter to Sen. Robert Byrd, December 5, 1980. Counsel's Office: Cutler, Box 54, Anti-Busing, 11–12/80, PPJC.

101. "Message to the House of Representatives Returning H.R. 7584 Without Approval," December 13, 1980. The American Presidency Project: http://www.presidency.ucsb.edu/ws/index.php?pid=44407#axzz1GsSAm4iE.

102. Reagan On Mandatory School Busing, Campaign Handout. Domestic Policy Staff: Goldstein, Box 35, Reagan, Ronald W., Busing, PPJC.

3

RONALD REAGAN AND THE
LEADERSHIP CONFERENCE
ON CIVIL RIGHTS

Battles Won and Wars Lost

MARY FRANCES BERRY

In the 1980s, the Leadership Conference on Civil Rights (LCCR) appeared to have President Ronald Reagan on the run. For three decades, the LCCR had been one of the most important legislative advocates for civil rights in the United States. In the 1980s, the LCCR and its allies defeated Reagan and his congressional allies four successive times in legislative battles over the meaning and direction of federal civil rights law and policy. The victories included enacting the Voting Rights Act Extension of 1982, the Civil Rights Restoration Act of 1988, the Fair Housing Amendments Act of 1988, and the Civil Rights Commission reauthorization in 1984. The LCCR also succeeded in killing Robert Bork's Supreme Court nomination. It accomplished these feats even though until 1986 Republican Senators Orrin Hatch (UT) and Strom Thurmond (SC) controlled the Senate Judiciary committee, from which most civil rights legislation emerges.[1]

Although an LCCR-led coalition of civil rights organizations and activists won significant legislative victories, they eventually lost the law and policy struggle to Reagan and his progeny. Reagan's biggest victories came through the courts. He appointed three associate justices and elevated William H. Rehnquist to chief justice of the Supreme Court. He also named to the lower federal courts a youthful cohort of 376 judges. In the thirty years since Reagan's election, the federal courts have redirected the law in ways that conservatives have cheered and advocates for civil rights have lamented.

Reagan also succeeded in gutting the United States Commission on Civil Rights. Since its inception in 1957, the Commission had been an independent instrument of investigation, education, and moral suasion with regard to the nation's achievements and shortcomings in civil rights. It was a symbol of the nation's commitment to equal opportunity for minorities, women, and the disabled, and it had not hesitated to criticize government at all levels, including presidents, when its investigations led it to conclude that criticism was warranted. Reagan and his advisers bristled at the Commission's criticism of his administration, and they could not abide the fundamental conflict between the Commission's view of its role and their desire to turn civil rights law and policy on its head.[2]

This essay discusses the post-war origins of the Reagan-era battles over civil rights and the course of those political struggles of the 1980s. It shows that while the LCCR achieved a series of important legislative victories, the Reaganites ultimately succeeded in changing the direction of civil rights law and policy in the United States.

The Conservative Movement and the Rise of Ronald Reagan

Ronald Reagan's victory in the 1980 presidential election was decades in the making. Identity politics conflating race and class, opposition to the post-war black freedom struggle, and efforts to prevent and then reverse civil rights progress were central to the conservative movement that Reagan helped shape, that propelled him to office, and that his presidency boosted into the decades that followed.

In the 1950s and 1960s, intellectuals envisioned and advocated the alignment of segregationists and conservatives and created a politics that made explicit and implicit use of race and racial antagonism. Southerners among them, such as the journalist James K. Kilpatrick and the attorney Charles Wallace Collins, defended segregation, articulated a racially enhanced critique of New Deal liberalism, and labored to embed the creed of states' rights in the conservative psyche. In giving Kilpatrick and like-minded thinkers a national forum, the *National Review*, guided by its founder and editorial force William F. Buckley Jr., was a seminal venue for conservative discourse. It introduced its readers to racially loaded political argumentation in its efforts to create a common conservative identity. In its editorial columns, the *National Review* initially took the position that southern blacks were politically "retarded" and intimated that violence was an acceptable means for white southerners to maintain power and ensure the continuation of "civilization" in the region. Only later did it temporize as it adopted the states' rights mantra.[3]

While intellectuals honed the philosophy of racial conservatism, politicians put it to use. Dixiecrats like Strom Thurmond beat the drum of segregation and opposition to federal civil rights enforcement as they stood against the efforts of African Americans and their allies in the northern wing of the party and among moderate Republicans. These southern Democrats wielded sufficient power that a timid Kennedy administration, for all its progressive rhetoric and image crafting, did little to advance the cause of civil rights.

The legislative victories of 1964 and 1965, won because men and women put their lives and livelihoods on the line to challenge segregation and discrimination, further energized the race-minded denizens of the conservative movement. George Wallace demonstrated in two presidential campaigns the potential for linking southern whites' concern for their region's racial status quo with northern whites' fear for their economic status and their all-white neighborhoods and schools. Although Wallace's racially hued populist rhetoric appealed to many northerners, he proved too volatile and frightening to successfully contest for national office before being gunned down in an assassination attempt in 1968. Senator Barry Goldwater, however, recognized the potential in Wallace's message in 1964. He worked to draw the South into a new Republican Party, attracting significant southern support for a presidential candidate for the first time in the party's history. While Goldwater's crushing 1964 defeat to Johnson seemed a terrible blow to the conservative movement, Goldwater went on to lead the GOP in its embrace of the thinly veiled racism of states' rights and law and order that it would use to capture the White House and ultimately Congress.

Richard Nixon figured out how to successfully apply the conservative race strategy on a national scale. As John Skrentny shows in his essay for this volume, Nixon came to the presidency at a time when the political meaning of civil rights was in flux. Advocates of public-school integration pressed the federal courts to make real the promise of *Brown v. Board of Education*, civil rights activists turned their attention toward economic inequality and job and residential segregation in the North, and urban blacks lashed out at the fallacy of the American dream by rioting in cities across the country. Recognizing and cultivating white northerners' feelings of being under economic and cultural siege, Nixon built on the foundations laid by the intellectuals, the Dixiecrats, Goldwater, and Wallace. He wove populist, racial, and law-and-order conservatism into the political construct of the "silent majority," crystallizing a conservative political identity among millions of Americans across regions.

Nixon was in many ways a transitional political figure. He sought to hold on to Republican moderates while attracting the right wing of the GOP and cleaving southern whites and northern working-class whites from the New Deal coalition. In supporting the Equal Rights Amendment and promoting federal government action to aid education and protect the environment, he proved too liberal for conservative purists. They had distrusted Nixon since he made a deal with Nelson Rockefeller at the 1960 Republican convention, accepting Rockefeller's moderate planks into the party platform. Southern Republicans were particularly incensed at a provision promising aggressive action on civil rights. Eight years later Nixon firmly opposed busing to achieve public-school integration, but that did not mollify conservatives angered by his support for policies intended to remedy the effects of discrimination in areas such as government contracting, as symbolized by the Philadelphia Plan. GOP conservatives tried to convince Reagan, the governor of California and a rising star of the right, to challenge Nixon for the party's 1968 presidential nomination. Reagan seriously considered it but declined. Ultimately Nixon defeated the liberal stalwart Hubert Humphrey in 1968 and demolished George McGovern in 1972.

After Nixon's disgrace and exit from office left the country bitterly divided, Gerald Ford was not much better to conservative minds. But it was Jimmy Carter's difficult tenure that provided Reagan and his supporters the opportunity to finally seize the presidency. During a decade of economic turbulence, revelations of bipartisan government deceit on Vietnam, Nixon's epic abuse of power, and the ongoing demands of African Americans, joined by other racial and ethnic minorities, women, gays and lesbians, and others seeking full citizenship, conservatives consolidated the gains and honed the rhetoric that they had been developing since the 1950s. In 1980, Reagan embraced the opportunity to lead them nationally. When he launched his general election campaign in

August with a speech pledging to defend states' rights, he left no doubt about a central tenet of his political strategy. He made that speech at the Neshoba County Fair Grounds in Philadelphia, Mississippi: the very spot where three civil rights workers had been murdered in 1968. It was ingenious theater calculated to resonate with voters whose identities had been shaped by decades of racial politics, who desperately wanted to control the federal government, and who would put him in the White House if sufficiently motivated. Three months after the Philadelphia speech, he won the election.

In the early years of his administration, Reagan achieved remarkable success with Congress, including the enactment of a large tax cut in 1981 and greatly increased military funding, and for a time he avoided fights on divisive social issues such as civil rights. Southern congressional Democrats, whose constituents had voted for him, gave him a reliable bipartisan majority on many issues, but when the administration began addressing civil rights issues, it found that Republican moderates were uncooperative. They represented constituencies that resisted backsliding on civil rights.

Whatever his personal views, Reagan extended the racially polarizing strategies that Republicans had used since the 1950s. He and Edwin Meese, his longtime counselor and the United States attorney general from February 1985 to August 1988, worked to drive deeper the wedge between the Democratic Party and northern white workers, who resented efforts to remedy long-standing discrimination in employment and education. Meese and Reagan also enhanced the party's courting of southern whites, the Christian Right, and economic conservatives, seeking to completely and permanently fracture the New Deal coalition and create a new conservative majority. Key to Reagan's and Meese's strategy was implementing their shared objective of turning back the clock on civil rights.[4]

Voting Rights

The first legislative battle was fought over voting rights. The Voting Rights Act of 1965 had transformed the electorate in the South, where registration had risen from 29 percent of eligible black voters in 1965 to 57 percent in 1980. Critical to the act's success were the provisions of

Section 5 requiring Justice Department or federal court preclearance of any proposed change to voting practices in jurisdictions where blacks had been systematically prevented from voting by violence and intimidation and by means such as poll taxes, literacy requirements, and sham tests of constitutional knowledge. The covered jurisdictions included the states of the former Confederacy in their entirety and a number of smaller jurisdictions elsewhere. Initially scheduled to expire in 1970, the "temporary" provisions had been renewed that year and again in 1975. They were scheduled to expire again in 1982. Their renewal was the first front in the battle over voting rights.[5]

A second front opened in April 1980, when the Supreme Court decided *Mobile v. Bolden*.[6] Five years earlier, the veteran civil rights activist Wiley L. Bolden and other African American residents of Mobile, Alabama, filed a lawsuit challenging the at-large electoral system for the city's three commissioners, who exercised all executive and legislative power in the city. Although African Americans constituted 35 percent of the city's population, none had ever been elected commissioner. The plaintiffs contended that the system violated the First, Thirteenth, Fourteenth, and Fifteenth Amendments to the Constitution, Section 2 of the Voting Rights Act of 1965, and the Civil Rights Act of 1871 by diluting African American votes. District court judge Virgil Pittman ruled on only the Fourteenth and Fifteenth amendment claims, finding that the city had violated both by intentionally discriminating against African American voters, and he ordered that a new mayor-council system be installed. The Court of Appeals for the Fifth Circuit affirmed, and the Supreme Court granted the city's petition for review.

The case raised a complicated question about how to interpret and enforce the Voting Rights Act. To challenge an electoral system as discriminatory and in violation of the Voting Rights Act, would one have to prove it had a discriminatory *effect*, or would one have to prove as well the *intent* to discriminate—a much more onerous standard that was difficult to demonstrate? As it stood at the time, Section 2 of the Voting Rights Act provided:

No voting qualification or prerequisite to voting, or standard, practice, or procedure shall be imposed or applied by any State or political subdivision to deny or abridge the right of any citizen of the United States to vote on account of race or color.[7]

Before *Mobile v. Bolden*, there was little case law interpreting Section 2, but it was generally agreed that, based on the legislative history of the act and its 1970 extension, the statute required only a showing of discriminatory *effect*: that a challenged electoral system infringed the voting rights of racial minorities, regardless of the motivations of those who created and ran the system.[8]

The Supreme Court disposed of the case in a variety of conflicting opinions, an exercise in obtuseness that was becoming typical and the bane of the lower courts, lawyers, parties, and anyone else seeking guidance from an increasingly fractious Court. A plurality of four, in an opinion by Justice Potter Stewart joined by Chief Justice Warren Burger and Justices Lewis Powell and William Rehnquist, addressed the Section 2 claim even though the lower courts had not ruled on it. Stewart declared that to establish a claim under Section 2 plaintiffs must demonstrate that the challenged electoral system was established with the *purpose* or *intent* to discriminate against minorities. He ignored relevant parts of the statute's legislative history in holding that Congress intended to require the same showing under that statute as required for Fifteenth Amendment claims. Then Stewart pointed to just one fact in finding that Mobile's system did not violate either the Fifteenth Amendment or the Voting Rights Act: African Americans in Mobile registered and voted without hindrance. He ignored voluminous evidence that minority voting strength had been intentionally diluted.[9]

Justice John Paul Stevens concurred in the decision in an opinion that made explicit what was perhaps implicit in the plurality opinion: he feared ruling in a way that might spawn litigation and draw the judiciary into what he termed the "political thicket" of electoral district drawing. While his legal analysis differed from the plurality's, Stevens was equally willing to sacrifice African Americans' voting rights to other considerations.[10] Justice Byron White forcefully dissented, but not from the requirement of discriminatory intent for Section 2. He argued that the facts of the case established the necessary intent for the constitutional claims.[11]

So while it was not exactly clear, it appeared that five, perhaps six, justices agreed that the scope of Section 2 was the same as that of the Fifteenth Amendment. The four justices in the plurality clearly required proof of discriminatory intent to demonstrate a violation of the statute. They ignored abundant evidence from which intent could be inferred.

Justice White also seemed to adopt the intent requirement, although he explicitly addressed only the constitutional claims. Justice Stevens similarly seemed disposed to require proof of discriminatory intent.

On remand, Judge Virgil Pittman ordered a new trial to take additional evidence bearing on the question of intent. Remarkably, the plaintiffs were able to find a turn-of-the-century document in which one of the system's designers acknowledged that such devices were intended to deny African Americans meaningful electoral participation. On April 15, 1982, the judge found that "one of the principal motivating factors for the at-large election system for the Mobile City Commission was the purpose (intent) to discriminate against blacks, and to deny them access to the political process and political office . . . [and] that the effects of this discriminatory intent continues [sic] to the present." Mobile's at-large system therefore violated Section 2 of the Voting Rights Act, as well as the Civil Rights Act of 1871 and the Fourteenth and Fifteenth Amendments.[12]

Elsewhere, the consequences of the Supreme Court's decision on Section 2 were immediate and devastating to voting rights claims. What was obvious to both proponents and opponents of meaningful voting rights—namely, that it would be difficult to enter the minds of officials of the distant past and that sophisticated racists would take care to leave no evidence of their invidious motivations—was borne out in practice. Because six justices seemed to require discriminatory intent for both constitutional and Section 2 claims, and because the plurality's evidentiary reasoning was so restrictive, cases decided under the previous standards were vacated and remanded for new proceedings. Lower courts in those cases and others repeatedly rejected challenges to at-large voting systems because of insufficient evidence of intent. With one exception, challenges were sustained only when plaintiffs, like those in *Mobile v. Bolden*, managed to produce a smoking gun.[13]

The case also showed why the Section 5 preclearance provisions were still needed. After Judge Pittman's decision on remand, the defendants offered to negotiate a resolution. The parties agreed to a settlement calling for a district-based electoral system beginning with the next scheduled election, in 1985. The specifics of the new system were to be determined by the Alabama legislature, which enacted a statute providing for the city's voters to decide between two specified plans. The voters chose a mayor-council system that was virtually identical to the system Judge

Pittman had ordered nearly nine years earlier. On July 30, 1985, the first three African Americans since Reconstruction were elected to the city council. It had taken the plaintiffs nearly ten years and $2.2 million in legal fees (which the city ultimately paid as part of the settlement) to replace a discriminatory electoral system with one that afforded African Americans effective participation in the political process.[14] Unless the preclearance provisions were renewed, election officials could engage in the kind of practices that Mobile's leaders had perpetrated in 1911, secure in the knowledge that lengthy, expensive, and uncertain litigation would be the only recourse for those whose rights they violated.

Nothing could be done to change the court's ruling on the constitutional claims in *Mobile v. Bolden* without a change in the court's membership, which was unlikely with Reagan in office. Congress, however, could correct the ruling on Section 2 of the Voting Rights Act by specifying an effects standard along with renewing Section 5. As the deadline approached, the LCCR geared up to lead the fight.

The Leadership Conference on Civil Rights

The LCCR was founded in 1950 by A. Philip Randolph, head of the Brotherhood of Sleeping Car Porters; Roy Wilkins of the NAACP; and Arnold Aronson, a leader of the National Jewish Community Relations Advisory Council. Its lobbying was instrumental in securing the passage of every federal civil rights statute since its founding, all of which Reagan had opposed. Those legislative victories included the Civil Rights Act of 1957, the Civil Rights Act of 1960, the Civil Rights Act of 1964, the Voting Rights Act of 1965, and the Fair Housing Act of 1968. The LCCR helped organize the 1963 March on Washington and was an early advocate of establishing a Civil Rights Division in the Justice Department. It also led the fight for Title IX of the Education Amendments of 1972, which prohibited gender discrimination in educational programs or activities receiving federal funding; Section 504 of the Rehabilitation Act of 1973, which prohibited discrimination against people with disabilities in federally assisted programs; and the Age Discrimination Act of 1975, which prohibited age discrimination in programs or activities receiving federal funds.

The LCCR also contributed greatly to the bipartisan support that civil rights enjoyed in Congress and much of the nation into the 1980s. As the veteran public-interest lobbyist Michael Pertschuk has observed, the LCCR was unmatched in its ability to mobilize grassroots activism, structure the media, formulate and implement legislative strategy, provide expertise in the substance of the law and legislative drafting, build and sustain relationships with congressional leaders, and identify and prepare witnesses for congressional hearings. From its black-labor-religious base, it had grown by 1981 to include 165 national organizations representing 65 million individuals, among them women, disabled persons, American Indians, Asian Americans, Latinos, older Americans, and gay and lesbian Americans. The LCCR operated under the direction of Ralph Neas, its newly hired executive director. Neas, a white, Republican Catholic, was the former chief legislative assistant to the liberal Republican Edward Brooke, the first black senator from Massachusetts. He was experienced at working across party lines. He used his considerable political acumen to keep his diverse coalition pulling together and to work with supportive legislators to shepherd the Voting Rights Act extension through Congress.[15]

The Reagan administration entered the voting rights battle on the side of those who wanted to eliminate or weaken the preclearance provisions. It opposed replacing the *Mobile* intent requirement with an effects test. The president claimed that an effects standard would require minority representation on elected bodies in proportion to their presence in the population and, he contended fantastically, "You could come down to where all of society had to have an actual quota system." Reagan also came out in support of a cynical proposal from Jesse Helms (R-NC), backed by Orrin Hatch and Strom Thurmond, to apply the preclearance requirements nationally, which they knew would overwhelm the Justice Department and render enforcement impractical.[16]

In the House of Representatives, the Judiciary Committee and its subcommittee on Civil and Constitutional Rights were chaired by strong civil rights advocates Peter Rodino (D-NJ) and Don Edwards (D-CA), respectively. Edwards' subcommittee staff worked with the LCCR to develop hearings in Washington and in the South and Southwest, which demonstrated that systematic, disguised discrimination persisted where it had historically been worst. As a result, Henry Hyde (R-IL), who had been the leading House opponent of renewing the preclearance provisions, was convinced to change his mind. The House Judiciary Committee reported a bill amending Section 2 to incorporate a results test and extending the Section 5 pre-clearance requirements intact. On October 5, 1981, the House passed the Judiciary Committee's bill by an overwhelming majority, 389–24.[17]

Within two months sixty-one senators had co-sponsored a bill in the Senate identical to the House bill. By spring 1982, the number of Senate co-sponsors had risen to sixty-five, nearly enough to override a veto. However, the Senate Judiciary Committee's Subcommittee on the Constitution, chaired by Orrin Hatch, rejected the effects test. In its report, the Subcommittee majority recommended "the retention of the intent standard in place of the new results standard adopted in the House-approved measure," and it defended the *Mobile v. Bolden* standard. The proposed bill then went before the full Senate Judiciary Committee, chaired by Strom Thurmond, who had the power to delay consideration of the bill as the deadline for renewing Section 5 approached, which all knew would weaken the LCCR's hand.

Bob Jones University and Goldsboro Christian School cases

The coalition was helped when the unexpected occurred: Reagan's fiasco involving Bob Jones University and the lesser-known Goldsboro Christian School. Both were private Christian institutions that excluded African Americans. Bob Jones University, located in Greenville, South Carolina, was founded in 1927. The Goldsboro Christian School was founded in 1963 at the height of southern resistance to *Brown* and just before school desegregation began in the North Carolina county where it was located. Until the 1970s, both enjoyed exemption from federal taxation under section 501(c)(3) of the Internal Revenue Code, which exempted corporations organized exclusively for educational purposes, among others. Donations to 501(c)(3) organizations were deductible from the donor's income under section 170(a). In 1970, after a federal court enjoined extension of the tax-exemption to private schools discriminating in Mississippi, the Internal Revenue Service concluded that it could no longer maintain the tax exemption for any school engaging in racial discrimination. After nearly five years of legal wrangling the IRS formally revoked Bob Jones University's tax-exempt status in 1975. The school sued the agency in federal court in South Carolina to block the revocation, arguing that the policy was inconsistent with section 501(c)(3) and violated the school's First Amendment right to the free exercise of religion. The school prevailed at trial, but the Court of Appeals for the Fourth Circuit reversed the district court, agreeing with the IRS on both the statutory and constitutional grounds.[18]

While the *Bob Jones University* case proceeded, the Goldsboro Christian School made similar arguments for tax-exempt status in federal court in North Carolina. The district court there found for the IRS, and another panel of the Fourth Circuit summarily affirmed the lower court, citing the decision a few months earlier in the *Bob Jones University* case. In October 1981, the Supreme Court agreed to review the decisions in a consolidated appeal. The government supported review in order to resolve the important questions. In its brief, filed nine months after Reagan took office, it argued that the Fourth Circuit decisions were correct and that the IRS policy was constitutional and consistent with the statute.[19]

Much had changed in the eleven years since the IRS initiated its policy. In 1970, memories of Jim Crow and school segregation were fresh. Also fresh was the violence hurled at civil rights activists and the resistance to school integration in the South, which included the establishment of thousands of private academies, many of them Christian, aimed at preserving white-only elementary and secondary schools. Moreover, the federal courts in the early 1970s were fully engaged in trying to achieve integrated public schools. By 1981, however, the racial origins of private religious schools like the Goldsboro Christian School had faded, and the conservative view of civil rights had gained ground. Nixon, Reagan, and many in the new Republican Senate majority had entered office decrying efforts to achieve school desegregation. They were supported by Christian fundamentalists, an increasingly potent political force.[20]

In his brief on the merits before the Supreme Court, the veteran Deputy Solicitor General Lawrence Wallace (who was in charge of the case because Solicitor General Rex Lee had represented the Mormon Church in a similar case) stated his intention to continue supporting the IRS ruling.[21] But he would soon be overruled by an administration seeking to reverse national civil rights law and policy. Soon after the Supreme Court granted certiorari, segregationists, supported by Strom Thurmond, a Bob Jones University trustee, began lobbying the administration, urging that it reverse its position. House Majority Whip Trent Lott (R-MS) wrote to Lee urging reversal of the IRS rule. As Edwards described him at the time, Lott was one of a group of young House Republicans pushing hard for a rollback of civil rights law: "Tough, eloquent, great speakers, they won't give you nothin.' Trent Lott is the toughest of that band; he's a tough son of a bitch, I'll tell you, and he won't give you an inch."[22]

Lott did not persuade Wallace to reverse the government's position, but when his letter reached key members of the administration his entreaties found sympathetic ears, ultimately including Reagan's. Next to the entry in the presidential Log outlining Lott's argument for saving Bob Jones University's tax exempt status, Reagan signaled his agreement succinctly, writing, "I think we should." Over Wallace's objections, Justice's Civil Rights Division head William Bradford Reynolds (who had consulted Meese) and Treasury Secretary Donald Regan set about reversing the government's position before the court and restoring the school's tax-exempt status. Concerns expressed by some in Justice and Treasury about potentially negative political consequences were brushed aside. Michael Deaver, Howard Baker, and officials in public affairs and the congressional liaison office, who might have anticipated adverse congressional and public reaction, were not consulted. On January 8, 1982, the Treasury Department announced the reversal of its legal position, declaring that only Congress could deny the exemptions by changing the statute and saying that it would restore the school's exempt status.[23]

The uproar was immediate. Alarmed civil rights organizations attacked the administration's support of what they saw as a racist policy. Their leaders denounced the administration's action. NAACP head Benjamin Hooks called it "criminal." Democratic leaders in Congress called it "part of a pattern of capitulation to the segregationists." Many Republican leaders were also critical. Employees of the Civil Rights Division, including half of the division's attorneys, protested the administration's reversal in a letter to Reynolds.[24]

Deaver and Baker were livid at the ideologues, and the administration set about trying to calm the political waters. In January 1982, Reagan released a statement, written by communications director David Gergen, averring that the president was opposed to racial discrimination, which was consistent with his private protestations against being considered prejudiced, and that the policy reversal was solely out of concern for agencies' not overstepping their bounds. A few days later the administration sent a draft bill to Congress that, not surprisingly, proposed to deny tax-exempt status to racially discriminatory schools.[25]

The administration's dance satisfied almost nobody. Democrats and many Republicans in Congress rejected the bill on the ground that the IRS had the power to establish its policy, and it went nowhere. Conservative groups felt betrayed. The LCCR and its member organizations rejected the bill for the legal reasons and as the face-saving ploy that it was, and they filed amicus briefs urging the Supreme Court to uphold the IRS rule. Wallace was so aghast at the ideologues' conduct that he refused to sign the government's brief until Lee persuaded him to do so while noting his disagreement with much of it in a footnote. The Court took the extraordinary step of appointing a lawyer, William T. Coleman, to argue the government's original position in favor of the exemption. When the court upheld the IRS rule in an 8–1 decision, it was widely seen as an embarrassing rebuke to the administration. Neas later commented,

> We were fortunate that the attorney general, over time, was to do so many foolish things. . . . [H]is effort in the Bob Jones case to allow segregated schools tax-exempt status underscored our general theme: "These guys are wrong substantively, and politically, and they are out of touch with almost all Republicans in the country." We could therefore leave room for moderate, mainstream Republicans.[26]

The embarrassing episode put Republicans on the defensive in the debate over the Voting Rights Act extension, and it made public what Edwards well knew about the Reagan Justice Department. As he explained at the time, "the Justice Department wouldn't answer our telephone calls, they refused to testify; about 80 career lawyers, people who had been filing their cases for 15 years almost had a revolt down there . . . because Justice was not enforcing the law."[27]

Senator Robert Dole of Kansas, a moderate, mainstream Republican who had previously been uncommitted within the Judiciary Committee, anxiously bridged the gap between Democrats and moderate Republicans and the right-wing Republicans in the Senate, suggesting a compromise and guiding it to acceptance. Edwards later opined that "Bob Dole pushed the magic button."[28] In the compromise bill crafted by Senators Dole, Edward Kennedy (D-MA), and Charles "Mac" Mathias (R-MD) that emerged from the Judiciary Committee, a revised Section 2 specified the results standard and provided that the standard could be met based on the totality of the circumstances. Another provision placated reluctant Republicans by providing that proportional representation of minorities was not required. The Section 5 preapproval requirements were renewed for twenty-five years—three and a half times longer than any previous extension. Provisions requiring bilingual assistance for voters were also extended.[29]

The bill passed the Senate by a large margin, and Dole persuaded the White House that it could get nothing better. The House approved the Senate bill overwhelmingly, and on June 29, 1982, a smiling Reagan signed the bill into law, looking and sounding like he had been its greatest supporter. Neas commented, "It's extraordinary chutzpah to take credit for something they fought until the very, very end of the process."[30]

Grove City College Case

The next, considerably more difficult and lengthy fight began when the Supreme Court decided *Grove City College v. Bell*. Grove City College was and remains a bastion of conservatism and the religious Right. A liberal arts college in western Pennsylvania whose students were supported by federal financial aid, the school refused to comply with Department of Education regulations implementing Title IX of the Education Amendments of 1972, which prohibited discrimination on the basis of sex by institutions receiving federal funding. The Carter administration instituted an administrative action against the college to enforce compliance, and the college sued the government, seeking an injunction to halt the process on the ground that federal aid to students did not constitute aid to the institution.[31]

After the Court of Appeals for the Third Circuit held that the college received aid within the meaning of Title IX and that the statute applied not only to the specific program receiving aid but also to the entire institution, the college appealed to the Supreme Court. Reversing the government's previous position, the Reagan administration argued before the court for the program-specific application. On February 28, 1984, in an opinion by Justice White, the court ruled that federal grants to students constituted aid to the college, but it also ruled that students' receipt and use of federal grants "does not trigger institution-wide coverage under Title IX." The prohibition against discrimination, the court held, applied only to the limited aspect of the institution's operations that specifically received the federal funding, in this case the financial aid office, not to the institution as a whole.[32]

The result of the court's reading of Title IX was that institutions receiving federal funding could discriminate on the basis of sex despite the statute's explicit prohibition against sex discrimination. Congressional Democrats and moderate Republicans and the LCCR were shocked. The decision logically jeopardized all the civil rights laws with identical language forbidding discrimination by recipients of federal funds, including Title VI of the Civil Rights Act of 1964 (upon which all subsequent legislation was based, outlawing discrimination on the basis of race, color, or national origin); the Rehabilitation Act of 1973 (outlawing discrimination against handicapped persons); and the Age Discrimination Act of 1975 (outlawing discrimination based on age).[33]

The Reagan administration, which sought the use of federal funds for religious purposes as part of the Republican political strategy, applauded the decision. Attorney General Smith, for example, said he was "very pleased." Further, the administration took the position that the ruling also applied to discrimination on the basis of race, color, religion, national origin, age, or physical handicap, and the Justice Department immediately began to act on that position. Within weeks of the court's decision it began closing civil rights investigations. Within three months it shut down twenty-three enforcement investigations, narrowed eighteen others, and was reviewing thirty-one more. The cases involved not only allegations of sex discrimination but also disability rights and claims of discrimination by racial minorities.[34]

The Leadership Conference on Civil Rights set to work to undo the court's ruling. The LCCR characterized its legislative effort as a Civil Rights Restoration Act, an effort to restore existing law, and it argued that taxpayers would not want their taxes distributed to those who discriminate based on sex, race, age, national origin, or disability. Within two weeks of the court's decision, legislation to remedy it was introduced with bipartisan support in both houses of Congress. The House bill passed by an overwhelming margin in June, but in the Senate Orrin Hatch vowed "to fight it with everything I've got." Hatch made good on his promise. He stalled by filibustering and, after that was stopped, offering more than 1,000 amendments. Senator Barry Goldwater (R-AZ) opined at one point that his colleagues were "beginning to look like a bunch of jackasses," to which Malcolm Wallop (R-WY) added: "Why do you say we're *beginning* to look like a bunch of jackasses? We're already there." Unmoved, Hatch and his conservative bloc succeeded in killing action on the bill for the rest of the session.[35]

As the wrangling dragged on into 1985, the United States Conference of Catholic Bishops injected the abortion issue. In May, the House Education and Labor Committee approved a version of the bill that included an amendment to repeal a 1975 law requiring universities to offer student and employee health insurance coverage for abortions as well as childbirth and forbidding the expulsion of women who had abortions or excluding them from honorary societies and other activities. The previous day, the Judiciary Committee, which shared jurisdiction on the issue, had approved a bill without the amendment. Realizing there were enough votes in both houses to add an anti-abortion amendment to any legislation, women's groups and Don Edwards delayed floor consideration of the bill, and another Congress failed to enact a Civil Rights Restoration Act.[36]

Robert Bork Nomination

The fight that erupted over Reagan's nomination in July 1987 of Robert Bork to the Supreme Court poisoned the atmosphere in Congress still further. The LCCR and its allies ultimately defeated the nomination because moderate Republicans in the Senate agreed with the Democratic leadership that it was an attempt to move the court rightward, imperiling privacy rights and civil rights generally. The LCCR carefully framed the debate to exclude abortion rights from the discussion. Instead, they focused on the paper trail Bork had left over the course of a twenty-five-year career in government, on the bench, and as a law professor. Senators asserted the Senate's power and right to be an equal partner in the process of seating justices on the high court, not just to rubber stamp a president's nominees.

The LCCR and other opponents of the nomination also worked to shape public opinion about Bork's qualifications and views. People for the American Way, an LCCR member organization, produced an effective television advertisement featuring the actor Gregory Peck, who had given an Oscar-winning performance as the principled lawyer Atticus Finch in the 1962 film adaptation of Harper Lee's *To Kill a Mockingbird*.

In the ad, Peck said of Bork, "He defended poll taxes and literacy tests, which kept many Americans from voting. He opposed the civil rights law that ended whites only signs at lunch counters. He doesn't believe the Constitution protects your right to privacy." Bork's defenders countered that these were merely his views about what was legally permissible under the Constitution and that he had modified some of them, but People for the American Way noted that if his views had prevailed, the results would be exactly as the ad stated.[37]

Bork and Reagan lost in the end. The Senate defeated the nomination in a 58–42 vote; the 42 nays were the most ever cast against a Supreme Court nominee. After initially stating that he would put forward a nominee that his opponents would dislike even more than Bork, and after the unfortunate nomination and withdrawal of Douglas Ginsburg, Reagan settled on the confirmable Anthony Kennedy. Ever since, "stealth" nominees for the court—those without extensive paper trails—have been the most easily confirmed, and all have avoided engaging in substantive discussions of the law during their confirmation hearings, including Elena Kagan, who as a law professor had criticized the confirmation process for lacking substance.[38]

The Bork fight seemed to have so poisoned the atmosphere that no civil rights laws could be enacted. But Senate Majority Leader Robert Byrd (D-WV) had boldly scheduled the Civil Rights Restoration Act as the Senate's first order of business after Democrats regained control of the body in the 1986 election, and the LCCR continued pushing for passage. Then, in early 1987, the coalition experienced division after the moderate Republican John Danforth (MO) insisted on a right-to-conscience anti-abortion amendment, which permitted federally funded hospitals and their medical personnel to refuse to perform abortions and allowed educational institutions to exclude abortions from health and disability leave plans. Described by its supporters as abortion neutral, the amendment also prohibited discrimination against women who had abortions, as a result of which leaders on the Christian Right opposed it. The Reverend Jerry Falwell of the Moral Majority claimed that it would require churches to hire "a practicing homosexual drug addict with AIDS to be a teacher or youth pastor," leading mainstream religious leaders to hold press conferences to counter his characteristically outlandish attack. Among civil rights advocates, the Danforth Amendment angered the pro-choice organizations in the LCCR, causing conflict within the diverse coalition, but the amendment passed despite the pro-choice opposition. The Senate passed the bill in a vote of 75–14 in January 1988, and in March, fully four years after the *Grove City College* decision, the House passed it in a 315–98 vote.[39]

Remarkably, Reagan vetoed the bill despite its bipartisan congressional support. It was the first veto of a civil rights bill in 120 years. Vice President George Bush abandoned his career-long pro-choice record and supported the president, saying that it was "not the time to become disloyal." With his bid for the Republican nomination to succeed Reagan under way, it certainly was not. Congress easily overrode the veto, and the Civil Rights Restoration Act became law on March 22, 1988.[40]

The LCCR's third important legislative victory came more readily than the previous two. Working with Hamilton Fish (R-NY), the coalition easily obtained passage of the Fair Housing Amendments Act of 1988, which strengthened the statute's enforcement provisions. It also prohibited discrimination against families with children and people with physical or mental disabilities. The LCCR secured the amendments by working out a bipartisan compromise with realtors, led by the National Association of Realtors, who had become believers in the LCCR's power as a result of the Bork fight and its success in pushing the Civil Rights Restoration Act. In the same period, the LCCR helped secure passage of the Martin Luther King Jr. federal holiday and redress for Japanese interned during World War II.[41]

Packing the Civil Rights Commission

As they accomplished these victories, coalition members expected to prevail when Reagan moved to gut the United States Commission on Civil Rights. The success they appeared to achieve in that battle was ephemeral, as Reagan used chicanery to tarnish it and turn the Commission from an independent body into an administration mouthpiece.[42]

The administration's effort to co-opt the Commission was prompted by two publications that the Commission issued during Reagan's first year in office. In October 1981, after conducting hearings in cities around the country on police practices, the Commission issued a report describing serious civil rights problems and offering a host of suggestions for improving police-community relations. The criticism of police angered

Meese, a former prosecutor, who reportedly liked to unwind at night by listening to the police band on his radio. Earlier in the year the Commission had published a draft report on affirmative action in employment, describing shortcomings and seeking public comment. To Meese, the Commission's independence and willingness to criticize government at all levels threatened the shift in civil rights law and policy that the White House had in mind.[43]

Although the Commission appeared to be an obstacle to the administration's plans, Meese and the president concluded that they could manipulate it to make it useful. With the right members, the Commission could help the administration by applauding the change in direction that Reagan wanted to make. In its effort to change the Commission from a watchdog to the president's lapdog, the White House sought to vitiate the Commission's major role, and a principal reason for its independence, which was monitoring the executive branch. Meese's and Reagan's disregard for public and Congressional respect for the practical and symbolic keystone of Commission independence would prove a political miscalculation that they struggled to overcome. Based on tradition and the law under which the Commission operated, there was no expectation that commissioners would resign at the beginning of each new administration. Instead, commissioners left voluntarily when they no longer felt useful or they tired of further service. Only Nixon had pressured a commissioner to step aside. After Commission Chair Father Theodore Hesburgh announced before the 1972 election that he was disappointed in Nixon and would resign if he were elected, Nixon, through John Erlichman, pressed him to do so, and Hesburgh eventually relented. But Nixon did not publicly take the position that he could fire a commissioner, and Hesburgh conceded only that the president could name a chair.[44]

To reinvent the Commission, Meese as point man for the administration began the process by identifying potential replacements for the sitting members. Meanwhile, the Commission, oblivious to the White House's plans, continued its work, including denouncing Reagan's attempt to extend tax-exempt status to segregated institutions in the Bob Jones University matter. Soon Meese had his candidates, and Reagan acted. In November 1981, without discussion or notice, he fired Chairman Arthur Flemming and Vice Chairman Stephen Horn, both moderate Republicans. After objecting to the administration's assault on the Commission's independence, Flemming and Horn left quietly, hoping to end the firings.

After some false starts in finding a replacement for Flemming, Meese settled on Clarence Pendleton, an African American whom San Diego mayor Pete Wilson recruited to head the city's Model Cities program in 1972, when Meese was a professor at San Diego State University. In 1975, Pendleton became president of San Diego's Urban League chapter, and by 1980, through his ties to Wilson and Meese, he had become a Republican. He was the only head of an Urban League chapter to support Reagan for the presidency. When Pendleton replaced Flemming he became the Commission's first black chair.[45]

To replace Horn, Reagan chose Mary Louise Smith of Iowa, former national chair of the Republican National Committee and a women's rights activist. Because Flemming and Horn left without a fight and Smith had a strong reputation as a feminist, civil rights groups, though concerned about Pendleton and the assault on the Commission's independence, struggled to mount opposition, and the Senate confirmed both nominees in March 1982.[46]

Emboldened by the imminent success of the Pendleton and Smith appointments, the White House announced in February 1982 the appointment of Rev. B. Sam Hart to replace Commissioner Jill Ruckelshaus, a moderately liberal Republican and ERA supporter and former Special Assistant for Women's Rights in the Nixon administration. Hart, an African American evangelist from Philadelphia, would satisfy the president's Christian Right constituency. Ruckelshaus, like Flemming, was told that the president wanted allies who supported his philosophy on the Commission. Criticism from members of Congress, civil rights leaders, and the public condemning Reagan's attempt to replace Ruckelshaus with Hart flooded the White House.[47]

Hart's nomination might have survived the criticism, but it did not survive press scrutiny or the administration's failure to consult Pennsylvania's Republican Senators John Heinz and Arlen Specter before naming him. Hart owed back taxes and rent payments on property in a Philadelphia suburb. His radio station had defaulted on a $100,000 federal loan from the Small Business Administration and was far behind on repayments to a Pennsylvania minority loan program. He had never registered to vote. After Heinz and Specter abandoned him, Hart asked Reagan to withdraw his name in February 1982.[48]

Despite the Hart fiasco, Reagan relished the fight over the Commission because it attracted public notice to what he claimed was a battle against a radical view of civil rights. When he announced in May 1982 that he would replace the remaining commissioners—Murray Saltzman, Blandina Cardenas Ramirez, and me—with a trio of new appointees, the battle's intensity and the public's attention grew. One of the candidates, a foe of abortion rights who satisfied another Reagan constituency, was Robert A. Destro, an associate professor at Marquette University law school and General Counsel for the Catholic League for Religious and Civil Rights in Milwaukee.[49] Destro's academic and professional qualifications made him a defensible selection, but the other two nominees, Constantine Nicholas Dombalis and Guadalupe Quintanilla, were disastrous. They had no relevant experience and could not explain the Commission's role. Dombalis, the head of a Greek Orthodox church in Richmond, made public statements showing he knew nothing about the Commission. He told reporters that he felt "in full concurrence" with President Reagan's statements on civil rights, but he also assured the press that he knew of no Commission policies with which he disagreed. Since the president and the Commission were so far apart on civil rights issues, Dombalis's statements left reporters dumbfounded. He also reminded many of Pendleton's 1981 reply to a reporter's question about whether he concurred with Reagan's opposition to affirmative action. "Whatever the administration's policy is in this respect," Pendleton said, "I have no choice but to support that policy, which must have come up through some previous advice." Fired up on both occasions, civil rights groups argued that the Commission needed to remain independent. Key senators, stating their concern about any attempt to replace a commissioner involuntarily, announced that they would not permit the Destro, Dombalis, and Quintanilla nominations to move forward, and the Senate returned the nominations with no action in December 1982.[50]

As the conflict over the three non-Reaganite commissioners went on, Pendleton eagerly sought public recognition as the administration's spokesman on civil rights. He used White House talking points supporting the president's policies as the basis for speeches across the country. In addition, he attacked civil rights leaders as "new racists" who betrayed their members' interests and worse. So valuable was he that the president tolerated his occasional flamboyant remarks and his announcements of commitments the president either had never made or did not want made public.[51]

Pendleton also frequently presented his views as those of the Commission. His conduct led fellow Reagan appointee Mary Louise Smith, already angered by the president's attempt to replace her fellow Republican women's rights supporter Ruckelshaus with Hart, to begin criticizing Pendleton and to agree on approving Commission reports in the pipeline over Pendleton's opposition.[52]

Unbowed by the Senate's rejection of his first attempt to replace the commissioners who troubled him, in May 1983 the president announced a dream team of Reagan Democrats as nominees to replace Saltzman, Ramirez, and me. He renominated Robert Destro and added John H. Bunzel and Morris B. Abram. The White House press office described Bunzel, a former president of San Jose State University, as an "early supporter of the civil rights movement." Abram, a partner in a major New York law firm, had been president of Brandeis University, co-chair of the White House Conference on Civil Rights in 1967 and 1968, and chairman of the United Negro College Fund. The White House described him as one who "broke with [Carter]" over his "misguided civil rights policies" to support Reagan's election and his policies.[53]

Contrary to White House expectations, the nominations ignited a firestorm. Most of the correspondence and public statements from advocacy groups and individuals lamented the effort to compromise the Commission's independence. In response, the White House tried to tout the nominees' credentials, but its frustration grew when its tactic had little effect in Congress. Longtime members of the oversight committees were familiar with the Commission's work and recognized the value of its independence. They were reinforced by protests stimulated by the civil rights organizations. The president could not overcome the independence argument, and the hostility generated by Pendleton's flamboyance and his revelation that he had been urging the White House to replace the incumbents did not help the administration's cause. The nominations languished in Congress through the summer, and they and the Commission neared death in early autumn, as confirmation hearings led nowhere and negotiations over reauthorizing the Commission failed to produce a compromise by September 30, when the Commission's statutory mandate expired and it entered a sixty-day wind-up period.[54]

It appeared that the administration would prefer to let the Commission die, but the president was not finished with his attempt to make it his. On October 24, 1983, the news was consumed with the tragedy of the previous day, when a delivery truck loaded with explosives drove into the United States Marine Corps barracks in Lebanon and exploded, killing 220 marines and 21 other service members. On the same day, United States forces invaded the Caribbean nation of Grenada. On that morning, counting on a distracted media, Reagan fired the remaining Commissioners in an effort to force the confirmation of his nominees. He angered key members of Congress by acting two hours before the Judiciary Committee was scheduled to consider a compromise to resolve the impasse. The president engaged the issue of the Commission's independence directly, saying that he did not like the criticism he had received from the Commission.[55]

Lawyers from the NAACP Legal Defense and Educational Fund and the Mexican American Legal Defense and Educational Fund went to federal court representing Commissioner Ramirez and me to argue that the firings violated the Commission's independence and were illegal. On November 14, Judge Norma Johnson agreed, announcing that you cannot fire a watchdog for biting. Surprised and outraged, the administration filed a notice of appeal, but the litigation would be moot before Johnson's decision could be reviewed.[56]

On November 11, 1983, in a bipartisan effort, after extended debate in Congress and hard negotiations with the LCCR, Senators Howard Baker (R-TN), Robert Dole, Joe Biden (D-DE), and Arlen Specter announced an agreement with Meese, who was with the president in Tokyo. The Commission would be reconstituted as an eight-member, independent, bipartisan presidential-congressional agency, with half of the members appointed by Congress and half by the president. Dole told the civil rights advocates that the three recently "fired" Commissioners would be reappointed by Congress and that Pendleton, Smith, Abram, and Bunzel would be appointed by the White House, leaving one Congressional appointee to be decided. The White House, it appeared, had lost. The president had to sign the bill. Senator Biden asserted, "Never again will this president, or the next president, or any other president, be able to fire a Commission member because that member differs with his views."[57]

That may have been true, but Biden's apparent optimism about Commission independence was misplaced. After the bill signing, Office of

Management and Budget Director David Stockman told the president that Meese's agreement to keep Smith and Ruckelshaus "poses real risks" to the administration. "If at least five members of the new Commission do not support a changed Commission direction, an impasse could occur over our statutory designees for the Chairman, Vice Chairman, and Staff Director, since, as noted above, the bill requires those three designees to have the concurrence of a majority of the Commission's members."[58] Meese and the president knew that Smith and Ruckelshaus could not be relied upon to support Pendleton, so Reagan reneged on the promise to appoint them. Instead, he appointed Esther Arroyo Buckley, a high-school science teacher from Laredo, Texas, and the Webb County Republican chair, after making sure that she would vote to confirm Pendleton and would follow administration policy. The administration then agreed with Republicans in the House to appoint Destro instead of Ruckelshaus. Reagan had his five votes to make Pendleton chair and Chavez staff director.[59]

Reagan had made good on a boast to Pendleton, who had come to see him on November 15, 1983, after the president's return from Tokyo. Reagan wrote in his diary that Pendleton had complained about the "so-called compromise to keep me from making appointments," but, Reagan added, "I think I can snooker them."[60]

Succinctly summing up what had happened, Neas observed, "The White House has accomplished the goal it has been seeking for six months—to pack the Commission." The reconstituted Commission became a lobbying arm for the White House for the rest of the Reagan presidency. It was no longer a forum in which Commissioners with different perspectives reasoned together and reached mostly unanimous recommendations across ideological and party lines. It had become yet another arena for political jockeying. It was essentially destroyed, even as it limped along for years thereafter.[61]

Reaganizing the Judiciary

The president's victory in the battle over the Civil Rights Commission was important, but his biggest success in affecting civil rights came in an arena where the LCCR had the least practical opportunity to shape the course of events: the Reaganization of the federal judiciary. While the coalition played an important role in defeating the Bork nomination,

Reagan succeeded in seating three justices and promoting William Rehnquist to chief justice. Moreover, the sheer number of positions that Reagan filled on the lower federal courts meant that, practically speaking, only a small percentage of his nominees could be questioned. Successful challenges were few (the most notable was Jefferson B. Sessions III), and in addition to Justices O'Connor, Scalia, and Kennedy, Reagan placed more than 350 judges on the federal bench, more than any other president. When he left office his appointees accounted for half of the judiciary. At the beginning of his presidency, the judiciary was divided by about three to two between Democratic and Republican appointees. When he left office, the proportions were reversed. Fewer than one in ten of his nominees were women; he named only four to the courts of appeals. He named only six new African American judges and elevated one other from a district court to a court of appeals. Just one African American woman met his requirements to serve.[62]

Reagan made no secret of his ambition to reshape the judiciary. With few exceptions his nominees were thoroughly vetted for their qualification to advance his political agenda. The 1980 Republican platform signaled, in characteristically euphemistic terms that have entered the political lexicon, the administration's plan. Potential judges would be tested on having "the highest regard for protecting the rights of law abiding citizens," playing the racially loaded law-and-order card that Goldwater had introduced and Nixon perfected. Candidates would have to demonstrate their ideological purity for moving the federal government out of the role of protecting individual rights by showing that their "judicial philosophy" was "consistent with the belief in the decentralization of the federal government and efforts to return decision making power to state and local elected officials." And they would have to narrowly view women's rights and be anti-abortion by showing that they "respect traditional family values and the sanctity of human life." As Sheldon Goldman has observed, "By framing his appointment goals in terms of the judicial philosophy he believed would accomplish his political purposes, Reagan placed a more legitimate public and professional face on his policy agenda for the judiciary."[63]

Once in office, the administration submitted candidates to an elaborate screening process designed and implemented by a cadre of operatives in the Justice Department and the White House. This process was presaged by the politicized selection of judges during Reagan's tenure as governor of California, despite his claims at the time and later that it was nonpolitical. During his 1966 gubernatorial campaign, Reagan criticized the outgoing governor Pat Brown for appointing political cronies and promised to take politics out of judicial appointments. In public statements, personal correspondence, and his 1990 autobiography, *An American Life*, Reagan characterized the process as apolitical. In *An American Life*, for example, he wrote, "In a country ruled by laws, it seemed to me that nothing was more important than removing politics from the process of choosing judges. . . . So I sent out an order to set up a new system to take politics out of the selection of judges." The system, as he described it, involved getting input from lawyers in the community, a citizen's group in the same community, and judges sitting in the district. Their recommendations, he continued, were sent to him and ranked. "Without exception," he wrote, "I chose the person at the top of the rating. Politics or party membership played no part in the selection."[64]

Paul Haerle, who directed judicial selection for Governor Reagan, told a different story. He described a thoroughly political process. Haerle set up the committees to which Reagan alluded. The lay members "were usually people who had been active in the Reagan campaign," Haerle explained, and "[t]he judge I'd usually pick in consultation with a Republican lawyer." Close Reagan associates not on the committees were also involved. William French Smith participated in Los Angeles County, while Meese vetted candidates in Alameda County (comprising Oakland and Berkeley). The process identified plenty of Republican candidates, whose names were submitted to the state bar association for rating, and Reagan's nominees were selected from those rated "qualified" or better. Political cronyism existed as well. Haerle described cases in which, contrary to Reagan's claims, he rejected recommendations in favor of political allies. In Monterey County, Reagan appointed his local campaign manager over two qualified candidates who were recommended by the selection committee. He appointed his aide Bill Clark to successively higher courts, rejecting committee recommendations. Reagan also traded judgeships for legislators' votes on several bills.[65]

So by the time Reagan entered the Oval Office, he, Meese, and Smith were experienced in politicized judicial selection. In the 1980 Republican platform they criticized Jimmy Carter for "his partisan nominations" and pledged "to reverse that trend," echoing Reagan's criticism of Brown and his promises in California. Then they took political-ideological judicial selection to a new level. To begin with, they dispensed with the pretense of desiring independent input, and they worked to diminish the power of senators and local party leaders in selecting candidates and to marginalize the ratings of the American Bar Association's Standing Committee on the Federal Judiciary.[66]

Having asserted greater control, the administration subjected candidates for the district courts and courts of appeals to an unprecedented, systematic screening process for adherence to Reagan's plan for the judiciary's role in achieving the legal and political change he sought. The process was directed by the White House counsel (Fred Fielding, then Peter J. Wallison, then A. B. Culvahouse), as well as by Smith and especially Meese, who as attorney general campaigned publicly for the reversal of decades of constitutional jurisprudence in civil rights, privacy rights, the rights of those accused of crimes, and federalism. In the Justice Department the process was centered in a newly created Office of Legal Policy, the name of which connoted its political purpose. It included the attorney general, the assistant attorney general for legal policy, the special counsel for judicial selection, and some of their staff. This group made recommendations to the Federal Judicial Selection Committee, another Reagan administration innovation, which was based in the White House. Later called the Working Group on Appointments because it also dealt with filling United States attorney positions (which George W. Bush's Justice Department shamelessly politicized twenty years later) and United States marshal positions, this body institutionalized and formalized the White House role. Beyond receiving recommendations from Justice, the White House group generated its own roster of candidates. It met in the White House, signaling its primacy in judicial selection and the importance of molding the judiciary to advance the president's agenda.

At Justice and in the White House, candidates' records were scoured and analyzed to gauge their ideological and political bona fides. Finalists were subjected to daylong interviews (another Reagan administration novelty, which many candidates found offensive) in which they were asked about their judicial philosophy as well as positions on specific issues, especially abortion. In short, the process delivered nominees who passed a litmus test designed to assure their devotion to interpreting the law in accordance with Reagan's political objectives. The Selection Committee's consensus recommendations were presented to the president, who generally did not play an active role in the process and rarely failed to approve the candidates placed before him.[67]

When Stephen Williams was seated in June 1986, Reagan's appointees made conservative judges a majority on the Court of Appeals for the District of Columbia Circuit, the second most important federal court. Conservatives celebrated this development as one of the most important victories of Reagan's presidency. By the end of his presidency, Reagan appointees were the majority on the Courts of Appeals for the Second, Sixth, and Seventh Circuits, and they were a near-majority elsewhere, where they joined Nixon's and Ford's appointees to make Republican appointees predominant.[68]

To its exceptional effort to seat judges dedicated to the president's political agenda, the Reagan administration added an exceptional commitment to ensuring they do so for a long time. The justices Reagan placed on the Supreme Court (average age 49.3) were notably younger than president Clinton's nominees (average age 57.3). Presidents George H. W. Bush and George W. Bush followed Reagan's lead (average age 49.3). Although President Obama's nominees are older on average than those of the Republican presidents, he seems to recognize the value of the Republican youth strategy (average age 52.5).[69]

Similarly, with conservative politicians pushing Reagan to nominate young judges to the lower courts, the administration, as White House counsel Fred Fielding acknowledged, did just that. During Reagan's first term, 11.4 percent of his appointees were under 40, a higher percentage than that of any recent predecessor, and the average age of his appeals court judges in his first term was 51.5, the youngest average among his and the previous four administrations. Youth was especially emphasized during Reagan's second term, when his nominees to the district and appellate courts were younger than those of any other president in the twentieth century. Of his second-term judges, 34.2 percent were under 45. The next-highest percentage of nominees under 45 was 22 percent, by Theodore Roosevelt. Notable examples of the Reagan youth movement were Richard A. Posner (Seventh Circuit, age 42), Frank Easterbrook (Seventh Circuit, age 35), Kenneth Starr (D.C. Circuit, age 36), J. Harvey Wilkinson (Fourth Circuit, age 39), Alex Kozinski (Ninth Circuit, age 34), and Edith Jones (Fifth Circuit, age 36).[70]

The Supreme Court's right turn, which began before Reagan's presidency and continued with his associate justice appointments, his elevation of Rehnquist, and the subsequent Republican appointments of Clarence Thomas, John Roberts, and Samuel Alito (all of whom were Reagan administration veterans), is undeniable and widely recognized. It is perhaps unsurprising that O'Connor and Kennedy, while contributing to the court's rightward shift, became swing votes in cases involving disputes over divisive issues like abortion and affirmative action, since their nominations were atypical in ways that short-circuited the process of guaranteeing their conservative qualifications. O'Connor was simply not subjected to the kind of screening applied to other nominees. Doubts were raised about her fidelity to the anti-abortion creed, but with a president concerned to keep a campaign pledge to name a woman to the first opening on the court, and with Goldwater and Rehnquist backing her, those charged with vetting her set aside the doubts, and Reagan chose her after a brief Oval Office meeting. Anti-abortion activists and other forces of the GOP Right had little opportunity to mount effective opposition. Kennedy was thoroughly screened and was passed over repeatedly for lacking the necessary conservative bona fides. But with an election year looming, he was a safe nominee for Republicans in the wake of the Bork defeat and the Ginsburg embarrassment. Rehnquist, on the other hand, continued performing as chief as he had as an associate justice, and Scalia has performed as Reagan and Meese knew he would for nearly thirty years. Justice John Paul Stevens trenchantly observed on the eve of his retirement that, with the exception of Ruth Bader Ginsburg and potentially Sonia Sotomayor, each of the eleven justices who had joined the court since 1975, including him, was more conservative than the justice he or she replaced. As a group, the Republican nominees moved the court sharply in that direction.[71]

Less well recognized is how Reagan's expectations have been realized in the lower federal courts, where cases are so numerous and generally lacking in publicity as to elude widespread appreciation. Analysis of their jurisprudence is beyond the scope of this essay, but a sophisticated quantitative study of the appellate courts by the political scientist Nancy Scherer suggests the degree to which politicized judicial selection affects outcomes. Scherer compares the voting behavior of judges appointed by Presidents Nixon through Clinton in cases decided by the courts of appeals between January 1, 1994, and December 31, 2001, involving four types of issues: claims of race discrimination; federalism issues under the Ninth and Tenth Amendments; abortion; and the legality of searches and seizures under the Fourth Amendment. The race discrimination cases, obviously, bear discussing here; the cases involving federalism issues do as well, because of their implications for the role of the federal government in protecting civil rights. In cases involving claims of race discrimination, Scherer found that, using Clinton appointees as a baseline and holding a host of other variables constant, the probability of a vote against a minority plaintiff increases by 28 percentage points with a Reagan or Bush appointee, and to a lesser extent with a Nixon appointee. Carter appointees vote about the same as Clinton appointees. In the cases involving federalism issues, again using Clinton appointees as a baseline and holding other variables constant, the likelihood of a vote against the federal government increases by 21 percentage points with a Reagan appointee and by 27 percentage points with a Bush appointee. Nixon appointees are more likely to vote against the federal government by 16 percentage points and Carter appointees less likely by 7 percentage points.[72]

Given that Reagan's appointees vote about the same way as the other Republican appointees, especially those of Bush, his vice president and successor, it can be argued that their impact has come not so much from the exceptional screening process to which they were subjected as from their exceptional numbers and Reagan's emphasis on youth. Scherer's analysis reveals their prolonged presence on the bench. Reagan-appointed judges (97) in the race discrimination cases well outnumber judges appointed by any other president (85 for Clinton), and Reagan's judges cast far more votes than any other president's appointees (Reagan's 486, Carter's 317). They constitute nearly a third of all the judges and cast more than a third of the votes. (The Republican presidents' appointees outnumber Democrats' appointees 164 to 130 and cast 58 percent of the votes.) Similarly, in the federalism cases, Reagan appointees well outnumber those of any other president and cast far more votes; they constitute a third of the judges and cast a third of the votes. (The Republican presidents' appointees outnumber the Democrats' appointees 85 to 57 and cast 62 percent of the votes.)[73]

Shortly before Reagan left office, Gary L. Bauer, one of his domestic policy advisors and later head of the Christian Coalition, asserted that although Reagan might not have succeeded in pushing through most of his conservative social agenda, he had pleased conservatives by appointing federal judges who would promote the Right's policy views.

"You've got to look at where the courts are going," added Dan Lungren (R-CA), who sat on the House Judiciary Committee. "They're far more conservative."[74]

The satisfaction of conservatives for whom Bauer spoke and Lungren's confidence in the courts' direction were well placed. Ronald Reagan's election to the presidency and the changes it wrought brought to fruition and propelled forward a decades-long effort by the Right to reshape the national discourse and redirect federal law and policy on civil rights. Reagan lost every legislative battle he fought with the civil rights coalition, but in capturing the federal courts and using the Civil Rights Commission to help shape public opinion, the Reaganites won. In their struggle against one another in the 1980s, Reagan and the LCCR alike were winning while losing. But while the LCCR won some important battles, Reagan won the war.

Notes

The author would like to thank Robert S. Natalini for his invaluable assistance.

1. Mary Frances Berry, *And Justice For All: The United States Commission on Civil Rights and the Continuing Struggle For Freedom in America* (New York: Alfred Knopf, 2009), 190–92.

2. Ibid., 182–215.

3. Robert C. Smith, *Conservatism and Racism, and Why in America They Are the Same* (Albany: SUNY Press, 2010), 77–90.

4. Kiron K. Skinner, Annelise Anderson, and Martin Anderson, eds., *Reagan: A Life in Letters* (New York: Free Press, 2003), 330–40; Lou Cannon, *Reagan* (New York: G.P. Putnam & Sons, 1982), 381–86; William Johnson, "The Push to the Right: Reagan's Alter Ego Meese Stands at Pinnacle of U.S. Law Enforcement," *Globe and Mail*, August 29, 1985.

5. Charles S. Bullock III and Katharine Inglis Butler, "Voting Rights," in *The Reagan Administration and Human Rights*, ed. Tinsley E. Yarbrough (New York: Praeger Publishers, 1985), 29–31; Michael Pertschuk, *Giant Killers* (New York: W.W. Norton & Co., 1986), 148.

6. Mobile v. Bolden, 446 U.S. 55 (1980).

7. 79 Stat. 437, as amended, 42 U.S.C. § 1937.

8. Frank R. Parker, "The 'Results' Test of Section 2 of the Voting Rights Act: Abandoning the Intent Standard," 69 *Va. L. Rev.* 715, 726–29 (1983).

9. *Mobile*, 446 U.S. at 60–61, 65.

10. *Mobile*, 446 U.S. at 84 (Stevens, J., concurring).

11. *Mobile*, 446 U.S. at 94–103 (White, J., dissenting). Justice Marshall forcefully dissented in a lengthy opinion. He argued that on any of the claims plaintiffs need only show

that the impact, or effect, of an electoral system was to discriminate against minority voters. He further argued, like White, that even if intent to discriminate were required, it had been shown. 446 U.S. at 103–41. Justice Brennan dissented in two sentences. He agreed with Marshall that discriminatory impact was sufficient and, in agreement with Marshall and White, that if proof of intent were necessary, intent had been proven. He did not distinguish between the constitutional and statutory claims. 446 U.S. at 94. Justice Blackmun concurred in the result only. He wrote that assuming that proof of intent to discriminate is required for the plaintiffs' constitutional claim (a requirement that he did not address, nor did he specify whether he was referring to the Fourteenth or Fifteenth Amendment claim, although presumably he meant both), he was "inclined to agree" with Justice White that the facts supported such a finding. However, severely chastising Judge Pittman, Justice Blackmun found fault with the remedy that the district court had ordered, so he argued for reversal and remand for reconsideration of an appropriate remedy. 446 U.S. at 80–83.

12. Bolden v. City of Mobile, 542 F. Supp. 1050 (1982). Judge Pittman offered several suggestions for a new system, but, perhaps because of Justice Blackmun's chastisement, he withheld imposing a remedy to give the Alabama legislature and Mobile voters a chance to devise a new system.

13. Parker, "The 'Results' Test of Section 2 of the Voting Rights Act," 69 *Va. L. Rev.* at 735–37.

14. Keith Nicholls, "Politics and Civil Rights in Post-World War II Mobile," in *Mobile: The New History of an Old City*, ed. Michael V. R. Thomason (Tuscaloosa: University of Alabama Press, 2001), 271–72.

15. The Leadership Conference on Civil and Human Rights/The Leadership Conference Education Fund, http://www.civilrights.org/about/history.html; Steven F. Lawson, *Black Ballots: Voting Rights in the South, 1944–1969* (New York: Columbia University Press, 1976), 144–45, 385n22; Robert Frederick Burk, *The Eisenhower Administration and Black Civil Rights* (Knoxville: University of Tennessee Press, 1984), 206–7; Paula F. Pfeffer, *A. Philip Randolph: Pioneer of the Civil Rights Movement* (Baton Rouge: Louisiana State University Press, 1990), 108; Pertschuk, *Giant Killers*, 149–50. LCCR membership has since grown to 180 organizations.

16. Bullock & Butler, "Voting Rights," in *The Reagan Administration and Human Rights*, (quoting *Congressional Quarterly Weekly Report*, December 26, 1981, 2605).

17. Bullock & Butler, "Voting Rights," 32; Pertschuk, *Giant Killers*, 157–59, 176. Hyde later wavered, but it did not prevent the legislation's passage.

18. Olatunde Johnson, "The Story of Bob Jones University v. United States: Race, Religion, and Congress' Extraordinary Acquiescence," in *Statutory Interpretation Stories*, ed. William N. Eskridge Jr., Philip P. Frickey, and Elizabeth Garrett (New York: The Foundation Press, Inc., 2011), 128–43; Philip B. Heymann & Lance Liebman, eds., *The Social Responsibilities of Lawyers: Case Studies* (New York: The Foundation Press, Inc., 1988), 132–40 (copies of relevant documents are reprinted at pages 154–75); Norman C. Amaker, *Civil Rights and the Reagan Administration* (Washington, D.C.: Urban Institute Press, 1988), 52–53. Bob Jones University was not the only segregated school that maintained tax-exempt status for years after the IRS issued the rule denying it. In May 1978, the United States Commission on Civil Rights called attention to the

existence of at least seven segregated schools in Mississippi that still were tax exempt. Tinsley E. Yarbrough, "Tax Exemptions and Private Discriminatory Schools," in *The Reagan Administration and Human Rights*, 110–11.

19. Johnson, "The Story of Bob Jones University v. United States," 142–44; Amaker, *Civil Rights and the Reagan Administration*, 53.

20. Johnson, "The Story of Bob Jones University v. United States," 130–32, 144.

21. Johnson, "The Story of Bob Jones v. United States," 144–45; Heyman & Liebman, *Social Responsibilities of Lawyers*, 140.

22. Edwards, quoted in John Herbert Roper, "The Voting Rights Extension Act of 1982," *Phylon* 45, no. 3 (3rd Quarter, 1984): 193.

23. Johnson, "The Story of Bob Jones University v. United States," 145–46; Heyman & Liebman, *Social Responsibilities of Lawyers*, 140–47; Amaker, *Civil Rights and the Reagan Administration*, 5–54.

24. Johnson, "The Story of Bob Jones University v. United States," 146; Heyman & Liebman, *Social Responsibilities of Lawyers*, 149.

25. Johnson, "The Story of Bob Jones University v. United States," 147; Heyman & Liebman, *Social Responsibilities of Lawyers*, 149–50.

26. Johnson, "The Story of Bob Jones University v. United States," 147–48; Heyman & Liebman, *Social Responsibilities of Lawyers*, 150–52, 181–82; Bob Jones University v. United States, 461 U.S. 574 (1983); Neas, quoted in Pertschuk, *Giant Killers*, 177.

27. Edwards, quoted in Roper, "The Voting Rights Extension Act of 1982," 193.

28. Ibid., 196.

29. Voting Rights Act Amendments of 1982, Pub. L. 97–205, June 29, 1982, 96 Stat. 131, § 2.

30. Steven Roberts, "President Backs Bipartisan Plan on Voting Law," *New York Times*, May 4, 1982; Remarks on Signing H.R. 3112 into Law, 18 Weekly Comp. Pres. Doc. 846 (June 29, 1982); Howell Raines, "Voting Rights Act Signed by Reagan," *New York Times*, June 30, 1982; Bullock and Inglis Butler, "Voting Rights," 32 (citing Nadine Cohodas, "Administration Defends Civil Rights Record," *Congressional Quarterly Weekly Report*, February 4, 1983, 266).

31. Through alumni and friends, the college maintains extensive ties to conservative think tanks and Republican politicians. Lee Edwards, *Freedom's College: The History of Grove City College* (Washington, D.C.: Regnery Publishing, Inc., 2000), 274–75. In its official materials the college highlights its consistent ranking by the Young America's Foundation and Free Congress Foundation as one of the most conservative schools in the country, as well as its teaching and advocacy of free-market economic theory. Grove City College, http://gcc.edu.

32. Grove City College v. Bell, 465 U.S. 555, 557–76 (1984).

33. Bob Packwood, "Discrimination Aided," *New York Times*, April 20, 1984 (Packwood was a Republican senator from Oregon); Robert Pear, "Justice Dept. Open to New Rights Bill," *New York Times*, March 3, 1984 (civil rights advocates concerns); Amaker, *Civil Rights and the Reagan Administration*, 59.

34. Smith quoted in Linda Greenhouse, "High Court Backs Reagan's Position On A Sex Bias Law," *New York Times*, February 29, 1984, A1; Robert Pear, "Justice Dept. Open to New Rights Bill," *New York Times*, March 3, 1984 (quoting William Bradford

Reynolds on Reagan administration position); Robert Pear, "23 Cases On Civil Rights Closed After Court Rules," *New York Times*, June 3, 1984; Hugh Davis Graham, "The Storm Over Grove City College: Civil Rights Regulation, Higher Education, and the Reagan Administration," *History of Education Quarterly* 18, no. 4 (Winter 1998): 418 (DOJ action, citing "Injustice Under the Law: The Impact of the *Grove City College* Decision on Civil Rights in America," n.d., Leadership Conference on Civil Rights Papers, Manuscript Division, Library of Congress).

35. Robert Pear, "Bill to Extend Rights Coverage Sets Off Dispute," *New York Times*, March 7, 1984; Pear, "Trying to Tie Strings to Federal Aid," *New York Times*, March 11, 1984 (bills introduced); Martin Tolchin, "Senate Crushes a Move to Block Civil Rights Bill," *New York Times*, September 30, 1984, Section 1, 11 (Goldwater, Wollop quotations); "House Approves Civil Rights Bill," *Associated Press*, June 27, 1984 (House approval, Hatch quotation); Martin Tolchin, "Civil Rights Plan Shelved As Senate Moves On Spending," *New York Times*, October 3, 1984, A1.

36. Larry Margasak, "Bill to Restore Civil Rights Protections Advances, But Abortion Fight Looms," *Associated Press*, May 23, 1985; "Abortion Limits Rejected In Bill," *New York Times*, May 23, 1985.

37. Stuart Taylor, "Ad Against Bork Still Hotly Contested," *New York Times*, October 21, 1987. The ad is available for viewing on the website of People for the American Way. http://www.pfaw.org/video/fair-and-just-courts/1987-robert-bork-tv-ad-narrated -gregory-peck.

38. Elena Kagan, "Review: Confirmation Messes, Old and New," *The University of Chicago Law Review* 62, no. 2 (Spring 1995): 919–42.

39. Irvin Molotsky, "Senate to Override Court, Votes a Bill Extending Anti-Bias Laws," *New York Times*, January 29, 1988, A1; Irvin Molotsky, "House Passes Bill To Upset A Limit On U.S. Rights Law," *New York Times*, March 3, 1988, A1; Helen Dewar, "Religious Leaders Assail Moral Majority's 'Scare Tactics' Over Civil Rights Bill," *Washington Post*, March 19, 1988; David Anderson, "Civil Rights Leaders, Abortion Foes Clash Over Legislation," *United Press International*, March 26, 1987.

40. Charlotte Saikowski, "Will Civil Rights Stand Come Back to Haunt Bush Campaign?" *Christian Science Monitor*, March 23, 1988, 1; Civil Rights Restoration Act, Pub. L. No. 100–259, 102 Stat. 28 (1988). Soon after the statute was enacted Grove City College prohibited students from accepting federal grants, in 1996 it prohibited their accepting Stafford and Plus loans, and it has continued those policies and accepted no other federal funding, enabling it to avoid complying with Title IX. As of May 2011, the full-time faculty of 148 included only 44 women, nearly half of whom were concentrated in three academic departments: modern languages (7), education (6), and physical education (6). Men chaired 20 of the 23 departments. Among 11 top-level administrators listed in the 2010–11 college catalogue—president, provost, vice presidents, deans, and assistant deans—there was one woman.

41. Pub. L. No. 100–430, 102 Stat. 1619 (1988) (amending 42 U.S.C. §§ 3601–19 (1982)) (Fair Housing Act Amendments); Pub. L. No. 98–399, 98 Stat. 1473 (1983) (King holiday); Pub L. No. 100–383, 102 Stat. 903 (1988) (redress for Japanese internment); Author's interview with Ralph Neas, March 2009.

42. For a complete examination of the controversy over the Civil Rights Commission, on which this section is based, see my history of the Commission, Berry, *And Justice for All*, 182–215.

43. United States Commission on Civil Rights, *Who Is Guarding the Guardians?*, October 1981; United States Commission on Civil Rights, *Affirmative Action: Dismantling the Process of Discrimination*, January 1981. The journalist Leslie Stahl describes Meese's leisure activity in her memoir, *Reporting Live* (New York: Simon & Schuster, 1999), 123. Contemporary accounts in major urban dailies included Aaron Epstein, "Attorney General Gets A Stern Rebuff From High Court Over Miranda Rule," *Philadelphia Inquirer*, March 16, 1986; Chris Reidy, "First Crony Meese Faces The Law From Other Side," July 27, 1987.

44. Berry, *And Justice for All*, 132–34.

45. Robert J. Thompson, "The Commission on Civil Rights," in *The Reagan Administration and Human Rights*, ed. Yarbrough, 188; Author's interview with Clarence Pendleton. Pendleton later told me that the Commission's report on the police had called Meese's attention to the Commission.

46. Thompson, "The Commission on Civil Rights," 187. After leaving the Commission, Flemming pursued an active career as a leading advocate for services to the elderly and preserving Social Security until his death at age 91 on September 7, 1996. Horn remained president of California State University at Long Beach until 1988. Elected to Congress in 1993, he served until 2003.

47. Thompson, "The Commission on Civil Rights," 189. Examples of opposition to the Hart nomination include Yzaguirre to President, February 19, 1982; Judith Lichtman, Executive Director, Women's Legal Defense Fund to President, February 16, 1982; Antonia Hernandez, MALDEF Associate Counsel to President, February 17, 1982; Kathy Wilson, National Chair, National Women's Political Caucus to President, February 12, 1982; Mary Purcell, President, American Association of American Women to President, February 13, 1982; Mary Louise Uhlig, President, Federally Employed Women to President, February 19, 1982; Ted Weiss and 24 others to President, February 23, 1982; Norman Dicks to President, February 25, 1982; Leonard Denardis to President, February 19, 1982; Phillip Burton to President, February 16, 1982; Albert Lee Smith to President, February 15, 1982; Gordon Jones to President, February 11, 1982. All of these documents are located in the White House Subject Files, FG 93, Ronald Reagan Presidential Library. Unless otherwise indicated, manuscript collections cited in this paper are in this library.

48. Thompson, "The Commission on Civil Rights," in *The Reagan Administration and Human Rights*, ed. Yarbrough, 190–91; Bill Peterson, "Hart Owes Back Taxes of $4,400 in Pa. Town," *Washington Post*, February 24, 1982, A3; Steven R. Weisman, "Reagan Rescinds Rights Nominee in Wake of Outcry," *New York Times*, February 27, 1982, A1.

49. Destro, a native of Akron, Ohio, was educated at Miami University of Ohio and Boalt Hall Law School at the University of California, Berkeley. Destro was deeply interested in issues of religious liberty and had, according to Congressman James Sensenbrenner (R-WI), "a record of able representation of conservative issues, most recently and significantly the right to life cause." Congressman Clement J. Zablocki

(D-WI) added that Republican Congressman Henry Hyde of Illinois and other anti-abortion officials supported Destro. Sensenbrenner to President, October 13, 1981; Zablocki to President, October 27, 1981.

50. Thompson, "The Commission on Civil Rights," 191–92 (Dombalis and Quinta-nilla nominations); Felicity Barringer, "New Defiant Tone: Civil Rights Commission Gets Tough," *Washington Post*, December 6, 1982, A9; Robert Pear, "Advocates Fear For Autonomy of Civil Rights Commission," *New York Times*, October 2, 1982, A1; Judith Cummings, "Blacks In San Diego Divided Over Nominee To Civil Rights Post," *New York Times*, November 28, 1981, I10 (Pendleton comment). When Pendleton later said that he regretted the statement and believed that the Commission was independent, many were unconvinced.

51. Jacqueline Trescott and Eve Ferguson, "Chairman Clarence Pendleton, Jr.; The 'Wild Card' of the Civil Rights Commission," *Washington Post*, November 14, 1982; Robert Pear, "Rights Panel Head Calls For 'Summit,'" *New York Times*, September 15, 1982. I discuss the "summit" case of Pendleton's over-reaching, which Reagan toler-ated, and Pendleton's nationwide speaking tours in more detail in Berry, *And Justice for All*, 197–201.

52. Robert Pear, "Rights Unit Affirms Support For Court-Mandated Busing," *New York Times*, October 13, 1982; Robert Pear, "Rights Panel Criticizes President On Two Affirmative Action Stands," *New York Times*, January 12, 1983.

53. Thompson, "The Commission on Civil Rights," 193–94; Francis X. Clines, "Rea-gan Chooses 3 For Rights Panel," *New York Times*, May 26, 1983; Office of the White House Press Secretary, May 25, 1983.

54. Thompson, "The Commission on Civil Rights," 194–97; Juan Williams, "Beyond the Lunch Counter Victories; With Basic Rights Guaranteed, Reagan Wants Federal Role Limited," *Washington Post*, June 1, 1983, A3.

55. Thompson, "The Commission on Civil Rights," 198; Herrington to Berry, Oc-tober 24, 1983; Herrington to Ramirez, October 24, 1983; Herrington to Saltzman, October 24, 1983. In a memo to Herrington the same day, the president wrote, "I have decided to terminate effective today the appointments of the following members of the CAR on Civil Rights," and he directed Herrington to "notify these individuals and Chairman Pendleton of [his] decision as soon as possible." A press release stated that preauthorization before the Judiciary Committee would require him to keep the incumbents, "thwarting the President's ability to exercise his power of appointment," which he decided to vindicate by firing the "holdovers." After all, each "Certificate of Appointment" stated that commissioners served "at the pleasure of the President."

56. Berry v. Reagan, Civil Action No. 83–3182, 1983 U.S. Dist. LEXIS 11711 (D.D.C. November 14, 1983), vacated and remanded for dismissal as moot, 732 F.2nd 949 (D.C. Cir. 1983) (per curiam); George Lardner Jr., "Ex-members of Civil Rights CCR Attest to Its Independence," *Washington Post*, November 8, 1983; Helen Dewar, "Two Victo-ries Reprieve Rights Unit; Judge Bars Firing of Three Members; Senate Passes Bill," *Washington Post*, November 15, 1983.

57. Thompson, "The Commission on Civil Rights," 198–99 and sources cited therein; Biden and Mathias to Reagan, November 4, 1983; Martin Tolchin, "Senate Approves Rights Panel Bill," *New York Times*, November 15, 1983.

58. Stockman to President, November 25, 1983.

59. Buckley says that she knew nothing about the Commission and the controversy into which she was thrust until after appointment. The White House General Counsel staff interviewed her, asking questions about affirmative action and other issues. She had to tell them that in a community that was 99 percent Hispanic, discrimination issues were not a concern. Author's interview With Buckley, April 23, 2006.

60. Ronald Reagan, *The Reagan Diaries*, ed. Douglas Brinkley (New York: Harper Collins, 2007), 197, entry for November 15, 1983.

61. Robert Pear, "Rift Grows Wider Over Rights Panel," *New York Times*, December 9, 1973 (Neas quotation).

62. Details on all federal judges, who can be sorted by appointing president, among other ways, can be found on the website of the Federal Judicial Center, Biographical Directory of Federal Judges, http://www.fjc.gov; Sheldon Goldman, *Picking Federal Judges: Lower Court Selection from Roosevelt Through Reagan* (New Haven: Yale University Press, 1997), 308–9; Herman Schwartz, *Packing the Courts: The Conservative Campaign to Rewrite the Constitution* (New York: Charles Scribner's Sons, 1988), 58; Donald R. Songer, Sue Davis, and Susan Haire, "A Reappraisal of Diversification in the Federal Courts: Gender Effects in the Courts of Appeals," *Journal Of Politics* 56, no. 2 (May 1994): 425–39, 425n2.

63. Republican Party Platform of 1980, available at John T. Woolley and Gerhard Peters, *The American Presidency Project* [online]. Santa Barbara, Calif., http://www.presidency.ucsb.edu/ws/index.php?pid=25844#axzz1KwNtLc1O; Goldman, *Picking Federal Judges*, 297.

64. Ronald Reagan, *An American Life* (New York: Simon & Schuster, 1990), 174–75; Skinner, Anderson, and Anderson, eds., *Reagan: A Life in Letters*, 208 (letter to "Bob Circa 1974"); "Transcript of Ronald Reagan's Remarks at News Conference in Los Angeles," *New York Times*, October 15, 1980, A24.

65. Lou Cannon, *Governor Reagan: His Rise to Power* (New York: Public Affairs, 2003), 219–22.

66. Republican Party Platform of 1980, available at John T. Woolley and Gerhard Peters, *The American Presidency Project* [online]. Santa Barbara, Calif., http://www.presidency.ucsb.edu/ws/index.php?pid=25844#axzz1KwNtLc1O; Goldman, *Picking Federal Judges*, 287–91; Schwartz, *Packing the Courts*, 53–54, 61–62; Nancy Scherer, *Scoring Points: Politicians, Activists, and the Lower Federal Court Appointment Process* (Stanford: Stanford University Press, 2005), 18–19. Scherer argues that diminished senatorial and ABA influence in appellate court nominations has continued under succeeding administrations of both parties. All agree that Senate leaders successfully resisted administration efforts to weaken senatorial privilege with respect to district court nominations.

67. Goldman, *Picking Federal Judges*, 291–96; Schwartz, *Packing the Courts*, 60–61; David Alistair Yalof, *Pursuit of Justices: Presidential Politics and the Selection of Supreme Court Justices* (Chicago: University of Chicago Press, 1999), 142–44.

68. Adam Meyerson, "One Hundred Conservative Victories: The Reagan Years," *Policy Review* (Spring 1986) ("Confirmation of Stephen Williams as judge on U.S. Appeals Court for D.C. Circuit, added to earlier confirmations of Robert Bork, Kenneth

Starr, Laurence Silberman, James Buckley, and Antonin Scalia (later replaced by Douglas Ginsburg), gives conservatives a majority on nation's second most important court, formerly the bastion of liberal judicial activism."); Schwartz, *Packing the Courts*, 152.

69. The nominees' ages when they joined the Court, by nominating president:

Reagan—O'Connor (51), Scalia (46), Kennedy (51).
Clinton—Souter (50), Ginsburg (66), Breyer (56).
George H. W. Bush—Thomas (43).
George W. Bush—Alito (55), Roberts (50).
Obama—Sotomayor (55), Kagan (50).

70. Schwartz, *Packing the Courts*, 59–60, 133–34, 142–44.

71. Joan Biskupic, *Sandra Day O'Connor: How The First Woman On The Supreme Court Became Its Most Influential Justice* (New York: ECCO, 2005), 70–80; Adam Liptak, "Court Under Roberts Is Most Conservative in Decades," *New York Times*, July 24, 2010.

72. Scherer, *Scoring Points*, 68–72. The judges involved in the cases included circuit-court judges in active service, circuit-court judges on senior status, and district-court judges sitting by designation on the circuit courts.

73. Ibid., 199, 205, 213, 219. Similar numbers prevail in the other types of cases.

74. Steve Roberts, "Reagan's Social Issues: Gone But Not Forgotten," *New York Times*, September 11, 1988, sec. 4, 4.

4

REBUILDING INSTITUTIONS
AND REDEFINING ISSUES

The Reagan Justice Department and the Reconstruction of
Civil Rights

RICHARD L. PACELLE JR.

By the 1960s, issues of race and civil rights had provoked a lasting political realignment.[1] Franklin D. Roosevelt had avoided the subject for fear of dividing his party, but when Hubert Humphrey successfully advocated a strong civil rights plank for the Democratic platform in 1948, those fears were realized. Before long, the South turned to the Republican Party as opponents of civil rights abandoned the Democratic Party in droves. Race continued to divide the parties after the waning of the civil rights movement. As John Skrentny shows elsewhere in this volume, the divisions came into sharper focus during the Nixon administration, which had a mixed record on civil rights issues. By the election of Ronald Reagan in 1980, the partisan divide on race and civil rights was as wide as ever.

In this chapter, I assess the civil rights policies of the Reagan administration by examining the Department of Justice (DOJ) and the Office of the Solicitor General (OSG). It has been widely charged that the administration politicized the OSG and tried to use it to pursue its social goals, most notably overturning *Roe v. Wade* 410 U.S. 113 (1973) and rewriting civil rights law.[2] On abortion, there was mostly lip service. For civil rights, however, the Reagan administration pursued a concerted policy of retrenchment that involved three strategies for reshaping civil rights law: redefinition, replacement, and reconstruction. Since the administration aspired to use the courts and the bureaucracy to effect social change, it had to encourage the courts to rewrite precedent, a tactic that involved the *redefinition* of rights and responsibilities. Such an ambitious goal required a sympathetic audience on the bench. Hence, *replacement*: the administration would fill judicial seats with judges who supported retrenchment on civil rights. Reshaping civil rights law involved a third component: the *reconstruction* of government mechanisms that dealt with civil rights, most notably the Civil Rights Division (CRD) and the OSG.

Linchpin of Legal Strategy

The Office of the Solicitor General has an extraordinary influence over the interpretation and implementation of law, but its role is not well understood. Located within the Justice Department, it plays a key role in deciding which cases should be appealed to the Supreme Court and in arguing the government's case before the court.[3] In essence, the OSG is a small elite legal firm that represents the interests of the government. At the apex of the office is the solicitor general (SG) who, unlike the attorney general or the justices of the Supreme Court, is required to be learned in the law.[4] The solicitor general has become, in fact, what the attorney general is in name.[5] In many respects, the nomination of a solicitor general parallels that of a Supreme Court justice. The criteria are similar: both are well respected, have legal experience, and often share the legal philosophy of the administration. There is often an "agenda" issue that dominates the administration's concerns as a litmus test that might affect the choice of a justice and a solicitor general.[6]

Although the SG is appointed by the president and serves under the AG, the office itself has a long tradition of independence. Presidents are not free to use the OSG strictly to do their political bidding.[7] The frequency of participation in front of the Supreme Court makes the SG an important ally of the justices, who rely on the office's expertise to control their docket and help structure doctrinal development.[8] The Court in turn expects the SG to act as the attorney for the United States rather than for a particular president. Indeed, tradition helps the SG maintain support from the court and provides some autonomy from political forces. The SG also has an unmatched record of excellence. The OSG has hundreds of cases it could appeal to the Supreme Court, but the OSG carefully screens petitions to bring only the best cases. It wins approximately two-thirds of its cases, and as litigant it annually has a higher percentage of petitions accepted for review or has a higher success rate.[9] More significantly, the court often adopts, sometimes verbatim, the arguments that the OSG propounds in its briefs and oral arguments. As one justice's clerk put it: "We jokingly referred to the SG's petition as the answer sheet."[10] Given the excellence of its attorneys, its knowledge of the proclivities of the justices, and the number of potential cases, the office has an unmatched ability and opportunity to litigate strategically.[11]

The Institutional Context for Civil Rights

The power and influence of the SG made it a central player in the Reagan administration's strategy of retrenchment. To understand that strategy, and to see why the administration's use of the SG marked such a dramatic break with precedent, it is necessary to trace, albeit briefly, the recent history of the construction of civil rights policy. In the 1950s and early 1960s, Congress was a graveyard for meaningful civil rights legislation.[12] Southern Democrats who normally ran with little or no opposition dominated the committee chairs in both chambers due to seniority. They were able to block meaningful civil rights legislation, often killing it in committee. Should a bill make it to the floor of the Senate, southerners could (and often did) filibuster it to death.[13] The few civil rights acts that did pass tended to be minor and largely symbolic. They served to satisfy proponents of civil rights and blunt the momentum toward meaningful change.[14]

With the first branch of government blocking racial equality policies, civil rights advocates had to seek redress for their grievances elsewhere. They turned to the Supreme Court, which became the vehicle for meaningful civil rights change. Even before its momentous school-desegregation decisions, the court was in the incremental process of advancing civil rights. The court banned the white primary, ended government enforcement of restrictive covenants (contracts that could forbid the sale of a home often on racial grounds), and began to level the so-called "separate, but equal" barriers in graduate and professional schools.[15] In *Brown v. Board of Education* 347 U.S. 483 (1954), the court took a quantum leap forward, holding that in the area of public education, separate but equal was unconstitutional.[16] The other branches moved much more cautiously on civil rights. President Dwight Eisenhower responded indifferently to the *Brown* decision and moved decisively only after a crisis over desegregation erupted in Little Rock, Arkansas. President John Kennedy was similarly unwilling to draw on the moral credit of his office or expend his finite political capital to advance civil rights. Kennedy defended his reluctance to push civil rights as a function of his narrow electoral victory.[17] It took an assassin's bullet, a southern president, and an electoral landslide to push Congress into action. With the passage of the Civil Rights Act of 1964 and the Voting Rights Act of 1965, Congress finally reinforced the court's landmark decision.[18]

The decision in *Brown* triggered a constitutional revolution.[19] Not only did the court strike a direct blow for equality by desegregating the schools, but it also instigated a series of related changes to civil liberties and civil rights.[20] The importance of the court was not lost on civil rights advocates, who used carefully formulated litigation strategies to undermine hostile precedents and build favorable doctrine.[21] They acquired powerful allies in the Justice Department, most notably the Civil Rights Division and the OSG. The office would be a strong advocate, lending its considerable prestige through its briefs and oral arguments.[22]

With the blessing of President Harry Truman, the OSG would become more aggressive in its use of amicus curiae briefs. The amicus curiae— or friend of the court—brief permits a group or individual who is not a party to enter the case.[23] For the U.S. government, this meant that the DOJ, the SG, and the president could interject their views into a state case. This was a great opportunity for influence. From the Truman administration through the Johnson administration, the OSG always backed the civil rights claimant before the Supreme Court. For the most part, the Nixon administration's OSG did so as well, though it was not as consistently supportive of civil rights.[24]

For decades, the courts provided the pathways for civil rights reforms. With the president and Congress initially reluctant to intervene in civil rights, it was the court that took the initiative. Ultimately, presidents of all ideological stripes, from Truman through Carter, used the OSG to support and even extend the frontiers of civil rights, although some did so more forcefully than others.

Ronald Reagan, however, would represent a decisive break with this long-standing trend of using the SG to support civil rights. As Marissa Golden notes, "Between the time that President Dwight Eisenhower elevated the civil rights wing of the Justice Department to the status of a division and Ronald Reagan was elected to the White House, civil rights policy proceeded on a fairly straight path toward increased presidential commitment to its enforcement."[25] Thus when Reagan came to power, he was reversing the policies not just of the Democrats but also of his own party's presidents.

To appreciate the significance of the change, it is instructive to consider how his Republican predecessors dealt with the issue. Dwight Eisenhower hoped that the court would not order integration of the schools, even pressuring Chief Justice Earl Warren to retain the status quo.[26] There were serious doubts that Eisenhower would use the bully pulpit or send troops to enforce the court's directives. Ultimately, though reluctantly, he did enforce desegregation. Eisenhower wanted leadership on civil rights issues to come from the cabinet level. This was fortunate, because the DOJ was forceful in expanding the scope of civil rights. Attorney General Herbert Brownell submitted a bill to Congress that marked the turning point in the administration's policies.[27] Brownell wanted to separate the Civil Rights Section from the Criminal Division and expand the former's power. Thus the Civil Rights Act of 1957 created the Civil Rights Division, a move that empowered further change on civil rights through the courts. After *Brown*, the DOJ used authority and procedures that had not been invoked since Reconstruction. The goal was not to create a litany of new rights but to find legal means of enforcing the rights that were increasingly flowing from the court's decisions.[28]

As Robert Fredrick Burk has argued, "*Brown* meant that the full moral weight of the Constitution as interpreted by the Supreme Court was now on the side of the advocates of integration."[29] The decision increased pressure on the administration and subsequent presidents. Thus, the Eisenhower administration opted for a legal perspective over a political one. The SG went into court to protect the statutory power the Justice Department had obtained through the Civil Rights Act. Ultimately, the idea of "winning while losing" well describes civil rights in the Eisenhower era. Although proponents won a signal victory in *Brown* and the Civil Rights Division was empowered, progress was very slow indeed. Victories were symbolic. When the Supreme Court ordered desegregation with "all deliberate speed," it was clear that southern school districts would proceed deliberately slowly.

Richard Nixon's presidency was marked by a number of apparent contradictions. His civil rights policies were emblematic of these contrasts, as Skrentny shows in this volume. On the one hand, Nixon pursued a "southern strategy" as part of his attempts to build "an emerging Republican majority." On the other hand, his administration supported changes in employment discrimination policy that paved the way for affirmative action. In employment cases, the Equal Employment Opportunity Commission (EEOC) and OSG were responsible for a monumental expansion of employee rights.[30] With the blessing of the administration, in the case of *Griggs v. Duke Power Company* 401 U.S. 424 (1971), the court adopted the disparate impact standard, which meant that those challenging employment practices need not show that the employer intended to discriminate but only that the effects of the practices were discriminatory.[31] The prospects for affirmative action were much brighter after disparate impact became the standard, making *Griggs* the proverbial *Brown* of employment discrimination.[32]

Yet, on the whole, the Nixon years saw an important, albeit gradual, reversal in support for civil rights in the Justice Department and the courts. Many of these actions suggest that Nixon's "southern strategy" was more than just rhetorical.[33] The Justice Department, for example, reversed a number of policies pertaining to civil rights. Attorney General John Mitchell announced that the Justice Department would slow school desegregation.[34] Failing that, the Justice Department pursued a strategy of nonenforcement by the Civil Rights Division, which prompted a revolt and mass resignations by careerists.[35] During the proposed extension of the Voting Rights Act, the DOJ supported lifting mandatory preclearance requirements.[36]

Similarly, although the Nixon administration enunciated support for *Brown*, it tried to limit its applicability and the remedies used to further its principles. As Jerris Leonard, director of the CRD, said, "I knew my mandate: enforce the law, don't expand it."[37] The Nixon administration may have wanted to place limits on the expansion of civil rights, but its hand was stayed by doctrinal development and legal considerations. Both judicial precedent and political judgment suggested that it was prudent to avoid signaling an immediate retreat. Although the administration opposed busing as a means of achieving desegregation, for example, it enforced decisions that contradicted its desires.[38] As Leonard noted, "I never had a clue whether Richard Nixon and John Mitchell truly supported civil rights, but they supported the law."[39]

Still, as the court got more conservative and cases got more difficult, retreat was possible. Many of the desegregation cases argued during Nixon's presidency involved more complicated issues than those faced by his predecessors. Questions of broad remedies and what to do about northern de facto discrimination broke the consensus on the court. In addition, Nixon used his political resources to change the legal realm through his Supreme Court appointments.

Retreat was occurring. The Supreme Court, a traditional bastion for civil rights, was being slowly transformed into a less favorable forum for advancing racial equality. The administration was slowing the pace of civil rights. More importantly, for the first time in decades the U.S. government and the SG opposed civil rights advocates in briefs before the Supreme Court. Symbolically, the Nixon administration legitimized opposition to civil rights.

The Reagan administration, however, made a much more conscious effort to retreat on civil rights. The White House did not support the renewal of the Civil Rights Act and sought to weaken enforcement of the Voting Rights Act.[40] According to Norman Amaker, the record "clearly manifested an effort to turn back the clock on the enforcement of civil rights laws."[41] Officials in the Reagan administration aimed their guns at the remedies for discrimination: busing, the disparate impact standard, and affirmative action. There was a problem, however: Supreme Court precedents. These not only permitted but also often mandated the use of busing to achieve racial balance in the schools, disparate impact to shift the burden of proof in employment discrimination from employee to employer, and affirmative action to remedy past discrimination. Further rankling for the Reagan administration was the fact that these adverse precedents arose under the more conservative Burger Court and were set in motion by Republican presidents.[42] To attack these precedents the administration needed a new argument, a new audience, and a new mouthpiece.

The Politics of Retrenchment, Retreat, and Reorganization

Redefining issues is one of the most difficult tasks in American politics. Issues are largely path dependent; once they take on a certain character they do not normally deviate. Ronald Reagan was willing to buck the considerable odds. The administration made attempts to reverse or limit existing precedents and opposed the extension of the Voting Rights

Act.[43] To help in those efforts, the administration tried to redefine the central concepts and questions.

The task of redefining civil rights was particularly difficult given entrenched definitions and active civil rights groups. Precedent was not generally supportive to the new administration. Agency positions supporting civil rights had been long established, and previous solicitors general had argued in favor of civil rights for a generation. Yet, the administration tried the opposite tack: attempting to get the court and the OSG to revisit and reverse existing precedents, thus attempting to destabilize existing doctrine and change the law.[44] The administration tried to transform the policy environment. Part of that transformation entailed institutional reorganization: politicizing the OSG, reinventing existing institutions, and creating new mechanisms for furthering its agenda. The administration would seek to accomplish this largely through the courts, endeavoring to pack the judiciary with like-minded judges.[45]

Redefinition

The goal of redefinition is relatively simple in theory but difficult to implement: to undermine existing positions and to vet the new arguments in order to make them more respectable. Perhaps some law reviews would pick up the thread, and it would percolate through the legal system. Maybe a few groups would respond with amicus curiae briefs.[46] Maybe a district court judge would accept the argument, and it would decide a case. Even if such an argument was not upheld in the court of appeals, perhaps a judge would dissent, making the case more likely to be accepted by the Supreme Court.[47] Once the case was in front of the justices, perhaps the argument of the SG could arm a sympathetic ally, so that it would make its way into a dissent—a call to the future. And maybe, just maybe, between putting new justices on the court and distinguishing past decisions, a majority might be persuaded to create a new precedent.

The administration was accused of trying to turn back the clock on existing rights. As the issues and the facts in individual cases got more difficult, the administration could have attempted to distinguish the case of the moment from existing precedents. Bradford Reynolds, the assistant attorney general and head of the Civil Rights Division, thought otherwise. He did not want to lend support to a precedent that the administration would prefer to undermine. Rather, he sought to advance arguments that reconfigured the underlying theories the court used in deciding civil rights cases.[48] Opponents charged that Reynolds led "the Reagan administration's assault on civil rights."[49] They had a point. Reynolds reversed past Justice Department policies, opposed Supreme Court precedents, fought further school integration, argued for narrow interpretations of statutes, and reversed voting rights policies.[50] There were charges that Reynolds attempted to pressure the solicitors general into carrying the administration's agenda cases before the justices.[51]

At the core of the Reagan agenda was the elimination of remedies like affirmative action, quotas, timetables, and busing. In addition, the administration sought to limit the redress of discriminatory practices to clear intent and to restrict compensation for discrimination to cases in which individual victims could be identified. The target for these goals was the Civil Rights Division, the EEOC, the Office of Civil Rights, and the Civil Rights Commission. It was on civil rights that the Department of Justice was "pressing its most ambitious agenda."[52]

Reagan wanted to reverse trends by redefining the terms of the debate.[53] He helped reframe reproductive rights from the rights of women to the rights of the unborn, for example. Similarly, affirmative action was redefined as "reverse discrimination." Affirmative action was wrong because it used discrimination to remedy discrimination. The administration resurrected the concept of a "color-blind Constitution." Civil rights advocates had long sought a color-blind Constitution to advance equality. Now the administration argued that programs that mandated or supported constitutionally approved affirmative-action plans were not color-blind but discriminated against innocent whites.[54] The administration also wanted to attack the disparate impact standard, despite the fact that business actually supported it.[55]

Policies were dominated by the premise that claimants should be treated as individuals rather than as members of a group.[56] Thus the administration advocated a change of focus from group rights to individual rights. The administration used narratives about individuals who were victims of affirmative action.[57] The arguments were designed to counter the use of sweeping class-wide remedies. Remedies needed to be narrow and strictly tailored. If individual plaintiffs could show they were the victims of clear discrimination, then a specific remedy would be available.

Replacement

The redefinition of issues was an important component of attempts to retrench and retreat on civil rights. It was essential however to translate political debate into living policy. The administration needed a sympathetic audience for its arguments. It was unlikely that the Reagan administration could sell a majority of Congress on its redefined notions of civil rights, so the administration sought to tip the balance by packing the courts at all levels. Years of Republican rule made the court a more favorable forum for possible redefinition.

While Reagan fully appreciated the importance of Supreme Court appointments, he was likely the first president to embrace fully the notion that the lower courts were important loci of power.[58] Cases get shaped in the lower courts. Since the overwhelming majority of cases do not get to the Supreme Court, the decisions of lower courts carry additional weight. Lawyers sympathetic to the administration could fashion cases before conservative federal judges, preparing briefs to move into the appellate courts. If the administration did its job properly in choosing district and courts of appeals judges, then its positions on civil rights would be vetted and cases would be shaped to meet its designs. And if the administration was careful in filling vacancies on the Supreme Court, then the precedents moving back down the judicial hierarchy would be favorable to its policy preferences as well.[59]

The Court was certainly the most favorable institutional environment for the administration. According to David Rose of the employment section of the Civil Rights Division, "the Reaganauts made a conscious effort to use the courts as in the sixties. Courts would lead the way. It was better than using Congress or administrative regulations. The administration grabbed hold of the appellate process in the OSG and in the Appellate Section. They tried to control the flow of litigation."[60]

If the judicial branch was the primary target for the Reagan administration, the mission was clear: change the ideological composition of the courts, top to bottom. According to David O'Brien, Reagan so transformed the process of selecting judges that future administrations were "sure to follow Reagan's lead in vigorously pursuing their legal goals when picking judges."[61] Reagan had a more coherent and ambitious agenda for judicial selection than any of his predecessors had. Reynolds claimed, "The greatest accomplishment of the Department of Justice and the administration was the judicial appointments at all levels. There was a real sea change . . . in judicial attitudes beginning in the second term. The appointments explain in large measure how we were able to move the administration's agenda."[62]

These judges were instruments of presidential power and a way to ensure a president's legacy.[63] With the luxury of eight years in the White House, Reagan was able to accomplish a great deal. A longer perspective is even more telling—for twenty of twenty-four years, the GOP had the prerogative of judicial nominations. The result was clear. When Bill Clinton took office, over 70 percent of the federal judges had been appointed by Republican presidents.[64]

The influence, of course, was most visible at the Supreme Court level. One of the most telling editorial cartoons of the 1984 campaign showed nine justices who looked exactly like Ronald Reagan sitting on the Supreme Court bench chanting "forty more years."[65] Like Nixon, Reagan had the opportunity to remake the court in his own image, appointing three new justices and promoting Rehnquist to chief justice. More importantly, perhaps, the court was beginning to reconfigure its institutional role, rejecting the preferred-position doctrine that had been the basis of expansive rights and liberties.[66] The "new" philosophy, a return to past doctrine, advocated attention to the intent of the framers of the Constitution and a stricter construction of the document. In practical terms, a majority desired to balance individual rights and competing social interests on a more equal footing than the preferred-position doctrine allowed.[67] This theory was complemented by a willingness to defer to the elected branches in civil liberties and civil rights, rejecting the liberalism that had guided judicial policymaking.[68]

The change in the dominant philosophy underlying decision making was reflected in the decline in the aggregate percentages of victories for civil rights claimants. In the period before Nixon came to office, it was not unusual for the Supreme Court to support civil rights and civil liberties claimants over 70 percent of the time. By the time the Reagan years had tolled, that support was routinely around 30 percent.[69] Certainly, it is important to remember that many cases in the latter period were more difficult, thus requiring the drawing of finer lines. But the goal of the

Reagan administration was to undermine adverse precedents once the momentum swung in its favor. Not since the Johnson administration had the DOJ possessed such a politicized view of courts, judges, and the law.[70]

Given the lifetime tenure of federal judges, the judicial nomination process is the gift that keeps on giving. Long after presidents leave office, their appointees continue to make policy. The administration aimed, in the words of Edwin Meese, "to institutionalize the Reagan revolution so it can't be set aside no matter what happens in future elections."[71]

Reconstruction

Who would make the arguments that existing precedents should be overturned and civil rights should be redefined? These were the priorities of the political appointees in the DOJ. Those priorities were still one step removed from being aired in briefs and oral arguments. It became incumbent on the DOJ to rework the mechanisms of civil rights and litigation. Attorneys General William French Smith and Edwin Meese moved decisively to exert control over the three primary agencies charged with equal protection: the Civil Rights Division, the Civil Rights Commission, and the EEOC.

There are three means of changing the direction of a bureau or building what some call "the administrative presidency": leadership, budget, and reorganization. The Reagan administration chose the first: the appointment of ideological leadership.[72] The "administrative presidency" is a management strategy to help presidents achieve their policy goals by so-called taming the bureaucracy. It permits the president to work through the bureaucracy to pursue his goals rather than navigating the perilous congressional obstacle course. Both Nixon and Reagan used these strategies to overcome the perceived power deficit that presidents face in dealing with the bureaucracy. Typically, the deeper a president can push loyalists into the bureaucracy, the better the prospects for influence. For the Reagan administration, this translated into a significant attempt to micromanage the attorneys in the OSG and the CRD.[73] The administration appointed sympathetic directors and closely monitored the work of the line attorneys. Reynolds was given charge of the CRD and was the effective voice of leadership on civil rights. Later-to-be Justice Clarence Thomas assumed control of the EEOC, and Clarence Pendleton was appointed to head the Civil Rights Commission. Both were very conservative African Americans and largely toed the party line. The agencies that had been the vehicles for positive change were now being asked to be the agents of retrenchment.

Each new administration faces the same problem when it takes control of the White House: while it can replace a handful of people at the top of each agency, its ability to penetrate deeply into the rank and file is limited. This is a problem for an administration seeking to reverse policies—they are bucking tradition, precedent, and career bureaucrats used to different guiding principles. In some agencies, especially those dealing with civil rights, lawyers and civil servants who had dedicated their professional lives to a cause resisted attempts to undermine their hard-fought victories.

The Reagan administration sought to implement its objectives administratively and judicially rather than legislatively.[74] The administration believed not only that the existing policy positions of the agencies were fraught with problems but also that the agencies themselves had been captured by clientele groups. According to Hugh Davis Graham, Reagan "capitalizing on growing white resentment of minority preference policies . . . attempted to countercapture the offending Washington agencies."[75] He used each appointment opportunity to stack the agencies with conservatives. The administration sought to reverse policy, precedent, and case law in midstream.[76]

Of course, where federal agencies are concerned, there is a missing piece to the litigation puzzle. Control of the CRD could be undermined from above by the OSG. No agency can go forward to the Supreme Court without the permission of the OSG. So, if the administration was going to pursue a litigation strategy, it had to get the SG on board. Thus, the Reagan administration had to populate the CRD, other federal civil rights agencies, and the OSG with sympathetic leadership. It also had to change the ethos of each organization. The administration had to convince the agencies to reject their traditional policies and the SG to undermine its past litigation efforts. In short, the administration had to reconstruct the mechanisms of civil rights and litigation.

The relationship between any agency and the OSG is a complicated one. The agency is responsible for its policy position, but the SG decides which cases can be appealed to the Supreme Court. Agencies want to appeal as many of their defeats as possible. But the SG has to ride herd and think about the collective benefits and costs to the government. If the agency is unhappy with the SG's unwillingness to proceed, it can involve the attorney general and, in some cases, even the president.[77] They may decide to pressure the SG to reverse course. In most areas of law, regardless of the party controlling the White House, the position of the OSG would be unchanged. That was decidedly not the case in civil rights.[78] There were frequent battles between solicitors general who, though conservative, were trying to protect the office's relationship with the court, and the leadership of the agencies, most notably Reynolds, who were trying to advance the president's agenda against the backdrop of a finite ticking clock.

The ability of the Reagan administration to achieve its goals was dependent on the other institutional actors. A divided government constrained the administration. Congress was increasingly aggressive in protecting civil rights, but there was a counterbalance in the Supreme Court, which was increasingly sympathetic to the administration. Thus, a litigation strategy was critical for the administration.

The Civil Rights Division accrued significant power under Smith and Meese. The Division traditionally pursued a course of incremental progressive and nonpolitical law enforcement regardless of the administration. As Joel Selig, who served in the CRD, noted: "The Division's preference has always been for the middle ground; its approach has been neither maximalist as advanced by more militant civil rights advocates, nor minimalist as advanced by those committed to the narrowest possible interpretation of the civil rights laws. As a result, Division attorneys rightly consider themselves in a position to criticize approaches that partake of either extreme."[79] Under Reagan, the Division was charged with a radical departure from this tradition. Reynolds, in effect, created a shadow Civil Rights Division, circumventing the normal machinery. There were advantages to this for the administration, most notably a clearer responsiveness to its agenda. The costs of maintaining this shadow Division were inefficiency and low morale.[80]

According to Deputy Solicitor General Edwin Kneedler, "The Civil Rights Division wanted to enforce civil rights law, but there was a perception that Reynolds did not. There was a perception during the Reagan years that the Civil Rights Division's protector role was being cast off. . . . When the government seems to be arguing against long-standing institutional positions, it gives the Court some pause."[81] Reynolds increasingly tried to exert influence (some would say pressure) over the Office of the Solicitor General.[82]

The authority of the Division was strengthened when the administration weakened the authority of the EEOC, a potential rival. The CRD became involved in a number of disputes with the EEOC over the position the government would take in some important cases. The EEOC had been created with clear institutional weaknesses. Although the agency had some litigating authority, there were limits to that power. The EEOC needed clearance from the SG in order to enter a case.[83]

Clarence Thomas moved decisively to change many of the practices of the EEOC. He sought to abandon the use of timetables and numeric goals, which had resulted from the *Griggs* case and its progeny. Thomas also restricted the use of class-action suits that relied on statistical evidence of discriminatory effects. The EEOC lost important battles for power within the DOJ. The EEOC pleaded its position to the SG, but was told that it would have to accept the Justice Department's opposition to affirmative action.[84] According to Rose, "The Reagan administration pre-empted the EEOC, rather than attack it directly. It was clear that the Department of Justice was calling the shots."[85]

Institutionally, the emasculation of a rival would give the DOJ more authority to speak with one voice. Politically, weakening the EEOC would remove a voice that might oppose the Division's interpretation of civil rights. The EEOC was powerless to resist these impulses, and Congress failed to come to its rescue.[86] Reagan appointees began to reconstruct a potential ally, the Civil Rights Commission, as well as the EEOC itself.[87]

The relationship between political appointees and staff attorneys in the OSG and the Civil Rights Division was noteworthy. For decades, the OSG and the CRD supported a broad view of civil rights. The civil rights decisions created supportive precedents that Reagan solicitors general tried to limit or undermine. This caused problems for staff attorneys who had helped establish and buttress those precedents. Some exercised voice; others chose to exit.[88] According to Lincoln Caplan, staff attorneys viewed the political appointees as "social revolutionaries with no regard for the law," while the Reagan appointees viewed the careerists as "intransigent holdovers."[89]

The DOJ tried to reassign some of the Division's attorneys out of fear that they would undermine its agenda. There were charges that the OSG had become politicized, and a number of attorneys left the office.[90] Reynolds claimed, "For a number of years, we rewrote briefs in the front office. We reviewed every brief. Many late nights we reworked and rewrote the briefs. The crew in the office was pretty darn good attorneys. . . . They did not sabotage the briefs. At the same time, the briefs were not written with passion or enthusiasm. I edited them to put heart into them. It was not their fault—they did not believe in our position, but they were professionals."[91]

The disputes between the administration and the career attorneys were on display, almost from the beginning. The administration suffered a humiliating defeat in *Bob Jones University v. United States* 461 U.S. 574 (1983). The case had begun during the Carter administration when the DOJ brought the case to strip the university of its tax-exempt status because it discriminated in its admission policies. The Reagan administration announced that it was changing positions in the case and supporting the university. The case symbolized the tension between the careerists, who argued that the government should not support the university, and the Reagan Justice Department. According to Selig, "By refusing to avail itself of the moderating influence of career Department attorneys, the administration failed to take advantage of the institutional strengths at its disposal and instead set itself up for an embarrassing defeat."[92] The decision fueled a chain reaction. Career attorneys in the CRD had lost faith in an administration they thought was trying to reverse long-standing policies. At the same time, the Reagan appointees lost confidence in the careerists they felt were out to undermine their agenda.[93]

In addition to the changes in the civil rights agencies, there were changes internal to the OSG. The administration was charged with politicizing the office by making it more directly accountable to the attorney general. Lawrence Wallace, the deputy SG in charge of civil rights, was relieved of those cases. Voices argued that the SG needed a political ally, so to exert additional control the administration established the position of Principal Deputy.[94] The principal deputy, sometimes referred to as the political deputy, was to be an intermediary between the SG and staff attorneys.

Critics feared that the creation of the principal deputy would inject an unhealthy dose of politics into the office. There were fears that these deputies would be moles for the White House.[95] While the principal deputy did not have the feared impact, it demonstrated the vulnerability of the office's independence. According to Donald Ayer, the second person to hold the position, "The principal deputy argues the difficult, highly charged political issues. But he/she is not a political fix it man. The role of the principal deputy is not to carry political water on controversial issues. It is important that he or she pursue the ideals of the office, which include disinterested logical reasoning."[96] If the principal deputy did not fulfill the dire prophesies, it still became a symbol of the desire of political forces to influence the office.[97]

Ideologically, Reagan's two solicitors general, Rex Lee and Charles Fried, largely reflected the administration they served.[98] But they battled to hew a little closer to the idea that the SG serves the government and the people, not a particular administration's view. They were careful to try to protect the long-standing relationship between the OSG and the Supreme Court. Assistant Attorney General Reynolds, on the other hand, was more inclined to battle for principles, short-term consequences be damned. Caplan referred to Reynolds as the "Shadow Solicitor" and charged that he tried to usurp the role of the solicitor general.[99] In some of the agenda cases, Reynolds or a deputy would write an alternate brief when they deemed the solicitor general's brief unsatisfactory.

Clashes between the solicitors general and Reynolds, the politically motivated head of the Civil Rights Division, erupted on more than a few occasions. Rex Lee did his best to hold out. He argued that if he had done what Reynolds wanted and brought cases to further the president's agenda, he would lose those cases and the justices would not take him seriously.[100] Reynolds maintained, "Our differences were not philosophical but how to say what we want to say and to have the greatest impact on the Court. Rex brought to the table considerable background and expertise on how to get five votes. I brought a passion and vigor without modulating it too much."[101] Reynolds had control over the final briefs in the lower courts and some felt that he often made extreme arguments.

The clashes were much more frequent when Charles Fried became the SG. Reynolds maintained that his "differences with Rex [Lee] were over how to present the case, not what to present. But with Charles, the differences were substantive" and "more things would go to Attorney General [Ed] Meese." Reynolds noted, "Ed almost always sided with me. I think that stuck in Charles' craw."[102] For his part, Fried wrote, "Working with Brad Reynolds was the toughest part of my job."[103] Fried claimed, "Along with the browbeating he would threaten that if he did not get his way, then 'the AG' would hear about it." According to Rose, "It was clear that Brad Reynolds and Ed Meese were calling the shots on policy. The independence of the OSG was taken away under Fried."[104]

Lee and Fried were involved in thirty-six civil rights cases. In fifteen of those cases, Lee and Fried filed briefs or argued for the civil rights claimant. In the other twenty-one cases, they argued against the civil rights claimant. They were successful in twenty-three of the thirty-six cases. The data lend credence to the argument that Fried pushed a more conservative agenda than his predecessor did. While Lee filed briefs or argued eleven cases in favor of civil rights claimants and ten against, Fried argued just four cases for the civil rights claimant and he opposed those claimants in eleven cases. This translated to different levels of success: Lee won fifteen of his twenty-one civil rights cases, but Fried won just eight of his fifteen cases.[105]

Lee largely dealt with busing, employment, and affirmative action. He had some success when the office did not overreach. Caplan argued that Lee resigned because of increasing attempts by Meese and Reynolds to politicize the OSG, which Lee feared would damage the relationship between the solicitor general and the court.[106] Fried had the more difficult cases, which attacked affirmative action and disparate impact directly.[107] Both solicitors general succeeded in drawing the wrath of liberals and conservatives. Lee and Fried had their names on briefs seeking to arrest or reverse a number of civil rights precedents and attacking *Roe v. Wade*, earning the enmity of liberals. Both also infuriated conservatives because they tried to rein in the most extreme briefs.[108]

It is difficult to say whether the more ideological stances ended up hurting the OSG and Lee and Fried personally. Patrick Wohlfarth showed that the SG does pay a price when the court perceives the amicus briefs as too polemic.[109] There is no doubt that the court took umbrage on occasions. In a few cases, the Supreme Court was openly critical of the SG during oral arguments, in majority, concurring, and dissenting opinions, and in refusing the office some of its normal perks.[110]

To many, there was a sea change in the OSG, which was the result of politicizing the office. While Reagan gets the blame (and in part it is deserved), it may have been Jimmy Carter who opened Pandora's box. Past solicitors general had been respected legal scholars like Robert Jackson, Archibald Cox, and Erwin Griswold. They had the reputation and strength to stand up to a president. Carter, however, selected a lesser-known judge, Wade McCree, who lacked the professional standing to combat the political forces. Subsequent solicitors general, while qualified, were similarly chosen more for their political acumen than their legal clout.[111] Some argue that the nature of the SG has changed over time as a result. According to Andrew Frey, "There are two models of the solicitor general. The first is what I call the Harvard Law Professor Model: 'I know what is best for the Court. My job is to help the Supreme Court reach the right result.' The second see themselves as lawyers for a client, apart from their view of the general public interest. They see themselves as lawyers with the principal task of advancing the programmatic and litigation interests of the government." Frey used Cox and Robert Bork as examples of the Harvard Law Professor model. More recent solicitors general seem to fall into the second group. Relatedly, Philip Heymann argued that traditionally the SG could tell the president that the office could not take a certain position because it was contrary to the law. He argues that there has been a movement away from that. Recent solicitors general are more likely to be advocates for a position and to try to find grounds to argue that position.[112]

An Assessment of the Strategy

The administration achieved varying degrees of success through its tactics of redefinition, replacement, and reconstruction. As Gil Troy noted, "It took time for the Reagan Revolution to restrain the courts, weaken the bureaucracy, reorient the body politic."[113] The administration was successful at redefining the issues tied to race and getting the court to accept some of those definitions. The replacement strategy was largely successful, but the administration wished it could have done more. Had Reagan succeeded in getting Robert Bork on the court, it might have tipped the balance more decisively. George H. W. Bush was able to move the court by choosing Clarence Thomas to replace Thurgood Marshall. But David Souter (replacing William Brennan) was more moderate than advertised, thus marking a missed opportunity to shift the court farther right.[114]

Still, the administration had significant opportunities to change policy in a dramatic fashion. Although the court seemed to be sympathetic, the extreme nature of some of the arguments may have induced some of the moderate conservatives to support existing precedents. Not surprisingly, these cases mobilized civil rights groups in opposition, as Mary Frances Berry chronicles in her chapter. The divisions in the CRD, the EEOC, and the Civil Rights Commission were constantly on display for judges, justices, and members of Congress to see. Curiously, though, the administration often ran into problems within its own party. Republicans in Congress did not support some of Reynolds' gambles. This message was not lost on the court.

Although the administration did not achieve its ambitious goals, it did make progress in halting the development of civil rights law and in reversing some precedents. The most sustained success would have to wait for the Bush administration. The Court supported the administration on limiting busing but not on eradicating it. The real retreat would come in *Board of Education Oklahoma City v. Dowell* 498 U.S. 237 (1991) when Kenneth Starr was SG (under Bush). The Court was inconsistent in its affirmative-action decisions but ultimately placed limits when the program would result in someone being laid off. Similarly, the court limited the minority business enterprises or set-aside programs.[115]

On the eve of the end of Reagan's second term, Charles Fried argued his biggest case: *Ward's Cove Packing v. Atonio* 490 U.S. 642 (1989). Fried viewed *Ward's Cove* as a chance to "tame" *Griggs*, the case that had so transformed the landscape for discrimination in employment. Fried's amicus brief tried to move the court from an effects test to an intent test. Justice White's opinion in *Ward's Cove* paraphrased and endorsed the points made by Fried's brief and shifted the burden from employers to employees in such cases.[116] The Court ruled that the existence of disparities was not proof of discrimination in and of itself. Workers had to show that companies had no legitimate need for the challenged practices. The opinion disposed of the language of *Griggs* that pressured employers to use quotas.[117]

The victory was short-lived, however. Congress passed the Civil Rights Act of 1990 to nullify the court's interpretations. President Bush vetoed the bill, claiming it would lead to quotas. The Senate failed by a single vote to override the veto. The Civil Rights Act of 1991 was passed with a few compromises. Bush's hand was forced by a number of events and by an election less than a year away that made it impossible for him to veto this version. According to James Simon, "Most of the conservatives' narrow victories in civil rights cases were blunted by the Civil Rights Act of 1991."[118] The legislation not only repudiated the *Ward's Cove* reinterpretation of *Griggs*, but it struck more deeply, providing opportunities to challenge discrimination in seniority systems.[119]

The greatest anxiety for the civil rights community came from *Patterson v. McLean Credit Union* 485 U.S. 617 (1988). Brenda Patterson sued under Section 1981 for racial and sexual harassment. In Fried's view, the extension of the statute to private activity was a terrible stretch. But in the original brief, Fried wrote that the interpretation of *Runyon v. McCrary* 427 U.S. 160 (1976), though distorted, was well established and should be respected.[120] Civil rights proponents were shocked when a narrow majority ordered reargument on the question of whether the court should reconsider *Runyon*, an important case that had set an expansive civil rights precedent.[121] Symbolically, coming just four days after Anthony Kennedy had replaced Justice Lewis Powell, it seemed to portend a judicial turn to the right. In practical terms, this was a threat "to one of the foundation decisions in civil rights."[122] At a meeting with the attorney general, some argued that the OSG needed to make a strong argument to help stiffen the resolve of its allies on the court.[123]

Fried felt that the case was a trap and decided not to file a brief: "I saw no reason to bait the various bears a second time. I did not think a reconsideration of *Runyon* was a good idea. I did not think that the Court would overturn it." Further, he argued: "Our silence now would be an eloquent but respectful way of saying to the five members of the Court who had asked for reargument that this was a misconceived enterprise."[124] Conservatives excoriated Fried, with one saying he was "running a renegade operation that looks more like a Dukakis solicitor general's office."[125] Despite tremendous pressure, Meese did not overrule Fried.

There were good reasons for this strategic discretion. In previous cases and in an earlier version of this case, Fried had supported the precedent. To argue otherwise now, he felt, would look like the last gasp of a departing administration.[126] It was not lost on Fried that 66 senators, 119 representatives, 47 state attorneys general, and 112 civic groups joined briefs supporting *Runyon*.[127] Given the widespread support for the precedent, if the court overturned it, Congress would undoubtedly respond by restoring the status quo. Finally, Fried felt that urging the court to overturn

Runyon would be a futile gesture that would jeopardize his attempts to overturn *Griggs*. The court unanimously upheld *Runyon*, a move that kept this key civil rights precedent in tact.

The Court invited the SG to participate in *Thornburg v. Gingles* 478 U.S. 30 (1986), which the DOJ considered the most important voting rights case of the 1980s. A few years earlier, in *Mobile v. Bolden* 446 U.S. 55 (1980), the court had ruled that the government must prove discriminatory intent in voting dilution cases. Congress reversed the decision with an amendment to the VRA holding that proof of discriminatory effects is sufficient. *Thornburg v. Gingles* involved the amendment that the administration had actively opposed.[128] Under Reynolds' direction, the Justice Department sided with a southern state for the first time in a voting rights case. According to Fried, the case presented real problems: "The statute made no sense. The 'good guys' were lined up against us. It was an uphill fight from the word go."[129]

The brief argued that the lower court interpretation of the VRA was "fundamentally flawed." Robert Dole and nine other senators filed a brief arguing that the administration had misinterpreted congressional intent. In essence, the case permitted the court to revisit the debate between disparate impact and intent, this time in the context of voting rights. The SG was again arguing for intent, but the congressional brief argued that disparate impact was sufficient.

The Court's decision followed the lines that Dole's brief had suggested.[130] The opinion seemed to rebut the solicitor general's argument point by point.[131] Reynolds professed surprise at the decision in *Thornburgh*. These cases would return in an altered form and the administration's position would ultimately be vindicated. According to Reynolds, "The post-*Gingles* voting cases were close to our arguments. This was due, in part, to the fact that we rewrote internal guidelines in the Voting Rights Act. We wanted to make damn sure that the 'effects' did not overtake enforcement."[132]

Political considerations dominated legal ones in the Reagan administration, and this was increasingly the case as time went on. The goals of the solicitors general were to maximize the Reagan agenda in the courts. The AG and the CRD tried to push the SG to go even further. Typically, the SG acts strategically, with legal positions tempering political stances. Rex Lee tried to moderate the positions of the political operatives with mixed success. Charles Fried was not as fortunate. Like McCree, Lee and

Fried were the newer brand of solicitor general. They lacked the independent base of authority that would permit them to withstand the brisk political winds.

The administration wanted to destabilize precedent and doctrine. But the court was not ready for a wholesale reversal. The administration, on a finite clock, did not have time to do the background work to distinguish between precedents and undermine them in an incremental fashion. Although the court was sympathetic, the stridency of the SG in the agenda issues likely cost the administration the votes of moderate justices. Fried conceded that this was a widely held perception: "It may have influenced Powell and Stevens."[133] Congress mobilized to counter the administration's gambols. Bradford Reynolds lamented the apparent lack of success: "We thought probably naively that with two terms we could be successful in getting the affirmative action train turned around, getting the legal approach to desegregation turned around, and getting *Roe v. Wade* reversed. We fell short on all these fronts. You can't turn the ship of state on a dime."[134] But all was not lost. As Simon noted, "For more than three decades, the modern Supreme Court has served as the crucial national institution that had encouraged the civil rights movement by broadly interpreting the Constitution and federal laws to protect racial minorities. The 1988 Court term, in which *Patterson* was decided, marked the end of that historic judicial era. With the advent of the conservative Rehnquist Court majority, Congress, not the Court, became the channel for civil rights activism."[135]

The notion of "winning while losing" is not an accurate descriptor for civil rights during the Reagan presidency. It might better be described as "surviving while losing." The administration launched an assault on civil rights remedies that took a visible toll. In the end, though, Congress came to the rescue and the court did not support the most extensive attacks. Civil rights proponents were surviving.

If the administration did not fully succeed in getting many issues redefined, it helped change the context for decision making. The major advance may have been the steady reduction in institutional barriers that had constrained the solicitors general. This reduction extended beyond the court. As Reynolds noted: "There were more and more places to shoot the cannon as time went on. There were more places to go that were receptive. More doors were open to advance our arguments." And if the administration left without accomplishing its goals, success was imminent. As Reynolds noted, "At the end of the second term and Bush's years, the courts were very receptive to our ideas. A great deal of our agenda eventually got through."[136]

The Waning of Support for Civil Rights

A comparison of the Eisenhower, Nixon, and Reagan administrations highlights the significant changes that had taken place by the 1980s in civil rights law and policy. Each administration faced differing institutional contexts with respect to civil rights, as shown in table 4.1. First, the types of issues that each administration faced were quite different. The clear de jure discrimination that confronted the Eisenhower administration had been replaced by the more difficult de facto discrimination issues under Nixon, and the Reagan administration had to deal with even more difficult questions of remedies.[137] The Eisenhower Justice Department was headed by what Nancy Baker called a "neutral."[138] In terms of the law enforcement–political continuum, Attorney General Brownell was closer to the legal end. Under Nixon, Attorney General John Mitchell was a political appointment in every sense of the word, and his Justice Department was more mixed in its approach. There was little shading with the Reagan administration. It fell much closer to the political end of the spectrum.[139]

Of the agencies that dealt with civil rights issues, the Eisenhower administration built and empowered some (e.g., the CRD) and maintained others (e.g., the OSG). The Nixon administration centralized power in the Justice Department. While this appeared ominous for civil rights advocates, the results were mixed. It was the Reagan administration that attempted to reorganize the civil rights agencies, emasculating one (the EEOC) and completely reorienting the direction of the other two (the CRD and the Civil Rights Commission). The administration then tried to bend the OSG to its will with some success.[140]

The Eisenhower administration reluctantly carried out its duty. The Nixon administration balanced its policies, dragging its feet on northern desegregation and remedies but building an impressive legacy combating employment discrimination. The Reagan administration attempted a full-blown retreat. No previous administration, according to Amaker, "manifested a tendency to subvert in any fundamental way the protective goals of civil rights law."[141]

Whereas presidents such as Truman, Eisenhower, Kennedy, Johnson,

Table 4.1. Republican administrations and civil rights policy

President	Type of Issue	Context and Position		Policy Responses
		Justice Dept.	Institutions	
Eisenhower	De Jure	Legal	Construction/ Maintenance	Grudging Compliance
Nixon	De Facto	Mixed	Reorganization/ Devolution	Careful Line Drawing
Reagan	Remedies	Political	Reconstruction	Retreat and Reversal

and even Nixon to some degree used the Oval Office to further civil rights, Reagan used it to slow and even reverse progress. While Congress in the 1950s and early 1960s was a barrier to civil rights, Congress in the 1980s was a barrier to retrenchment.[142] Democrats controlled the House and many Republican representatives and senators had large black constituencies they did not want to offend.[143] The agencies that had been the vehicles for positive change were now being asked to be the agents of retrenchment. The judiciary, which stood as the beacon of equal protection, was now to be the vehicle for slowing civil rights.

There was a certain irony in that the Reagan administration's three-pronged plan was designed to reverse the policies and weaken the institutions that his party had established. After all, it was Eisenhower who helped establish a viable Civil Rights Division and Civil Rights Commission, and it was Nixon whose CRD and solicitor general supported the disparate impact standard that led to affirmative action as a remedy for past discrimination.[144]

Analysts disagree about how much retrenchment of civil rights policy can actually be attributed to Ronald Reagan personally.[145] Reagan set the overall priorities for his administration but was distant and remote from the details and specifics of policy.[146] Troy argues that he was often "disengaged."[147] He was "notoriously innocent at policy specifics, but gifted at evoking larger themes."[148] Although he was not the architect of the policies, "more than any other president, Reagan used public rhetoric to change the public agenda in civil rights."[149] However one assesses Reagan's personal role, without question his administration made fundamental and enduring changes in American politics and policy, especially on civil rights.

Notes

1. James Sundquist, *Politics and Policy: The Eisenhower, Kennedy, and Johnson Years* (Washington, D.C.: Brookings Institution, 1968); Edward Carmines and James Stimson, *Issue Evolution: Race and the Transformation of American Politics* (Princeton: Princeton University Press, 1990).

2. Lincoln Caplan, *The Tenth Justice* (New York: Vintage Books, 1987); Patrick C. Wohlfarth, "The Tenth Justice? Consequences of Politicization in the Solicitor General's Office," *Journal of Politics* 71 (2009): 224–37.

3. Rebecca Salokar, *The Solicitor General: The Politics of Law* (Philadelphia: Temple University Press, 1992), 10.

4. Peter Ubertaccio III, *Learned in the Law and Politics: The Office of the Solicitor General* (New York: LFB Scholarly Publishing, 2005).

5. Richard L. Pacelle Jr., *Between Law and Politics: The Solicitor General and the Structuring of Race, Gender, and Reproductive Rights Litigation* (College Station: Texas A&M University Press, 2003).

6. Ubertaccio, *Learned in the Law and Politics*; Salokar, *The Solicitor General*.

7. Pacelle shows that in most areas of law, like federalism, regulation, and criminal cases, there is no difference in the position taken by the SG regardless of which party controls the White House. In addition, Bailey, Kamoie, and Maltzman show that the respect for the SG is the highest when the office argues a position that appears at odds with the ideological position of the president. Richard L. Pacelle Jr., "The Emergence and Evolution of Supreme Court Policy," in *Exploring Judicial Politics*, ed. Mark C. Miller (New York: Oxford University Press, 2009), 174–91; Michael Bailey, Brian Kamoie, and Forrest Maltzman, "Signals from the Tenth Justice: The Political Role of the Solicitor General in Supreme Court Decision Making," *American Journal of Political Science* 49 (2005): 72–85.

8. Pacelle, *Between Law and Politics*.

9. Pacelle, *Between Law and Politics*; Kevin McGuire, *The Supreme Court Bar: Legal Elites in the Washington Community* (Charlottesville: University of Virginia Press, 1993); Charles Epp, *The Rights Revolution: Lawyers, Activists, and Supreme Court in Comparative Perspective* (Chicago: University of Chicago Press, 1998), 60–63.

10. H. W. Perry, *Deciding to Decide: Agenda Setting in the United States Supreme Court* (Cambridge, Mass.: Harvard University Press, 1991), 132–33.

11. Kevin McGuire ("Repeat Players in the Supreme Court: The Role of Experienced Lawyers in Litigation Success," *Journal of Politics* 57, 1 (Feb. 1995): 187–96) argues that expertise is the crucial determinant of the office's success.

12. Hugh Davis Graham, *The Civil Rights Era: Origins and Development of National Policy, 1960–1972* (New York: Oxford University Press, 1990).

13. Sarah Binder and Steven Smith, *Politics or Principle?: Filibustering in the United States Senate* (Washington, D.C.: Brookings Institution, 1997).

14. Pacelle, *Between Law and Politics*, 75.

15. Charles Zelden, *The Battle for the Black Ballot: Smith v. Allwright and the Defeat of the Texas All-White Primary* (Lawrence: University Press of Kansas, 2004); Clement

Vose, *Caucasians Only: The Supreme Court, the NAACP, and the Restrictive Covenant Cases* (Berkeley: University of California Press, 1959).

16. Richard Kluger, *Simple Justice* (New York: Knopf, 1975).

17. Paul Light, *The President's Agenda: Domestic Policy Choice from Kennedy to Carter* (Baltimore: Johns Hopkins University Press, 1982), 104.

18. Brian Landsberg, *Enforcing Civil Rights: Race Discrimination and the Department of Justice* (Lawrence: University Press of Kansas, 1997).

19. Robert McCloskey, *The American Supreme Court* (Chicago: University of Chicago Press, 1960); Richard L. Pacelle Jr., Bryan W. Marshall, and Brett W. Curry, "Keepers of the Covenant or Platonic Guardians: Decision Making on the United States Supreme Court," *American Politics Research* 35 (2007): 694–724.

20. Mark Tushnet, *The New Constitutional Order* (Princeton: Princeton University Press, 2003); Richard L. Pacelle Jr., *The Transformation of the Supreme Court's Agenda: From the New Deal to the Reagan Administration* (Boulder: Westview Press, 1991). In addition to delivering on the promise of civil rights, the court realigned the First Amendment and expanded the rights of the accused. A number of free-speech cases involved protests by civil rights activists in the South. The landmark decision that redefined libel law, *New York Times v. Sullivan*, was based on a civil rights advertisement in the newspaper (Anthony Lewis, *Make No Law: The Sullivan Case and the First Amendment* [New York: Vintage Books, 1991]). In criminal procedure, the court restarted the process of incorporating provisions of the Bill of Rights into the states to help protect minorities in the South. Samuel Walker, *In Defense of American Liberties: A History of the ACLU* (New York: Oxford University Press, 1990); Richard Cortner, *The Supreme Court and the Second Bill of Rights: The Fourteenth Amendment and the Nationalization of Civil Rights* (Madison: University of Wisconsin Press, 1981).

21. Stephen Wasby, "How Planned is 'Planned Litigation'?" *American Bar Foundation Research Journal* 32 (1984): 83–138; Stephen Wasby, *Race Relations Litigation in an Age of Complexity* (Charlottesville: University of Virginia Press, 1995); Jack Greenberg, *Crusaders in the Court* (New York: Basic Books, 1994).

22. Timothy R. Johnson, *Oral Arguments and Decision Making on the United States Supreme Court* (Albany: State University of New York Press, 2004); Pacelle, *Between Law and Politics*.

23. Paul Collins Jr., *Friends of the Supreme Court: Interest Groups and Judicial Decision Making* (New York: Oxford University Press, 2008).

24. There were forty-four cases in which the SG had taken a position prior to the Nixon administration, and in each one, regardless of the administration, the office supported civil rights claimants. The Nixon solicitors general supported civil rights claimants in 22 of the 28 cases argued during his term and a half. Pacelle, *Between Law and Politics*.

25. Marissa Martino Golden, *What Motivates Bureaucrats?: Politics and Administration During the Reagan Years* (New York: Columbia University Press, 2000), 83.

26. Eisenhower invited Warren to a dinner and sat the chief justice between himself and former solicitor general John Davis, who was arguing the case on behalf of the school districts. Eisenhower praised Davis and expressed the hope that little

white girls would not have to go to school with big black boys. Robert Frederick Burk, *The Eisenhower Administration and Black Civil Rights* (Knoxville: University of Tennessee Press, 1984), 142.

27. John Anderson, *Eisenhower, Brownell, and the Congress: The Tangled Origins of the Civil Rights Bill of 1956–1957* (Tuscaloosa: University of Alabama Press, 1964), 43. David Nichols, *A Matter of Justice: Eisenhower and the Beginning of the Civil Rights Revolution* (New York: Simon & Schuster, 2007).

28. Robert Dixon, "The Attorney General and Civil Rights 1870–1964," In *Roles of the Attorney General of the United States*, ed. Luther Huston, Arthur Selwyn Miller, Samuel Krislov, and Robert Dixon (Washington, D.C.: American Enterprise Institute, 1968), 122.

29. Burk, *The Eisenhower Administration and Black Civil Rights*, 143. Nichols, *A Matter of Justice*.

30. Alfred Blumrosen, *Modern Law: The Law Transmission System and Equal Employment Opportunity* (Madison: University of Wisconsin Press, 1993).

31. Fried, *Order and Law*, 122–27.

32. William Eskridge, *Dynamic Statutory Interpretation* (Cambridge, Mass.: Harvard University Press, 1994); Pacelle, *Between Law and Politics*.

33. Pacelle, *Between Law and Politics*; Landsberg, *Enforcing Civil Rights*.

34. Pacelle, *Between Law and Politics*.

35. Cornell Clayton, *The Politics of Justice: The Attorney General and the Making of Legal Policy* (Armonk, N.Y.: M.E. Sharpe, 1992).

36. Under the Voting Rights Act, states with a history of discrimination in voting laws and procedures could not implement changes to voting procedures without "preclearing" proposed revisions with the Department of Justice.

37. Interview with Jerris Leonard.

38. Landsberg, *Enforcing Civil Rights*, 144–45.

39. Interview with Jerris Leonard.

40. Robert Detlefsen, *Civil Rights Under Reagan* (San Francisco: Institute for Contemporary Studies, 1991).

41. Norman Amaker, *Civil Rights and the Reagan Administration* (Washington, D.C.: Urban Institute, 1988), 157.

42. Bernard Schwartz, *The Ascent of Pragmatism: The Burger Court in Action* (Reading: Addison-Wesley, 1990).

43. Amaker, *Civil Rights and the Reagan Administration*, 157–59.

44. Pacelle, *Between Law and Politics*.

45. Sheldon Goldman, *Picking Federal Judges: Lower Court Selection from Roosevelt Through Reagan* (New Haven: Yale University Press, 1997).

46. Following a script laid out by liberal groups, there was a rise of conservative public law interest groups who filed amicus briefs, lobbied the legislature, and fought for and against judicial nominees. They helped the Reagan administration structure litigation and monitored the lower courts. Lee Epstein, *Conservatives in Court* (Knoxville: University of Tennessee Press, 1985); Steven Teles, *The Rise of the Conservative Legal Movement: The Battle for Control of the Law* (Princeton: Princeton University Press, 2008).

47. Perry, *Deciding to Decide*.

48. Pacelle, *Between Law and Politics*.

49. Herman Schwartz, *Packing the Court: The Conservative Campaign to Rewrite the Constitution* (New York: Scribners, 1988), 182.

50. Raymond Wolters, *Right Turn: William Bradford Reynolds, the Reagan Administration, and Black Civil Rights* (New Brunswick, N.J.: Transaction, 1996), 24–33.

51. Caplan, *The Tenth Justice*; Pacelle, *Between Law and Politics*.

52. Golden, *What Motivates Bureaucrats?*, 84–88.

53. William Gormley, *Taming the Bureaucracy: Muscles, Prayer, and Other Strategies* (Princeton: Princeton University Press, 1989), 173–74.

54. Kim Isaac Eisler, *A Justice For All: William J. Brennan, Jr., and the Decisions That Transformed America* (New York: Simon & Schuster, 1993), 263.

55. Once the disparate impact standard was put into effect, it became an easy way for businesses to show that they were complying with anti-discrimination laws. Eskridge, *Dynamic Statutory Interpretation*.

56. William French Smith, *Law & Justice in the Reagan Administration: Memoirs of an Attorney General* (Stanford: Hoover Institution Press, 1991), 90–93.

57. Civil rights advocates, most notably the Legal Defense Fund, were famous for personalizing their cases. Constitutional principles were funneled through portraits of Ada Sipuel, Lloyd Gaines, and Linda Brown to humanize the cases for the justices. Now it was Paul Johnson and Wendy Wygant, whites who did nothing to discriminate but were victims of affirmative-action programs.

58. Henry J. Abraham, *Justices, Presidents, and Senators* (Lanham, Md.: Rowman and Littlefield, 1999); Lee Epstein and Jeffrey Segal, *Advice and Consent: The Politics of Judicial Appointments* (New York: Oxford University Press, 2005).

59. Stephen Macedo, *The New Right v. the Constitution*. 2nd ed. (Washington, D.C.: Cato Institute, 1987).

60. Interview with David Rose.

61. David O'Brien, "The Reagan Judges: His Most Enduring Legacy?" in *The Reagan Legacy*, ed. Charles Jones (Chatham: Chatham House, 1988), 63.

62. Interview with W. Bradford Reynolds.

63. O'Brien, "The Reagan Judges."

64. Reagan alone appointed just under 50 percent of the federal judges in his two terms. Cal Jillson, *American Government: Political Change and Institutional Development* (New York: Routledge, 2007), 338.

65. Richard Pacelle, *The Role of the Supreme Court in American Politics: The Least Dangerous Branch?* (Boulder: Westview Press, 2002).

66. The preferred-position doctrine comes from footnote 4 in the *United States v. Carolene Products* decision. Justice Stone argued that civil liberties and the rights of insular minorities should be held in a preferred position. This ultimately led to a majority opinion and became the dominant standard on the court. The doctrine stood for the proposition that the burden of proof for a restriction on rights or liberties fell on the government. Pacelle, *The Transformation of the Supreme Court's Agenda*.

67. Tushnet, *The New Constitutional Order*; Pacelle, *The Transformation of the Supreme Court's Agenda*.

68. Tinsley Yarbrough, *The Rehnquist Court and the Constitution* (New York: Oxford University Press, 2000).

69. Lee Epstein, Jeffrey Segal, Harold Spaeth, and Thomas Walker, *The Supreme Court Compendium*, 3rd ed. (Washington, D.C.: Congressional Quarterly, 2003), 232–35.

70. O'Brien, "The Reagan Judges."

71. Ibid., 62.

72. Golden, *What Motivates Bureaucrats?*, 85.

73. Ibid., 5–8.

74. Ibid., 85.

75. Graham, *The Civil Rights Era*, 8.

76. Golden, *What Motivates Bureaucrats?*, 83–86.

77. Pacelle, *Between Law and Politics*.

78. Richard L. Pacelle Jr., "*Amicus Curiae* or *Amicus Praesidentis*? Reexamining the Role of the Office of the Solicitor General in Filing *Amici*," *Judicature* 89 (2006): 317–25.

79. Joel Selig, "The Reagan Justice Department and Civil Rights: What Went Wrong?" *University of Illinois Law Review* (1985): 789.

80. Landsberg, *Enforcing Civil Rights*, 68; Selig, "The Reagan Justice Department and Civil Rights," 787–88.

81. Interview with Edwin Kneedler.

82. Pacelle, *Between Law and Politics*, 168.

83. Neal Devins, "Unitariness and Independence: Solicitor General Control over Independent Agency Litigation," *California Law Review* 82 (1994): 297–99.

84. Ibid., 293.

85. Interview with Rose.

86. Devins, "Unitariness and Independence," 294.

87. Steven Shull, *A Kinder, Gentler Racism? The Reagan-Bush Civil Rights Legacy* (Armonk, N.Y.: M.E. Sharpe, 1993), 112–17.

88. Golden, *What Motivates Bureaucrats?*

89. Caplan, *The Tenth Justice*, 218–20.

90. Ibid., 218–28.

91. Interview with Reynolds.

92. Selig, "The Reagan Justice Department and Civil Rights," 820.

93. Selig, "The Reagan Justice Department and Civil Rights," 821; Golden, *What Motivates Bureaucrats?*

94. Caplan, *The Tenth Justice*, 61–62.

95. Salokar, *The Solicitor General*.

96. Interview with Donald Ayer.

97. Interview with Kneedler.

98. Salokar, *The Solicitor General*, 55.

99. Caplan, *The Tenth Justice*, 87–99.

100. Wolters, *Right Turn*, 232.

101. Interview with Reynolds.

102. Interview with Reynolds.

103. Charles Fried, *Order and Law: Arguing the Reagan Revolution* (New York: Simon & Schuster, 1991), 41–42.

104. Interview with Rose.

105. Pacelle, *Between Law and Politics.*

106. Caplan, *The Tenth Justice,* 107.

107. Interview with Reynolds.

108. Caplan, *The Tenth Justice,* 102–7.

109. Wohlfarth, "The Tenth Justice?"

110. Pacelle, *Between Law and Politics.*

111. It was not unusual for the position of solicitor general to be a stepping-stone to a seat on the Supreme Court. Certainly, many solicitors general have been seriously considered when a vacancy occurred. But there had been none between Thurgood Marshall and Elena Kagan (Robert Bork was nominated). Part of this may have been a function of the lesser rank of recent solicitors general, but more likely it has to do with the fact that many became political lightning rods while serving as SG, which hurt their chances of gaining Senate confirmation to the court.

112. Pacelle, *Between Law and Politics,* 269.

113. Gil Troy, *Morning in America: How Ronald Reagan Invented the 1980s* (Princeton: Princeton University Press, 2005), 42.

114. Tinsley Yarbrough, *David Hackett Souter: Traditional Republican on the Rehnquist Court* (New York: Oxford University Press, 2005).

115. Thomas Keck, *The Most Activist Supreme Court in History: The Road to Modern Judicial Conservatism* (Chicago: University of Chicago Press, 2004).

116. Wolters, *Right Turn,* 283.

117. Fried, *Order and Law,* 129.

118. James Simon, *The Center Holds: The Power Struggle Inside the Rehnquist Court* (New York: Simon & Schuster, 1995), 81.

119. Blumrosen, *Modern Law,* 285.

120. Fried, *Order and Law,* 122–24.

121. David Savage, *Turning Right: The Making of the Rehnquist Supreme Court* (New York: Wiley, 1992), 191.

122. Simon, *The Center Holds,* 4–8.

123. Justice Scalia expressed dissatisfaction with the attorneys trying to overturn *Runyon.* In response to a point, Scalia said, "If that's all you have, I'm afraid it is nothing." Savage claimed, "Scalia would need ammunition to fight for overturning *Runyon,* but the attorneys had not given him any." Savage, *Turning Right,* 223.

124. Interview with Charles Fried.

125. Fried, *Order and Law,* 125–29.

126. Ibid., 125–26.

127. Simon, *The Center Holds,* 42.

128. Caplan, *The Tenth Justice,* 240.

129. Interview with Fried.

130. Wolters, *Right Turn,* 113–21.

131. Caplan, *The Tenth Justice,* 243.

132. Interview with Reynolds.

133. Interview with Fried.

134. Interview with Reynolds.

135. Simon, *The Center Holds*, 81.

136. Interview with Reynolds.

137. Interview with Lawrence Wallace.

138. Nancy Baker, *Conflicting Loyalties: Law and Politics in the Attorney General's Office, 1789–1990* (Lawrence: University Press of Kansas, 1992).

139. Ibid.

140. Caplan, *The Tenth Justice*.

141. Amaker, *Civil Rights and the Reagan Administration*, 28.

142. Gary Orfield, "Congress and Civil Rights: From Obstacle to Protector," in *African Americans and the Living Constitution*, ed. John Hope Franklin and Genna Rae McNeil (Washington, D.C.: Smithsonian Institution Press, 1995); Stephen Wasby, "A Triangle Transformed: Court, Congress, and Presidency in Civil Rights," *Policy Studies Journal* 21 (1993): 565–74.

143. Southern hegemony over the committees had been broken by the passing of some veteran southern Democrats and the migration of others to the Republican Party.

144. Bernard Schwartz, *The Ascent of Pragmatism: The Burger Court in Action* (Reading, Mass.: Addison-Wesley, 1990).

145. Stephen Skowronek, *The Politics Presidents Make: Leadership from John Adams to Bill Clinton* (Cambridge, Mass.: Belknap Press, 1997), 411.

146. Fred Greenstein, *The Presidential Difference: Leadership Style from FDR to George W. Bush*, 2nd ed. (New York: The Free Press, 2004), 150.

147. Troy, *Morning in America*, 340.

148. Norman Thomas and Joseph Pika, *The Politics of the Presidency*, 4th ed. (Washington, D.C.: CQ Press, 1997), 182.

149. Andrew Busch, *Ronald Reagan and the Politics of Freedom* (New York: Rowman & Littlefield, 2001), 28.

5

CIVIL RIGHTS POLICYMAKING
IN THE CLINTON
ADMINISTRATION

In Reagan's Shadow

ROBERT C. SMITH

Bill Clinton was elected, and to some extent governed, in the shadows of Ronald Reagan. Reagan was a "reconstructive" president. That is, like FDR, Lincoln, Jefferson, and Jackson, he brought an end to one "political time" and started a new one that changed the terms or conditions of electoral competition and political debate. This paper examines the impact of Reagan's reconstructive presidency on the Clinton administration's civil rights policymaking. Specifically, I compare the policies of Reagan and Clinton on two fronts: affirmative action and welfare reform. In each of these policy areas Clinton's initiatives consolidated and legitimated the Reagan revolution and extended its time. This comparative assessment of the two presidencies demonstrates in all its complexities and contradictions the volume's theme of winning while losing in the post–civil rights era.

Reagan's Reconstructive Presidency

In his innovative study, *The Politics Presidents Make*, Stephen Skrowronek identifies Reagan as one of the most transformative American presidents. When Skrowronek identifies Reagan as a great president, however, he is not playing some presidential rating game. Rather, he is locating presidents in "political time," that is, not in relationship to their individual achievements per se but rather in relationship to previously established governing regimes. According to Skrowronek, Reagan is a reconstructive president because he repudiated an old regime and inaugurated a new one. By contrast, LBJ is a mere "articulator" since his landmark accomplishments (Medicare, civil rights, environmental regulations, and aid to education and the arts) simply continued the work of FDR's reconstructive presidency.[1]

Reagan's reconstructive presidency, however, lacked a generation-defining policy and its principal success was repudiating New Deal liberalism.[2] He successfully discredited liberalism, arguing that it was inconsistent with the nation's founding principles and values. Reagan's greatness as a leader is, therefore, negative and lies not in what he accomplished but in what he prevented. In other words, he closed off the opportunities for further liberal, activist government. Reagan accomplished this because "like no other politician since Franklin Roosevelt he made very good use of language and sentiments to tap into the wellspring of traditional beliefs and values which were associated with an old fashioned patriotism, on the one hand, a commitment to free markets and individual opportunity, on the other."[3] In doing this Reagan became the "Roosevelt of the right."[4]

This was a historic accomplishment for sure, but it was more symbolic than substantive. Despite the potency of symbolism, Skrowronek argues that Reagan's policy accomplishments were far from great or reconstructive. Putting aside his contested role in bringing about the collapse of the Soviet Union and the end of the Cold War,[5] Skrowronek concludes that in general the "Reagan revolution was a single shot affair," largely the adoption in its first year of huge tax cuts and a massive increase in military expenditures.[6] The result of these policies was huge deficits and debt—a deficit trap—perhaps intentionally created to "starve the beast," the federal government.[7]

In general, then, Reagan's major "reconstructive" accomplishment was delegitimizing liberalism, turning it by the time he left office into the dreaded "L" word to be avoided by politicians with presidential ambitions.[8] Related to this delegitimization of liberalism was the reinforcement in the political culture of skepticism toward the role of government—especially the federal government—as an agent of positive change. And, finally, related to both, Reagan turned taxes into the dreaded "T" word to be avoided as well by politicians with national ambitions. Thus, in Reagan's reconstruction, taxes became not the price of civilization but nutrients for the beast of a wasteful welfare state.

Reagan's delegitimization of liberalism specifically relied on undermining the victories and framework of the civil rights movement. Throughout his career Reagan opposed all civil rights legislation, contending that such legislation infringed on either the rights of the states or the rights of individuals. And while he was hostile to the welfare state in general, he reserved his most venomous rhetoric for those parts of it designed for or disproportionately serving the needs of the poor and African Americans. Thus, he repeatedly attacked the "failed" Great Society programs of the 1960s, that is, affirmative action and "welfare." He declared that affirmative action was reverse discrimination. With respect to welfare—specifically Aid to Families with Dependent Children (AFDC)—through his rhetoric Reagan reinforced in American lore the idea of the welfare recipient as the "welfare queen": the lazy, promiscuous, Cadillac-driving black woman who would rather live off the labor of others than work.[9]

Overall, Reagan helped to popularize the neoconservative reframing of the policy debate on race. Although today's "neocons" are better known for their concerns about foreign policy, the rise of the movement in the late 1960s and early 1970s was largely built upon domestic issues— the student rebellions, the ghetto riots, black power, the Great Society, and the emergent feminist movement.[10] By the time Reagan assumed the presidency, neoconservatives had reframed the debate on race, shifting the responsibility for dealing with the problem of racialized poverty away from the government and toward the black community itself.

Conservative and neoconservative intellectuals began to attack the black community in the late 1960s on cultural grounds, arguing that the problem of poverty among blacks was not systemic (functions of structural unemployment and racism) but cultural, the functions of morally irresponsible sexual behavior, the absence of individual initiative and willingness to work, the decline of "family values," and the absence of community self-help.[11]

Reagan was a product of this movement. That is, Reagan was not simply a conservative in the sense that Eisenhower, Nixon, and Gerald Ford were conservatives. Reagan was a movement conservative. Indeed, after Goldwater's defeat in 1964 Reagan became the movement's most articulate and popular spokesman. As Burnham puts it, Reagan was the conservative movement's "charismatic prophet."[12]

In the Shadow of the Reagan Democrats: The Politics of Preemption

Reagan's reconstruction destabilized the dominant party coalition by turning key Democratic Party constituencies into reliable Republican voters. The conservative movement's destabilization of FDR's coalition began in 1964 when Barry Goldwater won the Republican nomination. Although Goldwater lost the general election to LBJ's landslide, his nomination effectively secured conservative control of the Republican Party. In addition, by winning four Deep South states, Goldwater launched the party's "southern strategy" that would in the long run result in the white South abandoning FDR's coalition to become the core GOP constituency. This disruption, however, was anticipated, with LBJ telling Bill Moyers on the evening of his signing of the 1964 Civil Rights Act, "I think we just delivered the South to the Republican Party for a long time."[13] What was not so easily anticipated was the emergence of a conservative, racist bloc in the North.

In the 1964 Democratic primaries Alabama Governor George Wallace challenged President Johnson and won 43 percent of the vote in Maryland, 34 percent in Wisconsin, and 30 percent in Indiana. In late 1964 David Danzig wrote that in cities throughout the North, Italian, Jewish, Irish, and Polish Americans—what by the end of the Reagan presidency would be called Reagan Democrats—were beginning to rebel against government efforts to promote racial equality. Foreseeing the coalition Reagan would consolidate in the 1980s, Danzig wrote, "the old conservative slogans that served in the fight against the New Deal and the welfare state—'federal tyranny,' 'preservation of the Constitution,' 'American individualism'—are being applied to the civil rights struggle and used as a new rallying point cry for the right wing."[14] It was the maturation of this incipient racist, rightist bloc that helped bring Reagan to power in 1980.

After Reagan's landslide reelection in 1984 worried Democratic Party elites, they hired Stanley Greenberg, a Yale political scientist who had specialized in the study of racism in South Africa and the American South, to study why Reagan had done so well among traditional, working-class Democrats in the North.[15] Greenberg conducted a detailed study of Reagan Democrats in Macomb County, Michigan. Greenberg wrote, "The story of Macomb could be replicated with somewhat less drama in white, home owning, working and middle class enclaves across the United States."[16] Ninety-seven percent white, the typical Macomb resident was a high-school graduate working in manufacturing with an income above the national median. These Democrats, Greenberg found, voted for Reagan not out of concern for social or moral issues such as abortion or school prayer but because of race. Greenberg described their views as "awful . . . clearly racist."[17] First, they "rejected out of hand the social justice claims of black Americans. . . . They had no historical memory of racism and no tolerance for present efforts to offset it."[18] Second, they viewed blacks as violent, lazy, whining, and as a people who would rather live off welfare than work. Third, they viewed the Democratic Party as the party of blacks, while the Republican Party, because of its opposition to welfare, busing, and affirmative action and its support of "law and order," was viewed as the party of the hard-working, beleaguered white middle class.[19]

In 1960 JFK had won Macomb County with 63 percent of the vote and in 1964 LBJ won with 74 percent. In 1968 Nixon received no more votes than Goldwater did, but Wallace won 20 percent of Macomb County (in 1972 Wallace won 66 percent of the County in the Democratic primaries). In 1980 Reagan nearly equaled Johnson's proportion of the vote, winning 67 percent.[20]

After twelve years of Republican presidencies, Bill Clinton knew he had to get the votes of Reagan Democrats. When Clinton decided to run for president in 1992, he asked Greenberg to become his pollster. In order to win and govern effectively, Clinton, Greenberg said, had to appeal to the interests and sentiments of the voters of Macomb County. That is, he was advised to distance his campaign from the concerns of blacks and the poor and to embrace nontraditional Democratic positions on crime, welfare, and affirmative action.[21] Although Clinton was said to have been "appalled" by Greenberg's findings, he heeded his advice in the conduct of his successful 1992 campaign.[22] He nevertheless lost Macomb, winning 38 percent of the vote compared to George H. W. Bush's 43 percent and independent Ross Perot's 20 percent.[23] Despite failing to return Macomb to the Democratic Party column, Clinton ascended to the White House.

In His Own Shadow: Bill Clinton and the Question of Character

As the first Democratic president after Reagan, Clinton was what Skrow-ronek calls a "preemptive president." According to the political scientist, preemptive presidents play a kind of juggling act. That is, they seek to simultaneously maintain the allegiances of their party's traditional constituencies, institutional and ideological, while preempting or co-opting aspects of the reconstructive president's constituencies and agenda. Preemptive presidents attempt to do this in both campaigning and governing in order to "assuage" their own base while "aggravate[ing] interest cleavages and factional discontent within the dominant coalition, for therein lies the prospect for broadening their base of support and sharpening their departure from the received formulas."[24]

On several salient issues of race, Clinton implicitly or directly repudiated Democratic Party orthodoxy. However, on other issues he rejected the Reagan reconstruction. For example, he sought to expand the New Deal by pursuing a Great Society welfare state with national health insurance. In terms of social and moral issues, he supported full reproductive rights for women and became the first president to endorse civil rights protections for homosexuals.

Preemptive presidents, Skrowronek writes, "are often singled out for flaws of character."[25] This was certainly the case with Clinton, who during the 1992 campaign was referred to as "slick Willie." James MacGregor Burns, author of perhaps the best book on leadership, is the harshest critic of Clinton's lack of leadership character.[26] In his assessment of the Clinton presidency, Burns writes that the only constant in Clinton's career was "his continuously recalculated self-interest."[27] Elsewhere he described Clinton as "pragmatic," as having "no values, no ideas that are not up for trade," and as the "wavering Clinton . . . between centrism and somewhere left of center."[28]

Yet even Burns acknowledges that if Clinton was firmly committed to any one cause it was racial justice, writing, "deep in his heart Bill Clinton always had a passionate desire for justice and equality. . . . It was etched in his soul, his music, his marriage and his early life experiences."[29] David Maranis, the author of the best Clinton biography, concurs, writing of Clinton's days at Oxford that Clinton was the house liberal on civil rights "a Martin Luther King man through and through. . . . He had memorized King's famous "I Have A Dream" speech. . . . Race had always been the issue with which he defined himself as a progressive son of the new South."[30] Arthur Schlesinger Jr. wrote of Clinton, "Racial justice appears to be his most authentic concern."[31] On race, then, Clinton was caught between the light in his soul and the shadows of Reagan and Macomb.

Two Issues in the Shadows: Affirmative Action and Welfare

Scholarship on the civil rights movement has often ignored African American concerns with the economy and the welfare state, but as Charles and Dona Hamilton make clear, "in every decade beginning with the inception of the modern American welfare state in the New Deal . . . there have always been two agendas—civil rights and social welfare."[32] Indeed, the famous 1963 March on Washington was initially planned as a march for jobs rather than civil rights.[33] In the last year of his life Dr. King's Poor People's Campaign focused on the economy and the welfare state, proposing full employment and a guaranteed income.[34] And at a major post–civil rights era meeting of black leaders, the economy and the welfare state were central items on its "Seven Point Mandate." The first two items on this 1976 agenda were a full-employment economy and welfare reform to include "a guaranteed annual income . . . not laden down with punitive counterproductive (forced) work requirements."[35]

The civil rights leadership viewed affirmative action as the cornerstone of post–civil rights era policy. Although affirmative action in employment goes back to the New Deal, in its modern form it started in the middle 1960s as a policy designed to remedy or compensate groups for past discrimination and to enforce the nondiscrimination provisions of the Civil Rights Act of 1964.[36] Today supporters view affirmative action as the core of post–civil rights era policy because it is believed to be an indispensable mechanism for bridging the disparities between blacks and whites in terms of education, employment, and income. Affirmative-action policies continue a long tradition of the dual agenda of civil rights and social welfare.

Concern with economic issues is as old as the post–Civil War era quest for forty acres and a mule as a means to provide an economic underpinning for the emancipated slaves. However, until the New Deal, blacks, like most Americans, tended not to look to the government for solutions to the problems of poverty and joblessness. The Great Depression and the New Deal changed all of this, as the federal government for the first time assumed responsibility for the employment and income security of the people. As discussed below, African Americans were unsuccessful in their efforts to shape the Social Security Act in a nondiscriminatory way. Nevertheless, since the New Deal African American civil rights organizations have focused on the economy—full employment and welfare—and some kind of race-based allocation of jobs.[37]

Affirmative action and welfare reform then are excellent cases for studying the shadow of Reagan over civil rights policymaking in the Clinton administration. Reagan throughout his public career had inveighed against the welfare state in general and "welfare" (AFDC) specifically. He opposed affirmative action from the beginning, arguing that it violated fundamental American principles of individualism and the civil rights movement's principle of a color-blind society.

Affirmative Action

President Johnson laid out the philosophical rationale for affirmative action in his 1965 commencement address at Howard University. The President said, "You do not take a person who, for years, has been hobbled by chains and liberate him, bring him up to the starting line of a race and then say 'you are free to compete with others,' and still justly believe you have been completely fair."[38] President Nixon codified Johnson's philosophy in his 1971 revision of Johnson's Executive Order 11246 requiring government contractors to develop affirmative-action plans with "goals and timetables" for training, hiring, and promoting blacks and other minorities. Nixon's order became the model for affirmative-action plans in all sectors of American society and at all levels of government.

From its beginning neoconservatives attacked affirmative action, commencing with Nathan Glazer's influential 1975 polemic, *Affirmative Discrimination*.[39] Although neoconservative critics objected to affirmative action on multiple grounds (contending it was racially divisive, stigmatized minorities, and lowered educational and employment standards), their fundamental concern was that it violated the classical liberal principle of individualism, the idea that people should be treated as individuals and not as members of groups. The neoconservatives and Reagan also contended that Nixon's goals and timetables were mere euphemisms for racial preferences and quotas and for a racial "spoils system" in employment, higher education, and government contracting.

Thus, it was widely anticipated that Reagan would, once elected, keep his promise to with a "stroke of the pen" revise or revoke Nixon's order.

President Reagan almost certainly wanted to substantially revise or revoke the order. But in the decade since its promulgation Nixon's order had developed powerful constituencies, including the civil rights and feminist communities, important elements of the business community (including the National Association of Manufacturers and the Business Roundtable), and moderates and traditional conservatives within Reagan's own party and cabinet.[40] Neoconservatives, "movement" conservatives, small businesspeople, and some elements of the Jewish community joined together in a loose "color blind coalition" to support revocation of the order.[41] White House assistants Edwin Meese and Patrick Buchanan strongly supported overturning Nixon's order. But traditionalist conservatives and moderates in the administration were equally strong in support of its retention. Support among moderates was based partly on a sincere commitment to the purposes of the order, as well as on a concern that any attempt to change it would be portrayed as racist or anti–civil rights, which might undermine the Republican Party's appeal to minorities and women. There was apparently also some concern that an attack on affirmative action might adversely affect the president's chances for reelection, so it was decided to postpone any decision until after the 1984 election.[42]

After Reagan was reelected, Meese became attorney general. Shortly thereafter, Meese sent to the White House a comprehensive set of recommendations proposing to revise 11246 "to prohibit the use of quotas and numerical goals and timetables on the part of firms that contract with the federal government."[43] In addition, the attorney general's package included numerous draft documents: a presidential letter to members of Congress, letters to newspapers, talking points for the White House press secretary, and letters to Republican congressional leaders asking for their support. Clearly Meese and his Justice Department colleagues planned for rapid implementation of the recommendations and a massive public relations campaign.

Instead of transmitting the recommendations to the president, White House Chief of Staff Don Regan on October 22, 1985, (seven months later) convened a meeting of the White House Domestic Council to consider what, if any, recommendations should be sent to the president.[44] The Council was deeply divided. Joining with Meese and Buchanan

(White House communications director) in favor of the revisions was Bradford Reynolds, the acting associate attorney general; Clarence Pendleton, chair of the Civil Rights Commission; William Bennett, the education secretary; and Clarence Thomas, chair of the EEOC. The opposition was lead by William Brock, the secretary of labor (the department responsible for administering the order) and included Secretary of State George Shultz (who was labor secretary in the Nixon administration when Executive Order 11246 was adopted), Treasury Secretary James Baker, Transportation Secretary Elizabeth Dole, and HUD Secretary Samuel Pierce.[45]

The divided Council decided to send Reagan four options: 1) revising the language to strengthen the existing ban on quotas; 2) allowing federal contractors to voluntarily use goals and timetables; 3) completely banning the use of goals and timetables; and 4) implementing no changes in the existing order.[46]

Although it is not completely clear from the available records at the Reagan Library, apparently given the divisions in the Council, Don Regan decided not to submit any options to the president.[47] Regan was aware of widespread opposition in Congress. By June 1986 69 senators and 182 representatives had publicly announced their opposition to any changes in the order, and many had sent personal letters to the president. Opposition was almost unanimous among Democrats, and among those publicly opposed to any revisions were Republican congressional leaders Bob Dole and Bob Michaels.

Although Reagan might have had the votes at least in the House to sustain a veto of legislation, the battle would have divided his cabinet and his party in Congress and led to a rancorous, racially polarized debate throughout the country.

In the speech prepared by the Justice Department for Reagan's delivery on national television announcing his revocation of the order, Reagan would have said, "'Affirmative action' is discrimination pure and simple. . . . Purely and simply, affirmative action as it has developed in this country has nothing whatsoever to do with civil rights; affirmative action is in violation of every traditional value of civil rights."[48]

Reagan, of course, did not deliver the speech; by deciding not to decide, he maintained a policy he had unwaveringly opposed since its inception. How does one account for Reagan's failure to keep his promise? Reagan had two overarching goals: tax cuts coupled with reductions in the size of the domestic budget, and the expansion of the military. All else he generally left to his staff. And since the staff was divided, Reagan simply decided not to decide.[49]

Nevertheless conservative scholars are sharply critical of the president's failure to revoke 11246.[50] Nicholas Laham, for example, writes of Reagan's "confused, contradictory positions on affirmative action" and states that the president on affirmative action was a "self-serving politician who was willing to sacrifice his conservative philosophical beliefs in order to protect the interests of the Republican Party, especially its moderate wing, whose members shared the same liberal views on civil rights as their Democratic counterparts." Thus, like many conservatives, Laham concludes, "having survived the most conservative administration in modern history, affirmative action gained new legitimacy."[51]

On affirmative action Clinton operated in two shadows, Macomb County and Reagan's nondecision on the issue. The voters in Macomb were bitterly opposed to affirmative action, viewing it as a "give away" program. That is, respondents told Greenberg that affirmative action was taking jobs and places in school from qualified whites to give them to undeserving blacks—a view shared by more than three quarters of whites.[52] Thus, during the 1992 campaign Clinton waffled on the issue— supporting affirmative action but opposing quotas—caught between Macomb and Harlem. In this, he was following in Carter's footsteps, as Crespino and Smith show in their essay for this volume.

Once he assumed the presidency Clinton continued to waffle. An early indication of the president's ambivalence was the case of *Taxman v. Piscataway*.[53] The case involved the decision of the Piscataway, New Jersey, school district to lay off a white rather than a black teacher in order to maintain some racial diversity on its business-school faculty, which had one black faculty among thirteen. Taxman, the white teacher, sued claiming that while the black teacher was equally qualified in terms of credentials and tenure, to base the layoff decision openly and solely on race was a violation of Title VII of the 1964 Civil Rights Act. At the district and circuit courts she prevailed, and the school district appealed. The Supreme Court granted review and the elder Bush administration in its waning days filed an amicus brief supporting Taxman's position. Initially, the Clinton administration said it would rescind the Bush brief and refile in support of the school district. However, with the president's review and approval, the Office of the Solicitor General reversed this position.

In its brief filed with the Supreme Court the Clinton administration argued that while some race-conscious remedies were permissible under Title VII, the layoff of Taxman solely on the basis of race imposed an unjustified and unnecessary burden on her and therefore was legally impermissible.[54]

Although the school district's case seemed an eminently defensible one to many scholars of affirmative-action jurisprudence as well as to three dissenting judges on the Third Circuit, the Clinton administration's unwillingness to offer a defense and concern about the court's conservative tilt on affirmative action led black leaders to negotiate an arrangement that rendered the case moot.[55]

The administration's flip-flop on the case reflected the president's own shadow. He was strongly committed to affirmative action as a tool to remedy racial injustices, but he was also concerned that its racial nature engendered widespread concern among whites about preferences and quotas, some of which he viewed as legitimate. Although the president never considered outright revocation of the order, he apparently did give some consideration to the abolition of race-based affirmative action in favor of a class-based approach.[56] Dick Morris, his principal strategist, advocated this class approach, arguing that affirmative action based on income and residence would deprive the Republicans of the issue in the 1996 election.[57]

Several factors militated against adopting Morris' recommendation. First, the president's own sense that a class-based approach might not be adequate to deal with the problem of "continuing racial and gender disparities in employment, income and business ownership."[58] Second, most of his senior staff and cabinet supported retention of race-based affirmative action. Third, the black leadership establishment was unwavering in its support of the retention of Nixon's order. Related to this unwavering support, Clinton "knew if he wobbled on affirmative action, he would be susceptible to an electoral challenge from Jesse Jackson, either as an independent or in the Democratic primaries."[59]

In 1995 Clinton directed the White House staff to conduct a comprehensive review of all federal affirmative-action programs. The review was headed by George Stephanopoulos, a senior policy advisor, and Christopher Edley, an African American, who served as associate director of the Office of Management and Budget, both supporters of retention of the Order in its race-based form.[60] During the course of the review the

Supreme Court in *Adarand v. Peña* significantly narrowed the constitutionally permissible scope of affirmative action.[61] This allowed the administration to sharply cut back affirmative action while defending it in principle.[62]

On July 19, 1995, the president gave his "mend it, don't end it" speech before a largely black audience in Washington. Clinton said, "Let me be clear about what affirmative action must not mean and what I won't allow it to be. It does not mean the unjustified preference of the unqualified over the qualified of any race or gender. It doesn't mean numerical quotas. It doesn't mean and I don't favor rejection or selection of any employee or student solely on the basis of race or gender without regard to merit."[63] But he concluded, "Let me make this clear: Affirmative action is good for America. . . . Let's mend it, not end it. . . . When affirmative action is done right, it is flexible, it is fair, and it works."[64]

Clinton's decision making on affirmative action stayed in Reagan's shadow. Neither man revoked the order, but both cut back on its implementation.[65] At the end of both presidencies the controversial race-based program remained in place, yet the policy faced increasing attacks from a conservative Supreme Court.[66] Although many black leaders were critical of Clinton's waffling on affirmative action, Mary Francis Berry described it as "absolutely wonderful, given the way the courts had been cutting back on affirmative action."[67]

However, as the political scientist Linda Williams writes, Clinton did a great deal of "mending," including eliminating or modifying seventeen affirmative-action programs, adopting race-neutral language in many others, tightening eligibility requirements for minority-owned businesses, and abolishing the automatic presumption that all minorities are disadvantaged.[68]

Welfare Reform

African Americans have been interested in the reform of AFDC since its inception as Title IV of the Social Security Act. The Social Security Act established a two-tier welfare system. The first tier created a social insurance system for unemployed and retired workers. The second tier provided assistance to children from single-parent families. Although African American organizations strongly supported the Social Security Act, they were equally strong in their opposition to the two-tier system.

Opposition to the two-tier system arose mainly because the majority of blacks were excluded from the first tier. In order to get the support of southern members of Congress, FDR agreed to exclude the self-employed, domestic servants, and farm workers from the first tier. By excluding these workers, the system excluded 60 percent of all black workers and 80 percent of black women while covering 70 percent of whites.[69] The Hamiltons write that the NAACP and Urban League "correctly predicted that this would lead to continued dependency and subordination because many blacks would be forced to rely on tier 2 assistance when they could not work."[70]

When the AFDC program was established nearly 90 percent of the recipients were white, mainly widows with children. By 1961 more than 40 percent of the recipients were black, unmarried mothers and their children. Welfare thus became a "black" program. This transformation came about as a result of the first welfare reform bill, an amendment to the Social Security Act in 1939 that provided benefits to the widows and children of tier-one recipients. With this change the political scientist Gwendolyn Mink writes that AFDC "lost its only venerated constituency," namely, "worthy widows . . . mostly white" who were "always mothers of marital children" and "blameless survivors of stable marriages to regularly employed, socially insured men."[71] With the departure of these worthy, white widows—by 1961 only 7.7 percent of welfare mothers were widows—welfare became a program for "morally disdained, racially despised" black women.[72] After this 1939 reform, all subsequent welfare reform was aimed at morally disciplining the recipients and requiring them to work.[73]

Welfare reform involves a clash of values between conservatives and neoconservatives on the one hand and black leaders and the Left/liberals on the other. African American leaders and leftist/liberal critics of the American political economy see the disproportionate representation of African Americans as AFDC recipients as caused by the failure of the economy to produce enough jobs for all willing and able to work as well as the distribution of the resulting unemployment on a racial basis. The scholar Mack Jones states this view of black welfare dependency as a near axiom, namely, the "logical, perhaps even necessary, outgrowth of the American political economy conditioned by white racism."[74]

Conservatives and neoconservatives, in sharp contrast, view the problem as cultural, mainly the breakdown of male responsibility for the family. As Nathan Glazer put it, black poverty and welfare dependency could be dealt with only by requiring blacks to return to "traditional practices and restraints" regarding work, sexuality, and family.[75]

These clashing perspectives on welfare have shaped reform debate since the New Deal. As the Hamiltons write, "civil rights organizations have consistently emphasized three main points: (1) preference for a universal social welfare system that does not distinguish between social insurance and public assistance, (2) jobs for all in the regular labor market and (3) federal hegemony over social welfare."[76] Meanwhile, conservative welfare reform emphasizes individual initiative, work, the traditional family, and states' rights.[77]

These different perspectives may be gleaned from a brief review of welfare reform since the 1960s when welfare came to be viewed as a program for blacks. It should be noted, however, that in 1952 the Social Security Act was finally amended to include domestic and farm workers in the tier-one social insurance system, bringing most black workers under coverage for the first time.

The Congress in the Public Welfare Amendments of 1962 for the first time allowed the states to require that AFDC recipients participate in community work or training programs or else lose their benefits (mothers with children under six were exempted).[78] This legislation also created the AFDC-UP program, which allowed the states to provide benefits to families with unemployed fathers. In 1967 the Work Incentive Program (WIN) was enacted, allowing the states to require all employable mothers, whatever the age of their children, to work.[79]

In 1969 Richard Nixon proposed a radical change in welfare policy. Prodded by Daniel Patrick Moynihan, Nixon proposed that the federal government guarantee an income to all families with children.[80] Although Nixon's proposed Family Assistance Plan (FAP) included relatively stringent work requirements, the idea of a guaranteed federal income shocked movement conservatives. Reagan, then the governor of California, spearheaded conservative opposition.[81] Reagan objected to the federal takeover, arguing instead that AFDC should be turned over to the states. Reagan also argued that FAP would result in a vast expansion of the welfare rolls at enormous cost to taxpayers. Finally, Reagan contended that the very idea of a guaranteed income was antithetical to American values. Although he was initially reluctant to oppose a president of his own party on a major issue, as the debate went on he became increasingly aggressive, writing letters to every governor and member of Congress.[82]

The FAP was ultimately defeated through a coalition of conservatives and southerners who opposed any guarantee, and liberals and blacks who objected to the bill's work requirements and what they saw as the low level of the income guarantee.[83] Although the FAP was defeated, the Social Security Act was amended to create the Supplemental Security Income (SSI) program, which provides a guaranteed income to the elderly poor, the blind, and the disabled.

In 1971 President Carter proposed the Program for Better Jobs and Income (PBJI). PBJI would have consolidated AFDC and food stamps into a single program that would have required welfare recipients to work in public-service employment in exchange for their benefits (single mothers with young children were exempted). This legislation, like FAP, was defeated by a coalition of conservatives and liberals. Conservatives were opposed because they thought the program was too costly, while liberals and African American leaders contended the work requirement was unnecessary because it was based on the erroneous assumption that the poor did not wish to work.[84]

Throughout the welfare-reform debates of the 1960s and 1970s African American leaders argued that it was not that AFDC recipients were not willing to work but that the economy was not producing enough jobs. Thus, as an alternative to welfare they proposed a full employment strategy.[85] Absent full employment, they opposed work requirements in welfare reform as unfair and punitive. As the Hamiltons write, civil rights organizations "adamantly opposed a mandatory work policy in welfare reform legislation because it assumed that recipients preferred welfare over work. They argued that this policy was unnecessary; recipients preferred to work and would do so if jobs were available. What was needed was not welfare reform but a full employment policy."[86]

On January 6, 1981, President Reagan convened a meeting at Blair House with his senior advisors to discuss welfare reform. In addition to Reagan, the nine persons in attendance included James Baker, chief of staff, Richard Schweiker, secretary of Health and Human Services designee, Robert Carlson, Reagan's California welfare director, and Martin Anderson, a senior policy advisor and the author of an important conservative manifesto on welfare.[87] At this meeting Carlson presented a briefing book with thirty-six issues for discussion and presidential approval for submission to Congress.

At the core of the recommendations were proposals to create a series of block grants for the principal federal welfare programs for the poor, including AFDC, low-income energy assistance, and Medicaid. In addition, Carlson proposed that the thirteen categorical nutrition programs (food stamps, school lunch, summer feeding, the Women, Infants and Children program, etc.) be consolidated into a comprehensive nutrition program. Under each of these proposed block grants the states were given "complete discretion over eligibility requirements" as it was felt "they could best determine priorities for truly needy families and design systems which could be financed with block grants."[88]

Although Reagan approved Carlson's recommendations, they were not submitted to Congress as comprehensive welfare reform until the following year. It is unclear why Reagan delayed, although welfare reform, like everything else, had to take a back seat to the priorities of tax cuts and the military buildup, and some on the White House staff worried that the proposals would make the administration "appear mean and cruel to the poor."[89] In 1982, when Reagan presented the proposal, Congress ignored it. Moynihan suggests that "had it been proposed in the swirl of the first 100 days as it were, it might well have succeeded."[90] Thus, Reagan may have missed the opportunity to achieve the conservative movement's long-held wish to reform welfare on the basis of conservative principles.

In his 1986 State of the Union address Reagan made welfare reform an urgent priority of the administration and under the direction of Attorney General Meese appointed a task force to study the issue and make recommendations. In a February 5 radio address Reagan spoke of a "gathering crisis" in our "inner cities . . . especially among the welfare poor" caused by the "growing percentage of babies born out of wedlock."[91] Reagan blamed the crisis on the "insidious" welfare programs, which encouraged women to have children out of wedlock and usurped the role of the father as provider. "In some instances," Reagan said, "you have to go back three generations before you can find an intact family. It seems even the memory of families is in danger of becoming extinct."[92]

In July 1967 the president announced the creation of an Interagency Low Income Opportunity Advisory Board, headed by Charles Hobbs, assistant to the president for policy development. The board presented its recommendations to the president in December 1986. Unlike the Blair House recommendations, Hobbs's report avoided block grants and focused mainly on tightening eligibility and on a mandatory work requirement.[93]

Meanwhile in Congress the Democrats were proposing that the AFDC-UP program be made mandatory for all states. Under this program two-parent families with children qualify for welfare if the "principal wage earner" was unemployed. Optional under current law (in 1987 twenty-one states had adopted it), the program, the Democrats argued, promoted the breakup of families through its failure to pay benefits to intact families. Although Reagan in his radio address had lamented the impact of welfare on the breakup of families as "the most insidious effect" of the system, the administration opposed making AFDC-UP mandatory because it would increase cost and expand the number of recipients. In a compromise worked out between Senators Moynihan and Robert Dole, AFDC-UP was made mandatory and participation in training or work programs was required of all able-bodied recipients with children over the age of three (the government provided reimbursements for child care and transportation).

Conservatives in and out of the administration urged the president to veto the bill, claiming that instead of decentralizing the system the mandatory AFDC-UP further centralized power in Washington while expanding the cost and coverage of the program. In a memo to Ed Feulner, Stuart Butler wrote that the bill was a "disaster" because it "would raise welfare expenditures; raise benefit levels; expand welfare eligibility; micro manage welfare; and restrict work programs. In stark contrast to the whole thrust of the Administration's proposals, they fail to decentralize welfare in any meaningful way."[94] But Feulner wrote, "President Reagan will face a very unpleasant choice—either veto a bipartisan welfare bill and be denounced as anti poor, or sign it and expand the welfare state."[95]

Reagan signed the bill. A July 15, 1988, memorandum for the president from Ken Cribb, Joe Wright, and Chuck Hobbs urged the president not to veto the legislation. Hobbs's signature on the memorandum was likely crucial, since he was the major architect of the administration's welfare strategy. The memorandum conceded that conservative "criticisms are certainly significant" and the "bill is not the welfare reform bill we would sign onto if we had our druthers. . . . But the most important forward step, and the one best understood by the public, is the establishment for the first time in federal law of the principle that someone able to work for their welfare must do so."[96]

The Family Support Act of 1988 signed by Reagan was far short of the kinds of radical reforms envisioned by the president in his January 1981 Blair House meeting. Except for the requirement that one parent in a two-parent family work in a public or private sector job for at least sixteen hours a week, the Act did little to alter the system, although it did allow the states to seek waivers from the federal government to establish experimental welfare systems of their own.[97] But, again, the Reagan presidency was also a rhetorical presidency. The President's rhetoric throughout his presidency—indeed throughout his career—had sought to delegitimize welfare and stigmatize its recipients as lazy, shiftless welfare queens and young bucks.[98] Busch concludes that this rhetoric and the modest reforms of the 1988 Act, therefore, "served as a way station to the more fundamental reforms enacted in 1996."[99]

During the 1992 campaign Clinton promised to "end welfare as we know it" by requiring recipients to get a job within two years or lose support. Senator Moynihan, by now the leading congressional authority on welfare policy, described the president's campaign rhetoric as "boob bait for the bubbas," implying that it was a symbolic gesture toward anti-welfare sentiments among working-class whites in places like Macomb.[100] Symbolic gestures aside, the substance of Clinton's reform plan (based on the writings of David Ellwood, the Harvard policy analyst who subsequently became the assistant secretary for welfare in the administration) involved not just a two-year time period but an expanded program of social services including health, child care, job training, and public-sector jobs. Comprehensive reform of this sort would have cost more than the existing system.[101]

In part because of the difficulty of designing the program and finding the ways and means to pay for it, and because of the priorities of the budget and health insurance, the administration delayed submitting a proposal until the summer of 1994. This was too late for action before the fall elections.

When the Republicans gained control of Congress, they took Clinton's campaign pledge seriously and three times passed bills ending welfare as a federally guaranteed entitlement and imposing strict work and time requirements, without guarantees of health, child care, or job training.

The legislation also provided that Medicaid, nursing-home care, and food stamps would also be devolved to the states as block grants, and it denied various welfare benefits to legal immigrants.

Clinton twice vetoed the Republican bills, but after the block grant provisions on Medicaid, food stamps, and nursing homes were deleted he signed the third version of the legislation. Senator Moynihan and all except two members of the Congressional Black Caucus opposed the bill signed by the president. But it passed both Houses of Congress with overwhelming bipartisan majorities.

Debate on the bills was passionate and in the House racially rancorous; Elizabeth Drew described the House debate as "uglier than any in memory."[102] Moynihan in long, learned, passionate Senate-floor speeches concluded that the bill was the "most regressive event in social policy of the twentieth century,"[103] and said, "Those involved will take this disgrace to their graves."[104]

In addition to the opposition of the Congressional Black Caucus and other liberal interests (including the American Federation of Labor and Congress of Industrial Organizations), the legislation was opposed by all of the president's senior domestic-policy advisors except one (Bruce Reed) and by all of the cabinet and subcabinet officials with welfare policy responsibilities—three of whom resigned to protest the president's decision.[105]

Dick Morris, however, urged the president to sign the bill. Morris describes Clinton as in "agony" about the legislation, but the politics, he wrote, "pointed one way and only one way: signing."[106] Morris said he told the president that a veto would cost him the election, transforming a 15-percent win into a 3-percent loss. Years later in an interview with Jason DeParle, Clinton "chafed" at the idea that a veto would have cost him the election. "I was really steamed," Clinton told DeParle, "when everybody said, 'oh, Bill Clinton did this to win the ninety-six election!' Hell, I didn't have to do this to win the election. . . . I was going to win the election in ninety-six on the economy. I did it 'cause I thought it was right."[107] In his memoir Clinton wrote that he signed the legislation because he "thought it was the best chance America would have for a long time to change the incentives in the welfare system from dependence to empowerment through work."[108]

Clinton also invoked the shadows of Macomb and the Reagan Democrats as part of his reason for signing the bill, telling DeParle that ending welfare was a means of "reviving liberalism."[109] The two were linked, he thought, because of "how welfare had poisoned the politics of poverty and race. Welfare cast poor people as shirkers. It discredited government. It aggravated the worst racial stereotypes. It left Democrats looking like the party of giveaways."[110]

The bill signed by Clinton met all of Reagan's criteria for conservative reform. It, among other things, abolished the New Deal–era federal guarantee of aid to poor women and their children, giving the states authority to design their own welfare programs. Benefits were limited to five years over a lifetime, and most adult recipients were required to work within two years.[111]

Scholars more than a decade after the passage of the bill are uncertain as to its impact on the well-being of poor black women and children. All we know for sure is that as a result of the legislation "more women are working and poor, rather than nonworking and poor."[112] Bill Clinton, however, is certain, writing on the tenth anniversary of the bill's passage that it has been a "great success" and an excellent example of bipartisanship.[113]

Whatever our eventual understanding of the legislation's impact, its enactment is the longest shadow of Reagan and the conservative movement on civil rights policymaking in the Clinton administration and perhaps the starkest example of winning while losing of the entire post–civil rights era.

Conclusion

With respect to race Bill Clinton was a highly successful preemptive president. As a candidate he was able to appeal to the anti-black sentiments of Macomb while maintaining overwhelming support among African Americans. As president he was able to co-opt conservative positions on welfare while maintaining the highest levels of support among African Americans and their leaders. When he left office in January 2001, 87 percent of blacks approved of his performance as president, compared to 45 percent of whites. Nearly a decade later (1998) a poll indicated that among blacks he was more popular than Jesse Jackson, carrying 93 percent to Jackson's 87 percent.[114] The Nobel laureate Toni Morrison went so far as to describe Clinton as the first black president, writing that he displayed "almost every trope of blackness—single parent household, born poor, working-class saxophone-playing, McDonalds junk food-loving boy from Arkansas."[115] Dewayne Wickham, the *USA Today* columnist, concludes after interviewing more than two dozen black intellectuals and political leaders, "Bill Clinton was not the first black president, but in the long line of white men who ascended to this nation's presidency he was the next best thing."[116] Clinton was better, Wickham believes, than Lyndon Johnson who risked his presidency and his party's future to enact the most comprehensive civil rights and anti-poverty policies of any American president.

The observations of Morrison and Wickham testify to Clinton's remarkable preemptive skills on race. His position on civil rights reflected the shadow of the greatest conservative president of all time, yet somehow he managed to be regarded as "blacker" than the greatest civil rights president of all time.

Notes

1. Stephen Skrowronek, *The Politics Presidents Make: Leadership from John Adams to Bill Clinton* (Cambridge, Mass.: Harvard University Press, 1993).

2. William Muir Jr., "Ronald Reagan: The Primacy of Rhetoric" in *Leadership in the Modern Presidency*, ed. Fred Greenstein (Cambridge, Mass.: Harvard University Press, 1988).

3. Andrew Busch, *Ronald Reagan and the Politics of Freedom* (Lanham: Rowman & Littlefield, 2001), 253.

4. William Berman, *America's Right Turn: From Nixon to Clinton* (Baltimore: Johns Hopkins University Press, 1994), 97. Two book-length studies that make explicit comparisons between Reagan and FDR are John Sloan, *FDR and Reagan: Transformative Presidents with Clashing Visions* (Lawrence: University Press of Kansas, 2008) and Sean Wilentz, *The Age of Reagan: A History 1974–2008* (New York: Harper Collins, 2008). See also Steven Hayward, *The Age of Reagan: The Fall of the Old Liberal Order, 1964–1980* (Roseville, Calif.: Prima Publishing, 2001).

5. Wilentz reviews the research on Reagan's role in the fall of the Soviet Union. See *The Age of Reagan*, 245–87. See also James Graham Wilson, "Did Reagan Make Gorbachev Possible?" *Presidential Studies Quarterly* 38 (2008): 456–75.

6. Skrowronek, *The Politics Presidents Make*, 421.

7. See Mark Smith, *The Right Talk: How Conservatives Transformed the Great Society into the Economic Society* (Princeton: Princeton University Press, 2008), 161. See also Bruce Bartlett, "Starve the Beast: Origins and Development of a Budget Metaphor," *The Independent Review* 12 (2007): 5–26.

8. On the use of the "L" word by Reagan during the 1988 campaign, see Charles O. Jones, "Meeting Low Expectations: Strategy and Prospects of the Bush Presidency" in

The Bush Presidency: First Appraisals, ed. Colin Campbell and Bert Rockman (Chatham, N.J.: Chatham House, 1991), 37–68.

9. On the use of Reagan's iconic welfare queen rhetoric to disparage African American recipients, see David Zucchiro, *Myth of the Welfare Queen* (New York: Scribners, 1999); Angie-Marie Hancock, *The Politics of Disgust: The Public Identity of the Welfare Queen* (New York: New York University Press, 2004); Franklin Gilliam, "The 'Welfare Queen' Experiment: How Viewers React to Images of African American Mothers on Welfare," Center for Communication and Community, Paper # 007, UCLA, 1999.

10. See Peter Stienfels, *The Neoconservatives: The Men Who are Changing America's Politics* (New York: Simon & Schuster, 1979); Gary Dorrien, *The Neoconservative Mind: Politics, Culture and the War of Ideology* (Philadelphia: Temple University Press, 1993).

11. These themes were advanced by numerous neoconservative intellectuals including Nathan Glazer, Aaron Wildavsky, Charles Murray, Thomas Sowell, and Glen Loury. See Robert C. Smith, *Conservatism and Racism and Why in America They are the Same: A Study in Ideas and Movements, 1950–1980* (Albany: State University of New York Press, 2010), 91–106.

12. Walter Dean Burnham, "The 1980 Election Earthquake: Realignment, Reaction or What?" in *The Hidden Election: Politics and Economics in the 1980 Presidential Campaign*, ed. Thomas Ferguson and Joel Rogers (New York: Pantheon, 1981), 99.

13. Randall Woods, *LBJ: Architect of Ambition* (New York: Free Press, 2006), 480.

14. David Danzig, "Rightists, Racists and Separatists: A White Bloc in the Making," *Commentary*, August 1964, 28.

15. Stanley Greenberg, *Race & State in Capitalist Development: Comparative Perspectives* (New Haven: Yale, 1980).

16. Stanley Greenberg, *Middle Class Dreams: The Politics and Power of the New American Majority* (New York: Times Books, 1995), 297.

17. Quoted in John Aloysius Farrell, "Realignment of the Party," *Denver Post*, August 23, 2008.

18. Greenberg, *Middle Class Dreams*, 39.

19. Ibid., 34, 39.

20. Ibid., 22–24.

21. Ibid., 21.

22. James MacGregor Burns and Georgia Sorenson, *Dead Center: Clinton-Gore Leadership and the Perils of Moderation* (New York: Scribner, A Lisa Drew Book, 1999), 247. See Jeremy Mayer, *Running on Race: Racial Politics in Presidential Campaigns, 1960–2000* (New York: Random House, 2002), 229–72; Kenneth O'Reilly, *Nixon's Piano: Presidents and Racial Politics From Washington to Clinton* (New York: Free Press, 1995), Chap. 10; Robert C. Smith, *We Have No Leaders: African Americans in the Post Civil Rights Era* (Albany: SUNY Press, 1996), 255–76.

23. Greenberg, *Middle Class Dreams*, 24.

24. Skrowronek, *The Politics Presidents Make*, 43.

25. Ibid., 44.

26. James MacGregor Burns, *Leadership* (New York: Harper & Row, 1978).

27. Burns and Sorenson, *Dead Center*, 49.

28. Ibid., 166.

29. Ibid., 242.

30. David Maraniss, *First in His Class: A Biography of Bill Clinton* (New York: Simon & Schuster, 1995), 105.

31. Arthur Schlesinger Jr., "Rating the Presidents: Washington to Clinton," *Political Science Quarterly* 112 (1997): 188.

32. Dona Cooper Hamilton and Charles Hamilton, *The Dual Agenda: Race and Social Welfare Policies of Civil Rights Organizations* (New York: Columbia University Press, 1997), 3–4. Stephen Lawson, "Freedom Then, Freedom Now: The Historiography of the Civil Rights Movement," *American Historical Review* 96 (1991): 456–71.

33. Hamilton and Hamilton, *The Dual Agenda*, 124.

34. Ibid., 167–74.

35. "Seven Point Mandate," *Focus* 14 (1976): 8.

36. Hamilton and Hamilton, *The Dual Agenda*, 20. Hugh Davis Graham, *The Civil Rights Era: Origins and Development of National Policy* (New York: Oxford University Press, 1990), chapters 21–23.

37. Ralph Bunche was critical of the New Deal civil rights leadership for this early focus on affirmative action in employment, arguing that it would tend to "widen the menacing gap between white and black workers." Instead, he argued for an interracial working-class movement devoted to the adoption of a policy that would "provide adequate numbers of jobs and economic security for the population." See his "The Programs of Organizations Devoted to the Improvement of the Negro," *Journal of Negro Education* 8 (1939): 542–43.

38. "To Fulfill These Rights," *Public Papers of the Presidents of United States of America: Lyndon B. Johnson, 1965, Vol. II* (Washington: Government Printing Office, 1966), 635–40.

39. Nathan Glazer, *Affirmative Discrimination: Ethnic Inequality and Public Policy* (New York: Basic Books, 1975).

40. Smith, *Conservatism and Racism in America*, 143–84.

41. Nicholas Laham, *The Reagan Presidency and the Politics of Race* (New York: Praeger, 1998), 94.

42. Smith, *Conservatism and Racism in America*, 143–84.

43. Mark Distler to Patrick Buchanan, March 10, 1986. Quoted in Laham, *The Reagan Presidency and the Politics of Race*, 94.

44. Minutes, Meeting of Domestic Council, October 22, 1985, *PQ WHORM*, Subject File, Ronald Reagan Library (RRL).

45. Ibid.

46. Ibid.

47. Several observers conclude that Regan "Kept the issue off the President's desk." See Rowland Evans and Robert Novak, "Stalemate Quotas," *Washington Post*, December 30, 1985; Hugh Davis Graham, "Civil Rights Policy" in *The Reagan Presidency: Pragmatic Conservatism and Its Legacies*, ed. W. Elliot Brownlee and Hugh Davis Graham (Lawrence: University Press of Kansas, 203), 285; Hedrick Smith, *The Power Game: How Washington Works* (New York: Random House, 1988), 304. Donald Regan

does not mention the issue in his memoir. See *For the Record: From Wall Street to Washington* (San Diego: Harcourt Brace Jovanovich, 1988).

48. Quoted in Laham, *The Reagan Presidency and the Politics of Race*, 79.

49. Graham, "Civil Rights Policy," 290.

50. See, for example, Terry Eastland, *Ending Affirmative Action: The Case for Color-blind Justice* (New York: Basic Books, 1996).

51. Laham, *The Reagan Presidency and the Politics of Race*, 92, 126.

52. The University of Chicago's General Social Survey in 1996 found that 76 percent of whites believed whites were likely to lose jobs or promotions because of racial preferences.

53. Taxman v. Piscataway, 91 F3d, 1544 (1996).

54. Brief for the United States, Piscataway v. Taxman, 11F. 3d1547, Third Circuit, 1996.

55. *Taxman*, see especially the opinion of Chief Judge Sloviter. By the time the case reached the Supreme Court, Taxman had been rehired; thus the only question at issue was about $400,000 in back pay and legal fees. Civil rights groups raised this amount and the case was withdrawn. See Steven Holmes, "Rights Groups Work to Keep Preferences," *West County Times*, November 23, 1997.

56. George Stephanopoulos, *All Too Human: A Political Education* (Boston: Little, Brown, 1990), 371; Linda Williams, *The Constraint of Race: The Legacies of White Skin Privilege in America* (University Park: Pennsylvania State University Press, 2003), 295.

57. Dick Morris, *Behind the Oval Office: Winning the Presidency in the Nineties* (New York: Random House, 1997), 214.

58. Bill Clinton, *My Life* (New York: Knopf, 2004), 663.

59. Ibid. Jackson's threat was direct and public, telling the *New York Times*, "'There is no question about it. My position on it was public, and I stated it to [Clinton]. I had no inclination to run. My choice was, rather, to support him. But if he had taken away the program for equal opportunity, he would have crossed the line." Steven Holmes, "On Civil Rights Clinton Steers a Bumpy Course," *New York Times*, October 20, 1996. In addition to Jackson's threat, the Congressional Black Caucus indicated that it would conduct street protests and economic boycotts.

60. A brief account of Stephanopoulos and Edley's work and Clinton's decision-making process is in Bradley Patterson Jr., *The White House Staff* (Washington: Brookings Institution, 2000). See also *Affirmative Action Review: Report to President Clinton* (Washington: U.S. Bureau of National Affairs, 1995); Stephanopoulas, *All Too Human*; Christopher Edley, *Not All Black and White: Affirmative Action, Race and American Values* (New York: Hill & Wang, 1996).

61. Adarand v. Peña, 903—1841, 1995 (slip opinion).

62. Steven Holmes, "Administration Cuts Affirmative Action While Defending It," *New York Times*, March 16, 1998; Williams, *The Constraint of Race*, 298–309.

63. "President's Clinton's Remarks on Affirmative Action," http://millercenter.org/president/speeches/detail/4594.

64. Ibid.

65. On Reagan's cutbacks on affirmative action, see Harrell Rogers Jr., "Fair

Employment Law for Minorities: An Evaluation of Federal Implementation" in *Implementation of Civil Rights Policy*, ed. Charles Bullock and Charles Lamb (Monterey, Calif.: Brooks/Cole, 1984), 93–177.

66. Edwin Meese contends that Reagan's strategy with respect to affirmative action was from the outset to use judicial appointments to eventually get affirmative action invalidated on constitutional principles. See *With Reagan: The Inside Story* (Washington: Regenery Gateway, 1992), 315–16.

67. Quoted in Dewayne Wickham, *Bill Clinton and Black America* (New York: Ballantine Books, 2002), 110.

68. Williams, *The Constraint of Race*, 308–9.

69. See Ira Katznelson, *When Affirmative Action was White* (New York: W.W. Norton, 2005), 42–50.

70. Hamilton and Hamilton, *The Dual Agenda*, 5.

71. Gwendolyn Mink, *Welfare's End* (Ithaca: Cornell University Press, 1998), 47.

72. Ibid. See also Hancock, *The Politics of Disgust*.

73. Mink, *Welfare's End*.

74. Mack Jones, "The Black Underclass As A Systemic Phenomenon," in *Race, Politics and Economic Development*, ed. James Jennings (New York: Verso Press, 1992), 23.

75. Nathan Glazer, "The Limits of Social Policy," *Commentary*, September 1971, 54. See also Charles Murray, *Losing Ground: American Social Policy, 1950–1980* (New York: Basic Books, 1984).

76. Hamilton and Hamilton, *The Dual Agenda*, 4.

77. Donald Matthewson and Shelly Arsneault, "Conservatism, Federalism, and the Defense of Inequality," *National Political Science Review* 11 (2007): 335–51.

78. Mink, *Welfare's End*, 38.

79. Mark Lincoln Chadwin, John J. Mitchell, and Demetra Smith, "Reforming Welfare: Lessons From the WIN Experience," *Public Administration Review* 4 (1981): 372–80.

80. Daniel Patrick Moynihan, *The Politics of a Guaranteed Income* (New York: Vintage Books, 1973).

81. Steven Hayward, "Welfare Reform: Another Win for the Gipper," John M. Ashbrook Center for Public Affairs, http://www.ashbrook.org/tools/printerpage.asp.

82. Ibid.

83. Moynihan, *The Politics of a Guaranteed Income*; see also Vee Burke, *Nixon's Good Deed: Welfare Reform* (New York: Columbia University Press, 1974).

84. Lawrence Lynn and David Whitman, *The President as Policy Maker: Jimmy Carter and Welfare Reform* (Philadelphia: Temple University Press, 1981).

85. The Congress in 1978, acting under pressure from African American organizations, did enact the Humphrey-Hawkins "Full Employment and Balanced Growth Act." However, at President Carter's insistence this legislation was so watered down that by the time it was passed it was little more than a symbolic gesture. See Smith, *We Have No Leaders*, 187–210; Timothy N. Thurber, *The Politics of Equality: Hubert Humphrey and the African American Freedom Struggle* (New York: Columbia University Press, 1999), 223–48.

86. Hamilton and Hamilton, *The Dual Agenda*, 175.

87. Martin Anderson, *Welfare: The Political Economy of Welfare Reform in the United States* (Stanford, Calif.: Hoover Institution, 1978).

88. Minutes of Meeting, A Welfare Program for the Reagan Administration, January 6, 1981, Martin Anderson Files, RRL.

89. Personal Interview with Martin Anderson, January 13, 2006.

90. Daniel Patrick Moynihan, *Come The Revolution: Argument in the Reagan Era* (New York: Harcourt Brace Jovanovich, 1988), 94.

91. Ronald Reagan, "Radio Address to the Nation on Welfare Reform," February 15, 1986, http://www.reagan.utexas.edu/archives/speeches/1986/21586a.htm.

92. Ibid.

93. "Up From Dependency: A New National Public Assistance Strategy," December 1986, Daniel Crippen File, RRL.

94. Memorandum from Ed Feulner to Stuart Butler, "Republicans and Welfare Reform," July 1, 1987, Juanita Duggins File, RRL.

95. Ibid.

96. Memorandum for the President from Ken Crib, Joe Wright, and Chuck Hobbs, July 15, 1988, Daniel Crippen File, RRL.

97. Mark Rom, "The Family Support Act of 1988: Federalism, Developmental Policy and Welfare Reform," *Publius* 19 (1989): 57.

98. Although Reagan never mentioned that the woman he referred to as the welfare queen was black, this was clearly the implication in his "frequently told, error-ridden, exaggerated account." See Sloan, *FDR and Reagan*, 347.

99. Busch, *Ronald Reagan and the Politics of Freedom*, 37.

100. Daniel Patrick Moynihan, *Miles To Go: A Personal History of Social Policy* (Cambridge, Mass.: Harvard University Press, 1996), 29. The slogan was developed and inserted in candidate Clinton's first major domestic policy speech by Bruce Reed. See Jason DeParle, *American Dream: Three Women, Ten Kids and a Nation's Drive to End Welfare* (New York: Viking, 2004), 3–4, 101–4.

101. David Ellwood, *Poor Support: Poverty in the American Family* (New York: Basic Books, 1988).

102. Elizabeth Drew, *Showdown: The Struggle Between Gingrich, Congress and the Clinton White House* (New York: Simon & Schuster, 1996). For a sample of the rancorous debate, see *The Congressional Record, House*, March 24, 1995, PH3742.

103. Quoted in Barbara Vobeja, "Moynihan Observing From the Wings," *Washington Post*, June 4, 1995.

104. Moynihan, *Miles to Go*, 41.

105. None of the officials who resigned were African American. Unlike in the affirmative-action case, Jesse Jackson did not threaten to challenge the President's renomination or reelection, nor did the Congressional Black Caucus threaten protests or boycotts. It should be noted also that African American opinion was generally supportive of the major elements of the bill signed by Clinton. See Katherine Tate, "Welfare Reform: Scrapping the System and Our Ideals," in *African Americans and the Political System*, 4th ed., ed. Lucius Barker, Mack Jones, and Katherine Tate (Upper Saddle River, N.J.: Prentice-Hall, 1999), 350–59.

106. Morris, *Behind the Oval Office*, 301.

107. DeParle, *American Dream*, 150.

108. Clinton, *My Life*, 720. Hillary Clinton in her memoir, however, does suggest that politics entered into the President's decision, writing "pragmatic politics entered. . . . If he vetoed welfare reform a third time, Bill would be handing the Republicans a potential political windfall. In the wake of the disastrous 1994 elections, he was concerned about further Democratic losses that would jeopardize his leverage to protect social policies in the future." Hillary Rodham Clinton, *Living History* (New York: Simon & Schuster, 2003), 369.

109. DeParle, *American Dream*, 150.

110. Ibid.

111. Personal Responsibility and Work Opportunity Reconciliation Act of 1996, Public Law 104–93, 110 Stat. 2105, enacted August 22, 1996.

112. Rebecca Blank, "Was Welfare Reform Successful?" *Economist's Voice* (March 2006), 4–5. For detailed studies of how women struggle to survive under welfare reform, see Lynneil Hancock, *Hands to Work: The Stories of Three Families Facing the Welfare Clock* (New York: William Morrow, 2002); Dàna-Ain Davis, *Battered Women and Welfare Reform: Between a Rock and a Hard Place* (Albany: SUNY Press, 2006); DeParle, *American Dream*.

113. Bill Clinton, "How We Ended Welfare, Together," *New York Times*, August 22, 2006.

114. Wickham, *Bill Clinton and Black America*, 1–2.

115. Toni Morrison, "Clinton as the First Black President," *New Yorker*, October 1998, 11.

116. Wickham, *Bill Clinton and Black America*, 239.

OLD VINEGAR IN A NEW BOTTLE

Vote Denial in the 2000 Presidential Election and Beyond

CHARLES L. ZELDEN

Wallace McDonald of Hillsborough County, Florida, did not vote on the day of the controversial 2000 election, though he had voted in many earlier presidential elections. McDonald, who had been convicted of misdemeanor vagrancy in 1959 (he had fallen asleep on a park bench while waiting for a bus), had recently received a letter from the Hillsborough County election supervisor, Pam Iorio, informing him that, as an ex-felon, his name had been removed from the voters' roll and thus he would not be allowed to vote in this election. McDonald was surprised by this ruling. "I could not believe it, after voting for all these years since the 50s, without a problem," he said. McDonald noted that, even by Florida's harsh standards, his offense did not amount to a felony—but here was the letter telling him that he could not vote. "I knew something was unfair about that. To be able to vote all your life, then to have somebody reach in a bag and take some technicality that you can't vote," McDonald said. "Why now? Something's wrong."[1]

Cathy Jackson, an African American woman from Broward County, Florida, faced a different problem that day. Jackson had been a registered voter in Broward County since 1996. She had been a regular voter in her precinct since registering to vote there. Yet when she showed up to vote on November 7, she was told that her name was not on the voter list. Although she insisted that she had voted in that precinct before, the poll workers refused to allow her to vote and even (erroneously) sent her back to her former polling place in Miami-Dade County. When the

Miami-Dade poll workers properly refused to allow her to vote, Jackson returned to Broward. There, the poll workers told her to wait while they checked her registration status. While she waited, Jackson was angered to observe "a poll worker from another precinct within the same polling place allow an elderly white voter, whose name did not appear on the rolls, to fill out an affidavit and vote." When Ms. Jackson asked if she could do the same, the poll workers explained that she could fill out an affidavit but could not vote until they had verified her registration. Unfortunately, the phone line to the county supervisor of elections office was busy. After hours of waiting for a verification that never came, Jackson left and went to work. Still, Jackson did not give up. After work, she returned to her precinct a third time to try to vote. The poll workers, however, never could verify her registration status and refused to allow her to cast her ballot.[2]

Near Tallahassee that same day, Darryl Gorham was driving some neighbors to vote when he saw something he thought was a forgotten thing of the past. Turning a corner about a mile from the precinct, Gorham saw "four Florida highway patrolmen standing in the middle of the street. They were stopping everybody. They had seven or eight cars stopped on the side of the road and waiting. They inspected the headlights, tail-lights, indicators, license, registration, tags, everything. . . . I've lived in Florida most of my life, but I have never ever seen a roadblock like that." Gorham was convinced that the white policemen were trying to slow down the flow of black voters in a tight election. "It took maybe 15, maybe 20 minutes. But many people were taking time out from work, or going to work, and it was making them late. Some just turned round and went back."[3]

Across the state of Florida, tens of thousands of voters—most of them minorities—experienced problems similar to those described above as they tried to vote in the 2000 presidential election. Even before the polls had closed on November 7, angry minority voters inundated the offices of the supervisors of elections and local media outlets with complaints about their inability to vote. The complaints included: use of highly inaccurate voting machines in largely minority precincts that did not properly register their vote; registered voters not being permitted to vote due to incorrect purging from the voter rolls or misspelled names on voter rolls, which kept otherwise valid voters from casting a ballot; inability to communicate with local election offices to confirm or deny registration; switching of precincts without prior notification; misinformation at precincts that kept legitimate voters from casting a ballot; polling places closing early or being moved without notice; problems with absentee ballots; and inadequate or nonexistent support for non-English speaking voters. There were also scattered complaints of police intimidation.[4] It was, in fact, with this type of disorganization in mind that former President Jimmy Carter remarked, "If we were invited to go into a foreign country to monitor the election, and they had similar election standards and procedures, we would refuse to participate at all."[5]

The complaints were not only numerous—they were accurate. True, the battle had been won against the more formal and systematic forms of disenfranchisement instituted in the Jim Crow era (and present well into the 1960s and even 1970s). Yet as the 2000 presidential election made clear, many subtle institutional forms of race-based disenfranchisement remained entrenched in the nation's electoral system. Although often implemented through technically race-neutral legal provisions and administrative procedures, the net effect was observable, focused on minority voters, and, in the end, effectively disenfranchised voters. And while it is also true that the total number of voters affected by these disenfranchising efforts were relatively small in terms of absolute numbers (thousands and tens of thousands in an electorate of millions), the impact on minority voting communities was proportionally significant. More to the point, in the unique situation of the 2000 election—one of the most contentious elections in modern U.S. history whose resolution nearly provoked a constitutional crisis of unprecedented nature as the State of Florida and the U.S. Supreme Court fought over how to count disputed votes and determine which candidate (Bush or Gore) would be the next President of the United States—it was also a potentially decisive factor in the final outcome of that election.

The elections that followed, in turn, showed the events of 2000 to be more than just an accident or fluke. What could have been mere error or mistake or administrative incompetence in 2000 continued unchecked and largely ignored in 2002, 2004, and 2006. Even the election of Barack Obama in 2008 merely hid from sight the ongoing patterns of administrative, race-based disenfranchisement.[6]

Hence, while most of the essays in this book address the theme of "winning while losing"—chronicling and analyzing battles won but wars lost in the sphere of civil rights—such was not the case with voting rights. In 2000 and beyond, African American voters learned that, despite their having seen many victories for the cause of voting rights in the decades preceding the election, echoes of "the bad old days" remained. To those disenfranchised in these elections, and to students of the history of voting rights, the story of minority voting rights since 2000 thus looks more like an especially demoralizing case of "losing while winning" rather than "winning while losing."

A Pattern of Disenfranchisement

Following the 2000 election, the United States Commission on Civil Rights held hearings on the Florida vote. In these hearings, the Commission found that "the percentage of spoiled [i.e., rejected] ballots [was] positively correlated with both the percentage of the population that [was] African American" and/or was "a member of a minority group." In all, "thirty-four percent of the variation in the percentage of spoiled ballots across counties [could] be explained by the size of the African American population in the counties." To prove this point, the Commission noted that in "the top 10 counties with the highest percentage of African American voters, nine out of 10 . . . [had] spoilage rates higher than the Florida average of 2.93 percent." Conversely, the lowest spoilage rates were found in white majority precincts.[7] The Commission concluded that "African American voters were nearly 10 times more likely than white voters to have their ballots rejected in the November 2000 election."[8]

These differences grew out of various interlocking administrative and legal failures by Florida election officials. The first two were the distribution of voting machines and the way these machines counted votes. A *New York Times* study found that "nearly 4 percent of the type of punch-card ballots most widely used in Florida were thrown out because the machines read them as blank or invalid. By contrast, the more modern, optical scanning systems rejected far fewer votes—only about 1.4 percent of those cast." Most minority voters in the state voted using the less accurate punch-card ballots. As the *Times* analysis showed, "64 percent of the state's black voters live[d] in counties that used the punch cards while 56 percent of whites did so." In Miami-Dade County, these differences resulted in predominantly black precincts having "their votes thrown out at twice the rate as Hispanic precincts and nearly four times the rate of white precincts." In all, noted the *Times*, "1 out of 11 ballots in predominantly black precincts [in Miami-Dade] were rejected, a total of 9,904."[9]

A racial bias appeared even in the use of the more accurate Scantron-type voting systems. Gadsden County, a poor rural county in northern Florida with a heavily African American population, used the normally more accurate optical scanning system for its vote. The advantage of an optical scan system is that it can catch and correct voter mistakes, such as not filling in a vote or voting for more than one candidate for the same office, at least so long as the ballots are scanned in the precincts in the voter's presence. In such cases, voters can correct mistakes to reflect their intent more accurately and thus enable their ballots to be counted. Gadsden County, however, could not afford to place a scanner in every precinct. The principal cost of adopting an optical scanner system is for the optical reader, not for the ballots themselves. So, to save money, Gadsden County counted its votes at a central tabulation center. Consequently, mistakes that could have been—and most likely would have been—corrected at the precinct level could not be corrected, and Gadsden County officials had to discard ballots afflicted with those mistakes. Thus, while Leon County, just across the Ochlockonee River from Gadsden, had only a 0.18 percent spoilage rate with optical precinct tabulation, Gadsden with its centralized system had 12.4 percent spoilage—the highest rate in the state.[10]

Voter purges also figured in the Commission's analysis of the Florida vote. The Commission found that the voter purge lists issued by the state to exclude felons from the franchise (as required by Florida law) were not only highly inaccurate (for example, of the 5,762 names on a 1999 purge list for Miami-Dade County, 14.1 percent of those named successfully challenged their inclusion on the list) but also racially biased. The Commission reported, "African Americans in Florida were more likely to find their names on the [purge] list than persons of other races." Further, the Commission estimated that African Americans made up 65 percent of the names on the purge list while totaling less than 20 percent of the total state population.[11]

Worse yet, state officials knew that these lists were highly inaccurate but distributed them anyway for use in screening actual voters. A private company, Database Technologies (DBT), working under guidelines provided by the Florida Secretary of State's office and the state Division of

Elections, had produced the felon list. These guidelines required DBT to use only the first names, last names, and birthdates of registered voters in compiling its list of ex-felons, and to do so in no particular order. As a result, John Phillip Smith and Phillip John Smith (or even John Smith Phillip) were treated as a match for inclusion on the felony ban list despite being different individuals. Similarly, the state guidelines required DBT to include individuals whose first or last name *approximated* the spelling of a listed ex-felon—so long as the spelling was "90 percent" the same, the name was included on the voting-ban list. When DBT officials reported these inaccuracies to state authorities, they were informed that the state "wanted to go broader" and thus "we [DBT] did it in the fashion that they requested." As a result, DBT produced a list that sought to "capture more names that possibly aren't matches and let the supervisors make a final determination rather than exclude certain matches altogether."[12]

Whereas it was true that, just before the election, the Division of Elections sent letters to the county supervisors of elections informing them of the potential for mistakes, the damage had already been done. In most counties, letters had already gone out informing those on the lists that their names had been dropped from the voting rolls. Although many who received the letters responded angrily that they were not felons and sought to restore their names to the voting lists, most reacted as Wallace McDonald did and did not even try to vote.[13]

Other types of complaints were harder to document but were potentially just as damaging to these voters' access to the polls. As with Cathy Jackson, some voters complained that minority voters were more likely to be wrongfully turned away from the polls when their names were not immediately found on the voter lists than were white voters, who were given the opportunity to sign affidavits and vote. Based on anecdotal evidence, the Commission found extensive "disparity between black and nonblack voters" in terms of their voting experience—a disparity "supported by the testimony of witnesses at the Commission's hearings" and exhibiting a clear pattern of race-based voter denial.[14]

Similarly, evidence of police checkpoints near largely minority precincts existed, although direct proof of an exclusionary intent in setting up these checkpoints was diffuse. The *Guardian* (UK) newspaper reported: "Major Ken Howes, a spokesman for the Florida Highway Patrol, said the four policemen had set up the checkpoint without authority from senior officers . . . but . . . insisted [that] the sergeant in charge had not intended to affect the vote." The lack of evidence of exclusionary intent offered little comfort to those who had felt intimidated by the sight of these checkpoints. For instance, Robert Chamber, a black resident who lived near the Woodville checkpoint, was skeptical of the claimed lack of discriminatory intent. He believed the checkpoint's message was clear. "It is putting fear in people's hearts," he said. "It means: 'We'll catch them before they get there.' The racism here may be underground but it's strong. There are places around here we just know not to go."[15]

A Matter of Intent

This summary of electoral failures in Florida's 2000 vote makes clear the pattern of race-based voter denial that pervaded the 2000 Florida presidential election. As the Commission's chair, Mary Frances Berry, noted, "The enormity of inequities" found in the Florida vote was "astounding."[16] In the end, the Commission found that "the problems Florida had during the 2000 presidential election were serious and not isolated"; that in many cases, these negative results "were foreseeable and should have been prevented"; and that "the failure to do so resulted in an extraordinarily high and inexcusable level of disenfranchisement, with a significantly disproportionate impact on African American voters."[17] Although unspoken, the underlying message of the Commission's report was that race-based voter disenfranchisement was alive and well in Florida.

The specter of race-based disenfranchisement could not have happened at a less opportune place or time in American history. Through a perfect storm of events, the 2000 presidential election was deadlocked, and the deadlock stretched from a day to a week to a month and ultimately to almost forty days. Over 100,000,000 Americans voted in this election—and yet no clear winner had emerged. True, Al Gore had won a majority of the national popular vote, but it is the electoral vote that determines who gets to be president—and in this election neither candidate had an electoral majority with the Florida vote still waiting for resolution. The Florida vote, in turn, had divided evenly between the two candidates. Out of some 5 million votes cast, 1,600 votes separated Bush and Gore in the Sunshine State on November 8—less than .005 percent of the votes cast. Subsequent recounts would lower that margin to just over 500 votes. In the end, no true accounting of the actual vote in

Florida was reached. Rather, a controversial U.S. Supreme Court ruling in *Bush v. Gore* declared Florida's vote-counting system unconstitutional and then asserted that the time for recounting votes was over—and thus that George W. Bush (who was ahead in this unconstitutional counting process) was the winner in Florida, and the nation.

The message of the Civil Rights Commission's report was clear. In an election in which only a few hundred votes separated the candidates (and yet still effectively picked the next President of the United States), thousands, perhaps tens of thousands, of Florida voters had been denied fair and legal access to the ballot or had had their votes wrongfully excluded from the final count. Had the Florida electoral system worked the way it was supposed to work, the outcome of the election—and by implication, the identity of the next president of the United States—could well have been different. And with this difference, the subsequent history of the nation could have been very different had Al Gore become president instead of George W. Bush.

The question remains: Just how important was the voter disenfranchisement in Florida in 2000, especially when viewed from a long-term perspective? Was this voter disenfranchisement the same as voter disenfranchisement of the past? Was it *intentional* discrimination with the goal of disenfranchising thousands of minority voters or just a series of *unintentional* mistakes? While not lessening the immediate impact of these actions, the lack of intent would imply a much less serious long-term problem for the nation.

Those who experienced the events in Florida were largely convinced that they were intentional acts, that the "mistakes" of Florida election officials reflected deeper patterns of discrimination and racism. They pointed to such experiences as that of Kandy Wells, who never received a voter's registration card despite registering to vote well before the registration deadline. Her white husband, on the other hand, who registered to vote at the same time that she did, received his card two weeks before the election. "You've got to remember that only 40 or 50 years ago blacks couldn't vote," Wells noted. "Things like this have been happening in Florida all along. It's just that this time it's so close and they got caught." Marvin Davies of Tampa, a veteran of the 1960s civil rights struggle, was even more convinced that what happened in Florida was little more than a continuation of the struggles of the 1950s and 1960s.

"When you go into that ballot box, the black man has the same power as the white man, so the white man will use all his money and all his power to stop the black man getting there," argued Davies.[18]

The Commission was less certain that this was the case. In its Executive Summary, the Commission's Report noted, "The highest officials of the state [did not] conspire to disenfranchise voters." What was happening in Florida in 2000 was not a *purposeful* attack on the voting rights of African Americans and other minorities. What happened in Florida was a tragedy, but it was a tragedy with its roots in administrative failure, unacceptable overconfidence verging on incompetence, underfunding of basic electoral processes, and a lack of planning and leadership on the part of Florida's election officials. At worst, the Commission declared, "state officials failed to fulfill their duties in a manner that would prevent this disenfranchisement," noting that while reforms were needed to see that this never happened again, this was as far as the Commission was willing to go.[19]

Yet if the discrimination experienced by minority voters in Florida during the 2000 presidential election was not intentional, if it was not a conspiracy by public officials to exclude minority voters from the franchise, how should we evaluate these events? Leaving aside the immediate impact of these excluded votes and voters, the long-term implications of a racially biased electoral process—intentional or not—are huge. The United States is a constitutional democracy. The legitimacy of American political power is founded on the consent of the governed. To exclude significant portions of this population—and to do so based on racial or ethnic standards—undermines the process's legitimacy, as well as the legitimacy of the results the process generates. Even if the taint is unintentional, the result poses a grave crisis for American democracy. Yet how much worse would it be if it were done intentionally? That significant numbers of African Americans in Florida could conclude that they had been victims of intentional acts of discrimination at the polls points to a much bigger problem.

The best way to evaluate this quandary is to examine the 2000 presidential vote in Florida in its historical and contemporary contexts. We need to understand what came before and what came after to evaluate the place of this event in history and to determine what lessons, if any, we can draw from it. While contextualizing our inquiry might not illuminate the actual intent of Florida's election officials on November 7, 2000, it can enable us to evaluate the seriousness of the events of 2000 and to elucidate their long-term implications.

"White Folks Ain't Going to Let Blacks Folks Vote"

In the years following the Civil War, hope dawned for millions of African Americans that freedom would bring with it a full entry into American public life—an entry best represented by the right to vote. Most Americans understood the Thirteenth Amendment's requirement that "neither slavery nor involuntary servitude . . . shall exist within the United States" to mean that newly freed blacks would acquire all aspects of freedom, including the right to vote. The Fourteenth Amendment's promise of equal protection and its defense of the "privileges or immunities of citizens of the United States" added support to claims of newly freed African Americans to the franchise. And then, seeming to clinch the matter once and for all, the Fifteenth Amendment declared: "The right of citizens of the United States to vote shall not be denied or abridged by the United States or by any State on account of race, color, or previous condition of servitude." Combined with the various Civil Rights and Enforcement Acts passed by Congress to implement these amendments and the presence of the U.S. Army empowered and directed to enforce congressional Reconstruction of the South, including establishing black voting rights, it appeared that African Americans would have a clear and simple path to the polls.

Events proved otherwise. For several years, southern black males did freely exercise their franchise. In 1867 and 1868, blacks across the South allied with white Republicans to elect large numbers of delegates, many of them black, to new state constitutional conventions. These Republican-dominated conventions, in turn, wrote extremely liberal constitutions granting full civil rights, including the right to vote, to African Americans. Hundreds of thousands of blacks quickly registered to vote; and in later elections they exercised this right in large numbers.[20]

By the early 1870s, however, things had begun to fall apart. Most white southerners detested Reconstruction and opposed the Republican-dominated (and black-led) Reconstruction state governments. As early as 1866, white terrorist organizations—the best-known being the

Ku Klux Klan—sought to block all efforts to transform the South's social and political relations. Seeking to frustrate the rise of Republican-led governments, these insurgents launched waves of race-based violence and terror that spread across the South. Republican Party meetings were broken up. Prominent blacks were attacked and often killed. Before long, even average blacks were assaulted for being "impudent" toward whites or "not knowing their place"; in 1870 alone, the death toll reached the hundreds and the number of injured rose into the thousands. In the worst episodes of racialized violence, white mobs attacked entire groups of blacks, terrorizing most and killing many. In one notorious 1873 incident, in Colfax, Louisiana, a white mob attacked and trapped 150 blacks in the county courthouse for three days; by the siege's end, fifty blacks had been massacred—after they had tried surrendering under a white flag.[21]

Bad economic times, well-publicized political scandals, and heavy campaigning by Democrats among the region's white voters added to the Republicans' woes. Combined with the chilling effects of violence on black voting, the result by the mid-1870s was that Democrats had recaptured all but three southern states. When, in 1877, after a bitter and inconclusive presidential election, the Republicans agreed to end Reconstruction as the price for the Democrats' acquiescence in the questionable granting of the presidency to Republican presidential candidate Rutherford B. Hayes, the end was near. Soon afterward, the remaining three Republican state governments fell. By the 1880s, political power in the American South was firmly in the hands of those opposed to black civil and political rights, under the banner of the Democratic Party.[22]

Acting quickly to cement their victory, southern white officials began a slow, steady campaign to blot out every trace of African American voting. Blacks' access to the polls declined slowly over a twenty-year period. As late as the 1890s, many blacks continued to participate in Republican Party politics and the electoral process. Yet in the face of such continued electoral activity, the general trend after 1877 was toward vote dilution and outright vote denial, with blacks as the targets. Southern white society could not accept the idea of black equality, for, in their eyes, blacks were not capable of being equal to whites. As one southern newspaper promised in 1875, although the Fourteenth and Fifteenth Amendments might "stand forever . . . we intend . . . to make them dead letters on the statute-book[s]."[23]

The result was a concerted, ongoing, and ultimately successful campaign of race-based disenfranchisement. Hoping to discourage black voters from exercising the franchise, for example, southern election officials in the 1870s and 1880s set up polling places in areas inconvenient for blacks—either at distant locations or in the middle of white sections of the town or county, with some even put in businesses owned by known opponents of African American voting. Such arrangements were at least intimidating, and often outright dangerous, for those blacks brave enough to seek to vote. A parallel approach limited the hours when predominantly black polling places were open; a few local officials refused to open these polling places at all.[24] Even more disturbing were laws designed to keep blacks from being listed on the voting rolls or to allow local officials to purge black voters from the voting lists. Epitomizing the most common approach was an 1873 Georgia law (echoed by laws adopted in North Carolina and Alabama) permitting local election supervisors to close their registration rolls to new applicants *except* during those times when black farmers were too busy to register, such as planting or harvest time. Some states added the requirement that voters show proof of registration before they could vote or face immediate disqualification. Given the long gap between registering and voting in most southern states, many blacks (as well as whites) could not meet this test.[25] Virginia went one step further, mandating separate registration books for white and black voters; not surprisingly, black registration books regularly were declared "missing" when blacks wished to register or were "lost" on voting day.[26] Finally, in an increasingly common practice in all the southern states, legislators added to the list of felonies that disqualified a felon from voting ever again those crimes considered most likely to be committed by blacks—arson, bigamy, and petty theft. "White crimes," on the other hand, such as grand larceny, carried no such limits.[27]

By the early 1890s, southern whites expanded their attacks on black voting to the next stage: total vote denial based on race. As one delegate to Virginia's 1901 constitutional convention noted, the intent after 1890 was "to disfranchise every Negro that [they] could disfranchise under the Constitution of the United States, and as few white people as possible."[28] Although operating mostly through technically race-neutral structures, between 1890 and 1905 state governments across the South updated their election laws and revised their constitutions to exclude black voting more fully. Mississippi devised the first and most successful of these disenfranchisement plans. Written into the state's new constitution in 1890, the four-step Mississippi Plan included: a $2 poll tax payable before registration; a literacy test in which voters had to read, understand, or interpret any section of the state constitution to the satisfaction of a white (and usually hostile) election official; long-term residency rules demanding two years domicile within the state and one year within the voting district; and permanent disenfranchisement for crimes deemed most likely to be committed by blacks.[29]

The Mississippi Plan was popular with whites at home and also appealed to whites in other southern states; each soon copied Mississippi's new approach to vote denial. In 1895 South Carolina required all voters to read and/or explain any section of the state constitution provided by the local voting registrar, as well as to meet a two-year residency requirement.[30] Louisiana built similar literacy requirements into its 1898 constitution, along with a new poll tax and rules denying felons the vote unless pardoned by the governor. Concerned with the potential that these rules might bar poor and illiterate whites from the polls, the state also adopted a grandfather clause allowing those who had voted before 1867 (when blacks could not vote), or whose fathers and grandfathers had voted then, to waive the new requirements.[31] Two years later, as its primary tools of vote denial, North Carolina imposed a poll tax and adopted literacy tests administered by local registrars (who had full discretion as to which parts of the state constitution applicants had to read); the state also adopted a grandfather clause similar to Louisiana's to protect poor white voters.[32] Similar outcomes followed as Alabama in 1901, Virginia in 1902, Texas in 1904, and Georgia in 1908 revised their constitutions.[33]

The results of such efforts were immediate and drastic. By 1896 all forms of black voter participation in Mississippi had declined to a mere 9 percent (fewer than 9,000 out of a potential 147,000 voting-age blacks). In Louisiana registered black voters declined by 99 percent to just 1,300 in 1904; eight years earlier it had stood at 130,000. Alabama recognized only 3,000 registered black voters in 1902, a precipitous drop from the state's pool of 181,000 voters in 1900. In Georgia, as of 1910 only 4 percent of black males were even registered to vote. In Texas, black voting had declined to a mere 5,000 votes by 1906. In the new century, across the entire South, voter turnout fell from a high of 85 percent of all voters during Reconstruction to less than 50 percent for whites and single-digit percentages for blacks.[34]

By the early 1900s, the southern whites' fight against black voting was largely complete. As of 1915 no southern state was without some sort of vote-denial program. These measures would stay in force throughout much of the first two-thirds of the twentieth century. Even successful attacks in the federal courts on these techniques launched by such civil rights organizations as the National Association for the Advancement of Colored People (NAACP) resulted only in these methods being revised and modified—but not abandoned.[35]

In Alabama, for instance, such time-tested disfranchisement techniques as the poll tax, literacy tests, long-term residency requirements, and the precondition of gainful employment to vote (all in place by 1900) were updated by such drastic procedures as a 1946 amendment to the state constitution (the Boswell Amendment) limiting registration to those who, in the view of local registrars, "could 'understand and explain' any article of the federal constitution"—a requirement that few blacks seemed to meet. Even more extreme was the 1957 gerrymandering of the municipal boundaries of Tuskegee, Alabama, to exclude from city elections all but 4 or 5 of the city's 400 or so qualified black voters (but no white voter). Less drastic, but perhaps more effective, was a 1951 Alabama law prohibiting "single-shot" voting in at-large county elections. In at-large elections, all the candidates run against one another, with the top vote-getters filling the available seats. Single-shot voting occurs where a particular sub-group of voters withholds some of their votes to ensure that their preferred candidate is one of the top vote-getters. Under the 1951 law, all ballots failing to include a full slate of preferences were disqualified, making single-shot voting impossible, and thus undermining the ability of blacks to elect even one candidate in an at-large election.[36]

Georgia focused its discriminatory efforts on undermining black voter registration. In 1949, the state legislature passed a "registration and purge" law. Under this statute, any voter who failed to vote in an election at least once in a two-year period was automatically expunged from the voter rolls. Further, anyone who re-registered following removal from the election lists (or who registered for the first time) had to pass the state's existing literacy test or to answer ten of thirty questions aimed at proving "good character" and the possession of an "understanding of the duties of citizenship." Enforcement of the literacy and "good character" tests, in turn, fell to the discretion of unsympathetic, and usually hostile, white local election officials whose standards were so demanding that even educated blacks had trouble passing these tests; for illiterate blacks, they proved to be almost insurmountable barriers.[37]

Similar patterns of exclusion appeared in states across the South. North Carolina centralized control over elections, established "intricate procedures for voter registration," and granted local registrars extensive powers to use these complex registration procedures to undermine black voting.[38] South Carolina responded to the court-ordered end of the all-white primary (which excluded black voting in the one election that had any real policy impact in the South) by removing from the statute books all 150 state laws regulating primary elections; the legislators hoped that making the Democratic primary a totally "private" affair would solve the constitutional problems with the all-white primary as a public process.[39] Texas placed its faith in a poll tax, which, though only a small amount of money ($1.75), was still prohibitively expensive for poor black and Hispanic laborers, to whom $1.75 was a day's wages.[40] Virginia allowed a proportionally larger black vote in primaries and general elections than other southern states—while at the same time trusting to the existing system of poll taxes, "understanding" requirements, and literacy tests to limit the electoral impact of black voting.[41] Louisiana used a constitutional "interpretation" test, along with a system by which any two registered voters could legally challenge the registration of another voter, to purge blacks from the voter rolls.[42]

The results of these exclusionary efforts, though not completely successful in stopping black registration or voting, were still considerable. As late as 1940, only 3 percent of voting-age southern blacks had been registered to vote—and in states adopting the all-white primary system, no black voter could take part in the one election that had practical meaning. In the 1950s, this situation began to change. By 1956, 25 percent of voting-age blacks were registered to vote; by 1964, this number had increased to 43.3 percent across the South. Raw numbers can be deceiving, however. Most registered black voters lived in the border states or in Florida; in the Deep South, where most blacks lived, as late as 1964 African American voter registration stood at only 22.5 percent, with Mississippi setting the lowest standard at 6.7 percent (though this figure was more than a threefold increase from a rate of 1.98 percent in 1962).[43] Worse yet, the application of such vote-dilution techniques as voting lists purges, at-large elections, and full-slate and majority-vote

requirements—not to mention the ever-present threats of economic re-
prisals and physical violence against any black trying to vote—meant
that, even in those areas where blacks could vote, no black candidate was
elected to office. Things got so bad that one observer maintained, "For
Negroes in some sections of the South, an attempt to exercise their right
of franchise as Americans seemed a greater risk in 1958 than at any time
since the outlawing of the white primary in 1944."[44]

Only with the passage of the Voting Rights Act of 1965 did these patterns begin to change—and even then, it would take over twenty years
of constant litigation and political pressure by the federal government
to force this reform to happen. Still, change did occur. As voting rights
scholars Chandler Davidson and Bernard Grofman note, "hundreds of
southern cities, counties, and other kinds of jurisdictions shifted from
at-large elections in the 1980s. . . . [with] remarkable gains in [minority]
officeholding." Numbering fewer than a hundred in 1965, black elected
officials in the seven southern states originally targeted by that year's
Voting Rights Act tallied some 3,265 in 1989—9.8 percent of all elected
officials in these states.[45]

Everything Old Is New Again

From the 1960s to the eve of the 2000 presidential election, the South
had undergone a virtual revolution in terms of minority participation in
the electoral process. Race- and ethnic-based vote denial seemed, if not
a thing of the past, at least a fading remnant of a bygone era; those who
complained that problems still existed, in turn, seemed out of touch with
the changes that had transformed America in general and the South in
particular. The age of disenfranchisement was over. Or was it?

The specter of a deeper problem in race relations than was reachable
by federal voting-rights statutes and enforcement made the events in
Florida in 2000 so troubling. As the events of November and December
2000 unfolded, many hoped that what had occurred in Florida concerning minority voting was an aberration. Reports from the Civil Rights
Commission and from the Florida Governor's Select Task Force on Election Procedures, Standards and Technology stressed that although many
problems did exist, they were not the result of intentional disenfranchisement efforts; in any case, both investigating groups agreed, these
problems could be fixed.[46] In Florida and throughout the nation, calls

for reform rang out, including promises of newer and more trustworthy electoral machines and procedures. "We will fix what is broken" was the message of the day.

Still, the idea that there could be purposeful disenfranchisement in the twenty-first century was a frightening prospect. Surely this could not be the case. The fault of what happened in Florida lay with error and mistake, not intent. Fix the machines, update the voter databases, and all would be fine. Or would it?

Sadly, as later events showed, all would not be fine. Although probes attributed much of what went wrong in Florida to error, overconfidence, and a lack of administrative oversight, underneath the surface lay troubling hints of a darker narrative of *intentional* exclusion, albeit one based more on political orientation and partisanship than on race.

The felon-purge-list problems in Florida in 2000 hint at the existence of this politically driven process. Lawmakers knew that African American men made up over 31 percent of the disenfranchised felon population in Florida. They also knew that the list that they were drawing up had a large number of "false positives." Despite warnings from DBT officials that names of non-felons appeared on the list, state officials still sent that list to county supervisors without adequate warnings as to the potential problems it contained.[47] Moreover, these officials knew or should have known that, given normal naming patterns, if large numbers of felons came from one group, then many of the false positives also would be from this group—and that pattern proved to be the case. As the Commission noted, "African Americans [had] a better chance of erroneously appearing on the Florida felon exclusion list" than members of other groups did.[48] In Miami-Dade County, for instance, "African Americans represented the majority of persons—over 65 percent—on . . . [the purge] lists," a percentage that "far exceed[ed] the African American population of Miami-Dade County, which [was] only 20.4 percent." Similarly skewed numbers could be found in other counties as well.[49]

So why exclude African American voters if race was not the primary motivating factor? Where is the negative intent? The answer lies in voting patterns. Statistics show that most African American voters cast ballots for Democratic candidates. In 2000, Al Gore received 90 percent of the African American vote. Four years later, John Kerry drew 88 percent of black votes. In 2008, 95 percent of African Americans voted for the Democratic candidate, Barack Obama. Statistics also showed that other

Democratic candidates received African American votes in similarly overwhelming numbers throughout this period as well.[50] Those in charge of Florida's electoral machinery—from the legislature enacting the laws requiring the felon ban list to the secretary of state commissioning the purge list to a majority of the county supervisors of elections administering the purge list—were Republicans. Hence, every "felon" excluded from voting meant at least a 31 percent (or 65 percent depending on how one counted the numbers) decrease in the chance of a vote for the other party. And, given the list's inaccuracies, many of those so excluded were, in fact, valid voters who legally should have been allowed to vote, indicating that the exclusions created an unearned partisan advantage.

Of course, what happened in 2000 could have been a mistake. There is no real proof that in 2000 the Republican officials who oversaw the purge list *intended* to exclude non-felons as a partisan ploy to win a close election. It could have been coincidence that the people wrongly excluded happened to vote for the other political party. Such was not the case, however, for the felon purge that the state carried out in 2004.

In early May 2004, the Florida Secretary of State's office sent county election supervisors a "scrub list" of 48,000 "potential felons" and asked county election offices to begin to remove those named on the list from the voting rolls. As in 2000, a private company had generated the list, in this case Accenture, Inc., from data supplied from the state's unified voter database (at a cost of $1.8 million). Along with the list came instructions from Secretary of State Glenda Hood to not distribute copies of the list to anyone, especially not the media.[51]

Hood had good reason to issue this order. Having obtained an advance look at the purge list, the *Miami Herald* reported on July 2 that "more than 2,100 Florida voters—many of them black Democrats—could be wrongly barred from voting in November because Tallahassee elections officials included them on a list of felons potentially ineligible to vote." It turned out that each of these former felons had had "their rights to vote . . . formally restored through the state's clemency process," but had not had their names removed from the list.[52] Five days later, on July 11, the *Sarasota Herald-Tribune* reported that "out of the nearly 48,000 names on the list, only 61 were Hispanic."[53] Given that many Florida Hispanics voted Republican and most Florida blacks voted Democratic, many saw in this statistic proof of a conspiracy to "fix" the election. At the least, the echoes of 2000's flawed voter purge resonated with such individuals.[54]

At first, state officials defended the list. "I can tell you with the utmost certainty that it was unintentional and unforeseen," responded Hood spokeswoman Nicole de Lara. When this argument did not work, state officials then denied responsibility for the purges. In a press conference, "Hood repeatedly stressed that county elections officials—not her office—are ultimately responsible for screening voters and protecting their rights."[55]

Local election officials, already burdened with trying to set things in motion for the November 2 election, objected loudly to this announcement. Ion Sancho, elections supervisor for Leon County, asked, "Why is the state doing this now? Within three minutes we identified an individual who should not be on the list. Right off the bat." Sancho noted that he had "never seen such an incompetent program implemented by the DOE." Kay Clem, from Indian River County, asked, "How do you make somebody prove on election day that they're not a felon?"[56]

In the end, such complaints proved effective. Under growing media and political pressure, on July 10 state officials finally agreed to withdraw the purge list. Given the widespread perception that the list was tilted to help the Republicans, Governor Jeb Bush felt that he had little choice but to pull the list. "It was the right thing to do," Bush explained. "The perception of all this begins to become reality." Despite withdrawing the list, Bush continued to defend his administration's actions. The omission of Hispanics was simply an "oversight and a mistake," Bush insisted. The governor chalked up the "swirl of conspiracy theories" being bandied about over the list to the "'political process' and to Democrats' hopes of turning out voters 'for their own cause.'"[57]

Although Bush downplayed the potential partisan impact of the purge list as a "conspiracy theor[y]," it is hard to ignore the list's potential—had it been used—to wrongly exclude African American voters who were likely to have voted for the other party. In a state where the victor in the last presidential election had won by just over 500 votes, the impact of even a few wrongly excluded votes could have been huge. More to the point, as the immediate reaction to the list's exclusion of Hispanic surnames showed, the political implications of the list's content were clear to everyone—including the election officials who commissioned the list.

Another example of the partisan inducement to exclude minority voters since 2000 arose in a non-southern state, Ohio. For weeks before Election Day 2004, word had been coming from Ohio of administrative rulings changing voting procedures and having the potential to exclude large numbers of (mostly Democratic) minority voters. The source of many of these reports was Republican J. Kenneth Blackwell, Ohio's secretary of state and chief elections official. Throughout September and October, Blackwell issued a series of administrative rulings that had the potential cumulative effect of excluding tens of thousands, even hundreds of thousands, of voters from the polls—or so charged the Democrats. Republicans disagreed, noting accurately that Blackwell's administrative rulings were perfectly legal and well within his authority. Democrats countered that although such justifications might be factually correct, they did not contradict the exclusionary effect of Blackwell's actions. Republicans failed to answer this charge.[58]

Blackwell's first ruling, which came on September 7, focused on registration forms printed on lightweight paper. His directive demanded that county boards of elections reject voter registration forms not "printed on white, uncoated paper of not less than 80 lb. text weight."[59] While on the surface there was nothing controversial about Blackwell's ruling, the timing of its initial publication less than one month before Ohio's voter registration deadline expired raised serious concerns. Many election officials feared that a change in procedures so close to the registration cut-off date would cause widespread confusion and chaos and result in fewer voters being registered. "It will create more confusion than the paper's worth," Jan Clair, director of the Lake County Board of Elections and a Republican, said. "It's the weight of the vote I'm concerned about on Nov. 2—that's the important thing."[60] Steve Harsman, deputy director of the Montgomery County board, worried that, given the backlog of application forms, there was a strong possibility that many voters who already had sent in a form (he estimated as many as 800) might not have their applications reprocessed in time to meet the registration deadline. With over 4,000 registration forms in backlog and more coming in every day, there was not enough time to process them all, given the delay that a second registration would entail. He also questioned the need for the ruling. "There is just no reason to use 80-pound paper," Harsman complained.[61]

It is impossible to tell how many potential voters could not vote as a result of Blackwell's initial ruling on registration forms. Anecdotal evidence suggests that "delays in processing new voter registrations kept many from being added to the rolls."[62] Statistical analysis conducted by the nonpartisan Greater Cleveland Voter Registration Coalition (GCVRC) suggested, "16,000 voters in and around the city were disenfranchised because of data-entry errors by election officials, and another 15,000 lost the right to vote due to largely inconsequential omissions on their registration cards." Statewide, the study concluded, "a total of 72,000 voters were disenfranchised through avoidable registration errors—one percent of all voters in an election decided by barely two percent."[63]

A similar problem arose in regard to voter registration as a whole. Ohio already was facing a registration tidal wave in 2004. On September 26, the *Associated Press* reported, "in Ohio's largest counties, election boards [were] getting nearly double the number of registration cards submitted in 2000." The scramble to register voters was "only expected to intensify . . . as the Oct. 4 registration deadline near[ed]." Despite hiring extra staff members and extending working hours to process cards, election boards across the state kept falling behind. Some boards were processing cards twenty-four hours a day and it still was not enough.[64] Most of these new voters were Democrats.[65]

The collision of large numbers of new, mostly Democratic voters with administrative confusion and delay was a troubling, potentially volatile combination. With voter lists in disorder, many of these new voters would have to vote provisionally. Surveys in two Ohio counties commissioned by the Democratic National Committee after the election showed that a large percentage of voters casting provisional ballots did so "in large part because election officials fail[ed] to process voter registrations and changes in registration occurring shortly before the election."[66] Any delays in processing registration cards, therefore, were more likely to affect Democratic than Republican voters. And although most of these voters probably would be allowed to cast provisional ballots, this prospect did not necessarily mean improvement. Provisional ballots raised their own troubling issues—issues made more complex by Secretary Blackwell's second administrative directive on voting.

Announced on September 17, this directive restricted the ability of voters to use provisional ballots. The new rule held that provisional voting was allowed only in the precinct where a voter lived. Where voters were improperly allowed to fill out a provisional ballot in the wrong precinct (on the mistaken belief that they were in the right precinct), their votes would not be counted.[67]

Democrats charged that, although this ruling was perfectly legal, in the Election Day confusion voters might be unable to locate their correct precincts. The large numbers of new registrations had necessitated the shifting of precinct lines, transferring many voters to new and unfamiliar polling places. Worse yet, Democrats complained, the ruling showed bias against poor, mostly Democratic voters. Lower-income people, many of them minorities, "moved frequently and were more likely to go to the wrong precincts," state and local party officials complained. The result would be widespread disenfranchisement predominantly affecting Democratic voters. So although the ruling might have been legal, its effects showed decided bias in favor of Blackwell's own party.[68]

Election Day proved these fears correct. As expected, provisional balloting proved to be a mess, with 155,428 voters filing provisional ballots.[69] In Pepper Pike, Ohio, Mark Cohn, a local lawyer, ran into exactly the problem that Democrats had warned against. When he arrived to vote at his usual place, his name was not on the registered-voter list for his precinct. He cast a provisional ballot, only to learn later that his name had been mistakenly included on the list for a different precinct. Even so, despite the clerical mistake that placed him on a different precinct list, he was informed that his vote was still invalid because he did not cast his provisional ballot in the "right precinct." Only after Cohn filed suit in federal court did the election board agreed to discard his provisional ballot and let him vote again.[70] In Toledo, Alexandra Hernandez described in later hearings her experiences with "a young African American woman who had come out" of a polling place "nearly in tears." "She was a new voter," Hernandez explained, "very first registered, very excited to vote, and she . . . had been bounced around to three different polling places, and this one had just turned her down again."[71]

Stories of this sort were common across the state. Reporters from the *Washington Post* found scores of longtime voters who had had their names dropped from the voter rolls. Forced to vote provisionally, they wondered if their votes would count. "I'm 52, and I've voted in every single election," Kathy Janoski of Columbus told the *Post* reporters. "They kept telling me, 'You must be mistaken about your precinct.' I told them this is where I've always voted. I felt like I'd been scrubbed off the rolls."[72] Frustratingly, many rejected provisional ballots such as Janoski's were filled out in precincts housed *in the same polling place* as the right precincts—but the poll workers, overworked and undertrained, did not direct the provisional voter to the right table in the same building.[73]

The numbers of lost votes were significant. In Cuyahoga County, the Greater Cleveland Voter Registration Coalition (GCVRC) registered about 10,000 voters, most of them minorities, yet found on Election Day that 3.5 percent of those applications either were not entered into the voter databases or were entered incorrectly. These problems effectively disenfranchised these applicants (for even had they been able to vote provisionally, their ballots would not have been counted).[74] In a study carried out after the election, the GCVRC estimated: "Based on the findings of our studies of both Board of Elections and voter entry errors in about 9,600 applications for registration or change of address, we project that nearly 7,000 Cuyahoga County voters were probably disqualified and about 12,500 voters were put at varying degrees of risk of disqualification." They added: "Over 900 provisional ballots may have been wrongfully rejected because of database problems alone." Overall, "2 out of every 5 provisional ballots that were rejected should have been accepted as legitimate." Simple factors, such as changing one's residence, exposed "voters to a 6% chance of being disenfranchised." Race and ethnicity also had an impact. "In fact, with respect to just provisional ballots," the report concluded, "we found a two-fold increase in rejection rate in predominantly African-American compared to predominantly Caucasian precincts."[75]

Perhaps the most notable example of arguably intentional efforts to limit voting in Ohio had to do with the placement of voting machines. According to a *Washington Post* investigation, "in Columbus, Cincinnati and Toledo, and on college campuses, election officials allocated far too few voting machines to busy precincts, with the result that voters stood on line as long as 10 hours—many leaving without voting." At Kenyon College, northeast of Columbus in central Ohio, "students were forced to stand in line for eleven hours before being allowed to vote, with the last voters casting their ballots after three in the morning."[76] Carolyn M. Sherman, a poll worker in an inner-city Columbus precinct, reported waits of up to eight hours to vote, as 1,500 voters found just three machines available to them.[77] The DNC report concluded that "not providing a sufficient number of voting machines in each precinct was associated with roughly a *two to three percent reduction in voter turnout* presumably due to delays that deterred many people from voting."[78] The human costs of such practices could be seen in the experience of Sarah Locke, 54, of Columbus. Her precinct, "a church in the predominantly black southeast [side of town] . . . was jammed. Old women leaned heavily on walkers, and some people walked out complaining that bosses would not excuse their lateness," Locke noted. Meanwhile, in the suburbs, voting machines were plentiful and lines were short.[79]

The primary cause of this discrepancy in time taken to vote between urban and suburban precincts was the significant lack of voting machines in busy inner-city precincts. One report showed that "at seven of eight polling places in Franklin County," all in the heavily populated city of Columbus, "there were only three voting machines per location." This was a notable change from the 2004 primary, when "there had been five machines at these locations." A *New York Times* investigation confirmed this discrepancy, noting that just before the election, Franklin County election officials—Republicans all—had reduced the number of voting machines assigned to downtown precincts and added them to the suburbs. They reassigned these machines by applying "a formula based not on the number of registered voters, but on past turnout in each precinct and on the number of so-called active voters—a smaller universe." In the Columbus area, "the result was that suburban precincts that supported Mr. Bush tended to have more machines per registered voter than center city precincts that supported Mr. Kerry."[80] Making matters worse, these same election officials in Columbus had limited themselves to only 2,866 machines, even though their own analysis showed that the county needed 5,000 machines for a smooth election—hence the shift of machines around the county.[81] Adding to the chaos, 77 machines broke down during the course of the day; meanwhile, in a warehouse sat some 81 voting machines that were never placed in any precinct on Election Day.[82]

Nor does the story stop here. In 2005, Republican-dominated Indiana (another non-southern state) adopted a law requiring voters to present a government-issued ID such as a driver's license in order to vote. In 2008 the U.S. Supreme Court upheld this rule, holding that "the state interests identified as justifications for [the law] are both neutral and sufficiently strong to require us to reject" the lawsuit. Unfortunately, studies have shown that "more than two thirds of Indiana adults have no passports and nearly 15 percent have no driver's licenses." Moreover, the vast majority of these eligible voters are "disproportionately African-American." And although it is true that they could, if they wished, seek out a non-driver's license ID from the state, for many the lack of transportation represented by their not having a driver's license makes this a difficult task, one that many are likely to abandon. The result, once again, was a potential diminution of the minority vote for partisan political gains.[83] In September 2008, Republican officials in Wisconsin brought suit "to enforce a 'no match, no vote' provision in state regulations, where voters must not only show a photo ID, but establish that it matches the name and number in the Department of Motor Vehicles or Social Security Administration database." The database, in turn, is riddled with errors, with the result that a close-match requirement, should it be adopted, would have the potential to exclude thousands of voters, many of them newly registered and minority.[84] Finally, there is Florida's recent experiment in "don't match, don't vote" requirements.[85]

Attacking the Republican officials who made these choices is not the point here. Were Democrats to see an advantage in excluding potential Republican votes by such exclusionary means, history suggests that they would act as the Republicans had done.[86] Rather, it is to point out how, in an age of extreme partisanship, where a shift of even a few votes could change an election's outcome, the chance exists to affect the results of voting by excluding from the polls those voters most likely to vote for the opposing party—and the temptation to take advantage of this opportunity is large. Moreover, given the current tendency of minority voters to vote Democratic, the result of this tendency (should Republicans in power take advantage of it) would be a sharp rise in minority vote denial—a rebirth of race-based and ethnic-based disenfranchisement—done by differing means and for differing motives but resulting in disenfranchisement nonetheless.

Conclusion

Americans remember the infamous 2000 presidential election for hanging chads, butterfly ballots, endless recounts, raucous allegations of constitutional and political misconduct, and a constitutional crisis—with the mess capped by a controversial Supreme Court decision that conferred the presidency on George W. Bush despite his having lost the national popular vote to Al Gore. We remember it for Florida's seeming inability to vote without error and for the state's disparate methods of counting votes from county to county. We remember it for a crisis that potentially threatened the nation's political and constitutional foundations.

Though these things are what Americans remember, they are not all the reasons why we should remember 2000. Eclipsed by the fight to name a new president was a darker story, one whose roots go back to the nineteenth century and a hundred-year fight for basic civil rights—a story many thought (and still think) to be long over and done with.

The 2000 presidential election in Florida exposed the ongoing difficulties faced by minorities who seek to exercise the hard-won right to vote. Voting should be a simple civic duty, but the tactics of vote denial spread a myriad of obstacles to that duty and in the process discourage all too many voters from taking the trouble to vote. Despite decades of successful legal and political efforts to combat race-based and ethnic-based voter denial, Florida in 2000 denied the vote to tens of thousands of legal voters, most of them minorities—and Florida authorities did this through perfectly legal legislative, administrative, and procedural means. Even if the intent to exclude was not present, the result was the same. In so doing, Florida in 2000 echoed past efforts by conservative forces in American—and especially southern—life to exclude from the electorate those deemed "unfit" on account of their race and ethnicity. It exposed the pervasive nature of vote denial and it pointed out the new and innovative means by which conservative and reactionary forces in American political life could—and did—continue their campaign to limit the franchise to those who in their eyes are "qualified" to vote. Events since 2000 have only reinforced these perceptions and the harsh realities to which they give rise.

Moreover, in line with the focus of this book, the events surrounding the election of 2000 and those that followed make clear that any investigation of the interaction of civil rights with the presidency must include a close look not just at the individual presidents and their policies regarding race but also a closer examination of the process by which those presidents have been elected. In other words, we need to look at the structural constraints under which the American people choose their leaders—a process that historically has raised serious concerns about the enfranchisement or disenfranchisement of thousands of minority voters and hence has shaped the electoral pressures on those elected to the presidency to meet the legitimate policy demands of minorities in this country.

Whatever the motivation for examining these events, the 2000 election and its progeny makes one thing abundantly clear: the ongoing civil rights fight for a fair and equitable ballot continues. Even though the bottle may be new, and the brewing methods may be different, the vinegar of disenfranchisement within remains essentially the same. The lesson is clear: if we do not pay attention to such considerations, and if we take for granted past constitutional victories in the battle for the franchise, then we will find that once again we are "losing while winning."

Notes

1. Julian Borger, "How Florida played the race card: 700,000 people with criminal past banned from voting in pivotal state," *The Guardian*, December 4, 2000, http://www.guardian.co.uk/world/2000/dec/04/uselections2000.usa. For other examples, see Robert E. Pierre, "Botched Name Purge Denied Some the Right to Vote," *Washington Post*, May 31, 2001, A1, http://www.washingtonpost.com/ac2/wp-dyn/A99749-2001May30.

2. United States Commission on Civil Rights, *Voting Irregularities in Florida During the 2000 Presidential Election*, unpaginated online text available at http://www.usccr.gov/pubs/vote2000/report/main.htm, chapter 2: "First-Hand Accounts of Voter Disenfranchisement," at note 4.

3. Borger, "How Florida played the race card."

4. See USCCR, *Voting Irregularities in Florida During the 2000 Presidential Election*, chapter 2; Martin Merzer, *The Miami Herald Report: Democracy Held Hostage* (New York: St. Martins Press, 2001), chapters 5 & 6.

5. Jingle Davis, "U.S. Voting Standards Fall Far Short, Carter Says; Nonpartisan Panel Opens Hearings on Ways to Improve Accuracy and Fairness," *The Atlanta Journal-Constitution*, March 27, 2001, 1.

6. This paper was originally written for a symposium that occurred prior to the 2008 election. As such it does not go into any detail as to the 2008 election. For a discussion of the ongoing administrative electoral problems (race-based and otherwise) in that election, see the "Postscript" of the second edition (A=abridged and updated) of Charles L. Zelden, *Bush v. Gore: Exposing the Hidden Crisis in American Democracy* (Lawrence: University Press of Kansas, 2010), 265–71.

7. USCCR, *Voting Irregularities in Florida During the 2000 Presidential Election*, chapter 1 at notes 48–54.

8. USCCR, *Voting Irregularities in Florida During the 2000 Presidential Election*, chapter 9 at note 5.

9. Josh Barbanel and Ford Fessenden, "Racial Pattern in Demographics of Error-Prone Ballots," *New York Times*, November 29, 2000, A19. A *Washington Post* analysis of Florida's spoilage rates came to a similar conclusion. According to the *Post*, "in Miami-Dade County, precincts where fewer than 30 percent of the voters are black, about 3 percent of ballots did not register a vote for president. In precincts where more than 70 percent of the voters are African American, it was nearly 10 percent." Similarly, the *Post* found that "As many as one in three ballots in black sections of Jacksonville, for example, did not count in the presidential contest. That was four times as many as in white precincts elsewhere in mostly Republican Duval County." The *Post* concluded, "Heavily Democratic and African American neighborhoods in Florida lost many more presidential votes than other areas because of outmoded voting machines and rampant confusion about ballots." John Mintz and Dan Keating, "Fla. Ballot Spoilage Likelier for Blacks: Voting Machines, Confusion Cited," *Washington Post*, December 3, 2000, A1.

10. USCCR, *Voting Irregularities in Florida During the 2000 Presidential Election*, chapter 8 at notes 15–20.

11. USCCR, *Voting Irregularities in Florida During the 2000 Presidential Election*, chapter 1 at notes 75–81; chapter 5 at notes 1–18. See also John Lantigua, "How the GOP Gamed the System in Florida," *The Nation* (April 30, 2001), which describes the efforts to limit minority voting via voting-lists purges and other similar means.

12. USCCR, *Voting Irregularities in Florida During the 2000 Presidential Election*, chapter 5 at notes 59–67, 74 (quoting from George Bruder, VP of Database Technologies and Emmett "Bucky" Mitchell, who headed the state purge effort); Lance De-Haven-Smith, "Florida 2000: Beginnings of a Flawless Presidency," in *Loser Take All: Election Fraud and The Subversion of Democracy, 2000–2008*, ed. Mark Crispin Miller (Brooklyn, N.Y.: IG Publishing, 2008), 49.

13. USCCR, *Voting Irregularities in Florida During the 2000 Presidential Election*, chapter 5 at notes 141–95, chapter 3 at notes 54–74.

14. USCCR, *Voting Irregularities in Florida During the 2000 Presidential Election*, Executive Summary.

15. Quoted in Borger, "How Florida played the race card."

16. Jim Lobe, "Black Voters Still Disenfranchised," *Inter Press Service*, December 11, 2000. See Also, USCCR, *Voting Irregularities in Florida During the 2000 Presidential Election*, chapter 1 at notes 75–81; chapter 2 at notes 4–26; Dewey M Clayton, "A Funny Thing Happened on the Way to the Voting Precinct: A Brief History of Disenfranchisement in America," *The Black Scholar* 34 (Fall 2004): 42–52; Revathi I. Hines, "The Silent Voices: 2000 Presidential Election and the Minority Vote in Florida," *Western Journal of Black Studies* 26 (Summer 2002): 71–74.

17. USCCR, *Voting Irregularities in Florida During the 2000 Presidential Election*, Executive Summary.

18. Both quoted in Borger, "How Florida played the race card." A *Washington Post* poll, conducted in conjunction with the Henry J. Kaiser Family Foundation and Harvard University, reported "that nearly half of all blacks believe problems with voting machines and ballots fell disproportionately on minority voters; 85 percent of those

respondents believe there was a deliberate attempt to reduce their political power." Pierre, "Botched Name Purge Denied Some the Right to Vote."

19. USCCR, *Voting Irregularities in Florida During the 2000 Presidential Election*, Executive Summary and chapter 9 at note 3.

20. Eric Foner, "From Slavery to Citizenship: Blacks and the Right to Vote," in *Voting and the Spirit of American Democracy: Essays on the History of Voting and Voting Rights in America*. ed. Donald W. Rogers (Urbana: University of Illinois Press, 1992), 62–63.

21. See generally, Charles Lane, *The Day Freedom Died: The Colfax Massacre, the Supreme Court, and the Betrayal of Reconstruction* (New York: Henry Holt and Co., 2008); LeeAnna Keith, *The Colfax Massacre: The Untold Story of Black Power, White Terror and the Death of Reconstruction* (New York: Oxford University Press, 2008).

22. Michael Perman, *The Struggle for Mastery: Disenfranchisement in the South, 1888–1908* (Chapel Hill: University of North Carolina Press, 2001), 9–36.

23. Quoted in Eric Foner, *Reconstruction: America's Unfinished Revolution, 1863–1877* (New York: Harper & Row, 1988), 590.

24. J. Morgan Kousser, "The Undermining of the First Reconstruction: Lessons for the Second," in *Minority Vote Dilution*, ed. Chandler Davidson (Washington, D.C.: Howard University Press, 1984), 32; Laughlin McDonald, Michael B. Binford and Ken Johnson, "Georgia," in *Quiet Revolution in the South: The Impact of the Voting Rights Act, 1965–1990*, ed. Chandler Davidson and Bernard Grofman (Princeton: Princeton University Press, 1994), 67–68.

25. Edmund Drago, *Black Politicians and Reconstruction In Georgia: A Splendid Failure* (Baton Rouge: Louisiana State University Press, 1982), 155; William Keech and Michael P. Sistrom, "North Carolina," in *Quiet Revolution in the South*, ed. Davidson and Grofman, 157; Peyton McCrary, Jerome A. Gray, Edward Still, and Huey L. Perry, "Alabama," in *Quiet Revolution in the South*, ed. Davidson and Grofman, 43.

26. Thomas Morris and Neil Bradley, "Virginia," in *Quiet Revolution in the South*, ed. Davidson and Grofman, 273.

27. Steven Carbó, Ludovic Blain, and Ellen Braune, *Democracy Denied: The Racial History and Impact of Disenfranchisement Laws in the United States* (New York: Demos, 2003), 4–5.

28. Alexander Keyssar, *The Right To Vote: The Contested History of Democracy in the United States* (New York: Basic Books, 2000), 113.

29. Armand Derfner, "Racial Discrimination and the Right to Vote," *Vanderbilt Law Review*, 26 (1973): 536–37; Frank R. Parker, David C. Colby, and Minion C. K. Morrison, "Mississippi," in *Quiet Revolution in the South*, ed. Davidson and Grofman, 137.

30. Orville Vernon Burton, Terence R. Finnegan, Peyton McCrary, and James W. Loewen, "South Carolina," in *Quiet Revolution in the South*, ed. Davidson and Grofman, 192–94; Perman, *The Struggle for Mastery*, 91–94.

31. Richard L. Engstrom, Stanley A. Halpin Jr., Jean A. Hill, and Victoria M. Caridas-Butterworth, "Louisiana," in *Quiet Revolution in the South*, ed. Davidson and Grofman, 105–6; Perman, *The Struggle for Mastery*, 125.

32. Keech and Sistrom, "North Carolina," 158; Perman, *The Struggle for Mastery*, 148–50.

33. McCrary et al., "Alabama," 43; Morris and Bradley, "Virginia," 271–71; Robert Brischetto, David R. Richards, Chandler Davidson, and Bernard Grofman, "Texas," in *Quiet Revolution in the South*, ed. Davidson and Grofman, 235; McDonald, Binford, and Johnson, "Georgia," 67. See also generally, Perman, *The Struggle for Mastery*, and Morgan J. Kousser, *The Shaping of Southern Politics: Suffrage Restriction and the Establishment of the One-Party South, 1880–1910* (New Haven: Yale University Press, 1974).

34. Keyssar, *The Right To Vote*, 114–15.

35. On this attack, see Charles L. Zelden, *Battle for the Black Ballot: Smith v Allwright and the Defeat of the Texas All White Primary* (Lawrence: University Press of Kansas, 2004).

36. McCrary et al., "Alabama," 45–47.

37. McDonald, Binford, and Johnson, "Georgia," 70–72.

38. Keech and Sistrom, "North Carolina," 157.

39. Burton et al., "South Carolina," 195.

40. Brischetto et al., "Texas," 235.

41. Morris and Bradley, "Virginia," 274.

42. Engstrom et al., "Louisiana," 108.

43. U.S. Commission on Civil Rights, *Political Participation* (Washington, D.C.: Government Printing Office, 1968), 122. See also Chandler Davidson, "The Voting Rights Act: A Brief History," in *Controversies in Minority Voting: The Voting Rights Act in Perspective*, ed. Bernard Grofman and Chandler Davidson (Washington, D.C.: The Brookings Institution, 1992), 23; Steven F. Lawson, *Black Ballots: Voting Rights in the South, 1944–1969* (New York: Lexington Books, 1999), 134.

44. Quoted in David J. Garrow, *Bearing the Cross: Martin Luther King and the Southern Christian Leadership Conference* (New York: Quill: 1986), 10–11.

45. Chandler Davidson and Bernard Grofman, "The Voting Rights Act and The Second Reconstruction," in *Quiet Revolution in the South*, Davidson and Grofman, 383.

46. "Revitalizing Democracy in Florida: The Governor's Select Task Force on Election Procedures, Standards and Technology," report issued March 1, 2001.

47. USCCR, *Voting Irregularities in Florida During the 2000 Presidential Election*, chapter 5 at notes 141–95.

48. In proof of this, the USCCR noted how, "in Miami-Dade County, over half of the African Americans who appealed from the Florida felon exclusion list were successfully reinstated to the voter rolls." In fact, "in the 2000 election, the supervisor of elections office for Miami-Dade received two lists—one in June 1999 and another in January 2000—from which his office identified persons to be removed from the voter rolls. Of the 5,762 persons on the June 1999 list, 327 successfully appealed and, therefore, remained on the voter rolls. Another 485 names were later identified as persons who either had their rights restored or who should not have been on the list. Thus at least 14.1 percent of the persons whose names appeared on the Miami-Dade County list appeared on the list in error. Similarly, 13.3 percent of the names on the January 2000 list were eligible to vote. In other words, almost one out of every seven people on this list were there in error and risked being disenfranchised." USCCR, *Voting Irregularities in Florida During the 2000 Presidential Election*, chapter 5 at note 14.

49. USCCR, *Voting Irregularities in Florida During the 2000 Presidential Election*, chapter 1 at note 80.

50. Melissa V. Harris-Lacewell, "Political Science and the Study of African American Public Opinion," in *African American Perspectives on Political Science*, ed. Wilbur Rich (Philadelphia: Temple University Press, 2007); Donna Brazile, "African American Voters Crucial to Democratic Voter," *The Black Commentator*, January 29, 2004, http://www.blackcommentator.com/75/75_guest_brazile.html; Cornell Belcher and Donna Brazile, "The Black and Hispanic Vote in 2006," *The Democratic Strategist*, March 29, 2007, http://www.thedemocraticstrategist.org/ac/2007/03/the_black_and_hispanic_vote_in.php; "Local Exit Polls-Election Center 2008-Elections & Politics." CNN.com, http://www.CNN.com/ELECTION/2008/results/polls/#USP00p1.

51. Rachel La Corte, "Activists Concerned About Purged Voters," *Miami Herald*, July 13, 2004, 3B; Jim Defede, "Voter List Mess Shows Officials Can't Be Trusted," *Miami Herald*, July 11, 2004, 1B.

52. Erika Bolstad, Jason Grotto, and David Kidwell, "Thousands Of Eligible Voters Are On Felon List," *Miami Herald*, July 2, 2004, 1A. See also, Mark Crispin Miller, *Fooled Again: How the Right Stole the 2004 Election & Why They'll Steal the Next One Too* (New York: Basic Books, 2005), 213–24.

53. Quoted in Defede, "Voter List Mess Shows Officials Can't Be Trusted."

54. Bob Mahlburg, "Felon Voting Chaos Persists: State Trying To Ease Fears About Glitches," *South Florida Sun Sentinel*, July 7, 2004, 5B. Defede, "Voter List Mess Shows Officials Can't Be Trusted."

55. Under state law, "County election officials are required . . . to verify names of suspected felons, send registered letters notifying them they are being dropped from rolls and advertise names in a local paper if they don't respond." Mahlburg, "Felon Voting Chaos Persists."

56. Quoted in Miller, *Fooled Again*, 219; Bolstad, Grotto, and Kidwell, "Thousands Of Eligible Voters Are On Felon List."

57. Lesley Clark, "List Abandoned, But Doubts Linger," *Miami Herald*, July 11, 2004, 21A. The state's recall of the list did not end the controversy. State law continued to demand that felons be barred from the ballot box. County election officials were still required by state law to verify names of suspected felons, to send registered letters notifying them they were being dropped from rolls, and to advertise names in a local newspaper if they did not respond. More to the point, they were still supposed to drop the names of anyone who did not respond to the letters sent from the election rolls—whether proof existed that the removal was legitimate or not. In point of fact, "supervisors in 14 counties—including Brevard and counties in North Florida such as Gulf and Wakulla—[had already] sent out letters informing voters they were included on the list" before the state's withdrawal of the purge list. Since "voters who fail[ed] to respond to county supervisors" were supposed to be purged from the rolls, the potential for excluding legitimate voters was a reality, not just theory. The state department of elections was finally forced into the embarrassing position of telling the county supervisors to ignore the state list and that "even if voters fail to respond to the election supervisors' letters, they should remain on the voting rolls." Embarrassing or not, this was too little and too late to placate angry members of the African American community and frustrated Democrats. Gary Fineout and Marc Caputo, "State Ceases Felon Voting Purge," *Miami Herald*, August 14, 2004, 6B; Donna

E. Natale Planas, "List Abandoned, But Doubts Linger," *Miami Herald*, July 11, 2004, 21A. See Miller, *Fooled Again*, 221–22.

58. William Hershey, "Suit Alleges Voter Impediments: Democrats Say Blackwell Trying To Limit Ballot Access," *Dayton Daily News*, September 28, 2004, B1. *Preserving Democracy: What Went Wrong in Ohio* (Washington: House Judiciary Committee Democratic Staff, January 5, 2005), 36–39, covers this issue in detail, http://www. openvotingconsortium.org/files/Conyersreport.pdf.

59. The directive also required that when county boards received such underweight registration forms they should treat them as "an application for a new registration form" and mail out a new application to the voter. Secretary of State J. Kenneth Blackwell, Directive No. 2004–31 (September 7, 2004). Quoted in *Preserving Democracy: What Went Wrong in Ohio*, 37.

60. Andrew Welsh-Huggins, "Some Election Boards Ignore New Order About Registration Paper," *AP Wire*, September 30, 2004.

61. Jim Bebbington, "Blackwell Rulings Rile Voting Advocates," *Dayton Daily News*, September 24, 2004, 1B.

62. The Voting Rights Institute, *Democracy at Risk: The 2004 Election in Ohio* (The Democratic National Committee, June 22, 2005), 170, http://a9.g.akamai. net/7/9/8082/v001/www.democrats.org/pdfs/ohvrireport/fullreport.pdf.

63. Quoted in Robert F. Kennedy Jr., "Was the 2004 Election Stolen," *Rolling Stone*, June 1, 2006, unpaginated online version at http://www.rollingstone.com/news/ story/10432334/was_the_2004_election_stolen. Kennedy also references a report by "state inspectors who investigated the elections operation in Toledo [and] discovered 'areas of grave concern.' With less than a month before the election, Bernadette Noe," head of the county elections board and Toledo's Republican Party, "had yet to process 20,000 voter registration cards. Board officials arbitrarily decided that mail-in cards (mostly from the Republican suburbs) would be processed first, while registrations dropped off at the board's office (the fruit of intensive Democratic registration drives in the city) would be processed last. When a grassroots group called Project Vote delivered a batch of nearly 10,000 cards just before the October 4th deadline, an elections official casually remarked, 'We may not get to them.'" "The most troubling incident uncovered by the investigation," Kennedy notes, "was Noe's decision to allow Republican partisans behind the counter in the board of elections office to make photocopies of postcards sent to confirm voter registrations." In point of fact, "on their second day in the office, the operatives were caught by an elections official tampering with the documents." All told, the state "investigators slammed the elections board for 'a series of egregious blunders' that caused 'the destruction, mutilation and damage of public records.'" See also, Norman Robbins, study leader, *Analyses Of Voter Disqualification, Cuyahoga County, Ohio, November 2004* (Greater Cleveland Voter Registration Coalition, May 9, 2006), 1–2, http://download11.rbn.com/rstone/ rstone/download/misc/AnalysesFullReport.pdf.

64. "Late Voter Registrations Could Cause Election Day Havoc," *AP Wire*, September 26, 2004.

65. A *New York Times* study in Ohio showed that the Democrats had "registered 250 percent more people in the first half of 2004 than they did in the same period in

2000." Quoted in "Ohio Registration Gains Matter," *Dayton Daily News*, October 2, 2004, A8.

66. Walter R. Mebane Jr., "Ohio 2004 Election: New Registrants, Provisional Ballots, Voting Machines, Turnout and Polls Open Elapsed Times in Franklin County Precincts," in *Democracy at Risk*, The Voting Rights Institute, 146.

67. Ibid. See also, Suzanne Hoholik and Mark Niquette, "Provisional Ballots: Election Directive Rattles Officials; What If Voters Get Unruly? Board Asks," *The Columbus Dispatch*, October 7, 2004, 1A; William Hershey, "Blackwell's Directive Draws Rain Of Ire," *Dayton Daily News*, October 10, 2004, B3; Mark Niquette, "Judge Blasts Blackwell: Secretary of State Faulted In Provisional-Ballot Case, Accused Of Failing Ohio," *The Columbus Dispatch*, October 21, 2004, 1A.

68. Hershey, "Suit Alleges Voter Impediments." See also, *Preserving Democracy: What Went Wrong in Ohio*, 5, 10, 12–13, 28, 30–41, 146. As to impacts, Steve Harsman, deputy director of the Montgomery County board of elections, estimated that had his county followed Blackwell's rules in 2000, 840 registered voters in Montgomery County alone would have had their votes denied for voting in the "wrong precinct." Quoted in Hershey, "Suit Alleges Voter Impediments." Ohio Governor Bob Taft believed that the new rules could affect over 100,000 voters in the November election. Gregory Korte and Jim Siegel, "Defiant Blackwell Rips Judge," *Cincinnati Enquirer*, October 22, 2004, 1A. Kay Maxwell, of the League of Women Voters, admitted while visiting in Ohio that neither she nor anyone else knew how many votes would be lost this way but argued, "any single voter who is disfranchised is one too many." Mark Niquette, "Ohio Won't Count Ballots Cast At Incorrect Precincts," *The Columbus Dispatch*, September 25, 2004, 1A.

69. Bob Fitrakis, "None Dare Call it Voter Suppression," *FreePress.org*, November 7, 2004. [Reprinted in *Did George W. Bush Steal America's 2004 Election: Essential Documents*, ed. Bob Fitrakis, Steve Rosenfeld, and Harvey Wasserman (Columbus, Ohio: CICJ Books, 2005), 28].

70. "Voting Issues Keep Courts Busy Up To Last Minute," *Cleveland Plain Dealer*, November 3, 2004, S9.

71. Bob Fitrakis and Harvey Wasserman, "Hearings on Ohio Voting Put Election in Doubt," *FreePress.org*, November 11, 2004. [Reprinted in *Did George W. Bush Steal America's 2004 Election: Essential Documents*, ed. Fitrakis, Rosenfeld, and Wasserman (Columbus, Ohio: CICJ Books, 2005), 40].

72. Michael Powell and Peter Slevin, "Several Factors Contributed to 'Lost' Voters in Ohio," *Washington Post*, December 15, 2004. A1.

73. "In Cuyahoga County, about 52% of this group of rejected provisional ballots were cast in the correct polling place, and, therefore, were due to poll worker failure to inform. Many of the remainder are likely due to registration errors on the part of the BOE or the voter, as explained above, and to occasional failures of the BOE website, which gave voters erroneous polling places." Norman Robbins, "Facts To Ponder About The 2004 General Election," (5–10–06 version), 2, http://www.clevelandvotes. org/news/reports/Facts_to_Ponder.pdf. See also, Spencer Overton, *Stealing Democracy: The New Politics of Voter Suppression* (New York: W.W. Norton & Co., 2006), 46,

who describes the experiences of Brandi Stenson, who along with her mother and brother stood in the wrong line in her polling place (which led her to the wrong precinct desk, located in the same building as the correct one, but without her name in the voting lists). "We were in the right building," Stenson noted. "We were in the wrong line." Rather than help Stenson find the right line, though, poll workers simply required her to vote provisionally. And since she voted provisionally in the wrong precinct, her votes were not counted. "I feel just like they didn't know what they were doing," Stenson said of the poll workers. "They wanted us to hurry up, because I was asking questions, my mom was asking questions, . . . They were trying to rush us out."

74. *Preserving Democracy: What Went Wrong in Ohio*, 68.

75. Robbins, *Analyses Of Voter Disqualification, Cuyahoga County, Ohio, November 2004*, 1–2. In a related report, the NAACP reported that it had "receiv[ed] over 1,000 calls related to voter registration issues, generally from individuals who were not on the voter rolls even though they had voted in previous elections, individuals with questions on how to register, and individuals with concerns about not receiving a voter registration card." Quoted in *Preserving Democracy: What Went Wrong in Ohio*, 67.

76. Kennedy, "Was the 2004 Election Stolen?" at note 132.

77. Carolyn M. Sherman, "Slip-Sliding Away in Columbus," *FreePress.org*, November 11, 2004 [reprinted in *Did George W. Bush Steal America's 2004 Election: Essential Documents*, ed. Fitrakis, Rosenfeld, and Wasserman (Columbus, Ohio: CICJ Books, 2005), 33–34]; Fitrakis and Wasserman, "Hearings on Ohio Voting Put Election in Doubt," *FreePress.org*, November 11, 2004, 39.

78. The Voting Rights Institute, *Democracy at Risk*, 48. (Emphasis added.)

79. Powell and Slevin, "Several Factors Contributed to 'Lost' Voters in Ohio." Kennedy, "Was the 2004 Election Stolen?" at note 136, argues, "[L]ong lines were not only foreseeable—they were actually created by GOP efforts. Republicans in the state legislature, citing new electronic voting machines that were supposed to speed voting, authorized local election boards to reduce the number of precincts across Ohio. In most cases, the new machines never materialized—but that didn't stop officials in twenty of the state's eighty-eight counties, all of them favorable to Democrats, from slashing the number of precincts by at least twenty percent." See also, Overton, *Stealing Democracy*, 42–48.

80. James Dao, "Voting Problems in Ohio Spur Call for Overhaul," *New York Times*, December 24, 2004, A1.

81. Powell and Slevin, "Several Factors Contributed to 'Lost' Voters in Ohio."

82. Bob Fitrakis, "How the Ohio Election Was Rigged for Bush," *FreePress.org*, November 22, 2004; Bob Fitrakis and Harvey Wasserman, "How a Republican Election Supervisor Manipulated the Vote, In Black and White," *FreePress.org*, November 23, 2004 [reprinted in *Did George W. Bush Steal America's 2004 Election: Essential Documents*, ed. Fitrakis, Rosenfeld, and Wasserman (Columbus, Ohio: CICJ Books, 2005), 48].

83. "High court upholds Indiana's voter ID law," CNN.com, April 28, 2008, http://www.CNN.com/2008/POLITICS/04/28/scotus.voter.id/.

84. Jonathan Alter, "'Jim Crawford' Republicans: The GOP is working to keep eligible African-Americans from voting in several states," *Newsweek*, September 11, 2008, http://www.newsweek.com/id/158392.

85. Mary Ellen Klas, "'No match, no vote' law to be enforced," *Miami Herald*, August 9, 2008, http://www.miamiherald.com/news/florida/story/679629.html; Steve Bousquet, "12,165 now on Florida's 'no match' vote list," *St. Petersburg Times*, October 28, 2008, http://www.tampabay.com/news/politics/state/article877094.ece.

86. This, in fact, may be happening in Ohio in 2008. The *Cincinnati Enquirer*, September 11, 2008, reported—in a story that eerily resembles the rulings of Secretary of State Blackwell in 2004—that "About one-third of the absentee ballot applications received at the Hamilton County Board of Elections have been ruled invalid because Republican Sen. John McCain's presidential campaign printed a version of the form with an extra, unneeded box on it. In a narrow interpretation of Ohio law, Democratic Secretary of State Jennifer Brunner says many of the McCain forms have not been completed properly. If the box stating the person is an eligible elector—or qualified voter—is not checked, Brunner said, the application is no good."

7

GEORGE W. BUSH,
COMPASSIONATE
CONSERVATISM, AND THE
LIMITS OF "RACIAL REALISM"

STEVEN F. LAWSON

When President George W. Bush reflected on his eight years in office, his most painful memory stood out sharply. Surprisingly, the 2001 terrorist attacks in New York City and Washington, D.C., the costly and contentious wars in Afghanistan and Iraq that followed, and the sharpest collapse of the economy since the Great Depression did not top Bush's list. Instead, two years after leaving the White House, the forty-third president still felt hurt that critics had branded him a racist for his handling of Hurricane Katrina's devastation of the majority-black city of New Orleans. "The suggestion that I was a racist," he lamented in his 2010 memoir, "represented an all time low." In 2005 when this catastrophe occurred, he told his wife, Laura, "it was the worst moment of my presidency." Five years later, he still felt "the same way."[1]

More than a year before Katrina, on January 15, 2004, President Bush chose to celebrate the Martin Luther King holiday at the Union Bethel African Methodist Episcopal Church, the largest black congregation in New Orleans and the place where Dr. King had spoken in 1961. The president marked the occasion by praising the 140-year-old church for its faith-based outreach to the poor neighborhoods of east New Orleans, the kind of program that his administration supported. More than a year later, five months after the hurricane, the president invited the church's pastor, the Reverend Thomas Brown Jr., to the White House Christmas party. The minister attended the event, but his church lay in ruins and his repeated calls to Washington for relief had gone ignored. When Bush returned to the Crescent City to observe the first anniversary of the terrible storm, Reverend Brown was not in attendance because he now lived in a federally constructed trailer park outside of Baton Rouge.[2]

President Bush did not understand how the plight of Reverend Brown and his parishioners could justify charges of racism against him. Indeed, the president believed that "racism was one of the greatest evils in society."[3] He had come of political age largely in the post–Jim Crow South, when public segregation fell with passage of the 1964 Civil Rights Act and African Americans regained suffrage and won election to public office following the 1965 Voting Rights Act. Bush proudly remembered that his father, then a congressman from Houston, had voted for the Civil Rights Act of 1968, designed to combat housing discrimination. He thought that as a result of the civil rights movement individuals, regardless of race, had an equal opportunity to succeed according to their own merits and that the government should use civil rights laws only to punish discrimination based on personal racial bias. Thus, being called a racist made no sense to Bush and violated his self-image.

However, Bush failed to recognize that racism had become more, not less, complicated. Despite the majestic accomplishments of the civil rights movement, vestiges of white supremacy remained embedded in the nation's political, economic, and social structures, thereby transcending individual bias and perpetuating the system of racial inequality. "The prejudices of centuries die hard," the sociologist Orlando Patterson explained, "and even when they wane, the institutional frameworks that sustained them are bound to linger."[4] As the president saw it, he cared about the welfare of those caught in the destruction of Hurricane Katrina without respect to race. Yet personal efforts and sympathy aside, the problems that Katrina exposed had roots in the institutional poverty left unresolved by the civil rights movement, the federal government, and private charity. To remedy conditions of deep racial and economic inequality required political and governmental involvement on a scale that conservatives deplored and most Americans seemed unwilling to back. President Bush could feel Reverend Brown's pain, but he did little to restore his church and give him back his community.

Still, George W. Bush's presidency cannot simply be dismissed as hostile to the interests of African Americans and other minorities. As other authors in this volume have argued concerning those presidents who came before him, civil rights during the conservative Bush regime showed a pattern of "winning while losing." Overall, the civil rights center held, while the rollbacks that occurred came mainly at the margins.[5] Through significant appointments, educational reform, celebration of milestones in civil rights history, support for reauthorization of the Voting Rights Act, and encouragement of minority entrepreneurship and homeownership, President Bush affirmed the legacy of the civil rights movement as he understood it. This was not enough, however, because the civil rights community had come to define the needs of African Americans and other minorities differently. Such core issues as affirmative action conflicted with the Bush administration's position on the value and enforcement of individual over group rights. As this essay will demonstrate, the Bush presidency retained much of the heritage of the civil rights struggle, but it departed from the scions of the movement, who saw the legacy of racism as more structural, pervasive, and persistent than did Bush and the Republican Party. On a number of important matters the president and civil rights supporters reached common ground, but their basic differences in assumptions about and remedies for racial inequality ultimately kept them at odds with each other. Beset by these basic disagreements, Hurricane Katrina reinforced the gulf between Bush and African Americans.

Becoming President

In his two terms as governor of Texas, from 1995 to 2000, Bush foreshadowed the approach he would take on civil rights issues when he became president. Like other Republican governors in the South, he appealed mainly to the conservative, white electoral base that President Ronald Reagan had expanded and solidified in the 1980s.[6] Yet Bush never wrote off the black or the Latino vote, which in the Lone Star State was significant. Both the governor and his chief political strategist, Karl Rove, agreed "that the nominee of the party of Lincoln had a moral obligation to fight for black voters regardless of whether it paid off in the short run."[7] Although Bush did not carry a majority of the African American vote in winning the Texas governorship, he did well for a GOP gubernatorial candidate in gaining 27 percent of black ballots. He did even better among Hispanics, capturing 49 percent of their votes and winning the largely Latino city of El Paso, the first time a Republican had done so.[8]

Bush's religious beliefs may help account for his appeal among blacks and Latinos. Governor Bush promoted the kind of faith-based initiatives that church-going minorities appreciated, even if they also expected government aid. "The government can hand out money," he remarked, "but it cannot put hope in a person's heart or a sense of purpose in a person's life."[9] This belief echoed the conservative Republican ideology of individual responsibility and limited government, but Bush sought to soften it through what he called "compassionate conservatism." For liberals and African Americans, the Reaganite rhetoric of individual liberty, free market competition, self-reliance, and the evils of big government harkened back to the late nineteenth century when Social Darwinists preached the harsh doctrine of "survival of the fittest." In much the same way that the steel tycoon Andrew Carnegie had spread the "Gospel of Wealth" among private philanthropists to remove some of the most ruthless aspects of laissez-faire capitalism, so too did George W. Bush propose the creation of "communities of promise . . . [to] help build the confidence and faith to achieve their own dreams." Bush believed that government had a role to play in standing "squarely on the side of opportunity."[10] Although the majority of African Americans rejected this conservative Republican, antigovernment, socioeconomic philosophy, Bush attempted to appeal to a long tradition in black communities: reliance on churches and civic and fraternal organizations to care for the unfortunate and the needy.

Nevertheless, Governor Bush did not always demonstrate the virtues of faith and compassion. Starting off in a positive direction, when two African American churches were set ablaze in Greenville, Texas, in June 1996, he visited the town, spoke out against violence and "old-time racism," and affirmed that the state had "no room for cowardice and hatred and bigotry."[11] In sharp contrast, two years later Bush refused to visit the East Texas town of Jasper after three white men murdered a forty-nine-year-old African American man, James Byrd Jr., by chaining his ankles and dragging him behind a pick-up truck for two miles. The assailants, avowed white supremacists, then dumped his lifeless body in front of a black cemetery. It remains unclear why Bush did not respond in the same manner as to the burning of the Greenville churches. He appeared even more insensitive by vetoing hate-crime legislation named after Byrd. Karl Rove later claimed that Bush's veto had nothing to do with race, as

Byrd's killers were apprehended, tried, and convicted. Even if race did not play into Bush's decision, sex and gender did. He rejected the bill mainly because it included crimes against gays and lesbians, and Bush's veto reflected conservative Republican opposition to gay rights.[12]

When Governor Bush had to deal with an issue more directly connected to the civil rights agenda, he tried to take a nuanced position. During his first year in office, in the case of *Hopwood v. Texas*, the Fifth Circuit Court of Appeals ruled unconstitutional the University of Texas's affirmative-action requirements for law school admission, which took racial considerations into account to promote a diverse student body.[13] Bush opposed affirmative-action plans like the one overruled in Texas, but he did support expanding educational opportunity for minorities. Most polls showed that Americans did not favor affirmative-action programs that they interpreted as providing racial preferences, and Republicans since Ronald Reagan had gained huge political mileage by challenging such plans as so-called reverse discrimination. Bush proved no exception, but he developed a "race-neutral" alternative designed to foster minority enrollments in higher education without antagonizing his conservative, white political base. His so-called percentage plan guaranteed that 10 percent of the graduates of each high school in the state could attend any four-year college in the University of Texas system. This ensured that schools with high percentages of black and Latino students would have adequate representation at the state university without specifying race as a criterion for admission. The question remained whether Bush and fellow Republican governors in Florida and California who adopted versions of this plan could avoid the political pitfalls of affirmative action while maintaining access to higher education for racial and ethnic minorities. With respect to Texas, Bush seemed a winner. Two years after the adoption of the 10-percent plan, black and Hispanic enrollment at Texas state universities stood at the same level or surpassed that under the previous "race conscious" program.[14]

Thus, when Bush campaigned for president in 2000 he had compiled a record that departed from both civil rights purists and hard-line conservatives. Instead of affirmative action he advocated "affirmative access," measures offering "every person . . . a fair shot based on his potential or merit."[15] He substituted compassion for rugged individualism and viewed the government as playing a necessary if limited role in encouraging equal opportunity for minorities. That said, Bush had a way to go to persuade African Americans that they could trust him as a civil rights advocate even as he sought to reassure conservative Republicans that he was one of their own. Mixing realism with hope, he admitted: "I know the current wisdom. Well he's a Republican, and therefore he has no chance to get the African-American vote. You know they may be right, but that's not going to stop me. So you'll find me in neighborhoods the Republicans usually don't go to."[16]

To help win over African American voters Bush and the Republican Party chose Colin Powell as keynote speaker at their national convention. The former national security advisor to Reagan, chairman of the Joint Chiefs of Staff under Presidents George H. W. Bush and Bill Clinton, and frequently mentioned presidential possibility, the popular retired Army general held far more moderate views on domestic policy than the conservative base of the party. Unlike most of those in attendance at the 2000 convention, including George W. Bush, Powell supported affirmative action and urged the delegates to understand the cynicism African Americans felt: "Some in our party miss no opportunity to roundly and loudly condemn affirmative action that helped a few thousand black kids get an education, but you don't hear a whimper when it's affirmative action for lobbyists who load our tax code with preferences for special interests."[17] Powell praised Bush for his compassionate conservatism— "just caring about people"—and for responding to the "deepest needs" of minorities in Texas.[18] Although relatively few black delegates attended the convention, compared to the number that attended the convention of the Democratic Party, the GOP spent over $1 million on radio ads targeting black communities and scheduled Bush to campaign in black areas.[19]

Bush's strongest appeal to black voters came in his appearance at the annual convention of the National Association for the Advancement of Colored People (NAACP). The first Republican presidential candidate to appear before this group since Ronald Reagan in 1980, the governor admitted "that the party of Lincoln has not always carried the mantle of Lincoln" and pledged strong enforcement of existing civil rights laws. Bush avoided the subject of affirmative action but reminded the audience of his educational reform efforts for minorities in Texas. Although the GOP candidate acknowledged that "discrimination is still a reality" and condemned racial profiling and housing discrimination, he quickly shifted his appeal away from race to economics where Republicans felt more comfortable. Lincoln had not only ended slavery, Bush asserted, but had also argued that "every poor man should have a chance." In pressing this point, Bush resurrected the Lincoln who had used the federal government to encourage the building of the railroads and the distribution of free land in the West to settlers. And "in the spirit of Lincoln's reforms," the Republican standard bearer proposed that government "remove obstacles on the road to the middle class." Prosperity would come not through government largesse, however, but through finding ways to give hardworking people an opportunity to own their own home, obtain adequate health care, and get the best schooling for their children. For those who needed extra assistance, the government would "rally the armies of compassion in neighborhoods all across America."[20]

This speech faithfully summed up Bush's approach as Texas governor and sketched out the course he would pursue as president. He hoped that African Americans would find their way back into the Republican Party through conservative appeals to their economic mobility and their religious values. Bush and his advisers never expected to capture anything close to a majority of blacks, but they hoped to improve on the meager 12 percent of the black vote that GOP presidential contender Robert Dole captured in 1996.

Hindering this prospect, Bush remained firm in his opposition to affirmative action. However much he tried to finesse the issue by presenting his position as "affirmative access," he still rejected "quotas" and "preferences," the buzzwords used by critics of affirmative action. Although he emphasized that his race-neutral program for admission into the University of Texas expanded the pool of minority applicants and "open[ed] the door so that more people [were] eligible to go to the university system," he gained little political leverage from this position.[21] His Democratic opponent, Vice President Albert Gore Jr., also denounced quotas, but he spoke out directly for retaining affirmative action as a means of "tak[ing] extra steps to acknowledge the history of discrimination and injustice and prejudice."[22]

Whatever overtures Bush made to African Americans proved fruitless. The NAACP rejected the olive branch Bush had extended at its convention. In the waning days of the campaign, the premier civil rights organization ran ads condemning Governor Bush for not signing the hate-crimes legislation passed in the aftermath of James Byrd's murder in

Texas. In NAACP radio commercials Byrd's daughter bitterly complained that Bush's veto "was like my father was killed all over again."[23] In the end, Bush did not convince African Americans that there was much compassion in his conservatism: he received a puny 8 percent of the black vote cast.[24]

The disputed results of the election further complicated Bush's relationship with African Americans. The clash over Florida's electoral returns is covered elsewhere in this volume, and it is sufficient to highlight here that the black electorate in the Sunshine State suffered disproportionately from deliberate efforts to disqualify them from voting and from equipment failures in black districts.[25] As a result, Democrats in general and blacks in particular considered Bush's presidency tainted from the beginning. A CBS poll showed that only 19 percent of Democrats and 12 percent of African Americans viewed Bush's election as valid. Jesse Jackson summed up the attitude of both groups: "We want Bush to understand that while he may occupy the White House, he will be there illegitimately."[26]

Unlike African Americans, Hispanics responded more positively to Bush's compassionate conservatism. As governor of Texas, Bush had drawn greater support from Latinos than from blacks. Personally, he had closer relationships with Latinos through family and business connections. He expressed "empathy" for recent Mexican immigrants in the state, but aimed his economic message mainly at a narrow segment of the Mexican population—businesspeople and the wealthy. The governor stoked the entrepreneurial efforts of Latino businesspeople to create investment opportunities and trade across the border. Largely ignored in Bush's plans were those working-class and poor Latinos more typically reliant on labor unions and government social-welfare measures to keep them afloat. Whereas African Americans overwhelmingly rejected Bush in the 2000 presidential election, Latinos gave him an estimated 35 percent of their vote, the highest percentage any Republican candidate had ever received.[27] With the nation's Latino population growing faster than that of either the black or white population and with Latinos replacing African Americans as the nation's largest minority, the Bush camp derived great encouragement from the substantial political inroads Republicans had made among Hispanics.

Diversity in the White House

Having lost a whopping 92 percent of the black vote, President Bush nevertheless refused to write off African Americans politically. Coming away with the narrowest of victories, if Bush made even small electoral gains among minorities he could reap rich dividends in 2004. With great fanfare, the president eschewed tokenism and made several high-level appointments of African Americans and Latinos at the start of his administration. Colin Powell became the first African American to serve as secretary of state and Condoleezza Rice the first African American woman to hold the rank of national security advisor and later secretary of state. Bush also selected Rod Paige, the reformist African American superintendent of schools in Houston, as secretary of education. He chose Alberto Gonzales, his Latino political ally from Texas, as White House counsel and later as U.S. attorney general. His cabinet also included two Asian Americans and another Latino, which compared favorably to the top appointments Bill Clinton had made in constructing a cabinet more reflective of the nation's diverse population. Overall, Bush selected more minorities to posts requiring Senate confirmation than any former Republican president.[28]

Bush chose the two most visible members of his team, Powell and Rice, for their foreign-policy expertise rather than their domestic views, but they did not check their racial awareness at the White House gates. Indeed, Powell considered his appointment as rooted in the civil rights movement. In taking office, he paid tribute, he said, "to so many people who helped me reach this position because the conditions weren't there and we had to fight to change those conditions." He hoped, in turn, to provide "inspiration to young African-Americans coming along."[29] Similarly, Condoleezza Rice recalled in her 2010 memoir the experience of growing up during the turbulent days of the civil rights movement in Birmingham, Alabama. Her father had forcefully stood up to racist terrorists, and one of her childhood friends, along with three other young girls, died in the 1963 bombing of the Sixteenth Street Baptist Church. Drawing upon her racial heritage, she convinced the president that he needed to commemorate the fortieth anniversary of passage of the 1964 Civil Rights Act with a public celebration in the East Room of the White House. After all, the act, she told her colleagues, "had made it possible for me to eat in a restaurant in my hometown."[30]

In addition, President Bush began making advances to black politicians, nearly all of them of the opposite political party. On his first day in office in 2001, he met with former Democratic Congressman William H. Gray of Pennsylvania, who then headed the United Negro College Fund and who told the president that he had to reach out to African Americans who felt bitter about their ballots being excluded in the presidential vote count in Florida. Besides promising to increase funds for historically black colleges and universities, Bush quickly followed up this conversation by inviting the Congressional Black Caucus (CBC) to meet with him nine days later on January 31, 2001. Despite hearing a good deal of criticism about black disfranchisement in Florida and the need for electoral reform, Bush declared that the meeting had gone well and "will be the beginning of hopefully a lot of meetings."[31]

However, this did not prove to be the case. The CBC did not get invited back to the White House until February 2004. In the interim, the September 11 attacks led to the Bush administration engineering the war with Iraq, and though Powell and Rice played important roles in this course of action, only 34 percent of African Americans supported the war compared to 57 percent of whites.[32] Despite strong black disapproval, the president continued to make symbolic gestures toward African Americans by addressing National Urban League conventions, leading celebrations on the Martin Luther King holiday, and commemorating the anniversaries of the historic *Brown v. Board of Education* decision and the signing of the 1964 Civil Rights Act. Yet these efforts did little to satisfy his civil rights critics. Making matters worse on one occasion, Bush responded to questions about his commitment to civil rights in a patronizing manner. In July 2002, when asked about his civil rights record he replied sarcastically: "Let's see there I was, sitting around . . . the table with foreign leaders, looking at Colin Powell and Condi Rice."[33]

This awkward comment reflected a deeper truth about Bush's attitude toward race and civil rights. Indeed, he often used diversity—his cabinet-level appointments and friendships with minorities—as the central measure of civil rights. Diversity may have given decision making in his administration a different complexion, but it did not provide an adequate substitute for forceful implementation of civil rights policies and federal efforts to combat intractable forms of racism. Bush did not ignore African American leaders, but he chose to deal mainly with those who might respond more positively to his message of uplift through self-reliance and faith-based initiatives. Consequently, Bush became the first sitting president since Herbert Hoover not to address the NAACP annual convention, choosing instead to speak to the National Urban League (NUL), which emphasized economic self-empowerment and focused on conciliation rather than protest. In conferring with the NUL and black church leaders rather than the NAACP, the president practiced diversity without satisfying the substantive civil rights demands of most African Americans.[34]

This was also true for Bush's appointment of judges to the federal courts, which often operated on the front lines of civil rights battles. According to the U.S. Commission on Civil Rights, traditionally a gadfly of presidential administrations, in making judicial appointments Bush "demonstrated a commitment to parity beyond any other president of his party." Of the selections he made in his first term, 20.7 percent were women, 8 percent were African American, and 10.3 percent were Hispanic. However, as the commission reported, "race and gender alone do not guarantee support for civil rights." A number of these appointments as well as some nonminority nominees were hotly contested by civil rights groups and their Democratic allies in the Senate who argued that they "would limit the scope and strength of civil rights laws." A couple of these nomination fights turned nasty, and in two instances Bush placed his candidates on the federal court of appeals through recess appointments.[35]

Racial Realism and Compassionate Conservatism

Bush embraced diversity because most conservatives believed that the federal government had done all it could to extend equal opportunities to individuals regardless of race. While they acknowledged that African Americans still faced prejudices, conservatives nevertheless contended that the kind of legalized racism the government could challenge had come mostly to an end. Declaring integration an accomplished fact, they called for a halt to race-conscious policies. "In a society that is genuinely open to black opportunity," the conservative scholar Abigail M. Thernstrom argued, "colorblind principles have no moral competition."[36]

Conservatives shifted the locus of racism from the government and society to the individual and culture. They defined racism as "motivated, crude, explicitly supremacist [actions] typically expressed as individual bias."[37] Continuing problems of poverty, educational inequality, and criminality rested not in the residue of state-supported segregation but in the failure of black individuals and families to avail themselves of the benefits of equal opportunity and throw off a culture of dependency. Conservatives maintained that the civil rights movement and the government response to it had leveled the playing field, leaving only minor bumps that with hard work, individual initiative, and charitable efforts could be overcome. "Racial realists," as the political scientist Clarence Lusane ironically labeled them, declared racism "a phenomenon of the past."[38]

Although Bush generally accepted the idea of racial realism, he also showed some awareness of its limitations. He had Condoleezza Rice, among others, to remind him. In 2003, Rice spoke bluntly to the National Association of Black Journalists: "When the Founding Fathers said 'We the People' they did not mean us. Our ancestors were considered three-fifths of a person."[39] Unlike conservative racial realists, Rice contended, "America is not color-blind and likely will never be. Race is ever present, like a birth defect that you learn to live with but can never cure."[40] Thus, within the framework of his conservative beliefs, Bush sought to ameliorate the lingering effects of the racism that Rice and Secretary of State Powell recognized.

For Bush, compassionate conservatism became much more than a slogan. Reining in the federal government did not mean he intended to abandon the poor and undereducated. Accordingly, the federal government had a responsibility to confer resources on state and local programs designed to improve educational opportunities, promote minority business enterprises and homeownership, and provide welfare services to the truly needy. Through a combination of public and private action—government agencies, civic groups, and religious organizations—Bush hoped to mobilize "armies of compassion" while reinforcing conservative principles of self-reliance and faith.[41]

The president saw as the international component of compassionate conservatism government aid to fight epidemics in Africa, an area of special interest to black Americans. Many of the religious groups that composed Bush's political base were committed to fighting poverty and ending genocide in Africa in places such as the Darfur region of Sudan. According to Representative Donald M. Payne of New Jersey, the black congressman and top-ranking Democrat on the House International

Relations Subcommittee on Africa: "The evangelical community raised the awareness of HIV and AIDS to the president. When the Bush administration came in, HIV and AIDS were not an overwhelming priority. Now we have seen a total metamorphosis."[42]

In pursuing this strategy, the Bush administration moved ahead in new directions while falling back in others that mattered a great deal to civil rights advocates. Bush chose to put his main political energy into educational reform because it relied on the cornerstone of conservative principles: localism, individual achievement, and opportunity for self-advancement. Nearly fifty years after *Brown v. Board of Education*, racial segregation in the schools no longer remained the law of the land. However, the achievement gap between white and black students remained wide and in many instances was growing. Federal aid to education had been a central tenet of liberal reform and one of the significant achievements of Lyndon Johnson's Great Society; yet the blight of educational inequality still existed. Hence by emphasizing quality education Bush intended to unite conservatives and liberals without injecting divisive issues of race into the mix. Still, the president could not avoid controversial differences between ideological foes concerning federal and state authority and secular and religious boundary lines. The No Child Left Behind (NCLB) Act emerged from these efforts.

No Child Left Behind

Bush had focused on educational reform as governor of Texas and considered the results a huge success. In fact, in running for the White House, he wanted to be "the education president."[43] He was appalled that in the year 2000 "nearly 70 percent of 4th graders from high poverty backgrounds couldn't read at grade level . . . [and] 40 percent of minority students failed to finish high school on time." These statistics, Bush contended, pointed to the existence of racial and ethnic bias against disadvantaged minorities, discrimination not produced by law but by the low expectations of government officials and educators of what blacks and Latinos could accomplish. In a stroke of ingenuity, Bush presented educational reform as "a piece of civil rights legislation."[44] In this way, he attempted to shift the civil rights focus from affirmative action, with its controversial racial preferences, to quality schooling, an idea at the heart of basic American values of uplift and fair play. In campaigning for president, Bush had told the NAACP that he would implement educational reform because "no child should be left behind in America."[45]

This course of action made good political sense. It appealed to African Americans and Latinos, and Bush's ideas fit comfortably into progressive thinking about school reform. The basic elements of NCLB—assessment, accountability, and expanded school options—had originated in the Clinton administration. Yet at the same time NCLB legislation posed some problems for the Democrats. Blacks and Latinos welcomed any measure that would improve their children's education, whereas teachers' unions, a staple of Democratic support, questioned attempts to gauge teacher performance mainly through standardized tests that took no account of poor socioeconomic conditions over which classroom teachers exercised no control but that influenced student achievement.[46]

The Bush administration placed NCLB at the top of its legislative agenda. The president signaled his commitment to its passage by appearing at the annual National Urban League Conference on August 1, 2001, and devoting his entire remarks to NCLB. Bush deplored the existence of the wide reading gap between black and white schoolchildren and asserted that it "leads to personal tragedy and social injustice." Declaring reading a civil rights issue, he noted that in "America literacy is liberation, and we must set all our children free." He refused to put the blame for failing schools on parents and the impoverished circumstances under which families lived; instead, he attributed the major portion of responsibility to school administrators and teachers who did not expect poor children to succeed. He adeptly termed this problem "the soft bigotry of low expectations." Money alone, he argued, would not solve the problem, as the federal government had invested $158 billion in aid to schools. "Just as faith without works is dead," the preacher-in-chief instructed, "money without reform is fruitless." The educational gap would not close without a regular testing regimen to show teachers "where and how to improve." Pushing hard for accountability, Bush reminded his largely sympathetic audience, "The purpose of education, after all, is not jobs for adults; it's learning for students."[47]

Bush's determination to obtain legislation proved as good as his words. Even before taking office, the president-elect met with a bipartisan group of lawmakers to plan strategy for passage of NCLB. He joined with key liberals, such as Congressman George Miller of California and Senator Edward Kennedy of Massachusetts, and conservatives, such as Representative John Boehner of Ohio, to hammer out a bill. Both sides agreed to compromise. Conservative Republicans gave up their proposal for school vouchers that families could use to send their children to private schools, and liberals accepted cost-cutting provisions that streamlined the administration of various programs and allowed states and localities more room for maneuvering.[48]

The final version of NCLB passed the House and Senate by wide margins. The measure, which Bush signed into law on January 8, 2002, required mandatory annual testing by the states to assess the performance of school children. The government would issue report cards for each school in the nation based on reading and math scores broken down by race, ethnicity, and socioeconomic status. By "disaggregating" results in this fashion, Bush fulfilled his pledge to minorities to spotlight educational achievement gaps and move to erase them. Toward this end, the act provided that if schools failed to meet assigned goals for three consecutive years, they must offer free tutoring services for children who needed them or else allow parents to transfer their children to a better performing school in the district. The law set 2014 as the year for achieving 100 percent proficiency in reading and math for all school children in the United States, an ambitious goal but one that Bush considered realistic and not merely symbolic.[49]

Bush initially succeeded in casting NCLB as a civil rights victory. Margaret Spellings, the education secretary of the NAACP, said of the act, it is "not just an education law. It's a civil rights law." Robert Gordon, a Democratic adviser to Senator John Kerry, went so far as to praise the act "as a form of affirmative action": "States must show that minority and poor students are achieving proficiency . . . or else provide remedies targeted to the school." Even the U.S. Commission on Civil Rights, whose liberal members usually clashed with the Bush administration, hailed NCLB as ushering in the "most sweeping public education changes in decades."[50]

However, praise for Bush's accomplishment proved short lived. From the beginning, many conservatives, skeptical of big government and "social engineering," questioned the expense of undertaking a massive federal overhaul of education. Expressing this concern, the conservative scholars Frederick M. Hess and Chester E. Finn Jr. criticized NCLB as too ambitious and impractical, calling it "a civil rights manifesto masquerading as an education accountability system."[51] The Bush administration gave liberals even greater reason to complain. Having embraced federal-sponsored reform, the president returned to more traditional conservative principles by cutting taxes and thereby reducing the revenue to fund NCLB adequately. In the years following the September 11 terrorist attacks and the subsequent war in Iraq, expenditures for homeland security and military defense skyrocketed, making a mockery of Bush and his party's pledge to rein in budget deficits.[52] Responding to conservative concerns, the president, just one month after he signed NCLB legislation, sliced $90 million from its appropriation. Over the next six years NCLB remained substantially underfunded, thereby raising liberal hackles.[53] In 2006, Congressman Miller issued a report card for NCLB: "I would give it an 'A' in terms of the goals that it has set," he declared, but "I would give it an 'F' for funding . . . and on implementation I would give it a 'C.'" Offering an even harsher assessment, Senator Kennedy blasted NCLB as "a symbol of controversial, flawed, and failed policy."[54]

The Bush administration rejected much of this criticism. The president pointed out that federal spending for education increased by 39 percent over his eight years in office, "with much of the extra money going to the poorest students and schools." Yet rather than dispute the fact that funding did not live up to demands, Bush shifted the focus of the argument. He responded to critics by saying that "success cannot be measured by dollars spent but judged by results achieved" and pointed out that when he left office the math and reading scores of fourth- and eighth-grade students had reached their highest levels and the performance gap between white and minority students had narrowed.[55] Unquestionably, NCLB has fallen short of expectations; gaps in educational achievement based on race, ethnicity, and income still exist among students, and they are not likely to close before the target date of 2014. At the same time, the United States has slipped in various measures of educational performance compared to the rest of the world. Still, Bush deserves greater recognition than he has received for departing from the strictures of conservative ideology to reform education in a manner not witnessed since the 1960s. In so doing he enlarged the scope of the traditional civil rights agenda to include reading and math literacy.

Affirmative Action

Although he may have defected from traditional, right-wing thinking with respect to education, President Bush embraced conservatives by challenging affirmative action. He opposed programs that took race into account for admission into colleges and universities, as he had done while serving as governor. The federal court of appeals had struck down the University of Texas affirmative-action admission's plan in the late 1990s, but the controversy remained unresolved nationally, being subject to a ruling by the U.S. Supreme Court. As president, Bush again confronted this thorny issue with much the same response.

By the time Bush became president, the judiciary had narrowed the scope of affirmative action. Although the Supreme Court had not overturned its landmark decision in the *Bakke* case (1978), which upheld the use of racial classifications to promote diversity in higher education, over the next two decades it prohibited affirmative-action plans in which racial considerations figured predominantly in their design and implementation. In the words of the court, to pass constitutional muster, affirmative-action programs had to be "narrowly tailored" to further "compelling state interests."[56] The court's rulings reflected public opinion. Polls showed that while Americans favored by a 2–1 margin attempts to increase the number of minority students in colleges and universities, they opposed by an even wider 3–1 margin extending favored treatment in admissions based on race and ethnicity. In November 1996, California voters passed a referendum preventing the state from granting preferential racial treatment in the fields of "public employment, public education, and public contracting."[57]

President Bush had voiced firm objections to quotas and preferences, but he had to walk a political tightrope on this issue. The problem for the president was figuring out how to satisfy conservative political supporters who took a dim view of affirmative action programs, regarding them as "reverse discrimination" against whites, while appealing to blacks and Latinos who favored expansive use of affirmative action. At first he tried to reach some kind of balance. In 2001, the Bush administration successfully argued before the Supreme Court in favor of a previously established Department of Transportation program that allowed federal contractors to award procurements to minority contractors as long as they did so under narrowly designated circumstances. Yet even this modest defense drew harsh criticism from affirmative-action opponents who attacked Bush for defending "a morally indefensible" program.[58]

The major challenge for Bush came with cases arising from the University of Michigan. The university had constructed an admission plan for undergraduates that automatically awarded African Americans, Hispanics, and Native Americans 20 points on a scale of 150, with 100 points needed for admission. With respect to entry into the law school, the university did not automatically grant specified points to minorities, but it sought to enroll a "critical mass" of under-represented minority students by considering the racial background of candidates as one of the criteria for selection. The Clinton administration had supported the University of Michigan, and the lower federal courts had upheld the university.

In contrast, the Bush administration challenged the university's affirmative-action program but not without first waging a fierce battle over what position to take. Led by Solicitor General Theodore Olson, conservatives backed the white plaintiffs and saw an opportunity to persuade the Supreme Court to overthrow what was left of *Bakke* and strike a final blow against affirmative action. On the other side, White House Counsel Alberto Gonzales and Deputy Attorney General Larry Thompson, a Latino and an African American, favored retention of affirmative action and worried that by coming out against it the president would damage his attempts to attract minority voters to the Republican Party. Powerful support for their position came from Colin Powell and Condoleezza Rice, the two most visible African Americans in the administration. Rice told the president that the "principle that race could be taken into consideration in admissions was worth defending."[59]

Complicating these deliberations further, Bush was confronted with a controversy surrounding Trent Lott, the Republican Senate Majority Leader from Mississippi. On December 5, 2002, at the celebration marking the 100th birthday of his GOP colleague Strom Thurmond of South Carolina, Lott praised the 1948 Dixiecrat candidate for president and declared that the country would have turned out better if the former segregationist had won the election. This statement unleashed a firestorm of criticism from blacks and Democrats, forcing Lott to resign as majority leader. Coming around the same time as the Michigan cases reached the Supreme Court, the Lott flap produced a good deal of political fallout. "The issue of race," Clinton Bollick, a leading conservative ideologue, asserted, "is radioactive for this administration."[60]

Yet in the end, Bush joined with Olson and the conservatives in arguing against the University of Michigan's affirmative-action plans. In January 2003, the president publicly announced that his administration would file an amicus curiae brief on behalf of the white challengers. Objecting to Michigan's policies as "divisive, unfair, and impossible to square with the Constitution," he denounced the affirmative-action plan as a quota system "that unfairly rewards or penalizes prospective students based solely on their race."[61] The brief filed in the undergraduate case, *Gratz v. Bollinger*, zeroed in on the twenty-points award for minorities as an outright quota benefitting minorities only. In the companion *Grutter v. Bollinger* case, the government argued that the attempt of the law school to admit a "critical mass" of certain racial minorities was really a quota in disguise. In both cases, Olson contended that the university relied on race as the "decisive factor" in making selections and instead should have used "race-neutral" criteria to recruit more minorities. By this he meant programs like the 10-percent admissions plans in Texas, Florida, and California and those that paid close attention to a student's socioeconomic status, a history of overcoming disadvantages, and participation in extracurricular activities that might result in the selection of a more diverse student body without violating the Constitution.[62]

Nevertheless, the Bush administration stopped just short of advocating a legal end to affirmative action, thereby paying some attention to the advice of his key minority advisers. The president refused to endorse Olson's recommendation to scuttle *Bakke* explicitly. However, affirmative-action proponents took no comfort from Bush's position and roundly condemned the government's brief. They understood that the Bush administration's reasoning, if adopted by the court, would result in overturning *Bakke* for all practical purposes.[63]

The Supreme Court refused to go this far. Because it singled out minorities to receive designated points toward admission, the undergraduate plan proved most vulnerable. In a six-to-three ruling in *Gratz*, the court struck down the policy for not paying sufficient attention to the individual characteristics of applicants and applying instead a rigid formula based on race to evaluate them. In legal terminology, Chief Justice William Rehnquist, speaking for the majority, found that the disputed "admissions policy is not narrowly tailored to achieve [the university's] asserted compelling interest in diversity." This opinion validated the Bush administration's arguments against quotas and preferences. However, on the same day a majority of five justices upheld the law school's affirmative-action admissions policy. In *Grutter* the court ruled that the law school admission plan considered race as only one of many factors in the selection of students. In her majority opinion, Justice Sandra Day O'Connor upheld the law school guidelines, which emphasized assessment of individual characteristics, because they furthered "a compelling interest in obtaining the educational benefits that flow from a diverse student body." Thus, the court did not discard *Bakke* nor did it require state universities to adopt race-neutral alternatives to attract minority students. The justices had weakened affirmative action without totally destroying it.[64]

Despite the mixed outcomes, Bush considered the rulings a victory. "Today's decisions seek a careful balance between the goal of campus diversity and the fundamental principle of equal treatment under the law," the president remarked, adding that he looked "forward to the day when America will be a color-blind society."[65]

However, to the dismay of civil rights advocates, the Bush administration acted as if this egalitarian moment had arrived. Subsequently, it filed briefs on behalf of white parents in public school districts in Seattle, Washington, and Louisville, Kentucky, challenging voluntary efforts to desegregate schools to reflect the racial and ethnic composition of the districts. In 2007, the Supreme Court agreed with the Bush administration that the school districts had improperly employed race to assign children. This decision limited further attempts by school districts to promote desegregation effectively.[66] In practice, these rulings ensured that the president's No Child Left Behind program, which he valued so highly, would operate within the segregated educational systems that continued to exist fifty years after *Brown*. The Bush administration had narrowed the reach of affirmative action, but it had done so in tandem with the Supreme Court and disgruntled white voters in states throughout the nation.[67]

Bush's opposition to affirmative action neutralized whatever advances among blacks he might have made from NCLB. Overall, the president failed to convince African Americans that they had much to gain from compassionate conservatism. In his reelection in 2004, Bush did only slightly better among African Americans than he had four years earlier. Gaining 11 percent of the black vote, up from 8 percent in 2000, he still received less than the post-1964 Republican average of 12 percent.[68] The president's thin support from African Americans got even slimmer in the wake of Hurricane Katrina.

Hurricane Katrina

The story of this tragic storm has been widely chronicled and needs little retelling here. On Monday, August 29, 2005, Katrina, packing winds of 145 miles per hour, pounded New Orleans and the Gulf Coast. Damaged by high winds, torrential rains, and a rampaging storm surge, the Crescent City did not encounter severe flooding until torrents of water from Lake Pontchartrain broke through several weakened levees. Nearly 50 percent of New Orleans lies below sea level, and in some low-lying areas, the water rose more than twenty feet above sea level, swamping homes and businesses.

African Americans composed 67.5 percent of New Orleans' 444,515 residents, and since 1978 blacks had served continuously in city hall as mayor. Before the hurricane struck, some 90 percent of New Orleanians had fled the Crescent City, leaving approximately 45,000 people to seek shelter in the Superdome and the Ernest N. Morial Convention Center. Over 1,400 New Orleanians perished in the storm. Slightly more than half the dead were black, which meant that a significant number of whites also died (many of whom lived in the wealthy lakefront district susceptible to flooding). However, given the racial composition of the city and the predominance of photographs and videos of black victims anxiously seeking help, Katrina became associated mainly with African Americans and the poor.[69]

The scope of the disaster was stunning, and for a week all levels of government failed in handling its consequences. "I've spent my whole life serving this country," Marine Colonel Terry Ebbert, New Orleans's emergency preparedness director, admitted three days after the hurricane hit and the levees broke, "and I know human misery. [I]f anybody in any leadership position had to stand where I am standing now and seeing this despair and human suffering they would feel like me, I'm ashamed of being an American."[70] Neither Ray Nagin, the city's mayor, nor Kathleen Blanco, Louisiana's governor, possessed either the skills or resources to tackle the problem.

Still, the greatest responsibility for the failure in managing the disaster fell on President Bush. When the hurricane made landfall, Bush was on vacation at his Texas ranch. Two days later, on his way back to Washington, he had Air Force One fly over New Orleans and the other devastated areas, choosing not to have the plane land so he could inspect the damage on the ground and show support for the victims. His appointee as the director of the Federal Emergency Management Agency (FEMA), Michael D. Brown, had no experience in this field, and despite his obvious failures in handling the situation, Bush publicly praised him (only to fire him a few weeks later). Furthermore, the president hesitated to send federal troops to New Orleans unless Governor Blanco formally made the request, which she refused to do. Bush accepted the blame for moving too slowly. "As the leader of the federal government, I should have recognized the deficiencies of local and state governments sooner and intervened faster," Bush recalled in his memoir. "The problem is not that I made the wrong decision. It was that I took too long to decide."[71]

African Americans attributed Bush's failures to more than poor timing. Even Bush admitted that blacks "came away convinced their president didn't care about them." He was correct in his assessment. Reflecting the attitudes of most African Americans, the hip-hop singer Kanye West bemoaned, "You know it's been five days [without aid], because most of the people are black. . . . George Bush doesn't care about black people."[72] Furthermore, public opinion polls revealed stark differences in how blacks and whites viewed the Bush administration's intentions. According to the Pew Research Center, 66 percent of blacks thought the government would have been more responsive if most of the victims had been white; in contrast, only 17 percent of whites believed this.[73]

Yet Bush's critics missed the point. The president cared about the human suffering inflicted by the hurricane, and his inaction did not stem from overt racism on his part. In focusing on personal blame, both Bush and his detractors ignored the deeper structural racism exposed by the catastrophe. The hurricane dramatically revealed that the country may have conquered legal inequality, but the debilitating effects of race and class remained embedded in American institutions. The legacy of racial discrimination had pulled a disproportionate share of blacks into poverty and left them less able to flee the storm's wrath. Like many cities, the Big Easy had two sides—one that housed prosperous whites and the small black middle class and the other in which the black poor lived. New Orleans was a microcosm of urban American, a metropolis split along lines of race and class. The median household income in 2004 was $27,355, about $8,000 less than that in Louisiana. At the same time, the proportion of residents living below the poverty line, 27 percent, exceeded that of state and national averages. Reflecting the reality of economic hard times, the population of the city had dropped by 40,000 between 2000 and 2004.[74]

The tragedy of Hurricane Katrina spotlighted race and class as matters of life and death. Blacks suffered most because they were disproportionately poor. Many blacks remained in the city with the storm approaching not because they were irresponsible but because they did not own automobiles and could not afford to pay the fares to exit on a plane or train. Also, they lived in places such as the Lower Ninth Ward precisely because their vulnerability to flooding made homes there less desirable and cheaper. Furthermore, housing in the city continued to reflect patterns of racial discrimination associated with the Jim Crow era, which exposed African Americans to the daily vicissitudes of crime, poor education, and health hazards and confined them to neighborhoods most likely to suffer the consequences of a hurricane. The damage inflicted by Katrina was not so much random as historically engineered. According to Chester Hartman and Gregory D. Squires, "If nobody is allowed to return to damaged areas, New Orleans will lose 80 percent of its black population, compared to just 50 percent of its white population."[75] Katrina vividly refuted the conservative argument that in the twenty-first century the United States had become a "color-blind society."

Katrina also exposed the weakness of the conservative philosophy of self-help and reliance, as well as conservative hostility to government. The tragedy revealed dramatically how broadly government intervention was needed, especially for those impoverished and with little means to escape or cope with this overwhelming disaster. The conservative hostility to government, perhaps best symbolized by the lamentable appointment of Brown as head of FEMA, left Gulf Coast residents more exposed to the ravages of the storm than they might have been with an administration that put a premium on governmental assistance and effectiveness.

By failing to see racism as institutional and its solutions as requiring much more than compassion, the president wound up concluding that he had satisfactorily made up for his initial leadership failures. Mounting a defense, Bush has pointed out that most of the population returned to New Orleans after the hurricane; tourism was flourishing again; the

Army Corps of Engineers repaired and strengthened floodwalls and levees; 70,000 citizens renovated or rebuilt their homes; schools reopened; and the Superdome, once an emergency shelter, hosted the 2010 Super Bowl victory of the home team New Orleans Saints.[76] Bush's claims, however, ignored the disproportionate toll Katrina had taken on the Big Easy's black citizens. Mardi Gras festivities resumed without missing a beat, the French Quarter managed to regain tourists, the wealthy built condominiums on higher ground, but the Lower Ninth Ward and other black neighborhoods remained something of a ghost town. Estimates of the Crescent City's population in mid-2007 ranged from 255,000 to 274,000 or from 50 to 55 percent of the pre-Katrina figure. Black residents comprised 60 percent of city residents in 2010, compared with 67 percent in 2000, whereas the proportion of white residents grew from 28 percent to 33 percent. Furthermore, the improvements that have occurred tended to help those best suited to compete within the free enterprise system, sacrificing those traditionally on the economic fringes. Also, just a year and one-half after the hurricane, the president failed to refer to Katrina or recovery in his State of the Union Address. Bush did not live up to his pledge that "we will do what it takes; we will stay as long as it takes" to rebuild New Orleans.[77] His administration never contemplated using Hurricane Katrina to launch a public discussion of the enduring impact of race and poverty that might have transformed this tragedy into a sustained campaign to relieve the plight of the nation's poorest and most neglected citizens.

The Politicization of Civil Rights Enforcement

If the mishandling of Katrina was not enough to drive an impenetrable wedge between African Americans and the president, the Bush administration itself only made matters worse. The president had told the National Urban League in 2004 that progress "for this country, for African Americans and all Americans, depends on the full protection of civil rights and equality before the law" and that the "Justice Department has vigorously enforced the civil rights laws."[78] Although the administration in general continued past approaches to enforcement, it shifted some priorities and reshaped others through its personnel policies. More so than previous administrations, Democratic or Republican, the

Bush Justice Department used a political litmus test in hiring staff that reflected its ideological positions.

By the time Bush became president, career civil rights lawyers in the Justice Department, especially in the Voting Section, had succeeded in enforcing the statutes passed at the height of the civil rights movement in imaginative and aggressive ways. As with most bureaucracies, career civil rights attorneys had provided continuity in enforcement no matter which political party occupied the White House. However, serious conflicts between political appointees and career officials arose in the Bush administration, thereby weakening enforcement. Joseph Rich, an attorney in the Civil Rights Division (CRD) of the Justice Department for thirty-seven years, bitterly underscored this point: "I was there in the Reagan years, and this is worse."[79] Between 2003 and 2007 more than 70 percent of CRD lawyers left the department, many of them forced to take early retirement, while others departed because of disagreements with department leadership. At the same time, those who stayed increasingly found their recommendations ignored and power diminished.[80]

The main problem centered in the CRD sections supervised by Deputy Assistant Attorney General Bradley Schlozman, especially those dealing with employment and voting. This Bush appointee manipulated hiring policies to employ Republicans, especially conservatives, to career positions while turning down liberal Democrats. According to a report by the department's Office of the Inspector General, Schlozman improperly considered political and ideological standards in making appointments as well as in forcing transfers from the sections under his control. In 2006, Schlozman privately informed a colleague of his thinking: "[When] we start asking about what is your commitment to civil rights? . . . [H]ow do you prove that? Usually by some membership in some crazy liberal cause." In other words he would not permit hiring members of any "psychopathic left-wing organization designed to destroy the government," singling out the American Civil Liberties Union and the Lawyers Committee for Civil Rights Under Law for special condemnation.[81]

Besides selective hiring, top Justice Department officials sought to reshape enforcement priorities. The department extended the administration's concern for conservative religious values by making protection of religious freedom a high priority in a manner once reserved for conventional civil rights issues. Under Attorney General Alberto Gonzales, who replaced John Ashcroft in 2005, the government aided groups that wanted public schools to send home religious literature with their children; argued for the exemption of places of worship from local zoning laws; and pressed an expansive definition of religious freedom under the First Amendment. In readjusting its mission, the Justice Department gave less attention to cases involving hate crimes, racial profiling, and voting rights. "Not until recently," Brian K. Landsberg, a law professor and former attorney in the Justice Department, commented, "has anyone considered religious discrimination such a high priority. No one has ever considered it to be of the same magnitude as race or national origin."[82]

The administration extended political calculations into other areas. To boost Republican Party fortunes, it waged a fierce campaign to crack down on alleged voter fraud, often targeting black communities with heavily Democratic majorities. Although government prosecutors filed 120 cases and obtained convictions in 86, a federal commission that studied electoral chicanery found that the pervasiveness of fraud was greatly exaggerated. Most of the problems stemmed from ignorance, confusion, and error rather than criminal intent to undermine fair elections. They were "isolated acts of individual wrongdoing" and not part of "organized schemes to subvert elections." A 2004 case in Milwaukee summed up the situation. A federal appeals judge found "mysterious" the prosecution and conviction of a woman on parole who mistakenly thought she was entitled to vote. Judge Diane P. Wood declared: "I don't know if the Eastern District of Wisconsin goes after every felon who accidentally votes. It is not like she voted five times, she cast one vote."[83]

Following a provision in the Help Americans Vote Act, enacted in 2002 following the controversial Bush-Gore election, the Justice Department backed use of voter identification cards to combat alleged fraud. To this end, in 2005, the Republican-dominated Georgia Legislature adopted a voter identification law. Under the regulation, a prospective voter needed a government-issued, photo identification card, such as a driver's license, to carry to the polls. Opponents argued that the requirement placed an unfair burden on impoverished Georgians, many of them black, who did not own a car or who could not afford the $20 for the approved identification card. Despite the advice of attorneys in the Civil Rights Division, the attorney general approved the law under Section 5 of the Voting Rights Act. The Eleventh U.S. Circuit Court of Appeals ruled otherwise. Judge Harold A. Murphy compared the law "to a Jim Crow–era poll tax that required residents, most of them black, to pay back taxes before voting" and struck down the measure. This victory for voting rights proved short-lived, however. After the state legislature made it easier for Georgians to obtain photo I.D.'s at no cost, Judge Murphy reversed himself and ruled that civil rights challengers had not proved that the law placed "an undue or significant burden" on the right to vote. When a similar case from Indiana came before the U.S. Supreme Court, voting rights proponents suffered a final blow. On April 28, 2008, in a six to three decision, the justices upheld the use of photo identification cards for voting and rejected the argument that the requirement to submit the card imposed an unconstitutional burden on the poor and minorities.[84]

In several important matters, however, politics did not lead to unfavorable civil rights enforcement by the Bush administration. Unlike African Americans, Latinos had shown critical support for the president in his 2004 reelection victory. He garnered around 44 percent of their vote, about nine points higher than in 2000.[85] This gain paralleled the increased support the Justice Department gave to Latino voters. Since 2002, the Voting Section had stepped up enforcement of the minority language provisions of the Voting Rights Act and raised its efforts to reach out to Hispanic voters in the jurisdictions to which the law applied. From 2002 to 2009, 70 percent of the government's voting rights cases (246 of 367) were filed on behalf of language minorities at a time when federal litigation involving African Americans was on the decline.[86]

Still, the Bush administration did not abandon black voting rights when its political interests were at stake. Since the 1980s the Republican Party had made great inroads in winning congressional and state elections in the South. This resulted in part from the creation of majority-black legislative districts that provided black voters a greater opportunity to elect candidates of their choice, usually African Americans. As the most faithful Democratic voters in the South, blacks elected Democrats to represent these districts. However, in shifting African Americans from neighboring areas to create these majority-minority districts, white Republicans also gained. What at first appears to be a strange outcome turns out to make perfect sense. Clustering African Americans in a few districts left fewer minorities in other districts to tip the scales in favor of moderate Democrats. Thus, racial redistricting helped produce more Republican victories. One of the Bush administration's first successful voting rights cases came in 2001 after Attorney General Ashcroft rejected a legislative redistricting plan in Georgia that would have reduced the number of potential majority-black districts as well as hamper Republican chances.[87]

Yet the administration's political concerns do not fully explain the lessening of government enforcement. Just as important, conservative court rulings greatly restricted enforcement opportunities. This was particularly true with respect to voting rights. Section 5 of the 1965 Voting Rights Act required covered state and local governments to submit any electoral change to the Department of Justice or the federal district court in Washington, D.C., for "preclearance" before going into effect. Also, the high tribunal had ruled that for a voting change to be judged suspect it had to "make matters worse for minority voters" than the existing situation did. The court referred to this principle as "non-retrogression." On January 24, 2000, before Bush was elected, in a five to four decision, the Supreme Court decided that with respect to Section 5 cases, a voting submission could pass muster, despite evidence of racial discrimination, if it did not *intend* to place minority voters in a worse condition ("retrogressive intent") than currently existed, a criterion difficult to determine. Thus, *Reno v. Bossier Parish School Board (Bossier II)* made it harder for the Department of Justice to wield Section 5 as a tool for guaranteeing minority voting rights. In the decade of the 1990s, the Civil Rights Division had reviewed numerous submissions of voting alterations and objected to approximately 250 of them on grounds of racial bias. After *Bossier II*, the department filed only forty-one objections from 2000 to 2004. And nearly all of these objections were based on discriminatory retrogressive effect rather than intent, a standard easier to prove.[88]

Reauthorization of the Voting Rights Act

Ironically, the *Bossier II* decision, which weakened civil rights enforcement, offered the Bush administration a superb opportunity to make its strongest statement on behalf of minority rights. Several provisions of the 1965 Voting Rights Act were scheduled to come up for renewal in 2007. These included Section 5 as well as the procedure for allowing jurisdictions to remove themselves from coverage. The act, first signed into law by the Democratic President Lyndon B. Johnson, had been reauthorized in 1970, 1975, and 1982 by the Republican Presidents Richard

M. Nixon, Gerald R. Ford, and Ronald Reagan. In each of the renewals, however, the Republican chief executives had tried unsuccessfully to weaken the measure before approving it.[89] Despite Bush's previous conflicts with civil rights proponents, he not only embraced renewal but also strengthened the law to overcome the restrictions imposed by the Supreme Court. That he did so in cooperation with a Republican-controlled Congress, considered "one of the most partisan and polarized ever," made the president's efforts all the more remarkable.[90]

Bush had not started out as a supporter of the Voting Rights Act. As governor of Texas, Bush, like most of his southern counterparts, condemned Section 5 as "an affront to the integrity" of the Lone Star State.[91] Yet Governor Bush supported other provisions of the Voting Rights Act, most particularly those that afforded assistance to language minorities. Mindful of the Latino vote, Bush consistently condemned proposals that required English only as the official language in conducting public business. Such measures, he remarked, was like "poking a stick in the eye of people of Hispanic heritage."[92]

Whatever burden Bush felt the federal government imposed on Texas when he was governor dissolved when he entered the White House. The Voting Rights Act had become part of the national consensus, a bipartisan fixture through Republican and Democratic administrations. Moreover, the Republican Party had benefitted at the expense of Democrats from the creation of more majority-black legislative districts in the South. In August 2005, the fortieth anniversary of the signing of the Voting Rights Act and two years before Section 5 and other temporary features were due to expire, President Bush marked the occasion with a proclamation reaffirming "this bedrock commitment to equality and justice for all." Signaling the administration's intentions, Attorney General Alberto Gonzales called the Voting Rights Act "enormously successful" but still necessary. He declared that the administration "looks forward to working with Congress on the reauthorization of this important legislation." Toward the end of the year, at a ceremony to sign legislation placing a statue of Rosa Parks in the U.S. Capitol, the president called upon Congress to "renew the Voting Rights Act of 1965."[93]

Reauthorization of the Voting Rights Act produced one of the rare examples of congressional bipartisanship during Bush's second term in office. Republicans controlled both Houses, and the president and party leaders lined up behind the renewal measure. In private meetings in the White House and with congressional leaders, the administration made it clear from the outset that it supported reauthorization. To oppose it, one official was quoted as saying, "would be political suicide." Fortunately for proponents of the bill, James Sensenbrenner, the Republican from Wisconsin, chaired the House Judiciary Committee. Sensenbrenner put aside the usual concerns he shared with fellow conservatives about federal encroachment on states' rights as represented in the preclearance requirements of Section 5. He had voted for renewal of the act in 1982, and now as committee chair he viewed its reauthorization as part of his legacy. The Wisconsin representative wanted to complete the renewal process as soon as possible, even before the official date in 2007 set for the special provisions to lapse. Unsure about the outcome of the 2006 congressional elections, which might result in the loss of the Republican majority, Sensenbrenner hoped to win approval for renewal while he and the GOP were in charge. Thus, he worked closely with Democrats on his committee to hold hearings and approve the measure before the 2006 elections. In agreement, House Republican Speaker Dennis Hastert of Illinois pledged his support.[94]

The series of House Judiciary Committee hearings held between October 2005 and April 2006 created a public record in favor of retaining Section 5. Since the previous renewal of the law in 1982, preclearance objections lodged by the attorney general to discriminatory voting changes had increased significantly. The committee found continued evidence of suffrage discrimination, especially the presence of racial bloc voting. Evidence also showed that minorities continued to file suits under the act to challenge voting bias, that the Department of Justice had sent federal observers to monitor contests in which minorities felt subject to electoral chicanery, and that the Civil Rights Division took increased action to ensure that the rights of language minorities were not violated. Reauthorization proponents also argued that Section 5 had a deterrent effect hard to measure by statistics, because it kept jurisdictions from adopting practices likely to disadvantage minority voters and result in federal disapproval. Based on this considerable evidence, the Judiciary Committee concluded that "voter inequities, disparities, and obstacles still remain for far too many voters and serve to demonstrate the ongoing importance" of retaining the Voting Rights Act.[95]

Sensenbrenner and the House Judiciary Committee in cooperation with a coalition of civil rights groups did not stop at simple reauthorization but added provisions to strengthen the law. In light of recent Supreme Court decisions weakening traditional enforcement of Section 5, the committee bill restored the pre-*Bossier II* standard allowing the attorney general to file objections based on discriminatory purpose, whether or not the intention was retrogressive.[96] When introduced on the floors of the House and Senate on May 2, 2006, not only did this bipartisan proposal preserve the Voting Rights Act, but it also extended the Justice Department's power to enforce it for another twenty-five years, until 2031. Given the toxic political climate of the time, growing out of the Bush administration's conservative foreign and domestic agendas of preemptive war and economic privatization, this was a notable accomplishment.

To his credit, the president and his congressional leaders held firm against a revolt by conservative Republican ideologues, mainly in the House. The key source of opposition revolved around objections to assistance for language minorities. Much of this concern about bilingualism and a belief in English-only standards stemmed from the debate over Bush's efforts around the same time to reform immigration regulations. Although the president failed in his attempt to make the path to citizenship easier for illegal immigrants who had lived and worked in the United States for an extended period, he and his congressional supporters kept the language-minority provisions of the voting rights bill in place. As a matter of fact, they turned back all attempts, including those related to Section 5, to amend the proposal. The House voted 390–33 to approve the Judiciary Committee's bill without any amendments proposed to weaken it.[97]

The Bush administration also rejected the arguments of those conservatives who contended that the Voting Rights Act was no longer necessary, that the country had made substantial progress in overcoming discrimination at the polls, and that continued attempts to draw majority-minority legislative districts only created "a black political class too isolated from mainstream political discourse."[98] Although Bush had accepted similar arguments against affirmative action in education, he, like most of his fellow Republicans, had little incentive to apply them to the political sphere. Despite the overwhelming black vote for Democratic presidential candidates and lawmakers, the national Republican Party did not give up on the possibility of gaining increased African American support; renewal of the Voting Rights Act was a painless step in that direction.

Nevertheless, Senate Republicans posed an unexpected challenge to reauthorization. Judiciary Committee Chairman Arlen Specter of Pennsylvania conducted his own hearings on the bill over three months, which slowed its progress. Along with fellow Republicans on the committee, Specter raised serious questions about the continued necessity for Section 5 and other provisions that targeted most of the southern states as well as scattered areas around the country. The Pennsylvania senator, usually counted as a moderate, believed along with the conservatives that since passage of the Voting Rights Act in 1965 discrimination had become more individual and less institutional and that color-blind approaches were now in order.[99]

Faced with dissent from within his party, President Bush rose to head it off. For the first time since he ran for president in 2000, Bush accepted an invitation to address the annual convention of the NAACP, one of the administration's severest civil rights critics. On July 20, 2006, on the eve of Senate debate on the bill, Bush expressed his wishes to the audience without equivocation: "I thank the members of the House of Representatives for re-authorizing the Voting Rights Act. . . . I look forward to the Senate passing this bill promptly *without amendment* [emphasis added] so I can sign it into law."[100] Aware that he and his party had made a poor showing with African American voters in the previous two elections and that the situation had only gotten worse following Hurricane Katrina, Bush believed that support for renewal could only improve the GOP's standing among blacks. "I consider it a tragedy," he asserted, "that the party of Abraham Lincoln let go of its historic ties with the African American community. For too long my party wrote off the African American vote, and many African Americans wrote off the Republican Party."[101] In response, Senate Republicans recalculated the political costs and followed the president. The reauthorization bill passed the Senate unanimously. In signing the law named in honor of civil rights pioneers Rosa Parks, Coretta Scott King, and Fannie Lou Hamer, on July 27, Bush acknowledged, in the "four decades since the Voting Rights Act was first passed, we've made progress toward equality, yet the work for a more perfect union is never ending. We'll continue to build on the legal equality won by the civil rights movement to help ensure that every person enjoys the opportunity that this great land of liberty offers."[102]

Passage of the reauthorization act marked the highlight of the Bush presidency with respect to civil rights. This achievement, however, did not do much to ingratiate the president's party with black voters, as the Democrats regained control of Congress in the 2006 elections. Over the final two years of Bush's term, the one serious incident to disrupt the racial peace did not directly involve his administration. It concerned instead deteriorating race relations in Jena, Louisiana. Following a series of events that included the hanging of nooses on the high-school grounds, clashes between white and black youths, and a suspicious fire at the main high-school building in late 2007, six black teenagers who beat up a white schoolmate were convicted for their crime and received unusually harsh prison sentences. The trial and the incidents surrounding it generated a good deal of national publicity in the news media and on the Internet. On September 20, some 15,000 to 20,000 civil rights demonstrators converged on Jena for a protest march, and thousands more rallied around the country in support of the Jena Six. The Justice Department monitored the case for possible civil rights violations, and President Bush publically applauded the demonstrations for being peaceful. He went so far as to express concern for the black youngsters. The president remarked that the reaction of the black community to the events did not surprise him, saying, "this notion of unequal justice harkens back to a previous time in our history that a lot of folks, including me, are working to get beyond."[103]

Conclusion: Winning While Losing

In an interview with the journalist Juan Williams a little more than a year before leaving office, President Bush looked back over his civil rights record with some satisfaction. He took pride in the passage of No Child Left Behind, which he considered an extension of the civil rights agenda, and in selecting minorities to high-level government positions, most notably Colin Powell and Condoleezza Rice. With respect to Hurricane Katrina, he chose to emphasize the rescue of people stranded from the rooftops of New Orleans as well as the $114 billion Washington sent to the battered Crescent City.[104] He could easily have added to this list signing the Voting Rights Reauthorization Act. Although he left out a good deal to the contrary—opposition to affirmative action, politicized civil rights enforcement, the initial mishandling of Hurricane Katrina— his scorecard stacked up reasonably well with his recent White House predecessors, including his father, George H. W. Bush, and Bill Clinton. Yet whatever his accomplishments, Bush could never overcome the troubling circumstances of his election in 2000. Most African Americans still felt that he had illegitimately won the presidency at the expense of disfranchised black voters in Florida.

George W. Bush remained unpopular with blacks and civil rights advocates not because he was a racist, which clearly he was not, but because his brand of conservatism left unresolved and even worsened conditions for many African Americans. Despite his views to the contrary, compassion, faith, and the free marketplace were not sufficient to overcome the enduring problems of poverty and discrimination embedded in the economic, political, and social structures of American society. The collapse of the financial system in 2008 followed by the greatest economic downturn in the United States since the Great Depression only reinforced the belief of most African Americans that Bush-style conservatism perpetuated their woes.[105]

They had plenty of evidence to support their skepticism. African Americans continued to trail behind whites in nearly all areas of achievement. When Bush put his signature on the Voting Rights Reauthorization Act in 2006, the median income for blacks was $30,939, compared with $50,622 for whites. Three-quarters of white households owned their own home compared with 46 percent of black households. The 2008 financial collapse made this situation worse. The Bush administration had encouraged efforts to provide home ownership to African Americans. With government support, lenders offered sub-prime mortgages aimed at marginal families who could not afford to repay these loans, especially when the housing bubble burst. For a substantial portion of blacks homeownership was not even a consideration. Approximately 24 percent of African Americans lived in poverty, nearly double the national rate of 12.3 percent, compared with only 8 percent of whites. Whereas 15.8 percent of Americans lacked health insurance, the rate for African Americans was still higher at 19.6 percent.[106]

Even some encouraging signs masked underlying problems. In the seven years following passage of No Child Left Behind the gap between whites and blacks in terms of high-school graduation rates narrowed by half (6.4 to 3.0), but the gap in college graduation between the races increased from 9.6 percent to 10.6 percent. Black men fared most poorly. In 2009, the percentage of black male college graduates (17.8) lagged far behind that of white men (30.6), white women (29.3), and black women (20.6).[107] The figures for African American men reflect a tragic reality experienced by black youth and young adults. In 2009, black males, with an incarceration rate of 4,749 inmates per 100,000 U.S. residents, were imprisoned at a rate more than six times higher than that of white males (708 inmates per 100,000 U.S. residents) and 2.6 times higher than that of Hispanic males (1,822 inmates per 100,000 U.S. residents). More than 28 percent of African American men can expect to be incarcerated over their lifetimes, while whites have only a 4 percent chance of imprisonment.[108]

Although African Americans achieved their greatest successes in the political sphere, they failed to reach their electoral potential. On the positive side, the number of black elected officials in the South, where the Voting Rights Act had its greatest impact, leaped from less than seventy-five in 1965 to over 9,000 in 2001, the latest figures that are available. Indeed, the majority of black elected officials nationwide are located in the South. Since the mid-1990s, black women have made the greatest gains in winning elected office, significantly outpacing black men (though overall they are still outnumbered by black men).[109] At the national level, there was a steady expansion of black legislators in the U.S. House of Representatives, with the Congressional Black Caucus containing 43 members at the end of Bush's tenure in the White House. Democratic control of the 110th Congress (2007–9) thrust veteran black lawmakers into the chairmanships of important House committees. Despite these impressive successes, in 2009 only one African American sat in the U.S. Senate and only two served as state governors.[110] These figures bear out the fact that overall blacks remained underrepresented as officeholders compared to their percentages in the population; constituting around 11 percent of the voting-age population, African Americans made up less than 2 percent of the total number of elected officeholders.[111] Furthermore, the disturbing racial disparity in rates of incarceration noted above has serious implications for black voting rights, for many states have laws on the books barring ex-felons from voting.[112]

Racial inequality persists not because presidents like George Bush and the majority of white Americans discriminate personally against African Americans but because it remains part of the unfinished legacy of the civil rights movement. The Second Reconstruction of the 1950s and 1960s succeeded in destroying the legal foundation of racial segregation and disfranchisement. However, it fell short of eradicating the effects of over three hundred years of white supremacy that continue to exist in the economy, housing, education, politics, and the criminal justice system. The Bush administration and the courts contributed to the problem by effectively shredding what was left of affirmative action, but even at its height this program never offered a comprehensive method for solving the problem of racial catch-up because it tended to favor those most able to take advantage of it, the middle class rather than the poor.

Notwithstanding affirmative action, the Bush administration did not overturn most accomplishments of the civil rights movement. The election of black politicians since passage of the 1965 Voting Rights Act and their rise to leadership positions in Congress helped restrain the efforts of Bush and conservative presidents before him to retreat on civil rights. They received critical backing from congressional Democrats and the national coalition of civil rights lobbying groups that had stayed on the scene and continued to exercise considerable power. Indeed, more than forty years after the heyday of the civil rights movement and the ascendency of conservatism, the Second Reconstruction has shown much greater staying power than the First Reconstruction, which came to a premature end after the Civil War. The most visible proof of its longevity came in 2008 with the election of Barack Obama as Bush's successor, the first black man ever to occupy the White House. It remains to be seen whether the Obama administration will be any more successful in achieving the unfulfilled goals of the civil rights movement. To do so will require the revival of something that was missing during the Bush presidency and the longer conservative era before it, something greater than a corps of black officials and powerful interest groups: a mass social movement connecting grassroots and national forces like the one that overthrew American apartheid in the 1950s and 1960s.

Notes

1. George W. Bush, *Decision Points* (New York: Alfred A. Knopf, 2007), 326. See also p. 325.

2. Robert Draper, *Dead Certain: The Presidency of George W. Bush* (New York: Free Press, 2007), 311–16, 353, 382.

3. Bush, *Decision Points*, 325.

4. Quoted in Jeremy Mayer, *Running on Race: Racial Politics in Presidential Campaigns, 1960–2000* (New York: Random House, 2002), 291.

5. For example, see John D. Skrentny, "Zigs and Zags: Richard Nixon and the New Politics of Race" in this volume.

6. Earl Black and Merle Black, *The Rise of Southern Republicans* (Cambridge, Mass.: Belknap Press, 2002).

7. Karl Rove, *Courage and Consequence: My Life as a Conservative in the Fight* (New York: Threshold Editions, 2010), 84.

8. Ibid., 122.

9. Bush, *Decision Points*, 278.

10. Speech to the NAACP, July 10, 2000, http://www.washingtonpost.com/wp-srv/onpolitics/elections/bushtext071000.htm, accessed April 21, 2011. Richard Hofstadter, *Social Darwinism in American Thought* (New York: G. Braziller, 1959); David Nassaw, *Andrew Carnegie* (New York: Penguin, 2006).

11. Bush, *Decision Points*, 277.

12. Rove, *Courage and Consequence*, 189; Clarence Lusane, *Colin Powell and Condoleezza Rice: Foreign Policy, Race, and the New American Century* (Westport, Conn.: Praeger, 2006), 70; and Draper, *Dead Certain*, 320.

13. Hopwood v. State of Texas, 78F.3d932 (5th Cir., 1996). The Supreme Court declined to review the case, and the ruling stood in Texas, Louisiana, and Mississippi, all under Fifth Circuit jurisdiction.

14. Barbara A. Perry, *The Michigan Affirmative Action Cases* (Lawrence: University of Kansas Press, 2007), 39. The Governor of Florida, who instituted a similar plan, was Jeb Bush, the brother of the Texas governor. Yet the results of such programs are disputed. See Mary Francis Berry, *"And Justice for All": The United States Commission on Civil Rights and the Continuing Struggle for Freedom in America* (New York: Alfred A. Knopf, 2009), 300, 329; Lusane, *Colin Powell*, 78. The problem was that while overall minority enrollment was maintained or increased, minority matriculation at the flagship University of Texas at Austin and Texas A & M decreased. "Sociology Professor Finds Ten Percent Plan Flawed," http://theop.princeton.edu/publicity/theop/Daily Princetonian020403.pdf, accessed April 21, 2011. Adam Liptak, "Bush's Affirmative Action Plan Unlikely to End Debate," January 19, 2003, http://aad.english.ucsb.edu/docs/janliptack.html, accessed April 21, 2011.

15. Gary Gerstle, "Minorities, Multiculturalism, and the Presidency of George W. Bush," in *The Presidency of George W. Bush: A First Historical Assessment*, ed. Julian E. Zelizer (Princeton: Princeton University Press, 2010), 263.

16. Mayer, *Running on Race*, 288. In the Republican Party primary in South Carolina, Bush had spoken at the controversial Bob Jones University, which banned

interracial dating, and he had refused to comment on whether the state should fly the Confederate flag on its Capitol. When one of his leading supporters jibed that the NAACP stood for the National Association for the Advancement of Retarded People, Bush called these remarks "unfortunate," a mild rebuke at best. At that stage in the Republican primaries, Bush was trying to outmaneuver his closest competitor, Senator John McCain, for conservative white support in the South.

17. Karen DeYoung, *Soldier: The Life of Colin Powell* (New York: Alfred A. Knopf, 2006), 293.

18. Ibid., 293, 294.

19. Mayer, *Running on Race*, 283.

20. Bush, Speech to the NAACP, July 10, 2000.

21. Steven F. Lawson, *Running for Freedom,* 3rd ed. (Malden, Mass.: Wiley Blackwell, 2009), 299. For the original see http://www.adversity.net/special/george_bush. htm, accessed 26 May 2011.

22. Lawson, *Running for Freedom*, 299; http://abcnews.go.com/Politics/story?id =122696&page=1, accessed May 26, 2011.

23. Mayer, *Running on Race*, 286, 288. Gore appeared at a rally with Byrd's daughter the last weekend of the campaign. Although not as well publicized or condemned, this advertisement ironically paralleled the Willie Horton ad that the Republican Party used to elect George H. W. Bush in 1988. Both advertisements distorted the actual situation.

24. Karl Rove is misleading when he writes that Bush "improved his record among African Americans by 20 percent from four years before." He must be referring to the number of votes and not the percentage. Overall, black voter turnout was significantly higher in 2000 than in 1996. Rove, *Courage and Consequence*, 72. More than for any one of his positions, African Americans overwhelmingly voted for Gore because of their embrace of Bill Clinton. Not only had Clinton meant sustained economic improvement, but Republican efforts to impeach and convict him made him something of a martyr among blacks who could identify with his victimization.

25. See Charles Zelden's essay in this volume and Zelden, *Bush v. Gore: Exposing the Hidden Crisis in American Democracy* (Lawrence: University Press of Kansas, 2008).

26. Rove, *Courage and Consequence*, 217, 229.

27. Gerstle, "Minorities," 257, 258, 267. Gerstle sees the Bush alliance with Latinos as "a conservative brand of multiculturalism," 261. Richard Nadler, "Bush's 'Real' Hispanic Numbers: Debunking the Debunkers," December 8, 2004, http://old. nationalreview.com/comment/nadler200412080811.asp., accessed May 15, 2011. Bush's sister-in-law Columba, Jeb's wife, is Mexican American.

28. Gerstle, "Minorities," 268. The United States Civil Rights Commission reported that of the 1,200 sub-cabinet appointments requiring Senate confirmation, Bush filled 9 percent with African Americans. However, this marked a decrease from the 15 percent appointed during the Clinton administration. See U.S. Commission on Civil Rights, Office of Civil Rights Evaluation, "Redefining Rights in America: The Civil Rights Record of the George W. Bush Administration, 2001–2004," Draft Report, September 2004, 26.

29. Lusane, *Colin Powell*, 2.

30. Condoleezza Rice, *Extraordinary, Ordinary People* (New York: Crown Publishers, 2010), 103. See also pp. 97–99. Rice's father, John Wesley, however, refused to support Dr. Martin Luther King Jr.'s Birmingham campaign because he did not believe in nonviolence or the use of children in demonstrations. On Powell and Rice's views departing from the Bush administration's, see Lusane, *Colin Powell*, 39, 45, 46, 47.

31. Draper, *Dead Certain*, 111, 112 (for the quote). Those in attendance also criticized the appointment of John Ashcroft, considered unsympathetic to civil rights enforcement, as attorney general.

32. Lusane, *Colin Powell*, 33. In contrast to their position on the Iraq War, the overwhelming majority of blacks, 94 percent, approved Bush's handling of the terrorist attacks in the immediate aftermath of September 11.

33. George W. Bush, "The President's News Conference, July 8, 2002," *Public Papers of the Presidents, 2002* (Washington, D.C.: Government Printing Office, 2002), 1191. See also DeYoung, *Soldier*, 425.

34. George W. Bush, "Remarks to the National Urban League, August 1, 2001," *Public Papers of the Presidents, 2002*, vol. 2 (Washington, D.C.: Government Printing Office, 2001): 934–37; "Remarks to the National Urban League, July 23, 2004," *Public Papers of the Presidents, 2004*, vol. 2 (Washington, D.C.: Government Printing Office, 2004): 1,406–15. Furthermore, Bush could not forgive the NAACP for its radio spots late in the campaign attacking him for opposing hate-crime legislation in the wake of James Byrd's murder.

35. U.S. Commission on Civil Rights, "Redefining," 15, 16, 17. Two of the most controversial recess appointments involved Charles Pickering Sr. of Mississippi and William H. Pryor Jr. of Alabama, both of whom were white. Bush made two appointments to the U.S. Supreme Court during his eight years in office, both white, conservative men: chief Justice John Roberts and Samuel Alito. He withdrew his nomination of Harriet Miers, a white woman, following charges on both sides of the congressional aisle that she lacked the requisite qualifications.

36. Abigail M. Thernstrom, *Voting Rights and Wrongs: The Elusive Quest for Racially Fair Elections* (Washington, D.C.: American Enterprise Institute, 2009), 173.

37. Lusane, *Colin Powell*, 48, 60 (for quote), 62.

38. Ibid., 60.

39. Ibid., 79.

40. Rice, *Extraordinary, Ordinary People*, 158.

41. DeYoung, *Soldier*, 292; Michael Kagin, "From Hubris to Despair: George W. Bush and the Conservative Movement," in *The Presidency of George W. Bush*, ed., Zelizer, 285.

42. Michael A. Fletcher, "Bush has Quietly Tripled Aid to Africa," *Washington Post*, December 31, 2006, http://www.washingtonpost.com/wp-dyn/content/article/2006/12/30/AR2006123000941.html, accessed June 3, 2011. Bush, *Decision Points*, 333–54.

43. Bush, *Decision Points*, 274; Frederick Hess and Patrick J. McGuinn, "George W. Bush's Education Legacy: The Two Faces of No Child Left Behind," in *Judging Bush*, ed. Robert Maranto, Tom Lansford, Jeremy Johnson (Stanford: Stanford University Press, 2009), 157.

44. Bush, *Decision Points*, 273–74.

45. Speech to the NAACP, July 10, 2000.

46. Hess and McGuinn, "George W. Bush's Education Legacy," 157, 158, 161. Bush's campaign for educational reform pulled him about even with Gore on the issue in the 2000 election, in contrast to four years earlier when Clinton outpolled the Republican candidate, Robert Dole, on education by 50 percent.

47. Bush "Remarks to National Urban League," August 1, 2001, quotes on p. 935.

48. John D. Graham, *Bush on the Home Front* (Bloomington: Indiana University Press, 2010), 68, 69, 70, 72. Bush, *Decision Points*, 275.

49. Hess and McGuinn, "George W. Bush's Education Legacy," 164; Graham, *Home Front*, 73, 74, 81, 87.

50. Hess and McGuinn, "George W. Bush's Education Legacy," 167–68, for the first two quotes in the paragraph. The U.S. Commission on Civil Rights statement can be found in USCCR, "Redefining," 45, which also assessed NCLB as deeply flawed in funding and methodology.

51. Hess and McGuinn, "George W. Bush's Education Legacy," 167; http://education next.org/crash-course/, accessed May 23, 2011.

52. Coincidentally, NCLB was linked to September 11 in another way. When the attacks occurred Bush was visiting the predominantly African American Emma E. Booker Elementary School in Sarasota, Florida, where he was reading to second graders. His appearance there was intended to provide a photo opportunity for pushing the NCLB forward through Congress. Draper, *Dead Certain*, 134.

53. Gerstle, "Minorities," 273; Draper, *Dead Certain,* 169; Graham, *Home Front,* 86; Christopher H. Foreman Jr., "The Braking of the President: Shifting Context and the Bush Domestic Agenda" in *The George W. Bush Legacy*, ed. Colin Campbell, Bert A. Rockman, and Andrew Rudalevige (Washington, D.C.: Congressional Quarterly Press, 2008), 281. Only $59.8 billion of the $116.3 billion authorized for the NCLB was funded.

54. Hess and McGovern, "George W. Bush's Education Legacy," 165, 159. Liberals were not alone in complaining about inadequate resources. The chronic underfunding of the program put enormous burdens on states and school districts to satisfy its requirements, thus irking governors and mayors of both political parties.

55. Bush, *Decision Points*, 277, for both quotes. The president also dismissed criticism of testing as a measure of performance. Karl Rove, *Courage and Consequence*, 237–38, offers a similar evaluation, though Rove put the increase in educational spending at 34 percent. See also Graham, *Home Front*, 91.

56. Bakke v. Regents of the University of California 438 U.S. 265 (1978); Adarand Constructors, Inc. v. Peña, 515 U.S. 200 (1995).

57. Perry, *Michigan Affirmative Action Cases*, 2007, 158, citing a Pew Research Poll in 2003. Lawson, *Running for Freedom*, 299.

58. Adarand Constructors, Inc. v. Mineta, 534 U.S. 103 (2001); USCCR, "Redefining," 54–56.

59. Rice, *Extraordinary, Ordinary People*, 302; Perry, *Michigan Affirmative Action Cases*, 87; Dana Milbank, "White House Split on Taking Affirmative Action Stance," *Washington Post*, December 18, 2002, http://aad.english.ucsb.edu/docs/xmay1.html,

accessed May 6, 2011. Olson was the chief counsel in the *Hopwood* case against the University of Texas affirmative-action program.

60. Perry, *Michigan Affirmative Action Cases*, 88. Another conservative foe of affirmative action, White House lawyer Bruce Fein, agreed that Lott's statements made it "politically unthinkable" for Bush to oppose affirmative action. See Milbank, "White House Split."

61. http://frwebgate2.access.gpo.gov/cgi-bin/PDFgate.cgi?WAISdocID=600em2 /2/2/0&WAISaction=retrieve, accessed May 6, 2011. Perry, *Michigan Affirmative Action Cases*, 48.

62. Theodore Olson et al., *Jennifer Gratz and Patrick Hamacher, Petitioners v. Lee Bollinger et al. On Writ of Certiorari to the United States Court of Appeals for the Sixth Circuit, Brief for the United States as Amicus Curiae Supporting Petitioner*, 13–14, 18; Theodore Olson et al., *Barbara Grutter, Petitioner v. Lee Bollinger, et al., On Writ of Certiorari to the United States Court of Appeals for the Sixth Circuit, Brief for the United States as Amicus Curiae Supporting Petitioner*, 10, 11, 34; Perry, *Michigan Affirmative Action Cases*, 89.

63. Liberal critics had good reason for their skepticism. As one conservative lawyer observed, the government brief came "as close to saying you can't use race as one can come without explicitly saying it." Perry, *Michigan Affirmative Action Cases*, 89, quoting Curt Levey. See also Amy Goldstein and Dana Milbank, "Use of Race is Called 'Divisive,'" *Washington Post*, January 10, 2003, A1 for similar comment by Bruce Fein.

64. Gratz v. Bollinger, 539 U.S. 244 (2003), 22; Grutter v. Bollinger, 539 U.S. 306 (2003), 21. In the short run, the overthrow of the undergraduate admissions plan did not prove harmful to minorities. For the 2004–5 academic year, immediately following the court's ban on racial preferences, the percentage of entering African American students grew from 5.8 to 6.9 and Latinos from 4.4 to 5. See Perry, *Michigan Affirmative Action Cases*, 162.

65. Perry, *Michigan Affirmative Action Cases*, 157. What the Supreme Court refused to render, Michigan's electorate did. A vigorous referendum campaign by anti–affirmative action proponents in 2006 resulted in passage of an amendment ending racial considerations like those used in Michigan's law school admissions program and upheld by the court. See Perry, *Michigan Affirmative Action Cases*, 170.

66. Parents Involved in Community Schools v. Seattle School District No. 1, 551 U.S. 701 (2007); Meredith v. Jefferson County board of Education, 548 U.S. 938 (2006).

67. In one instance, Bush's opposition to racial considerations in decision making proved beneficial to African Americans. In 2003, the Department of Justice issued guidelines prohibiting federal agents from considering race or ethnicity in routine enforcement decisions. It prohibited the use of generalized stereotypes. It did allow exemptions with respect to investigations of terrorism, which in the wake of September 11 most affected Muslim Americans. See USCCR, "Redefining," 79.

68. The Joint Center for Political and Economic Studies, "The Black Vote in 2004," http://www.iamsaam.org/userimages/BlackVote.pdf, accessed May 6, 2011.

69. Douglas Brinkley, *The Great Deluge: Hurricane Katrina, New Orleans and the Mississippi Gulf Coast* (New York: William Morrow, 2006); Michael Eric Dyson, *Come Hell or High Water: Hurricane Katrina and the Color of Disaster* (New York: Basic Books,

2006); Christopher Cooper and Robert Black, *Disaster: Hurricane Katrina and the Failure of Homeland Security* (New York: Times Books, 2006); Chester Hartman and Gregory D. Squires, eds., *There is No Such Thing as a Natural Disaster* (New York: Routledge, 2006); Lawson, *Running for Freedom*, 323.

70. Draper, *Dead Certain*, 325–26.

71. Bush, *Decision Points*, 310, 318, 331. Bush acknowledged that he should have visited Louisiana earlier and sent in troops from the 82nd Airborne. But, he defended his flying over the city without landing because his presence would have been a distraction, required extra security, and interfered with rescue efforts. Karl Rove agrees, *Courage and Consequence*, 450, 457, as does Presidential Press Secretary Scott McClellan, *What Happened: Inside the Bush White House and Washington's Culture of Deception* (New York: Public Affairs, 2008), 282–83, 290. Unlike Bush and Rove, McClellan argues that the Bush administration was caught "flat-footed" from the beginning and that its response lacked "imagination and initiative."

72. Bush, *Decision Points*, 310.

73. Lusane, *Colin Powell*, 185.

74. Lawson, *Running for Freedom*, 333–34.

75. Hartman and Squires, "Pre Katrina, Post Katrina," in *There is No Such Thing*, 6.

76. Bush, *Decision Points*, 331; Rove, *Courage and Consequence*, 458.

77. Michelle Kruppa, "New Orleans' official 2010 census population is 343,829, agency reports," *New Orleans Times-Picayune*, http://www.nola.com/politics/index.ssf/2011/02/new_orleans_officials_2010_pop.html, accessed May 9, 2011. Draper, *Dead Certain*, 411–12; Kent Germany, "The Politics of Poverty and History: Racial Inequality and the Long Prelude to Katrina," *The Journal of American History* 94 (December 2007): 751.

78. Bush, "Remarks to National Urban League," 1411–12.

79. Dan Eggen, "Politics Alleged in Voting Cases: Justice Officials are Accused of Influence," *Washington Post*, January 23, 2006, http://www.washingtonpost.com/wp-dyn/content/article/2006/01/22/AR2006012200984.html, accessed May 24, 2011.

80. "GOP's Civil Rights Problem," December 10, 2009, *Newsweek*, http://www.newsweek.com/2009/12/10/the-gop-s-civil-rights-problem.html, accessed May 24, 2011; Mark A. Posner, "The Politicization of Justice Department Decisionmaking Under Section 5 of the Voting Rights Act: Is it a Problem and What Should Congress Do?," *American Constitution Society for Law and Policy* (January 2006): 8. http://www.acslaw.org/files/Section%205%20decisionmaking%201-30-06.pdf, accessed May 24, 2011. For a conservative perspective on the conflict between political and career officials, see Thernstrom, *Voting Rights and Wrongs*, 116, 125, 140.

81. U.S. Department of Justice, Office of the Inspector General, "An Investigation of Allegations of Politicized Hiring and Other Improper Personnel Actions in the Civil Rights Division," July 2, 2008, 17, 33, 34. The Educational Opportunity, Housing, and Disability Rights Sections did not experience such problems. Under the Obama administration, hiring practices in the CRD have returned to the pre-Bush situation. Charlie Savage, "In Shift, Justice Dept. Hiring Lawyers with Civil Rights Backgrounds," *New York Times*, June 1, 2011, A19.

82. Neil A. Lewis, "Justice Department Reshapes its Civil Rights Mission," *New York*

Times, June 14, 2007, http://www.nytimes.com/2007/06/14/washington/14discrim. html?scp=1&sq=Brian%20Landsberg&st=cse, accessed May 26, 2011.

83. Eric Lipton and Ian Urbina, "In Five-Year Effort, Scant Evidence of Voter Fraud," *New York Times*, April 12, 2007, http://www.nytimes.com/2007/04/12/washington /12fraud.html?pagewanted=print, accessed May 26, 2011.

84. Crawford v. Marion County Election Board, 553 U.S. 181 (2008).

85. Richard Nadler, "Bush's 'Real' Hispanic Numbers: Debunking the Debunkers," December 8, 2004, http://old.nationalreview.com/comment/nadler200412080811. asp, accessed May 24, 2011.

86. Eileen R. Larence, "U.S. Department of Justice: Opportunities Exist to Strengthen the Civil Rights Division's Ability to Manage and Report its Enforcement Efforts," Testimony Before the Subcommittee on the Constitution, Civil Rights, and Civil Liberties, Committee on the Judiciary, House of Representatives, December 3, 2009, 9. http://www.gao.gov/new.items/d10256t.pdf, accessed May 24, 2011.

87. Georgia v. Ashcroft, 539 U.S. 461 (2003). This case showed the complications affecting voting-rights enforcements. Georgia Democrats, including the civil rights stalwart John Lewis, favored the Georgia plan because it might lead to more Democratic victories if blacks were scattered among some white districts. Black voters might lose a few additional black representatives but they would have more influence in electing Democratic candidates that represented their interests. The Supreme Court sided with Georgia over the Justice Department. In another case out of Texas in 2003, the attorney general approved a controversial Texas legislative reapportionment plan endorsed by conservative congressman Tom Delay that resulted in five additional Republican congressmen in 2004. The department did this over the objections of its Voting Rights Section attorneys. See League of United Latin American Citizens v. Perry, 548 U.S. 399 (2006); Posner, "Politicization," 15; Eggen, "Politics Alleged"; Thernstrom, *Voting Rights and Wrongs*, 136ff.

88. Reno v. Bossier Parrish School Board, 528 U.S. 320 (2000); Mark A. Posner, "The Real Story Behind the Justice Department's Implementation of Section 5 of the Voting Rights Act: Vigorous Enforcement, as Intended by Congress," *Duke Journal of Constitutional Law and Public Policy* 1 (2006): 190, 191; Peyton McCrary, Christopher Seaman, and Richard Vallely, "The End Of Preclearance as We Knew It: How the Supreme Court Transformed Section 5 of the Voting Rights Act," *Michigan Journal of Race and Law* 11 (2006): 313, 314, 322.

89. Steven F. Lawson, *In Pursuit of Power: Southern Blacks and Electoral Politics, 1965–1982* (New York: Columbia University Press, 1985).

90. James Thomas Tucker, "The Politics of Persuasion: Passage of the Voting Rights Act Reauthorization Act of 2006," *Journal of Legislation* 33 (2007): 207.

91. Ibid., 210. This remark came through his Secretary of State Antonio Garza Jr., who President Bush later appointed as ambassador to Mexico.

92. Ibid.

93. "40th Anniversary of the Voting Rights Act of 1965: A Proclamation by the President of the United States," August 5, 2005, http://edocket.access.gpo.gov/cfr _2006/janqtr/pdf/3CFR7916.pdf, accessed May 12, 2011. "Prepared Remarks of

Attorney General Alberto R. Gonzales at the Anniversary of the Voting Rights Act," August 2, 2005, http://www.justice.gov/archive/ag/speeches/2005/080205agvotingr ights.htm, accessed May 12, 2011; George W. Bush, *Public Papers of the Presidents, 2005*, vol. 2 (Washington D.C.: Government Printing Office, 2005), 1801. In April 2005, Republican National Committee chairman Ken Mehlman had already spoken out for renewal and reaffirmed that the Republican Party was the "party of Lincoln and Frederick Douglass." Tucker, "Politics of Persuasion," 212.

94. Thernstrom, *Voting Rights and Wrongs*, 290n21; Nathaniel Persily, "The Promise and Pitfalls of the New Voting Rights Act," *The Yale Law Journal* 117 (2007): 180; Tucker, "Politics of Persuasion," 213, 216, 217–18. Sensenbrenner worked closely with Democratic congressman from North Carolina Mel Watt. Watt's district had been the target of litigation during the 1990s challenging alleged racial gerrymandering. See Shaw v. Reno, 509 U.S. 630 (1993).

95. Tucker, "Politics of Persuasion," 217, 263; Persily, "Promise and Pitfalls," 199, 200, 204. For a trenchant criticism of the nature of the evidence gathered by the House Judiciary Committee, see Thernstrom, *Voting Rights and Wrongs*, 173, 174.

96. Tucker, "Politics of Persuasion," 222; Persily, "Promise and Pitfalls," 207–8; Thernstrom, *Voting Rights and Wrongs*, 135. The committee bill also added language that would nullify the court's ruling in Ashcroft v. Georgia.

97. Tucker, "Politics of Persuasion," 258.

98. Thernstrom, *Voting Rights and Wrongs*, 3. The quote comes from Abigail Thernstrom, who Bush appointed as vice-chair of the United States Commission on Civil Rights. Although Bush disagreed with Thernstrom on this issue, his appointment of her and other conservatives effectively polarized the agency and destroyed its effectiveness as a defender of civil rights. Berry, *And Justice for All*, 325ff; Lusane, *Colin Powell*, 72; Tucker, "Politics of Persuasion," 244, 254–56.

99. Tucker, "Politics of Persuasion," 261.

100. George W. Bush, "Address to the NAACP Annual Convention," Washington, D.C., July 20, 2006, 6. http://www.presidentialrhetoric.com/speeches/07.20.06.print. html, accessed May 13, 2011.

101. Ibid., 2.

102. George W. Bush, "Remarks Upon Signing the Voting Rights Act Reauthorization and Amendment Act of 2006," Washington, D.C., July 27, 2006, 2. http:// www.presidentialrhetoric.com/speeches/07.27.06.html, accessed May 26, 2011. The Chicano leader Cesar Chavez' name had been added in the Senate but for technical reasons it had to be scrapped. Because the House version had not included Chavez's name, this would have forced the two bills to a joint conference committee, which civil rights proponents wanted to avoid. They had good reason for this. Six days after Bush signed the bill, the Senate Judiciary Committee issued its report, which expressed doubts about the continued utility and fairness of the law's special provisions, including Section 5. Committee Democrats refused to sign the report. Persily, "Promises and Pitfalls," 186. In September 2006, the Justice Department filed its first objection against a submission from Georgia on the basis of the pre-*Bossier II* restored in the act. Tucker, "Politics of Persuasion," 267.

103. "Interview of the President by Juan Williams, Fox News," posted by Ed Morrissey, September 26, 2007, http://www.captainsquartersblog.com/mt/archives /013746.php, accessed May 26, 2011.

104. Ibid. In his memoir, Bush claimed the amount was $126 billion. Bush, *Decision Points*, 328. Karl Rove put the figure at $120.7 billion. Rove, *Courage and Consequence*, 458. See also Draper, *Dead Certain*, 411–12, quoting Bush as putting the figure at $110 billion.

105. On this point in general, see Robert C. Smith, *Conservatism and Racism: And Why in America They are the Same* (Albany: State University of New York Press, 2010).

106. Lawson, *Running for Freedom*, 339.

107. U.S. Census Bureau, *Statistical Abstract of the United States: 2011*, "Table 226. Educational Attainment by Race, Hispanic Origin, and Sex, 1970–2009." http://www.census.gov/compendia/statab/2011/tables/11s0225.pdf, accessed May 24, 2011.

108. Bureau of Justice Statistics, "Number of State Prisoners Declined By Almost 3,000 During 2009; Federal Prison Population Increased By 6,800," June 23, 2010. Black females (with an incarceration rate of 333 per 100,000) were more than 2 times as likely as Hispanic females (142 per 100,000) and more than 3.6 times as likely as white females (91 per 100,000) to have been in prison or jail as of June 30, 2009. http://bjs.ojp.usdoj.gov/content pim09stpyo9acpr.cfm/pub/press/, accessed May 24, 2011. For a disturbing treatment, see Michelle Alexander, *The New Jim Crow: Mass Incarceration in the Age of Colorblindness* (New York: The New Press, 2010).

109. David A. Bositis, *Black Elected Officials: A Statistical Summary, 2001*, 6. http://www.jointcenter.org/publications1/publication-PDFs/BEO-pdfs/2001-BEO.pdf, accessed May 24, 2011.

110. Roland Burris of Illinois was appointed to replace Barack Obama after his election to the presidency. Burris did not run for a full term and was succeeded by a white Republican. Deval Patrick was elected Governor of Massachusetts in 2007 and David Paterson, New York's Lieutenant Governor, became governor following the resignation of Eliot Spitzer in 2008. He did not run for another term. As of June 2011, no African Americans held a Senate seat and only Patrick served as governor.

111. Stephan Thernstrom and Abigail Thernstrom, *America in Black and White: One Nation Indivisible* (New York: Simon & Schuster, 1997), 288.

112. See Zelden, "Old Vinegar."

CIVIL RIGHTS AND THE FIRST
BLACK PRESIDENT

Barack Obama and the Politics of Racial Equality

RONALD W. WALTERS WITH ROBERT C. SMITH

Editorial Note

Ronald W. Walters wrote this paper in February 2009 for presentation at the Alan B. Larkin Symposium on the American Presidency at Florida Atlantic University. Seven months later, Professor Walters died of complications from lung cancer before he could complete his revisions. Robert C. Smith, a former student of Walters and a longtime friend and collaborator, willingly agreed to make the revisions. In revising the paper, Smith attempted to adhere as closely as possible to the style, structure, and substance of Professor Walters's original argument.

✳   ✳   ✳

In the 1940s, the great civil rights advocate and diplomat Ralph Bunche wrote that it was inconceivable that an African American could ever be elected president: a governor, a senator, a general, or a cabinet officer perhaps, but never president.[1] In 2008 the seemingly impossible happened. Newspapers across the country reported that Barack Obama's election was a momentous achievement—a historic occasion for African Americans and the nation as a whole. The *Chicago Tribune* summed up the sentiments held by many when it described Obama's election as the "crowning achievement of the Civil Rights Movement, the triumph of a black candidate in a nation with a history of slavery and segregation."[2] After hundreds of years of racial subjugation Obama's election came to embody Rev. Dr. Martin Luther King Jr.'s dream that one day in America, even in an election for president, individuals would be judged by the content of their character rather than the color of their skin. For many African Americans the election represented something more. Valerie Grimm, chair of Indiana University's African American Studies Department, reflected on this something else: "I have parents who are still living who are very enthusiastic about Obama. They live in Mississippi. For a time my parents couldn't vote, and when they could, their only choice was a white person. This means more than just seeing a black person on the ticket. It represents things they had been denied. It's being able to see the unbelievable, that the impossible might be possible. It represents for them a new day."[3]

Yet, the very same *Chicago Tribune* article that hailed the election as the crowning achievement of the civil rights movement told of another side to the story. It revealed that conservative activists were using Obama's victory as an argument to scale back the enforcement of civil rights, including affirmative action and the Voting Rights Act. Such efforts began almost immediately after election day. On November 11, 2008, for example, Abigail and Stephan Thernstrom, longtime opponents of affirmative action, wrote in the *Wall Street Journal* that the Voting Rights Act could now be loosened. The "doors of electoral opportunity in America are now open to all," they argued. "The aggressive federal interference in state and local districting decisions enshrined in the Voting Rights Act should therefore be reconsidered."[4] Given the long sordid history of denying African Americans the right to vote, as detailed by Charles Zelden elsewhere in this volume, talk of reconsidering the Voting Rights Act evoked deep concerns that black disenfranchisement might actually worsen in the wake of Obama's victory.

Such arguments point to a curious paradox arising from the 2008 election. While for the African American community the election of Obama represents a historic win in their ongoing struggle for equality, it also has the potential to represent a loss in that struggle. By creating the mistaken perception that the doors of equal opportunity are now open to all, when in reality institutionalized discrimination remains an irrefutable fact of modern American life, Obama's victory might have the effect of dampening the long-term effort to remedy the effects of centuries of racial discrimination. In other words, winning while losing—or at least not gaining—may be the outcome of the election of the first black president.

Multiple Dimensions of Civil Rights in the Obama Era

To understand this proposition, we must first correct a common perception about the meaning of civil rights in American history and politics. At least since the New Deal, the civil rights movement has had a dual agenda, focusing on both citizenship rights and social welfare.[5] Yet this dual agenda has been obscured by a narrow understanding that, in the popular imagination at least, equates civil rights only with political rights. In large part, such public perceptions have been trapped by a distorted historical memory stemming from the iconography of the civil rights movement of the 1960s. The movement is remembered primarily for its public protests, when in fact there was a much wider range of strategies and tactics used to advance racial equality. Similarly, historical memory generally distorts the movement's agenda by narrowly defining its goals as merely involving political rights, like the right to vote and run for office, rather than including the much broader spectrum of human rights and social justice that motivated civil rights activists at the time and has motivated them since.

The 1960s civil rights movement has thus been badly misinterpreted as having been devoted only to the acquisition of equal access to citizenship rights such as those made possible by the 1965 Voting Rights Act. However, human rights that related to what *one could do* with citizenship rights were the core of the 1964 Civil Rights Act—in equalizing access to public accommodations and athletics, as well as nondiscrimination in the use of federal funds—and the 1968 Fair Housing Act. The goal of expanding opportunities as well as protecting citizenship rights were likewise integral to Lyndon Johnson's Great Society programs, which focused on civic participation, community development, job training, and poverty elimination. So, too, has affirmative action been premised upon breaking down lingering barriers to economic and educational opportunity for disadvantaged groups. Such broad social objectives were both central to the welfare rights movement and to Dr. Martin Luther King Jr. at the time of his death.

Moreover, both civil rights and welfare rights have been enshrined in the Constitution for generations. The Fourteenth Amendment created *citizenship rights* for African Americans by theoretically extending equal citizenship to all Americans, allowing them "due process" of law and "equal protection of the laws." Furthermore, that the status of any citizen should also allow them access to the *human rights* has long been understood to be one of the basic purposes of government. In fact, the Preamble to the Constitution says that the American government was formed, in part, to "promote the general welfare," an objective that was included in Article 1, Section 8, directing Congress to "provide for . . . the general welfare."

Thus, although citizenship rights and welfare rights are often viewed separately, in fact they are joined. There is some support for this in the thinking of Supreme Court Justice Thurgood Marshall, who identified three elements in an interwoven pattern of rights.[6] First, there was the civil element of society, comprising the rights necessary for individual freedom, such as those protected by the Bill of Rights: liberty of person; freedom of speech, thought, and faith; and the right to own property, to conclude valid contracts, and to assert one's rights on an equal basis to all others. Second, there were political rights, or those that gave citizens participatory access to engage in making government decisions through the vote and their representative power. And finally there were social rights, including the right to economic welfare and security and the right to live life according to the prevailing social standards.

The civil rights movement of the twenty-first century and especially in the new era inaugurated by Obama's presidency will continue to struggle to close gaps in all three interwoven categories of rights: civil, political, and social. The task will be to protect and advance these rights at a time of contradictory reactions to Obama's victory. While many in the black community have heightened expectations of empowerment generated by the election of a black president, public policies that advance civil rights or that appear to "favor" African Americans are likely to be resisted by others who believe Obama's victory signals the endpoint of, rather than merely a way station along, the road to racial equality.

Citizenship Rights

As the *Chicago Tribune* article quoted at the beginning of this essay reveals, the election of Obama reinforced the impression among some that laws protecting citizenship rights are no longer needed. This, of course, is a matter of perspective, inasmuch as civil rights laws that passed in the 1960s restrained whites who dominated the political systems of the South and other regions from prohibiting blacks from enjoying integrated education, public accommodations, voting, higher education, fair housing, and other privileges of citizenship. Blacks, on the other hand, still continue to experience racial prohibitions today. While admittedly far less than in the 1960s, racism not only continues to limit black access to the old privileges but also has erected new limitations.

One sign of the lingering challenges facing African Americans may be found in a 2004 summary report on the attention to civil rights by the Bush administration.[7] Composed by the U.S. Civil Rights Commission, the report found egregious lapses in attention to civil rights enforcement by the Justice Department. It asserted that President Bush:

Seldom speaks about civil rights; implemented policies that have retreated from long-established civil rights promises; did not provide leadership to ensure timely and swift implementation of the Help America Vote Act . . . ; has not exhibited leadership on Affirmative Action, but instead promotes "race-neutral" remedies that do not account for past discrimination; [and his requests] for six major civil rights agency funds amount to a loss of spending power for 2004 and 2005.[8]

This strongly suggests that the civil rights of African Americans are not a settled affair, even if the new limitations stem less from individual manifestations of racism than from institutional racism. That such challenges continued in the era of Barack Obama is revealed in the field of voting rights. In two Supreme Court cases in 2009, for example, the conservative majority on the Supreme Court narrowed the reach of the Voting Rights Act by interpreting the law, in the words of law professor Richard Hasen, "in even stingier ways."[9]

Human Rights

The broader spectrum of human rights—including the alleviation of poverty and the promotion of the general welfare of citizens—remains of paramount concern and needs to address openly the racialized dimensions of poverty and opportunity in America. The Great Recession that started during 2008 had devastating effects on the well-being of the American people, increasing enormously human suffering. The loss of aggregate household wealth from both private and public investments has been estimated conservatively by a consensus of economists at 9 percent, or $5 trillion, in the last three months of 2008, double that for the entire year.[10] This loss was disproportionately devastating to African Americans, whose ratio of wealth to whites was 10:1 before the economic crisis. This loss was made even more difficult by the disproportionate loss of employment, which in terms of income mobility meant that the movement of whites from the bottom to the top quartile in income was 10.2 percent in 2008, whereas it was only 4.2 percent for blacks.[11]

The black middle class has experienced a substantial degree of immobility relative to the growth of the white middle class for nearly two decades, a position held by researchers in hearings before the U.S. Civil Rights Commission in 2005. Black middle-class incomes between 1980 and 2003 grew from 29 percent to about 40 percent but were unable to close a substantial gap with whites. The top quintile has grown by 66 percent, but the lower 10 percent has remained stagnant at twice the proportion of whites for the past 45 years.[12] The lack of growth by the black middle class relative to the rest of the economy made this group especially vulnerable to making debt with the instruments that were marketed in the housing field. Small wonder, then, that the black community is disproportionately represented in the home-foreclosure crisis.[13]

While there is some evidence that the comparative lack of educational access and performance is a critical variable, it is also important to note that black mobility has been constrained by the lack of attention by previous administrations to human investment policies. The weakening of affirmative action in higher-education, the lack of vigorous K-12 education financing, higher education financing changes that privilege loans instead of grants, and the retrenchment of minority-business contracting have done much to restrain the opportunities available to African Americans.

Most important, the lack of economic progress by the black middle class is related to the failure to curb intransigent poverty, creating community pressures that continue to fuel the drug trade in poor black neighborhoods, which, in turn, exacerbates the massive incarceration rate of blacks and the growth of female-headed households. The impact of this problem on the black community was vested in the 1994 Crime Control Act, passed under Bill Clinton but with the strong wind of the conservative Gingrich revolution at his back. Today, half (i.e., 48 percent) of everyone incarcerated in the United States is black. Professor Bruce Western of the Harvard Kennedy School, concludes: "Growing rates of incarceration mean that, in the experience of African Americans in poor neighborhoods, the advancement of voting rights, school desegregation, and protection from discrimination was substantially halted. Mass incarceration undermined the project for full African American citizenship and revealed the obstacles to political equality presented by acute social disparity."[14] The interaction among factors such as incarceration, poverty, and unemployment were important in shaping a rationale for increased voting by blacks in 2008, together with the equally alluring fact that an African American could be a credible candidate for president, yet it remains to be seen whether Obama will enact policies that remediate these conditions.[15]

The Obama Victory and the Civil Rights Agendas

In the immediate aftermath of the 2008 election, some commentators suggested that it may have constituted a classic, realigning election, one that reconfigured the electoral landscape and turned the page on the conservative era in American politics. Such speculation may have been premature. Obama's election appears to have signified not so much the advent of a new liberal age but a referendum on the last eight years of Republican rule and George W. Bush. The electorate wanted change and Obama was the change candidate. This made for an ideal climate for Obama or any Democrat to win. Throughout 2008 the Democrats maintained a double-digit lead on the generic ballot, which asks voters which party they would like to see win the presidency. As the general election approached, 90 percent of the population thought the country was headed in the wrong direction; the nation faced rising gas prices, two unpopular wars, a collapse in the housing market, a massive budget deficit, rising unemployment, and an incumbent president whose popularity was in the low 30s. Finally, a month before the election the stock market dramatically declined and the credit markets collapsed, requiring a $700 billion bailout from the federal treasury. Newspaper headlines and television newscasts raised the specter of another Great Depression. *Time*, for example, in its cover story of October 13, under the caption "The New Hard Times," showed men in long, Depression-era soup lines.

In this dismal strategic situation Obama should have won in a landslide. That he did not, many scholars attribute to "Ballot Box Racism." For example, Michael Lewis-Beck in his initial forecasting model predicted a victory for the Democratic nominee of 56.58 percent, but after including variables that take into account Obama's race, the margin dropped to a razor-thin 50.7 percent.[16] Ultimately, on Election Day Obama won by a margin of 53 percent to John McCain's 46 percent (the remainder was won by minor party candidates). He carried 28 states and the District of Columbia with 364 electoral votes to McCain's 163. Obama's "minority-majority" coalition resembled the typical Democratic presidential coalition since the 1960s; 95 percent of the black vote, 67 percent of Latinos, 86 percent of Jews, 66 percent of Asian Americans, and 70 percent of gays and lesbians.[17]

Although Obama lost the white vote to McCain 43 to 55 percent, his margin was slightly better than John Kerry's 41 percent in 2004. Yet as Alan Abramowitz writes: "Obama's 12 point deficit among white voters was identical to Al Gore's in 2000. However, the fact that white voters favored the Republican candidate by a double-digit margin in 2008 despite the poor conditions of the economy and the unpopularity of the incumbent Republican President suggests racial prejudice did affect the level of white voter support for the Democratic candidate."[18] In other words, Obama won in spite of his race and he did not win as decisively as he should have because of it.

Nevertheless, Obama's candidacy mobilized the black community in an unprecedented way. More so than even the Jesse Jackson campaigns, blacks participated in the process to a greater extent than whites. Forty-eight percent of blacks compared to 46 percent of whites reported following the election "closely," 31 percent reported making campaign contributions (compared to 21 percent of whites), and twice as many blacks (14 percent) reported working in the campaign. This is extraordinary, given that whites have always participated in presidential elections more than blacks.

Obama received a higher proportion of the black vote than any previous Democratic nominee: 95 percent compared to Lyndon Johnson's 94 percent in 1964. While the number of non-Hispanic white voters remained the same as in 2004, in 2008 two million more blacks turned out. Moreover, in 2008, for the first time the percentage of blacks who voted nearly equaled that of whites at 65 percent (versus 66 percent for whites).[19] In several states—Maryland, Mississippi, Missouri, Nevada, Ohio, and South Carolina—turnout among blacks surpassed 70 percent.

Among young people and women, blacks voted at a higher rate than whites.[20]

This heightened participation gave rise to empowerment expectations in the black community: expectations that the first black president would take their civil rights concerns into consideration in policymaking. However, Obama received this extraordinary outpouring of black support on the basis of racial identification and solidarity rather than because he addressed issues of specific concern to blacks. During the campaign, he avoided frank discussion of the particular challenges facing African Americans, framing his policies and proposals instead as ones that advanced human and welfare rights for all.

Of course, the danger of embedding human rights resources designed to achieve the viability of a racial group into broad social-policy aims is that they may fall into the naïveté of the view that "a rising tide lifts all boats." This has seldom been the case for African Americans. Indeed, the most authoritative student of race and poverty, Harvard Professor William Julius Wilson, noted that the issue of race should not be buried in public discourse but brought out into the open.[21] In a 2009 book synthesizing two decades of sociological research, Wilson convincingly documented the ways in which underlying structural issues—the historical legacy of slavery and discrimination, together with imbalanced public policies—served to create and sustain systematic poverty in the black community. Impoverished urban ghettos, for example, were themselves the products of government policies that segregated neighborhoods, denied mortgages to inner-city neighborhoods, reduced drastically federal aid to cities, and focused transportation resources on suburban over urban areas and of other policies that encouraged the middle class to flee the cities for the suburbs, leaving ghetto residents effectively cut off from mainstream society. Accordingly, Wilson suggested, measures designed to effect solutions for disadvantaged African Americans should be highlighted and dealt with openly so that the American people understand the gravity of their dimensions. Only an aggressive public policy response that addressed both cultural and structural contributions to economic inequality could begin to break the cycle of poverty for African Americans.

Professor Wilson took his cue from a speech on race that Obama delivered in response to the racially incendiary remarks of his former pastor Rev. Jeremiah Wright during the 2008 primary campaign. In that speech, Obama framed the problem of race in both structural and cultural terms. "We do need to remind ourselves," he said, "that so many of the disparities that exist between the African-American community and the larger American community today can be traced directly to inequalities passed on from an earlier generation that suffered under the brutal legacy of slavery and Jim Crow." Obama cited such things as segregated schools, legalized discrimination, a lack of economic opportunity for black men, and the lack of basic services in urban black neighborhoods as perpetuating economic disparities between blacks and whites. Yet he also addressed cultural issues within the black community that, he said, keep "us from squarely facing our own complicity in our condition," and he spoke of "taking full responsibility for our own lives." Although Obama identified specific policies and grievances that created the wealth and income gap between blacks and whites, he advocated what sounded like a race-neutral approach to remedying the situation. He urged African Americans to bind their "particular grievances—for better health care and better schools and better jobs—to the larger aspirations of all Americans." He implied that he would improve the condition of the African American community not so much by addressing its specific needs as by improving health care, education, and the economy for all.[22]

When subsequent speeches more strongly emphasized personal responsibility to the detriment of corrective public policy that would address structural problems, Obama drew criticism from Rev. Jesse Jackson Sr. and others. So, inasmuch as he has continued as president to emphasize personal responsibility to achieve social viability on the part of African Americans and others, the great anticipation is what public policies will be constructed to make the acceptance of such responsibility practical based on access to human resources that may be provided by the federal government.

The Obama Presidency and the Civil Rights Agenda

Obama continued to emphasize this broad human-rights approach to civil rights during the first two years of his presidency, consistently and persistently saying that as president he was required to subordinate race-specific needs to the broader human-rights dimensions. In his 100-day press conference he was asked by the correspondent for Black

Entertainment Television (BET) what specific policies would he propose to deal with the huge racial disparities in unemployment between blacks and whites (the rate for blacks was twice that of whites). The president responded by saying that his "general approach is that if the economy is strong, that will lift all boats as long as it is also supported by, for example, strategies around college affordability and job training; tax cuts for working families as opposed to the wealthiest, that level the playing field and ensure bottom-up growth."[23] Later, the president told April Ryan of American Urban Radio, "The only thing I cannot do is, by law I can't pass laws that say that I'm just helping black folks. I am president of the entire United States."[24] Responding to mounting criticisms among some black political and intellectual leaders, Obama cited the enactment of health-care reform as emblematic of his approach to race. He argued that since blacks were disproportionately without health insurance, they would benefit the most from health-care reform.[25]

Although the Obama administration and its African American attorney general did in its first year increase funding and enforcement of citizenship rights, reversing the Bush administration policy of neglect, it addressed the issue of civil rights indirectly and without a race-specific focus.[26]

"A Racial Pass"?

There are several contradictions at the heart of the first black president's policies on race. First, if it is a mistake to think about ethnic segments of the country in his governance, then why did the president sign an executive order mandating the increased participation of Asian and Pacific Islanders in federal programs, or say in a speech to the Hispanic Caucus that when their unemployment number reached over 10 percent that was not just a problem for Hispanics, it was a problem for the whole nation? No such statement was made by the first black president about the official 15.7-percent unemployment rate for blacks. Thus, a black president feels free to address the ethnic-specific concerns of Latinos and Asian Americans but not the more pressing needs of his own people.

During the campaign Obama and his staff were aware of polls showing that as much as half of whites thought he would favor blacks if he became president. Of that number only 32 percent said they would vote for him.[27] And during his first year in office there was a three-fold increase in the percent of whites who believed his policies favored blacks, from 11–13 percent in October 2008 to 37 percent in August 2009.[28] Thus, the first black president was acutely aware that he had to avoid any appearance of favoring blacks. To do otherwise would put at risk his presidency and his prospects for reelection.

So, where does this leave the black community, winners or losers? Many African Americans think they are winners. Public opinion polls during Obama's first two years show that his approval rating among African Americans rarely fell below 90 percent. "African Americans," the *Washington Afro* concluded, "have given President Obama a racial pass."[29] One reason for this "pass," said the capital's black weekly, was that "many believe the president is sensitive to Black issues and dedicated to solving them—albeit in his own way and his own time given the deluge of problems—recession, foreclosures, health care reform, two wars, etc.— he has to tackle. . . . That political maturity also recognizes that should Obama display even the suggestion of favoritism toward blacks, he would get a backlash from Congress and the public and would feed the conservative talk show machine for months."[30]

It appears, then, that for most blacks the mere fact that this talented, handsome, charismatic and *liberal, progressive* black man defied history and won the presidency is a win, win. But the final contradiction at the heart of the Obama presidency is that if he leaves office without having addressed both the citizenship and human rights dimensions of the civil rights agenda, his election will be a loss. Blacks have a right to demand a useful product from the political system in exchange for their participation and to evaluate the worthiness of politics on that basis. That is, it is valid for them to ask what difference it makes to the satisfaction of their interests that a black is elected president. To give him a pass is to ask for a loss. Because if a black president can ignore those interests, little can be expected from his white successors.

Notes

1. Ralph Bunche, *A Brief and Tentative Analysis of Negro Leadership*, ed. Jonathan Holloway (New York: New York University Press, 2005), 36.

2. Peter Wallsten and David G. Savage, "Voting Rights Act Opponents Point to Barack Obama's Election as Reason to Scale Back Civil Rights Laws," *Chicago Tribune*, March 15, 2009.

3. Quoted in Darryl Fears, "Black Community Increasingly Protective of Obama," *Washington Post*, May 10, 2008.

4. Abigail and Stephen Thernstrom, "Racial Gerrymandering is Unnecessary," *Wall Street Journal*, November 11, 2008.

5. For further elaboration, see the essay by Robert Smith in this volume.

6. Adam Seligman, *The Idea of Civil Society* (New York: The Free Press/Macmillan, 1992), 113–14.

7. U.S. Commission on Civil Rights, Office of Civil Rights Evaluation, "Redefining Rights in America: The Civil Rights Record of the George W. Bush Administration, 2001–2004," September 2004.

8. On the slow-down in enforcement of civil rights laws during the Bush administration, see also "Enforcement of Civil Rights Laws Declined Since 1999, Study Finds," *New York Times*, November 11, 2004; Dan Eggen, "Civil Rights Focus Shift Roils Staff," *Washington Post*, November 13, 2005.

9. Robert Barnes, "Supreme Court Restricts Voting Rights Act's Scope," *Washington Post*, March 10, 2009; David G. Savage, "Supreme Court Narrows but Preserves Voting Rights Act," *Los Angeles Times*, June 23, 2009.

10. Vikas Bajaj, "Household Wealth Falls by Trillions," *New York Times*, March 13, 2009.

11. Lawrence Mishel, Heidi Shierholz, and Jared Bernstein, "The State of Working America," Annual Report of the Economic Policy Institute, Washington, D.C., 2009, Table 2.4, "Income Mobility for white and black families . . ."

12. Briefing Report, "The Economic Stagnation of the Black Middle Class," U.S. Commission on Civil Rights, July 15, 2005, http://www.usccr.gov/pubs/122805_BlackAmericaStagnation.pdf.

13. Ruby Mendenrall, "The Political Economy of Black Housing: From the Housing Crisis of the Great Migration to the Subprime Mortgage Crisis," *The Black Scholar* 40 (2010): 20–37. As an example of the institutional racism referenced earlier, this article reports (31), "black communities are now experiencing reverse redlining as minority neighborhoods are often the target of subprime lenders. In neighborhoods where at least 80 percent of the population is black, those obtaining refinance loans were 22 times more likely to get a subprime loan than the national average. More striking is the fact that upper income borrowers living in predominantly black communities receive subprime loans at twice the rate of low income white borrowers."

14. Bruce Western, "Reentry: Reversing Mass Imprisonment," *Boston Review*, July/August 2008. http://bostonreview.net/BR33.4/western.php.

15. For a succinct overview of the social and economic well-being of the black community at the time of Obama's election, see the special issue of *The Black Scholar*: "The Political Economy and the Deteriorating Condition of African America in the Age of Obama," ed. Sundiata Keita Cha-Jua, volume 40, Spring 2010.

16. Michael Lewis-Beck, Charles Tien, and Richard Nadeau, "Obama's Missed Landslide: A Racial Loss?" Paper prepared for presentation at the annual meeting of the Southern Political Science Association, New Orleans, January 7–11, 2009.

17. These data are from the 2008 general election exit polls as accessed from http://www.CNN.comELECTION/2008/results/polls.main

18. Alan Abramowitz, *The Disappearing Center: Engaged Citizens, Polarization and American Democracy* (New Haven: Yale, 2010): 115.

19. Tasha Philpot, Daron Shaw, and Ernest McGowan, "Winning the Race: Black Turnout in the 2008 Election," *Public Opinion Quarterly* 73 (2009): 995–1022.

20. Ibid.

21. William Julius Wilson, *More Than Just Race* (New York: W.W. Norton and Co., 2009), 141–44.

22. Transcript of Barack Obama speech, "A More Perfect Union," March 18, 2008, http://www.npr.org/templates/story/story.php?storyId=88478467.

23. Presidential Press Conference, transcript, *New York Times*, April 30, 2009.

24. Howard Kurz, "Color of Change," *Washington Post*, December 23, 2009.

25. Sheldon Albert, "Obama Rejects Charges He's Ignoring Black People," Canada.com, December 22, 2009, http://www.canada.com/business/story.html?id=237/1848.

26. Charlie Savage, "Justice Department to Recharge Civil Rights Enforcement," *New York Times*, September 1, 2009.

27. Lewis-Beck, Tien, and Nadeau, "Obama's Missed Landslide," 14–15.

28. Michael Tesler and David Sears, *Obama's Race: The 2008 Election and the Dream of a Post-Racial America* (Chicago: University of Chicago Press, 2010), 144, 182.

29. Zenitha Prince, "Muffled Black Criticisms Reflect Racial Pride, Pragmatism," *Washington Afro*, March 18, 2010.

30. Ibid.

CONCLUSION

More Equal and Less Equal since the 1970s

THOMAS BORSTELMANN

In the ongoing struggle for racial justice over the last four decades, measures of victory and defeat were not always as clear as they tended to be in elections or on battlefields. Were civil rights advocates "winning while losing"? The answer depends on how one does the measuring. In sports, a percentage of success in one game looks very different in another. Consider the figure 40 percent. In baseball, a .400 hitter is a rarity and a superstar. In basketball, a 40-percent free-throw shooter is an embarrassment, a "brick-layer" tossing up shots with clanking imprecision. In elections, as Charles Zelden demonstrates in his essay here, problems with vote counting in Florida in 2000 and in Ohio in 2004 created serious doubts about the legitimacy of the outcome, but at least there were outcomes—the elections of George W. Bush—and concessions from the other contenders. In the long-term pursuit of social justice, by contrast, various advances and retreats mixed together over time in a manner that prevented ready mathematical evaluation.

It had not always been this way. Before 1970, as Richard Pacelle reminds us in his essay, the moral contours of the civil rights landscape were much clearer. When people by law were segregated and humiliated on the basis of their skin color, when they were kept in poverty and miseducation, when they felt the fist and the rope of white supremacy, it seemed fairly straightforward to understand right from wrong. The moral force of the black southern freedom struggle carried real weight and power. It also helped convince tens of millions of non-black Americans of the justice of that struggle. The civil rights movement was always more complicated, more calculating, and more willing to use force in self-defense than some traditional portraits have suggested.[1] But police dogs, Ku Klux Klan robes, and snarling white faces juxtaposed brilliantly with peaceful protesters. Amidst continuous Cold War moral rhetoric about the United States as a democracy and the "leader of the free world," the absence of equality and elemental justice for Americans of color revealed a glaring hypocrisy to most observers.[2]

The destruction of legal segregation and discrimination changed this situation. Mortally wounded by the *Brown v. Board of Education* decision of 1954, de jure Jim Crow finally fell before the combined blows of the Civil Rights Act of 1964 and the Voting Rights Act of 1965. The Immigration and Nationality Act of 1965 swept racial and ethnic criteria out of the nation's decisions about the places from which future Americans could come. No longer did American law aim to sustain a white nation. This was victory: just plain winning. Prejudicial attitudes did not, of course, disappear overnight, though they did decline steadily over subsequent decades. The larger problem now was how to implement equality, which meant overturning a vast inherited, racialized system of inequality, built over centuries and rooted in white theft of African American labor and government policies promoting white interests. The sins of the fathers had not disappeared but rather calcified into extensive black underprivilege in nearly every sphere of life.[3] Even the election of a black president in 2008, as Ronald Walters and Robert Smith note in their essay, did not necessarily lead to vigorous governmental policies to end inequality.

Affirmative action and busing offered compensatory tactics based on group identity that aimed to reduce some of this enduring racial gap. Such group identities seemed necessary but also deeply problematic— precisely the sort of barrier to individual achievement that the civil rights movement aimed to pull down. Could whites now be victims of discrimination? The moral landscape was much less clear than before. The U.S. Supreme Court in the *Bakke* decision of 1978 banned the use of quotas in educational admissions but allowed the limited use of race as one of many criteria, rooting affirmative action in the new rationale that diversity benefited *all* Americans.[4] As Steven Lawson makes clear in his essay, accumulated structural inequality was in many ways more difficult to address than the blatant discrimination of the earlier Jim Crow era. It was no longer quite so obvious what "winning" and "losing" might look like.

At first glance, it seems that a new conservatism gained the high ground in American politics in the 1970s and has stayed there ever since.[5] Richard Nixon's six years in the White House provided the hinge on which the voting public and the major parties began their swing to the right. Nixon's election in 1968 marked an end to his earlier career as a fierce anticommunist but a relatively racial liberal. Now he campaigned with straightforward appeals to the white South and to anxieties about "law and order"; he and his advisers spoke of "hunting where the ducks are" as he wooed former Democrats over to the party of Abraham Lincoln, initiating an epochal shift in presidential elections that would see the one-party white South flip almost entirely to the party once associated with the invading Union Army.[6] The third-party candidacy of gleeful segregationist George Wallace nearly derailed Nixon's strategy, but the Californian managed just barely to slip into the Oval Office. John Skrentny reveals in his essay how much Nixon's policies in office derived from partisan motivations rather than ideological commitments. The president's deepest determination was to win power and keep it, a drive that ironically led to the corruptions culminating in the Watergate scandal and his removal from the very office he most treasured. Along the way, Nixon did tend toward reducing enforcement of civil rights monitoring and did appoint a host of conservative judges to the federal bench. Regarding concern for racial justice, his administration represented the first shift of the federal government away from supporting civil rights after the great victories of the 1960s.[7]

This conservative trend was real, and it continued in subsequent presidential administrations. The only Democrats to win the White House between 1968 and 2008 were two southerners with distinctly pro-business orientations. Both Jimmy Carter and Bill Clinton also had strong African American support; they were quintessential New South governors, moderate Democrats who believed in racial equality and integration as well as entrepreneurship. Carter's devout evangelical Christian faith appealed to conservatives, as did Clinton's "good ol' boy" or "Bubba" personal friendliness. The very sound of southern accents, to most Americans, meant conservative. In their essay, Joseph Crespino and Asher Smith remind us of Carter's enthusiasm for deregulation, a major trend of the late 1970s that predated Reagan's presidency and enjoyed bipartisan support and great corporate enthusiasm. Likewise, in his essay, Robert C.

Smith emphasizes Clinton's historic role in ending a major thrust of the New Deal order when he signed the 1996 legislation removing the federal government from direct provision of welfare payments to the poor. Democrats in post-1970 America seemed less and less like Democrats of an earlier era.

The president receiving the most attention in this volume is Ronald Reagan. The preternaturally upbeat Midwesterner-turned-Californian served as the most visible and in many ways most attractive leader of contemporary conservatism. Reagan was most interested in cutting taxes and bolstering the nation's military forces—the highest priorities and chief governing accomplishments of the modern conservative movement.[8] Mary Frances Berry and Richard Pacelle, in their respective essays, demonstrate that Reagan's administration also frequently tried to chip away at civil rights protections, from voting rights monitoring, to anti-discriminatory tax regulations for schools, to pursuing employment discrimination cases. The 1980s saw the high-water mark of bureaucratic efforts to roll back civil rights gains. Civil rights defenders mostly succeeded in fighting off these specific efforts—"winning"—even while conceding political ground to Reagan—"losing"—in the rhetorical sphere of denigrating the role of government and in the bureaucratic and judicial spheres of appointing new personnel with far less concern for challenging embedded racial inequalities.

Here we can begin to see the broader pattern in American politics and culture that took shape in the 1970s and has continued since to become the pervasive common sense of life in the United States. This pattern involves both "winning" and "losing," from the perspective of those pursuing racial justice. This pattern is not simply conservative—it is closer instead to being socially liberal and economically conservative. It moves toward libertarianism, or neo-liberalism. And it is a pattern that extends far beyond the United States, setting American developments within a broader global set of developments.[9]

On the one hand, public culture in the United States from the 1970s onward grew markedly more inclusive and egalitarian. The key engine of change was the formal success of the black civil rights movement by the late 1960s in eliminating legalized racial discrimination and in delegitimizing explicit prejudice, particularly in public life. The African American freedom struggle inspired other Americans, who had also experienced something less than first-class citizenship, to organize and demand full respect and equality. Most important were women, whose possibilities and expectations in education, work, and relationships changed irrevocably. Likewise, gay and lesbian Americans moved with remarkable swiftness from an ignored or despised minority toward greater levels of respect and acceptance from the majority of their fellow citizens. Disabled Americans followed a similar upward path to inclusion in mainstream society, most notably with the passage of the Americans with Disabilities Act of 1990. The new wave of immigrants from Asia and Latin America, which followed the elimination of the discriminatory national-origins system in 1965, shifted U.S. demography from primarily black and white to increasingly multiracial and multicultural. Even animals gained a newfound respect with the passage of the Endangered Species Act in 1973, granting them not individual rights but, for the first time, a right of species to adequate habitat and survival.

In this more inclusive and egalitarian American society since the 1970s, public expressions of prejudice became increasingly unacceptable and came with real costs, as some politicians and other leaders found out the hard way. Being identified as "racist" became a major mark of shame. "Sexist" was not far behind, and "homophobic" was gaining ground rapidly. In the four decades after Richard Nixon's election, the United States emerged as a society where female authority over men in the workplace became as normal as its converse, where women ran large corporations, where the U.S. Supreme Court threw out restrictions on consensual homosexual behavior, where gays and lesbians could get married in several states and serve openly in the U.S. military, and where Barack Obama, a black man with a Kenyan father and an Islamic middle name shared by the tyrant in Iraq with whom the United States had just gone to war, was elected president in 2008. Indeed, even many of those who voted against Obama took pride in the fact of his election, which they saw as confirming the identity of the United States as a land of opportunity for all.[10] International observers across Europe and elsewhere registered enthusiastic approval, along with the rueful opinion that a member of an ethnic or racial minority would not likely be elected in similar fashion to the top office in their countries.[11]

On the other hand, in addition to the United States growing more socially egalitarian and inclusive since the 1970s, the country's political culture moved sharply toward viewing market mechanisms as the best solution to nearly all political and social, as well as economic, problems. From

Watergate and the deep economic recession and oil crises of the 1970s onward, Americans lost faith in the ability of government, particularly at the national level, to manage the economy successfully. Free markets and deregulation grew in popularity, while a citizen revolt against taxes spread from California across the country. The logic of markets was the logic of providing whatever consumers want to purchase. This included the rapid expansion of the gambling industry beyond Nevada—to Atlantic City, state lotteries, Indian casinos, and midwestern and southern riverboats—and the explosive growth of the pornography industry, fed by the development of videocassette recorders, DVDs, and the Internet. The logic of markets soon extended into other areas of American life. The nation's very security was provided by a military force no longer staffed through a draft of all eligible citizens but, after 1973, by a volunteer system that allowed national labor markets to determine who would serve the nation. Even access to abortion, the bête noire of the religious Right, became subject to the expanding discipline of the marketplace: three years after the U.S. Supreme Court legalized abortion in *Roe v. Wade* in 1973, the U.S. Congress passed the Hyde Amendment to prevent federal government health-care funding for the poor from paying for abortions. The result? A woman who wanted an abortion could have one if she could afford it, a true market solution.

In American politics by the new millennium, these two major tendencies—social egalitarianism and free-market commitment—each had one of the major political parties as its primary spokesperson. The Democrats were the party of inclusion, Republicans the party of free-market economics. But a wide swath of common ground encompassed both parties. Most Democrats no longer seemed eager to defend labor unions or the older New Deal/Great Society order of active federal government management of the economy and provision of social welfare to the poor. Most Republicans, for their part, rejected explicit racism and sexism— President George W. Bush, for example, had close black, female, and Latino advisers, friends, and family members. Behind the often-polarized rhetoric of contemporary partisan politics, American political culture since the 1970s had developed a significant common ground of egalitarian public inclusiveness and free-market enthusiasm.[12]

The United States did not stand alone in this pattern of political development. Across the globe, the 1970s proved to be the era when human rights came to the fore while the last remnants of colonialism and white supremacy began to topple. Aided by satellites, computers, and other innovations in communications technology, nongovernmental organizations focused on protecting human rights proliferated from that decade onward. Amnesty International won the Nobel Peace Prize in 1977. The Helsinki Accords of 1975 brought a Trojan horse of human-rights monitoring into the Soviet bloc, weakening Communist control and encouraging the establishment in Poland of Solidarity, the first independent labor union to be recognized in a Communist country—a clear sign of failure for a form of authoritarian rule supposedly dedicated to the welfare of workers. In southern Africa, the last great overseas European empire, Portugal, collapsed as Angolans and Mozambicans fought their way free of Lisbon's control. The white settlers next door in Rhodesia gave up their fight against the 95 percent of the country's residents with darker skins, allowing the creation of Zimbabwe in 1980. And young student protesters in Soweto in 1976 kick-started the final stage of the struggle to fell the last redoubt of global white supremacy: apartheid South Africa. Injustice and inequality at the hand of the state hardly disappeared across the world, but governments were forced to pay a higher price in public disapproval and opposition, both domestic and international, for the abuse of human rights. The trend of greater egalitarianism and inclusiveness in the United States was visible across much of the globe from the 1970s onward.[13]

In similar fashion, the enthusiasm for free markets in the United States that emerged in the 1970s fit into a broader pattern of global change. At the time, both Communists abroad and anticommunists in the United States believed that the Soviet Union was expanding its influence abroad. Socialism seemed on the march, from Vietnam to Angola to Nicaragua. But in retrospect it is clear that precisely the opposite was happening. The Soviet bloc was beginning its slow implosion, with Communists losing legitimacy in countries from Poland to Afghanistan. A decade later, Communist rule in Eastern Europe collapsed. In the Southern Cone of South America, fierce free-market enthusiasts seized control of Chile and Argentina. In Western Europe, Margaret Thatcher's election as prime minister of the United Kingdom marked a major shift toward privatizing the British welfare state. Most importantly, the People's Republic of China—the largest and most avowedly anti-capitalist nation—began its conversion to the use of private property and market mechanisms in 1978. World economic history has never been the same as a result. Even such outliers as Vietnam and Nicaragua would only aim at building socialism for another ten years before turning in the capitalist direction with the rest of the world. The shift toward market solutions, in other words, extended far beyond just the United States.[14]

A major obstacle to understanding trends in American political culture during the forty years between the elections of Nixon and Obama has been the lack of clarity about precisely what "conservative" means. Traditionally, the word connotes keeping the same, or not changing. But this has hardly been the case with conservatives in American politics since the end of the 1960s. These so-called conservatives have sought, above all else, to *bring* change—specifically, to overturn social and cultural developments seen as secular and corrupting, to sharply reduce governmental regulation of the economy, and to roll back a decline in U.S. power abroad. These three wings of contemporary conservatism have not always been the most natural of allies with each other.

Social conservatives, most but not all of them religious in orientation, focused on the behaviors and attitudes of Americans and how those had shifted in the 1960s and 1970s. They were troubled by declining deference to traditional authorities, both religious and secular. They feared feminism and the disruptions in family life that they expected to follow from women's rapid entry into the paid workforce. They rued the coarsening of public language, the growing informality of public dress, and the surge of explicit sexuality into every seam of public life. Social conservatives zeroed in on sexual issues above all, seeing abortion rights and homosexuality in particular as undercutting what they held to be the core institutions of American society, heterosexual marriage and family. Like traditional social conservatives dating back to Edmund Burke in seventeenth-century England, these conservatives wanted a government that would intervene in citizens' lives to the extent necessary to create and sustain what they saw as virtuous citizens. The job of the state was making good people.[15]

The second wing of contemporary conservatism, promoters of the free market, nurtured a rather different vision of the purpose of government. Instead of constraining people to be good by checking their deleterious impulses, these libertarian-leaning or economic conservatives believed above all in individual liberty. People should be as free as possible to partake of a free-market economy, buying and selling as they wished in the pursuit of their own happiness. These conservatives sought to reduce government constraints on free enterprise, to lower taxes, and thus to minimize the role of the state in society.[16] They believed capitalism underpinned liberty. But capitalism, in a historical sense, hardly conserved anything. Rather, it brought what the economist Joseph Schumpeter famously called "creative destruction"—the demolishing of older institutions and systems of production and trade in the pursuit of more efficient and profitable ones. Free markets brought change, as any resident of the U.S. rust belt could attest. Indeed, the expansion of capitalism around the globe since the fifteenth century had been perhaps the greatest force for change in the modern world.[17]

In addition to these two most important wings of modern American conservatism, a third wing in the 1970s and 1980s promoted a resurgent U.S. military presence abroad. This nationalist or neo-conservative wing looked outward at a world it feared was turning away from the United States, particularly after the U.S. defeat in Vietnam, and was determined to reverse this trend. These fierce anticommunists sought to reverse a decline in American willingness to assert the nation's interests overseas.[18]

These three major elements of modern American conservatism found a common home in the Republican Party, particularly under the amiable leadership of Reagan, who was able to convince all of them that he was on their side. Anticommunism certainly provided a common ground, since Communism threatened religious values, private property, and American global leadership. Despite the high profile of social conservatives on issues from school prayer to abortion rights to gay marriage, however, such concerns did not make progress in the same steady way that free-market and deregulation concerns did.[19] The Republican Party reaped the votes of social conservatives while delivering mostly to business conservatives—precisely the broader pattern we have seen of expanding social liberalism and increasing free-market conservatism.

The precise role of race and racism in modern American conservatism remains an open question. Without doubt, the conservative coalition built by Nixon, perfected by Reagan, and continued by both George Bushes grew initially, in part, in racist soil. There is simply no way to deny this: a large majority of white southerners left "the party of the fathers"—the Democratic Party—once it included African Americans on equal terms and moved wholeheartedly into the party of Abraham Lincoln. From 1964 through the 1970s and 1980s, this white backlash—joined by non-southern whites as well—bolstered Republican ranks.[20]

But by the 2000s and the 2010s, the element of white racial resentment was no longer so clearly dominant in the conservative movement, even as Republicans remained almost completely a white party. After all, such supposedly conservative values as patriotism, hard work, priority to families, and religiosity were deeply embedded in the lives of African Americans, Latinos, and other Americans of all colors. And younger white Americans increasingly did not share the prejudices and assumptions of their parents and grandparents, having grown up instead with a popular culture and public life that were dramatically more multicultural and integrated than those of previous generations. Prejudice was hardly dead, but historical change was visible.[21]

For Americans deeply committed to full human equality and an end to all forms of discrimination, the four decades following Nixon's election to the presidency in 1968 can, ultimately, be understood as an era of "winning while losing." In a Rip van Winkle–style scenario, a woman, a homosexual, a person of color, or a disabled person—that is, any of a majority of Americans—brought back directly from the late 1960s to the 2010s would be literally stunned by the extent of public social equality and inclusiveness. Yet this dramatic change happened alongside a comparable bipartisan conservative shift away from belief in an activist federal government and toward greater use of market mechanisms to try to solve public policy problems. The result has been a more purified form of individualism in American life, a terrain in which all citizens are expected to compete for material success, but with a sharply increasing maldistribution of wealth and income and a shrinking common commitment to minimum living standards. Americans are both more equal and less equal than they used to be.[22]

Notes

1. Timothy B. Tyson, *Radio Free Dixie: Robert F. Williams and the Roots of Black Power* (Chapel Hill: University of North Carolina Press, 1999); Simon Wendt, *The Spirit and the Shotgun: Armed Resistance and the Struggle for Civil Rights* (Gainesville: University Press of Florida, 2007).

2. Mary L. Dudziak, *Cold War Civil Rights: Race and the Image of American Democracy* (Princeton: Princeton University Press, 2000); Thomas Borstelmann, *The Cold War and the Color Line: American Race Relations in the Global Arena* (Cambridge, Mass.: Harvard University Press, 2001).

3. Thomas J. Sugrue, *Not Even Past: Barack Obama and the Burden of Race* (Princeton: Princeton University Press, 2010).

4. Regents of the University of California v. Bakke, 438 U.S. 265 (1978); Howard Ball, *The Bakke Case: Race, Education, and Affirmative Action* (Lawrence: University Press of Kansas, 2000).

5. Bruce J. Schulman and Julian E. Zelizer, eds., *Rightward Bound: Making America Conservative in the 1970s* (Cambridge, Mass.: Harvard University Press, 2008); Dominic Sandbrook, *Mad as Hell: The Crisis of the 1970s and the Rise of the Populist Right* (New York: Alfred A. Knopf, 2011); Laura Kalman, *Right Star Rising: A New Politics, 1974–1980* (New York: W.W. Norton, 2010); Philip Jenkins, *Decade of Nightmares: The End of the Sixties and the Making of Eighties America* (New York: Oxford University Press, 2006).

6. Kevin P. Phillips, *The Emerging Republican Majority* (New Rochelle, N.Y.: Arlington House, 1969); Harry S. Dent, *The Prodigal South Returns to Power* (New York: Wiley, 1978).

7. Dean J. Kotlowski, *Nixon's Civil Rights: Politics, Principle, and Policy* (Cambridge, Mass.: Harvard University Press, 2002).

8. This is a point made perhaps most evocatively by Thomas Frank in *What's The Matter with Kansas? How Conservatives Won the Heart of America* (New York: Henry Holt, 2004) but illuminated across the developing scholarly literature on recent American conservatism.

9. For a fuller elaboration of this argument, see Thomas Borstelmann, *The 1970s: A New Global History from Civil Rights to Economic Inequality* (Princeton: Princeton University Press, 2011).

10. See, for example, Peggy Noonan, "What I Saw at the Inauguration," *Wall Street Journal*, January 24–25, 2009.

11. See, for example, Brian Knowlton, "Global Views of U.S. Helped by Obama, Survey Says," *New York Times*, July 24, 2009.

12. For a much more detailed version of this argument, see Borstelmann, *The 1970s*, chapter 6 and conclusion.

13. Samuel Moyn, *The Last Utopia: Human Rights in History* (Cambridge, Mass.: Harvard University Press, 2010); Stephen Kotkin, *Armageddon Averted: The Soviet Collapse, 1970–2000* (New York: Oxford University Press, 2001); Ryan M. Irwin, *Gordian Knot: Apartheid and the Unmaking of the Liberal World Order* (New York: Oxford University Press, 2012).

14. Borstelmann, *The 1970s*, chapter 4.

15. Donald T. Critchlow, *Phyllis Schlafly and Grassroots Conservatism: A Woman's Crusade* (Princeton: Princeton University Press, 2005); Donald T. Critchlow, *The Conservative Ascendancy: How the GOP Right Made Political History* (Cambridge, Mass.: Harvard University Press, 2007); William A. Link, *Righteous Warrior: Jesse Helms and the Rise of Modern Conservatism* (New York: St. Martin's, 2008).

16. Kim Phillips-Fein, *Invisible Hands: The Making of the Conservative Movement from the New Deal to Reagan* (New York: W.W. Norton, 2009).

17. Joyce Appleby, *The Relentless Revolution: A History of Capitalism* (New York: W.W. Norton, 2010).

18. John Ehrman, *The Rise of Neo-Conservatism: Intellectuals and Foreign Affairs, 1945–1994* (New Haven: Yale University Press, 1995).

19. Ryan Sager, *The Elephant in the Room: Evangelicals, Libertarians, and the Battle to Control the Republican Party* (Hoboken, N.J.: Wiley, 2006).

20. Dan T. Carter, *The Politics of Rage: George Wallace, the Origins of the New Conservatism, and the Transformation of American Politics* (New York: Simon & Schuster, 1995); Rick Perlstein, *Before the Storm: Barry Goldwater and the Unmaking of the American Consensus* (New York: Hill and Wang, 2001); Rick Perlstein, *Nixonland: The Rise of a President and the Fracturing of America* (New York: Scribner, 2008); Kevin M. Kruse, *White Flight: Atlanta and the Making of Modern Conservatism* (Princeton: Princeton University Press, 2005); Matthew D. Lassiter, *The Silent Majority: Suburban Politics in the Sunbelt South* (Princeton: Princeton University Press, 2006); Joseph Crespino, *In Search of Another Country: Mississippi and the Conservative Counterrevolution* (Princeton: Princeton University Press, 2007).

21. Ellis Cose, *The End of Anger: A New Generation's Take on Race and Rage* (New York: Ecco, 2010).

22. Jacob S. Hacker and Paul Pierson, *Winner-Take-All Politics: How Washington Made the Rich Richer—and Turned Its Back on the Middle Class* (New York: Simon & Schuster, 2010); Larry M. Bartels, *Unequal Democracy: The Political Economy of the New Gilded Age* (Princeton: Princeton University Press, 2008); Joe Soss, Jacob S. Hacker, and Suzanne Mettler, eds., *Remaking America: Democracy and Public Policy in an Age of Inequality* (New York: Russell Sage Foundation, 2007); Tony Judt, *Ill Fares the Land* (New York: Penguin, 2010).

CONTRIBUTORS

Kenneth Osgood is the director of the McBride Honors Program in Public Affairs and is associate professor in the Division of Liberal Arts and International Studies at the Colorado School of Mines. For ten years, he taught at Florida Atlantic University, where he was the director of the History Symposium Series. Ken has been the Stanley Kaplan Visiting Professor of American Foreign Policy at Williams College (2010–11) and the Mary Ball Washington Professor of American History at University College Dublin (2006–7). He is the author of *Total Cold War: Eisenhower's Secret Propaganda Battle at Home and Abroad*.

Derrick White is associate professor at Florida Atlantic University in the Department of History. Professor White is the author of *The Challenge of Blackness: The Institute of the Black World and Political Activism in the 1970s*. His research areas include African American activism, Black Power, and sports history.

Mary Frances Berry has been the Geraldine R. Segal Professor of American Social Thought and Professor of History since 1987. She is the author of ten books including *Power in Words: The Stories behind Barack Obama's Speeches, from the State House to the White House* with Josh Gottheimer; *And Justice For All: The United States Commission On Civil Rights And the Struggle For Freedom in America*; and *My Face Is Black Is True: Callie House and the Struggle for Ex-Slave Reparations*.

Tim Borstelmann is the new Thompson Professor of Modern World History at the University of Nebraska–Lincoln. He spent twelve years in the History Department at Cornell University, where he was a prize-winning author and teacher. His most recent books include *The Cold War and the Color Line: American Race Relations in the Global Arena* and *Created Equal: A Social and Political History of the United States*.

Steven F. Lawson is professor emeritus at Rutgers University. He has written *Black Ballots: Voting Rights in the South, 1944–1969*; *In Pursuit of Power:*

Southern Blacks and Electoral Politics, 1965–1989; and *Running for Freedom: Civil Rights and Black Politics in America Since 1941,* 3rd edition.

Richard L. Pacelle Jr. is a faculty member in the Department of Political Science at Georgia Southern University. He is the author of *Between Law and Politics: The Solicitor General and the Structuring of Race, Gender, and Reproductive Rights Litigation.* His areas of concentration are judicial politics and public Law, American politics, and research methods.

John D. Skrentny is the director of the Center for Comparative Immigration Studies and professor of sociology at the University of California, San Diego. He is the author of *The Minority Rights Revolution.* His research focuses on public policy and law and inequality, especially as they relate to immigration and civil rights.

Robert C. Smith is professor of political science at San Francisco State University. He is the author or coauthor of more than forty articles and essays and nine books including *Race, Class and Culture: A Study in Afro-American Mass Opinion; Racism in the Post–Civil Rights Era: Now You See It, Now You Don't; We Have No Leaders: African Americans in the Post–Civil Rights Era;* and *African American Leadership.* He is associate editor of the *National Political Science Review* and general editor of the State University of New York (SUNY) Press African American Studies series.

Ronald W. "Ron" Walters (July 20, 1938–September 10, 2010) was an American scholar known worldwide for his knowledge of African American politics through his leadership and his writing. He was the director of the African American Leadership Institute and Scholar Practitioner Program, Distinguished Leadership Scholar at the James MacGregor Burns Academy of Leadership, and a respected professor in government and politics at the University of Maryland. He authored seven books and more than one hundred articles.

Charles Zelden is professor of political science in the Farquhar College of Arts and Sciences at Nova Southeastern University. A specialist in American legal and constitutional history, he is the author of *Bush v. Gore: Exposing the Hidden Crisis in American Democracy.*